War Isn't Hell,
It's Entertainment

War Isn't Hell, It's Entertainment

Essays on Visual Media and the Representation of Conflict

Edited by
RIKKE SCHUBART, FABIAN VIRCHOW,
DEBRA WHITE-STANLEY
and TANJA THOMAS

McFarland & Company, Inc., Publishers
Jefferson, North Carolina, and London

ALSO OF INTEREST

Super Bitches and Action Babes: The Female Hero in Popular Cinema, 1970–2006, by Rikke Schubart (McFarland, 2007)

We wish to thank the University of Southern Denmark for providing funding when it became necessary.

One article has been previously published and we are very thankful for permission to reprint it: Helga Tawil-Souri, "The Political Battlefield of Pro-Arab Video Games on Palestinian Screens," *Comparative Studies of South Asia, Africa and the Middle East*, vol. 27, no. 3, pp. 536–551. © 2007 Comparative Studies of South Asia, Africa and the Middle East. All rights reserved. Used by permission of the publisher, Duke University Press, and the author.

LIBRARY OF CONGRESS CATALOGUING-IN-PUBLICATION DATA

War isn't hell, it's entertainment : essays on visual media and the representation of conflict / edited by Rikke Schubart, Fabian Virchow, Debra White-Stanley and Tanja Thomas.
    p.   cm.
    Includes bibliographical references and index.

ISBN 978-0-7864-3558-6
softcover : 50# alkaline paper

1. Mass media and war. 2. War in mass media. 3. War and society — United States. 4. Popular culture — United States. I. Schubart, Rikke.
P96.W35W375 2009
303.6'6 — dc22   2009001465

British Library cataloguing data are available

©2009 Rikke Schubart, Fabian Virchow, Debra White-Stanley and Tanja Thomas. All rights reserved

No part of this book may be reproduced or transmitted in any form or by any means, electronic or mechanical, including photocopying or recording, or by any information storage and retrieval system, without permission in writing from the publisher.

On the cover: Laura Regan as P.f.c. Jessica Lynch in *Saving Jessica Lynch*, 2003 (NBC/Photofest); top border ©2009 Shutterstock

Manufactured in the United States of America

McFarland & Company, Inc., Publishers
  Box 611, Jefferson, North Carolina 28640
  www.mcfarlandpub.com

Table of Contents

Introduction (Rikke Schubart) — 1

Part One. The Public War Body

1. War Porn: Spectacle and Seduction in Contemporary American War Memorials (Erika Doss) — 13
2. Sporting Aces and the Military: Performance, Discipline, and Nationalism in the Fields of Honor (Fabian Virchow) — 31
3. The Camera at War: When Soldiers Become War Photographers (Mette Mortensen) — 44
4. Getting the Story Right: Myth, Meaning, and Gendered War Mythology in the Case of Jessica Lynch (Rikke Schubart) — 61
5. Celebrities and 9/11: "A Simple Show of Unity" (Sue Collins) — 77

Part Two. War and Entertainment

6. Gender Management, Popular Culture, and the Military (Tanja Thomas) — 97
7. "Tell Me That Wasn't Fun": Watching the Battle Scenes in *Master and Commander* with a Smile on Your Face (Anne Gjelsvik) — 115
8. Comic Situations/Endless War: *M*A*S*H* and War as Entertainment (Yvonne Tasker) — 132
9. Lavishing the Body Politic: *The Manchurian Candidate* (Debra White-Stanley) — 150
10. Hiroshima and Nagasaki: Image and Reality (Lawrence H. Suid) — 167

Part Three. Playing at War

11. The Authentic Illusion: Twentieth Century War Reenactors and the Ownership of History (Jenny Thompson) — 181
12. Digital War Games and Post 9/11 Geographies of Militarism (Marcus Power) — 198
13. The Political Battlefield of Pro-Arab Video Games on Palestinian Screens (Helga Tawil-Souri) — 215
14. Manufacturing Militainment: Video Game Producers and Military Brand Games (Matthew Thomas Payne) — 238
15. War/Games: The Art of Rules and Strategies (Bo Kampmann Walther) — 256

Abbreviations, Acronyms and Terms — 273
About the Contributors — 275
Index — 279

Introduction
RIKKE SCHUBART

One of the things transformed after 9/11 is our awareness of an altered relationship between war, media, and entertainment. "This is our second Pearl Harbor," said Senator Charles Hagel on CNN after September 11, 2001.¹ His comparison between 9/11 and the Japanese attack on December 7, 1941, was of course motivated by both events being unsuspected, both being carried out with planes, and the two attacks resulting in an almost equal number of casualties.² However, the comparison probably also sprang to mind due to the blockbuster movie *Pearl Harbor* (2001) starring Josh Hartnett and Ben Affleck, which a few weeks later on the fiftieth anniversary of Pearl Harbor had earned more than $430 million and had audiences cheering worldwide at a patriotic tale of romance and war.

The real Pearl Harbor was quickly forgotten. As the West struggled to comprehend the why and how of 9/11, media experts turned to entertainment and representation. When the World Trade Center collapsed on live television more than 160 million Americans and a billion people worldwide watched. Some — coming home and turning on their television — mistook the images for an American action movie.³ Commentators speculated that the attacks were inspired by Hollywood movies (either that the terrorists had watched American movies or, the philosophical take by Slavoj Žižek, by producing fantasies about disaster the United States saw the realization of its own long nourished desire for catastrophe).⁴ The attacks, said media experts, had been designed to ensure global media coverage. By choosing *twin* buildings the terrorists knew the media would be broadcasting when the second plane hit — and helicopters were indeed in the air a minute after the first hit, transmitting live the images of collapse that would haunt our television screens in the future.⁵

A link between entertainment, media, and war is not new. Since the production of the first American war film *Tearing Down the Spanish Flag* in

1898, war events have been used by the movie industry as inspiration for its stories, society has used war films as myths about good and evil (in the case of anti-war films simply reversing the terms), and the Pentagon has exploited the movie industry for propaganda purposes whenever possible.[6] The formal structures of war and entertainment, however, remained separate.

No, new is the *nature* of the link between entertainment, media, and war. In an almost uncanny prediction of a new relationship between war, media, and entertainment, James Der Derian in his book *Virtuous War: Mapping the Military-Industrial-Media-Entertainment Network* (2001) described what he called the MIME-network — the military-industrial-media-entertainment network.[7] Our digital technologies, claimed Der Derian, had altered the nature of war: "The new wars are fought in the same manner as they are represented, by military simulations and public dissimulations, by real-time surveillance and TV live feeds. Virtuality collapses distance, between here and there, near and far, fact and fiction."[8] Der Derian's book ends as the Institute for Creative Technologies opens in 1999, a forty-five million dollar collaborative project between the U.S. armed forces, the Hollywood entertainment industry, and the University of Southern California, "to pool expertise, financial resources, and tools of virtual reality for the production of state-of-the-art military simulations."[9] When Der Derian finished his last chapter it looked as if only the United States benefited from the MIME-network: bombings had been triumphantly transmitted as live-feeds in the Gulf War in 1991 where "smart bombs" took out enemy targets with minimal civilian losses, and advanced weapons technology practically eliminated the American losses.[10] Weeks after the war ended, CNN issued the CD-ROM *CNN: War in the Gulf* (1991) and Jean Baudrillard wrote the last of his famous three essays on the Gulf War — "The Gulf War Will Not Take Place" (January 4), "The Gulf War: Is It Really Taking Place?" (February 6) and "The Gulf War Did Not Take Place" (March 29)[11] — in denial that this was a war but instead a *simulation of* a war directed by the world's only superpower who used Iraq as setting for its tale of national victory. The MIME-network, it appeared, had "the power ... to seamlessly merge the production, representation, and execution of war."[12]

But when the planes hit the two towers, the MIME-network entered a new dimension. It took on a new function. What Der Derian had described as an American, or essentially Western, network between the military, the industry, the media, and entertainment, became *a global* network to be surfed by any media user — including those we in the West perceive as "the Other," "the opponent," or quite simply "the enemy." In planning the attacks, Bin Laden had used Western media and entertainment and turned them against the West, conscious of their function and visual appeal. However, the idea of using Western entertainment for local purposes was also being realized in less lethal ways: Thus, in 2001, Palestinian teenagers tired of playing war computer games in which they were American soldiers killing Arabs, could play the Arab war computer game *Under Siege* (2001) in which the heroes were Palestinians and the enemy were Israeli soldiers. As Helga Tawil-Souri discusses in her essay in this anthology, this was the first of many pro–Arab computer games. In *Special Force* (2003), released by the Hezbollah Central Internet Bureau, missions were based on Hezbollah missions during Israel's invasion of Southern Lebanon in the early 1980s. Suddenly, playing a computer game as an Arab meant enjoying *your own point of view*.

Today, almost a decade after Der Derian, the field of entertainment, media, industry, and war is much more than a network; it has become a condition of global civilization in the very same sense that the French philosopher Jean-Francois Lyotard used this term in his book *The Postmodern Condition* from 1979. This condition is not a roller coaster we can ride or skip as we please, not an option, but a condition we cannot escape. The network of entertainment, media, and war is a battlefield driven by commercial, social, and political interests, none of which can be innocent or "neutral." Thus, to be part of the MIME-condition means to be in a position pervaded by power and politics, whether this is the American army distributing its computer game *America's Army* online and free to further its military aims or it is Hezbollah producing Arab versions of war entertainment so that Arab children "would feel digital dignity," as one of the creators of *Under Siege* put it (see Tawil-Souri, chapter 13). The MIME-condition can be maneuvered and manipulated but it cannot be programmed and predicted; it seems to obey its own rules of communication (available and exploitable for every user) and is not easily "tricked." Thus, when the Pentagon used Ridley Scott's war movie *Black Hawk Down* (2001) as inspiration to stage the rescue of Pvt. Jessica Lynch on April 1, 2003, the bold propaganda backfired. The dramatic rescue of the captured American teenage soldier was filmed by the military's photographer and uploaded on the internet, and her story immediately turned into the television movie *The Rescue of Jessica Lynch* (Peter Markle, 2003). But seven weeks later, the BBC revealed her story as American war propaganda and her name has since become synonymous with war spin and media manipulation.

Whenever we try to establish a center or locate the exact positions of war, media, and entertainment—one is fought *here*, another reported *there*, and a third enjoyed *over there*—they seem to shift positions. Or, more precisely, to morph into one another as if absorbing each other's formal qualities. What is war becomes entertainment when soldiers record their actions, edit the material, and upload a video on the internet. What is entertainment becomes part of war when the same simulation programs are used as online entertainment and for military training purposes. Or entertainment may be indistinguishable from war when war reenactors take photographs of themselves, so realistic-looking that they end up on eBay sold as authentic war photographs.

The aim of the essays herein is not to separate media from war and entertainment, nor is it to "condemn" their interweaving. It is much too late for that. It is instead to investigate and trace their morphing into one another, to locate new developments, to critically discuss their use and signification, and if not map the territory (which is impossible) then at least shed light on the MIME-condition today. The fifteen essays engage their topics using diverse methods and theories ranging from qualitative interviews, ethnographic audience studies, cultural studies, film studies, media studies, and sociological theory. Key questions are *how war* is used as an imaginary site on which to stage dramas and create characters; *how entertainment* is used to engage viewers, audiences, gamers, as well as soldiers; *how boundaries* between war, media, and entertainment dissolve as new media alters the formal qualities (digital, online, global) of representation; and *what effect* the products of war and entertainment have on us as consumers of popular culture. The main title — *War Isn't Hell, It's Entertainment* — is both ironic and at the same time deadly serious. The title does not reflect a postmodern belief in ambivalence or the end of grand narratives, instead it acknowledges that the MIME-network is an inescapable condition of culture. Today, war is both a cruel and lethal theater of death and something else: an exciting, dramatic, heroic, or tragic narrative to be turned into films, television shows, computer games, news stories, reenactment plays, and banal militainment, and to be used for national, political, and commercial purposes as propaganda, as sites of resistance and opposition, and as "pure" entertainment providing spectacles of sublime beauty, intense joy, and larger-than-life heroes.

Part One, "The Public War Body," explores how war is aesthetized and narrativized in the public sphere. Thus *war memorials* are but one example of the last decade's renewed patriotism. Memorials today, argues art historian Erika Doss, boast recreational picnic areas, spectacular exhibitions, and high-tech museums and thus fetishize war itself as well as support militarism. Jean Baudrillard has called this "war porn."[13] The anti-war attitude of Maya Lin's Vietnam Memorial War has given way to nostalgic memorials honoring American soldiers as defenders of freedom and representatives of mythic American values and virtues. From a German perspective, military sociologist Fabian

Virchow looks at the *sport-soldiers*, who are top sportsmen and women who enlist in the army but devote all their time to training. In 1956 the German Democratic Republic (East Germany) began to use sports for military and political purposes, a strategy the Federal Republic of Germany joined in 1968 and which was continued after the reunification in 1990. Thus, at the Olympic Games in 2004, half of the German medal winners were sport-soldiers. Sport-soldiers are also used for recruitment in public events like the 2007 *Bundeswehr-Beachen* (a beach volley tournament), co-organized by the military.

From soldiers' physical bodies media scholar Mette Mortensen takes us into a digital realm where soldiers' recordings of war end on video-sharing web services like YouTube and LiveLeak, enriched with music scores and title sequences. Discussing authenticity, representation and self, and performance, Mortensen asks if such texts are entertainment, private statements, a democratic use of new media, or security threats? And how should we respond? In May 2007, the U.S. Army blocked access to several web sites, including YouTube, on its computers. In Denmark, however, the Danish Army issued a press release saying, "the army can not and will not censor private footage placed on the internet."[14]

Thus, media and war are handled differently by different nations. Another case was Pvt. Lynch, who was captured, rescued, and portrayed as a hero by Pentagon in 2003. "In reality we had two different styles of news media management," said a spokesman for the British army to *The Guardian*. "I feel fortunate to have been part of the UK one."[15] Discussing the Lynch case, film researcher Rikke Schubart does not focus on the incorrect facts (Lynch had not been abused and American soldiers shot blanks during the rescue) but on the rules of myth. According to historian Richard Slotkin a captured white woman stands at the center of American frontier mythology and historian George L. Mosse claims a woman cannot represent the nation as a combative war figure.[16] Lynch was rejected as a hero, says Schubart, because her gender did not fit American mythology. Less controversial media events were the telethon *America: A Tribute to the Heroes* and the *Concert for New York* where actors, musicians, and sports stars raised almost 300 million dollars after 9/11, each event earning more than any celebrity charity event to date. Such celebrity events, says media researcher Sue Collins, signal the convergence of the famous, the heroic, and the ordinary in media responses to the terrorist attacks. Celebrity functions as a cultural commodity, a promoter of capitalist consumption, and as a generator of intertextual meaning where activism intersects with economic power, spectacle, and nationalist unity.

Part Two, "War and Entertainment," deals with old-fashioned — one could say banal — links between entertainment and war. Outlining the gendered character of the military, cultural studies researcher Tanja Thomas discusses interaction between the military institutions and protagonists from the civilian sections of society. Media products like television soaps and documentaries are used to normalize soldiership as an ordinary profession and normalize certain kinds of gendered bodies and gendered practices. Following Michael Billig's term "banal nationalism,"[17] which designates the daily and ordinary routines that reproduce the nation, Thomas examines how the military use female actors, singers, and performers to recruit young people in what she calls "banal militarism."

The next four contributions turn to film and television. How can we take pleasure from watching scenes of combat and mutilation? asks film researcher Anne Gjelsvik. Because we respond with *mixed emotions* of fear, pity, excitement, and admiration. Taking Peter Weir's *Master and Commander* (2003) as her example, Gjelsvik dissects, for instance, our emotions when watching scenes of surgery performed without anesthesia. Drawing on philosophy and cognitive film theory, she argues that the spectator's pleasure comes from the mediated representation of war and not war itself, whereas emotions of pity and disgust correspond to the empathy and affects aroused in daily life.

Discussing the CBS television series *M*A*S*H* (1972–1983), film researcher Yvonne Tasker shows how the reading of this series, long praised for its anti-war credentials and characterized as a spoof of war films, has changed over time. By the end of the 1980s, critics drew attention to its individualist, masculinist aura and casual racism. *M*A*S*H* is significant for lasting longer than the UN police action it depicts and for outlasting the U.S. involvement in Vietnam, to which it had a more immediate cultural context at the time it originally aired. Combining elements of melodrama and tragedy with those of the situation comedy, *M*A*S*H* enacted war as "a process of living with war, and with moral outrage, via television," a process, says Tasker, which may be instructive today. Film researcher Debra White-Stanley also returns to the Korean War in her comparison of Jonathan Demme's 2004 remake of *The Manchurian Candidate* to the original film from 1962 and Richard Condon's novel from 1959. Themes of cold war, communist paranoia, and surveillance anxiety are replaced with anxieties about war casualties in Operation Iraqi Freedom, about prisoner abuse (at the time of filming Demme's remake Abu Ghraib was not yet a publicly known scandal), political corruption, and racial guilt. Ambiguously, Demme's film both problematizes historical memory and mourns the male sacrifices of war.

Finally, military historian Lawrence H. Suid looks at how depictions of the atomic bomb have oscillated in documentaries, film, and television fiction between being positive, negative, and neutral, using various strategies of authenticity and fictionalization. Thus, although Norman Taurog's film *The Beginning or the End* (1947) presented itself as historically correct and took its title from a comment by President Harry Truman, the film was in fact heavily fictionalized.

Part Three, "Playing at War," follows war into reenactment and, especially, computer games. Today, films play a lesser role in producing narratives of war and vicarious experiences of combat than do computer games, for which revenue and number of users long ago surpassed those of the film industry.

War reenactment is a growing area of entertainment in which participants create "authentic" war experiences by forming units, dressing in period uniforms, and recreating battles of past wars. As part of her ethnographic research Jenny Thompson attended forty-three of these "events" and gained first-hand evidence of "the hobby," as reenactors call their activities. Deeply serious, reenactors create their own war memories and war stories by living their own war experiences and, in their own way, reenactors place themselves in the history books: "No other collection that I can think of — like stamps or coins — you can't just shrink yourself into a stamp and put yourself in the book and go, you know, 'Oh, look! I'm a stamp!' Right? I mean this is something that you can actually collect and actually show off. Be a part of it."[18]

Our last four essays demonstrate that computer game producers and players are increasingly "a part of it" when they play at war. Long before the Institute for Creative Technologies was established in 1999, the military had been aware of the potentials offered by computer games for simulation and training. Already in 1962, the game *Spacewar* was produced by the Hingham Institute sponsored by the Study Group on Space Warfare, and in 1980 the U.S. Army collaborated with Atari in retooling the game *Battlezone* (1980) for target training use for gunners on the Bradley Fighting Vehicle, a tank. Providing a critical history of digital war games, in chapter 12 Marcus Power discusses the location of games in today's MIME-network. They "present a clean, sanitized and enjoyable version of war for popular consumption, obscuring the realities, contexts and consequences of war," but at the same time they also "provide players with coping strategies in a world full of geopolitical anxiety and uncertainty." Power is concerned that digital war games, with their disappearance of dead bodies and sanitized war free from "external political, moral, ideological, and humanitarian factors,"[19] do not sufficiently represent the reality of war.

But games also offer possibilities for political resistance. If Marcus Power — with Jean Baudrillard and James Der Derian — is concerned about the sanitization of war, Helga Tawil-Souri by contrast engages with the political potential of digital war games. Based on interviews with players, parents, and computer center owners in the Palestinian Territories, she examines the pro–Arab computer games *Under Siege* (Dar al-Fikr, 2001), *Under Ash* (Dar al-Fikr, 2003), and *Special Force* (Hezbollah Central Internet Bureau, 2003). They do not have eight million registered users like *America's Army* yet they are a huge success among Arab teenagers who play Arab heroes fighting Israeli soldiers. Situating the discussion of media violence within Orientalism and Western myopia, Tawil-Souri points to contradictions in the West's reactions: if the games are to be condemned for training terrorists and suicide bombers, what, then, about *America's Army* or *Ethnic Cleansing*, the latter a game where the player can be a Ku Klux Klansman or neo–Nazi skinhead? Rather than focus on effects and violence we should welcome these games as a challenge to Western hegemony. They reflect their users' worldview and as such "are entering a landscape already gripped by political unrest, displacement and collective violence" (Tawil-Souri, chapter 13). If they are not nice, then neither is the geopolitical world they represent.

We should ask ourselves what the military is thinking when producing computer games as instruments of public relations, recruitment, and training. This is exactly what Matthew Thomas Payne does in his essay based on interviews with the head producers of *America's Army* (2002), *America's Army: Rise of a Soldier* (2005), and *Full Spectrum Warrior* (2004). These producers become new media cultural brokers whose visions of war and opinions about representation and realism are immensely important in shaping the games that entertain millions of users globally. They are extremely aware of what they call *positive realism*—"the verisimilitude of real world topographies, physics, and ballistics"—and *negative realism*—"any element that deviates from codes and conventions of military realism" (Payne, chapter 14). Getting the weapons and the dirt on the walls right is positive realism, whereas swearing, blood, and dead bodies are negative realism. Payne offers a rare insight into the mind of producers who strategically design teen-rated games so they also appeal to eleven-year-old gamers: positive engagements with military environments, they believe, ease positive views of the military at a later age.

Finally, new media researcher Bo Kampmann Walther reflects on the relation between game and war. The two are miles apart when it comes to human involvement (war kills, computer games don't), yet share formal qualities like rules, strategies, and interaction patterns. Training and playing meet in what Dutch historian Johan Huizinga calls the "sacred playground" and Walther sheds light on the formal qualities that attract both the military and the individual gamer. However, playing also has a societal dimension. Danish new media researcher Jesper Juul has defined games as "half-real" because they are simulations ("play") yet we invest something in them ("a larger and fuzzier societal context") (Walther, chapter 15). A game is both play and not-play, like soccer players debating a referee's decision is both part of the game and not part of the game. Walther agrees with Sherry Turkle that simulations can be power tools in that "people who understand the distortions imposed by simulation are in a position to call for more direct economic and political feedback, new kinds of representation, and more channels of information." Playing at war incorporates formal qualities and also invites real investment. Which is precisely why Palestinian teenagers prefer to kill Israeli soldiers when gaming in the internet cafés.

The contributors differ in their opinion about the relation between war, media, and entertainment, but one thing is certain: the MIME–condition is here and we cannot leave it, like Neo pulling needles out of his body and quitting the program in the film *The Matrix* (1999). Our Matrix is *our* world, physically as well as virtually. But even if we cannot master it, we can do our best to understand how it works. Because the MIME-condition is *not* a "second Pearl Harbor" nor is it a second Matrix nor second anything else. It is a unique condition happening to us, around us, with us, right now.

Notes

1. Jesper Zimmer Hansen, "Pearl Harbor revisited? Den formaterede virkelighed efter 11. september" [Pearl Harbor revisited? The formatted reality after September 11] in *Mediernes 11. september* [The media's September 11], ed. Lars Qvortrup, 73–89, 73 (Copenhagen: Gads forlag, 2002).
2. Pearl Harbor had 2,402 death casualties in 1941; the 9/11 attacks had 2,998 death casualties in 2001. Numbers are from Wikipedia, accessed from http://en.wikipedia.org/wiki/Attack_on_Pearl_Harbor and http://en.wikipedia.org/wiki/9/11 on June 17, 2008.
3. Kirsten Drotner, "Når virkeligheden overgår fiktion: mediematricer mellem det kendte og det ukendte" [When reality surpasses fiction: Media matrixes between the known and the unknown] in Qvortrup 28–42, 33, *Mediernes 11. september*.
4. Astrid Söderbergh Widding discusses Žižek in "Filmretorik og den internationale politik" [Film rhetoric and international policy], *MedieKultur*, themed issue on media and war, ed. Rikke Schubart and Bent Steeg Larsen, no. 38 April (2005): 43–50. See also Slavoj Žižek, *Welcome to the Desert of the Real* (London: Verso, 2002) and Jean Baudrillard, *The Spirit of Terrorism* (London: Verso, 2002).
5. Drotner, "Mediematricer," 29.
6. See Robert Eberwein ed., *The War Film* (New Brunswick: Rutgers University Press, 2005) about the American war film as a genre. During the Second World War, Hollywood produced almost 2,500 war films with assistance from the Pentagon, James Der Derian, *Virtuous War: Mapping the Military-Industrial-Media-Entertainment Network* (Boulder: Westview Press, 2001), 168. An example of willing war propaganda is the seven episode

documentary series *Why We Fight* (1942–45), produced by Frank Capra under commission by the government.

7. The term alludes to the military-industrial complex (MIC), composed of a nation's armed forces, its suppliers of weapons systems, supplies and services, and its civil government. The term was made famous when President Dwight D. Eisenhower used it in his Farewell Address to the Nation on January 17, 1961. Information is from Wikipedia accessed from http://en.wikipedia.org/wiki/Military-industrial_complex on June 25, 2008.

8. Der Derian, *Virtuous War*, xviii.

9. Ibid., 162.

10. For a critical analysis of the Gulf War see H. Mowlana, G. Gerbner and H.I. Schiller (ed.), *Triumph of the Image: The Media's War in the Persian Gulf—A Global Perspective* (Boulder and Oxford: Westview Press, 1992) and Douglas Kellner, *The Persian Gulf TV War* (Boulder and Oxford: Westview Press, 1992).

11. "The Gulf War Will Not Take Place" appeared in *Libération* January 4, 1991, part of "The Gulf War: Is It Really Taking Place" appeared in *Libération* February 6 and fragments of "The Gulf War Did Not Take Place" appeared in *Libération* March 29. The articles were published together as *La Guerre du Golfe n'a pas eu lieu* (Paris: Galilée, 1991) and published in English in 1991 as *The Gulf War Did Not Take Place*. See *The Gulf War Did Not Take Place*, translated and with an introduction by Paul Patton (Bloomington: Indiana University Press, 1995).

12. Der Derian, *Virtuous War*, xx.

13. Jean Baudrillard, "Pornographie de la guerre," *Liberation* (May 19, 2004), reprinted as "War Porn" in *The Conspiracy of Art: Manifestos, Texts, Interviews* (Cambridge: MIT Press, 2005), 205–212, quoted from Erik Doss, this volume.

14. Press release of August 23, 2007, from the Army's Operational Command, quoted from Mette Mortensen, this volume. See Mortensen's article for a discussion of the Danish and American military responses to digital footage and public use of the Internet.

15. Al Lockwood quoted in John Kampfner, "The Truth About Jessica," *The Guardian*, May 15, 2003, accessed from http://www.guardian.co.uk/Iraq/Story/0,2763,956255,00.html on November 12, 2003, and quoted from Rikke Schubart, this volume.

16. Richard Slotkin, *Regeneration Through Violence: The Mythology of the American Frontier, 1600–1860* (New York: Wesleyan University Press, 1996, 1973); George L. Mosse, *Nationalism and Sexuality: Respectability and Abnormal Sexuality in Modern Europe* (New York: Howard Fertig, 1985).

17. Michael Billig, *Banal Nationalism* (London: Sage, 1995), quoted from Tanja Thomas, this volume.

18. Richard Paoletti, interview with the Jenny Thompson, February 1997, quoted from Jenny Thompson, this volume.

19. Adam Elkus, "Subliminal Militarization," accessed from http://82.165.179.211/warandpeace/35759/ on November 19, 2006, quoted from Marcus Power, this volume.

Part One
The Public War Body

1

War Porn
Spectacle and Seduction in Contemporary American War Memorials
ERIKA DOSS

Introduction: The Spectacle of Gratitude

Bursts of machine-gun fire sting the water; soldiers stumble out of landing craft and struggle to shore; bodies litter the beach. Welcome to the National D-Day Memorial in Bedford, Virginia, a nine-acre, multi-sculptured, $25 million tribute to "the sacrifices of the Allied Armed Forces who landed in Normandy, France on June 6, 1944."[1] Located on an 88-acre hillside in the southeastern part of the state, about ten miles from the Blue Ridge Mountains, the center of the memorial features a gigantic triumphal arch — exactly, symbolically, forty-four feet and six inches tall — inscribed with the word OVERLORD on its polished granite entablature: the code name of the military operation commanded by American general Dwight Eisenhower. The sprawling site also features formal gardens (including one planted in the design and colors of the Supreme Headquarters Allied Expeditionary Force shoulder patch), a circle of flags representing the twelve Allied nations, a "Necrology Wall" with the names of U.S. servicemen killed on D-Day, and a display of war matériel (anchors, propellers, and a restored Aeronca L-3 "Grasshopper" aircraft). Overlord Arch is capped with black-and-white stonework that imitates the stripes on Allied aircraft used during D-Day; nearby is "Final Tribute," a "fallen soldier" sculpture of a helmet hoisted on an inverted rifle that replicates battlefield memorials to soldier dead often raised by soldiers themselves.

Most visitors spend their time in the memorial's huge interior plaza, where the action on Omaha Beach is dramatically restaged — albeit reduced to a frozen tableau of a few life-sized bronze action figures slogging their way through a six-inch-deep reflecting pool toward a simulated sandy beach made of aggregate concrete. Every few seconds, water jets shoot up from various locations in the pool, in sync with a soundtrack of German machine gun fire. One fallen GI lies crumpled on the shore, his head resting near a waterlogged Bible; another screams in anguish while trying to scale a twenty-foot green metal wall standing in for the cliffs at Pointe-du-Hoc. Occasionally, the memorial is open at night for various events, and the grounds are flooded in red, white, and blue lights. Every Father's Day in June, it hosts the "World War II in Miniature Show and Contest," sponsored by the Roanoke Valley Chapter of the International Plastic Modelers Society. "This monument pays tribute to those who died on D-Day but also to those who lived to secure the beachhead and carry freedom inland," reads the memorial's entrance plaque. "Treasure it."

With its Disney-esque aesthetics and preposterous special effects, the National D-Day Memorial has all the humble solemnity and commemorative decorum of a water park. While framed as an international memorial to Allied forces, it is clearly beholden to the obligations and demands of American war memory. Authorized by Congress in 1997, it is located in Bedford because the town claims more losses on D-Day than any other American

National D-Day Memorial, Bedford, Virginia, dedicated June 2001 (photograph by Erika Doss).

town: nineteen of its thirty-five citizen soldiers died during the invasion, two more during the fighting in Normandy. However appalling this hokey memorial, "the order of the day is gratitude," intoned President George W. Bush at its dedication in 2001, held on the 57th anniversary of D-Day and attended by some 24,000 people. "Today we give thanks for all that was gained on the beaches of Normandy," he added. "We remember what was lost, with respect, admiration, and love."[2]

The Seduction of World War II

Americans certainly love D-Day: more than 800,000 visited the National D-Day Memorial in its first five years of operation. Likewise, the National D-Day Museum in New Orleans, which opened in 2000 and was re-named the National World War II Museum in 2006, attracted some 300,000 visitors a year before Hurricane Katrina, which put it in the top ten percent of museum attendance figures nationwide. *Saving Private Ryan*, a $70 million blockbuster which included a carnage-strewn twenty-five minute D-Day sequence that critics and movie goers couldn't stop talking about, was the most popular Hollywood release of 1998, generating a domestic gross alone of over $216 million and winning Steven Spielberg an Oscar for Best Director. Tom Hanks, who played the role of Captain John H. Miller in *Saving Private Ryan*, used his talents to endorse the National World War II Memorial, and helped raise over $52 million for the grandiose monument that was dedicated on the national mall, between the Lincoln Memorial and the Washington Monument, in 2004. Among the plethora of World War II computer and video games, titles like *Close Combat: Invasion Normandy* (2000), *Medal of Honor: Allied Assault* (2002), *Call of Duty* (2003), and *Brothers in Arms: D-Day* (2006) attest to D-Day's resonance in the gaming industry.[3] Some sixty year after the fact, D-Day continues to loom large in the American national imaginary.

So does Pearl Harbor, perhaps the most enduring symbol of World War II itself, endlessly circulated in America's political rhetoric and its culture industries in order to shore up various national scenarios. In the early 1980s, Pearl Harbor's fortieth anniversary prompted political and media hype about America's "trade war" with Japan being induced by an "economic Pearl Harbor." A decade later, Pearl Harbor's fiftieth anniversary was commemorated by a host of books, television shows, and museum exhibitions that crystallized December 7, 1941, as "the day" that World War II started for America — and cast aspersions on any competing narratives suggesting prior U.S.

knowledge of the Japanese attack, and hence of national compliance in the orchestration of that "good war." In 2004, the National World War II Memorial was dedicated in Washington, D.C., a grandiose monument described in its mission statement as "an important symbol of American national unity, a timeless reminder of the moral strength and awesome power that can flow when a free people are at once united and bonded together in a common and just cause."[4]

As Emily Rosenberg argues, Pearl Harbor's legacy has been to reinforce American beliefs that war is "event-driven," that Americans only "go" to war when attacked by the forces of evil, and that the United States is essentially an innocent and peace-loving nation.[5] Historical narratives that veer from these assumptions and attempt more nuanced interpretations, such as introductory films shown at the USS *Arizona* Memorial Visitors Center (which hosted 1.5 million visitors in 2000), or a planned Smithsonian exhibit in the mid–1990s on the *Enola Gay* and the "dilemmas of nuclear strategy," are savaged as anti–American and anti-patriotic, even treasonous.[6]

The $135 million movie *Pearl Harbor*, a three-hour epic that opened in May 2001, reaffirmed these cause and effect, good versus evil understandings of World War II (and war in general) for many Americans. So did its blitz of

National World War II Memorial, Washington, D.C., dedicated May 2004 (photograph by Erika Doss).

marketing tie-ins, from Hasbro's "Pearl Harbor GI Joe Collection" and ASAP's video game *Pearl Harbor: Zero Hour*, to military history books, war movie re-releases (such as a refurbished version of the 1970 film *Tora! Tora! Tora!*), and numerous television specials (like MSNBC's *Pearl Harbor: Attack on America*, hosted by General Norman Schwarzkopf). It is hardly surprising, then, that four months later, Pearl Harbor became the most "enduring analogy" to 9/11. On September 11, 2001, George W. Bush apparently wrote "The Pearl Harbor of the 21st century took place today" in his presidential diary, and the next day, the *New York Times* alone included some thirteen articles mentioning Pearl Harbor. Banners screaming "DAY OF INFAMY," which echoed President Franklin Delano Roosevelt's description of Pearl Harbor as "a date which will live in infamy," headlined many other U.S. newspapers.[7]

War Porn

Long before 9/11, of course, Americans had been pining for the glory days of World War II and, more generally, pursuing a giddy romance with all things war: the "war on drugs," "the war on AIDS," "the war to control the legal culture," as Robert Bork described his unsuccessful bid for the Supreme Court in 1987. However contradictory the uses of these multiple war metaphors, war itself is ingrained in contemporary American national consciousness because, as Michael Sherry argues, of longstanding and automatic assumptions that war alone is "the best way to mobilize Americans and to capture their problems and conflicts."[8] War is the great American distraction: mythologized as a patriotic project; articulated as an economic linch-pin; desired for its explicit, stimulating, visceral, and authenticating capacities. And war porn is the great American cultural expression, not as a form of sexual fantasy and social transgression but as an instrument of national consensus, conformity, and normalcy.

Jean Baudrillard likened war porn to the titillation derived from Abu-Ghraib's atrocity snapshots, while staff at *Adbusters* used the term to describe *Time Magazine*'s 2003 "Person of the Year: The American Soldier": a group of young, good-looking GI's pictured on the magazine's cover dressed in desert khakis and body armor, cradling M-16's, and described as "the face of America, its might and good will, in a region unused to democracy."[9] Constituting both the subjects and objects of the nation's martial authority, war porn characterizes the contemporary American lust for militarism, evinced not only in war movies, war games, war toys, and war memorials but in the general fetishization of war itself on every conceivable level of American society. Americans today are utterly seduced by war, argues Andrew Bacevich, and are especially swayed by a "new American militarism" that manifests itself in "a romanticized view of soldiers, a tendency to see military power as the truest measure of national greatness, and outsized expectations regarding the efficacy of force." He adds: "To a degree without precedent in U.S. history, Americans have come to define the nation's strength and well-being in terms of military preparedness, military action, and the fostering of (or nostalgia for) military ideals."[10]

Whether or not this "new American militarism" is all that new — Jackson Lears, Amy Kaplan, and Jonathan Hansen, among others, have discussed the nation's prevalent martial ethos at the turn of the 20th century — it is certainly central to contemporary American identity.[11] And it is increasingly realized in America's growing body of war memorials. From abstract to figurative memorials, from benches and walls to groves of trees, flagpoles, and street signs — Yuma, Arizona, mandates that new city streets be named after U.S. soldier dead — commemorating American militarism has become a shared national imperative. Their burgeoning numbers speak to a generally unquestioned American faith in militarism, and accommodate the nation's sense of itself as a military presence and power, as a force to be reckoned with.

Honoring Soldier Dead

The contemporary surge in war memorials stems in part from the popular and critical success of the Vietnam Veterans Memorial, a long, low horizontal sculpture featuring two intersecting walls of highly polished black granite. Designed by Maya Lin and dedicated in Washington, D.C., in 1982 despite considerable controversy, "The Wall" is the national capital's most popular memorial (3.8 million visitors were counted in 2005), and has spurred the making of hundreds of other Vietnam memorials across the country — over 500, estimates one author.[12] It has also influenced many other war memory projects, including Korean War memorials dedicated in Washington, D.C. (1995), Toledo, Ohio (2006), Lawrence, Kansas (2005), Baton Rouge, Louisiana (2004), Lake County, Indiana (2003), Philadelphia (2002), Wichita, Kansas (2001), and Wilsonville, Oregon (2000). Memorials to the Cold War, such as the Victims of Communism Memorial (dedicated in Washington, D.C. in June 2007) and to the Gulf War, including Operation Desert Shield/Desert Storm memorials erected in Greensburg, Pennsylvania (1992), Evansville, Indiana (1993), and Lincoln City, Oregon (1994), also dot the

American landscape. Memorials to the U.S. war in Iraq and Afghanistan have already been built in New Bedford, Massachusetts (2006), Lewiston, Maine (2006), and Blanca, Colorado (2004). In 2004, the Middle East Conflicts War Memorial was dedicated in Marseilles, Illinois. Commemorating U.S. soldier dead has also become a boon to the commercial monument industry, as seen in the burgeoning appearance of "memorial benches" and "fallen soldier" statues. Retailing for around $200, memorial benches to U.S. soldiers killed in Iraq — simple granite seats inscribed with their names, their birth and death dates, and epithets of remembrance — can be seen in cities ranging from San Clemente, California, and Sierra Vista, Arizona, to Independence, Indiana, and Lewiston, Maine. Likewise, "fallen soldier" statues marketed by the Large Art Company, a custom bronze sculpture firm headquartered in Baltimore, have been erected in towns across the country. Also called "Battlefield Cross" memorials, these bronze arrangements of boots, helmets, and rifles cost $4,400 and are among the most popularly requested items from Large Art; as of 2007, over seventy had been sold, including five erected in Iraq. As company owner and artist Richard Rist remarks, "I sense an eagerness to almost overcompensate in honoring our war dead."[13]

The Vietnam Veterans Memorial has had a big impact, too, on how this growing body of contemporary war memorials is defined and understood. Much as Maya Lin's memorial was commissioned as a "veterans" memorial, as a tribute to the military men and women who served in the Vietnam War, subsequent war memorials have been cast as "service" memo-

Fallen Soldier Memorial, Thornton, Colorado, dedicated July 2005 (photograph by Erika Doss).

rials: as tributes to soldiers rather than the wars they fought in. Such distinctions are specious: the nation does not build memorials to peacetime clerk typists.[14] Whatever they are called, American memorials that commemorate the nation's soldiers are war memorials. They are both copious and historically sweeping.

In 2004, for example, a memorial to the "Army of Occupation," the U.S. troops commanded by General Zachary Taylor during the Mexican American War (1846–1847), was erected in Corpus Christi, Texas. In 2006 in Kansas City, the Liberty Memorial — a World War I memorial originally dedicated in 1926 — was refurbished and expanded with the addition of the National World War I Memorial Museum. In San Francisco, plans are in place for the Abraham Lincoln Brigade Monument, the first national memorial to the 3,000 Americans who fought in the Spanish Civil War from 1936 to 1938. In 2004 in Iowa, a $10 million 4.6-acre Memorial Park & Education Center honoring black and female soldiers was dedicated at Fort Des Moines, where the first Officer Candidate School opened to African American men in 1917, and where the Women's Army Auxiliary Corps trained during World War II.

Recognizing the time-consuming and costly efforts of repeatedly raising new war memorials to commemorate the nation's nonstop history of conflict and combat, some communities have opted for "all-war" memorials that collectively remember all of America's soldiers and wars — and leave room for more. The Veterans Walk of Honor in Ripon, Wisconsin (dedicated 2001) is one; the Veterans Memorial in Palisade, Nebraska (2006), population 386, is another. Plans are underway in Picatinny, New Jersey, to establish a memorial "for the bygone, ongoing, and future sacrifices made by all New Jersey fallen soldiers."

Munster, Indiana's Community Veterans Memorial (2003), a $3.2 million seven-acre site, similarly commemorates "those who participated in the great wars of the 20th century — World Wars I and II, Korea, Vietnam, Desert Storm," and leaves lots of open space for the "great wars" of America's future. Designed by Julie Rotblatt and Omri Amrany (perhaps best known for their sixteen-foot statue of basketball star Michael Jordan installed in front of Chicago's United Center), Munster's memorial is located on a former landfill on the outskirts of town, next to a business park and Heartland Memorial Hospital. It features "actual war memorabilia" (P-51 Mustang fighter plane, 75mm Airborne Pack Howitzer, Huey helicopter) and life-sized bronze sculptures, which are sprinkled among landscapes meant to depict "the terrains of the countries in which the conflicts took place." World War II is represented by a recreation of Omaha Beach; Vietnam by a ruined Buddhist temple and a menacing Green Beret aiming a 40mm grenade launcher at anyone in his way. The Gulf War is recreated in piles of pea gravel simulating sand dunes, and a billowing ten-foot bronze cloud depicting the burning oil wells of Kuwait. Nearby, in a closing vignette titled "The Emptiness of War," a small boy clutching his father's dog tags surveys the entire wartime tableau from the vantage of his bombed-out house.

Like the National D-Day Memorial, Munster's all-war memorial is a highly affective space with intensely dramatic images, text panels, and audio guides ("Push to Hear History") describing each wartime scene. It is also shamelessly contrived as an all-war theme park modeled on a miniature golf course. Spiraling walkways made of memorial bricks — which visitors are encouraged to purchase as "a permanent tribute to loved ones who fought to preserve our freedoms" — link all-wars in an endless loop; winding their way from one park attraction to the next, visitors perpetually reanimate national war memory. Benches, ponds, fountains, and landscaped lawns lend a recreational air to the site, inviting visitors to throw frisbees and have a picnic while they also look at the bodies of dead soldiers and stroll past wrecked wartime dioramas. And visitors are enthusiastic: children crawl through the ruined buildings and climb on the Howitzer while their parents exclaim about the "lifelike" qualities of the bronze statues.

Although Rotblatt says the Munster memorial aims to address the "horrors of war" and "how we hope to evolve as a species to break the cycle of war," its spectacular sets, battle-ready cast of characters, heroizing script ("in the bush, without a helmet, he moves swiftly and silently" is the description of the Special Forces soldier), and dizzying theme park dynamics hardly inspire anti-war sentiment.[15] Rather, as one visitor observed: "Anybody that's an American that's in this country, that sits there and wants to pick at this and that, maybe they should come and look at this thing and see what the veterans are doing. They had a job to do and they did it." Considering such audience reception, it is not surprising that each September 11 since 2002, Munster's memorial hosts "Freedom Walk," one of 42 such walks organized across America by the United States Defense Department to rally support for U.S. troops in Iraq. In 2005, participants in Washington, D.C. donned free "Freedom Walk" t-shirts and marched from the Pentagon to the national mall, viewing war memorials along the route that Secretary of Defense Donald Rumsfeld said serve to remind Americans of "the sacrifices of this generation and of each previous generation that has so successfully defended our freedoms."[16]

While some of the nation's newer war memorials pay homage to the Minimalist and mournful aesthetics of the Vietnam Veterans Memorial, most feature figures, images, and expressions that romanticize American soldiers and celebrate a martialized American identity. Pittsburgh's Vietnam and Gulf War Veterans Memorial (1995), for example, a small monument erected on the city's south side, consists of a polished black granite wall inscribed with "Welcome Home" and with bronze plaques featuring the "POW/MIA" logo, the insignia of various military service units, and the "fallen soldier" motif. The Korean War Monument in New Bedford, Massachusetts (2001), similarly features a black stone wall angled in an accordion fold and etched with the names of soldier dead, military badges, photographs of tanks, aircraft carriers, Corsair fighter bombers, and U.S. soldiers, and the inscription "Korean War, 1950–1953, Freedom Is Not Free." That adage, also inscribed on a wall of the Korean War Veterans Memorial in Washington, D.C., has been widely adopted in contemporary American war memorials. However Orwellian — implying that freedom requires debt, entails costs, and demands sacrifices; declaring, by virtue of being inscribed on war memorials (and generally nowhere else) that war is the price of freedom and, in fact, requires the sacrifice of freedom: that freedom must be sacrificed to be free — it is an adage beholden to the culture of gratitude that informs contemporary American war memorials.

We Are All Warriors

Veterans of color are especially engaged today in war memory, which is not surprising given the U.S. military's prominent position today as a leading minority employer — and its historical authority as the first large-scale American institution to officially desegregate (in 1948). Until the past few decades, minority military participation was mostly neglected in American commemorative culture, save for notable exceptions like the Shaw Memorial (Boston, 1897), the Victory Monument (Chicago, 1926) and the All Wars Memorial to Colored Soldiers and Sailors (Philadelphia, 1934). Recently, however, black soldiers have been the subjects of multiple memorials to multiple wars, from the Revolutionary War to World War II. In 2005, a memorial to the 1st Rhode Island Regiment, a unit of black slaves and freemen authorized in 1775, was dedicated at Patriots Park in Portsmouth, Rhode Island; in 2006, the African American World War II Navy Memorial was dedicated in North Chicago. Memorials paying tribute to black Civil War soldiers are especially prevalent. In 1998, the African American Civil War Memorial, featuring Ed Hamilton's *The Spirit of Freedom*, a nine-foot bronze statue depicting black Union soldiers and sailors, was unveiled in Washington, D.C. In 2004, Kim Sessums' African American Monument, a $300,000 sculpture that depicts black contraband and commemorates "the service of the 1st and 3rd Mississippi Infantry Regiments, African Descent," was dedicated at Vicksburg National Military Park.[17] Aimed at crafting minority membership in the national imaginary, none of these war memorials reference the slavery economics that erupted in the American Civil War, nor do they address the demeaning conditions for black troops in a racist and segregated American military. Focused on gratitude, they glorify the "service" of black soldiers without critiquing the originating conditions of their servitude.

Nor are these memorials unique: in recent decades, enormous efforts have been expended to include all Americans in national war memory. In 2000, for example, Congress authorized the $65 million American Veterans Disabled for Life Memorial on a two-acre site near the U.S. Capitol. A memorial to honor Latino veterans is being built in Avondale, Colorado. Native American soldiers are commemorated by the Indian Memorial, the 2003 addition to the Little Bighorn National Battlefield Monument near Crow Agency, Montana; by the National Native American Vietnam Veterans Memorial (1995) at The Highground, a 140-acre veterans memorial park near Neillsville, Wisconsin; and by the Cherokee Warrior Memorial (2005) in Tahlequah, Oklahoma, which features a granite wall, two 105mm cannons, and 2,000 brick pavers honoring individual Cherokee veterans. The National Japanese American Memorial (Washington, D.C., 2000) pays tribute to the thousands of Japanese Americans who served in the U.S. armed forces during World War II, before they were accused of national disloyalty and forcibly interned in wartime "relocation" camps.

Women soldiers are commemorated by the Vietnam Women's Memorial (Washington, D.C., 1993), the Women in Military Service for America Memorial (Arlington, Virginia, 1997) the New York State Women Veterans Memorial (Albany, 1998), the Women Veterans Monument (North Hanover, New Jersey, 2003), and the Women's War Memorial (Broken Bow, Oklahoma, 2007). Historically, American women have played leading roles in national war memory, from organizing Civil War memorials at the turn of the last century to orchestrating the recovery and return of soldier dead to U.S. soil after World War I.[18] The daughters of many World War II veterans were instrumental in creating the Rosie the Riveter/World War II Home Front National Historical Park (2000), a memorial in Richmond, California, that replicates the frame of the Liberty cargo ships that female wartime industrial workers produced at the Kaiser Shipyards.

Women soldier memorials are often praised for their grassroots public processes and hyper-inclusionary ambitions: for the ways in which they seemingly challenge American memorial culture's mostly male domain (none of the 43 national memorials managed by the United States National Park Service, for example, focus specifically on women or women's history); for historically recovering the two million women who have served in the U.S. armed forces since the nation's beginnings; and for depicting American women as powerful and heroic figures. Yet none of them takes up the dynamics of gender in America's armed forces, or considers the processes and practices by which women are integrated into the U.S. military. In Charleston, West Virginia, for example, an eight-foot bronze statue of a woman soldier was commissioned for inclusion in the Veterans Memorial, a $3.8 million oval monument that features similarly huge statues of male soldiers. Yet the female figure, dressed in fatigues, t-shirt, and combat boots, was deemed "too masculine" by a review panel of female veterans, and the women's memorial was cancelled. Sculptor P. Joseph Mullins followed the directive to depict a "modern woman" soldier, but female vets said they wanted something that "looked more like a lady" instead of statues that "just look like another male." Scholars have argued that membership in the military body is predicated on masculine terms; as Heather J. Höpfl remarks, "one must become a man in order to demonstrate [the] discipline and commitment" that defines the modern military.[19] Yet that view is seemingly at odds with those held by female veterans.

Assumptions, in fact, that contemporary war memorials especially or only pay tribute to particular soldiers — black soldiers, Native American warriors, women veterans, etc.— and not the nation and its militarist agenda, are highly misleading. As Bryan Turner remarks, today's war memorials "are more concerned with the forgotten soldier, the mistreated, the disappeared.... Individuals, not states, get memorialized as, for example, in Maya Lin's Vietnam Veterans Memorial."[20] Yet these memorials are made because their patrons insist that they, too, are entitled to a voice, a place, and a historical presence in the national American imaginary. Even if they are individualized and localized, they are components of *national* war memory; however much they pay tribute to and maybe even mourn America's soldier dead, they exist because of, and hardly contest, the larger context of American militarism. Likewise, although the U.S. military rather confusedly marketed itself as an "Army of One" from 2000 to 2005, the fact is that military membership for all soldier bodies is predicated on their uniformity within a like-acting national military body that adheres to imperatives of strength, bravery, heroism, and authority. These imperatives have been traditionally associated with masculinity but as Judith Butler argues, gender is not what we are but what we perform and in the U.S. military, performance is geared toward the cohesion of the unit and the protection of the nation.[21] Most significantly in this light, individual memorials like women's war memorials perform the same role as other American war memorials: framing their subjects, and their audiences, in a militarized national narrative.

Bloodless Sacrifice

"Monuments to veterans are popular again," states the newspaper headline of a 2006 story on the war memorial "binge" in Southern California. In Riverside County, for example, tributes to Vietnam vets, Native American vets, women vets, and Medal of Honor vets are all underway, and memorials like *Letters Home* are already in place. Dedicated in 2004 in Temecula, California and designed by sculptor Christopher Pardell, the $472,000 memorial features a sixteen-foot semi-circular bench and a life-size bronze statue of a battle-ready, khaki-clad soldier, helmet on his knee, M-16 at his side. The sculptural equivalent of the similarly buff GI's pictured on the cover of *Time* in 2003, this young soldier sits on sandbags as he pens a letter, using his helmet as a writing table. A granite wall at his back is embellished with the texts of sixteen other letters written by American soldiers from the Revolutionary War to the war in Iraq; a "Path of Honor" leading to the bench consists of hundreds of memorial pavers ($65 each) engraved with the names of local soldiers. "Hopefully when people come here they will get a sense that these are not heroes," says Pardell, who calls *Letters Home* a "service memorial," not a war memorial. "These are your neighbors, your friends. The ordinary people who have always gone off to defend freedom."[22]

Located in a quiet suburban park designed like a golf course, facing a pond often filled with ducks, Temecula's memorial lets soldiers tell their stories as it simultaneously naturalizes their wartime experiences, and their deaths. Like the all-war memorial in Munster, Indiana, it blends war into a recreational landscape, normalizing it as an everyday part of American life: civilians and soldiers sit together in a peaceful, pastoral setting. "I think Chris' vision is extraordinary. It's a great tribute to these men and women because it humanizes them," remarks Andrew Carroll, author of the 2001 bestseller *War Letters: Extraordinary Correspondence from American Wars* (a source for many of the memorial's letters). "It keeps us mindful of the thousands who have served and for the principles for which they served. Their service pays us dividends every single day," adds Temecula mayor Mike Naggar.[23] "Tomorrow I may see if four years at West Point and $250,000 of taxpayer money has produced an effective leader," reads one of the memorial's engraved letters — an excerpt from a letter that 23-year-old 2nd Lt. Todd J. Bryant wrote to his wife on September 19, 2003. A month later he was killed in Fallujah.

Memorials like *Letters Home* are obviously nostalgic, geared toward American publics who harbor fantasies of other, mythical American wars. Today's soldiers don't write letters: they text message — and send photos of Abu Ghraib on their cell phones. But that contemporary wartime reality doesn't mesh with memorial culture visions of the soldiers depicted in Pardell's sculpture. While such memorials may "humanize" GI's like Todd Bryant, they also remember them on sentimental and soothing terms that utterly disguise their lives, and deaths, as modern soldiers. This is not, of course, peculiarly American: as Jay Winter explains, multiple modern European publics reckoned with the shock and horror of World War I and its aftermath by turning to "traditional" memory tropes like patriotism, valor, and glory to mediate their deep bereavement.[24] As a typical site of contemporary American war memory, Temecula's *Letters Home* similarly mediates the loss and devastation of war — the death of soldiers like Bryant — for American audiences with formal and iconographic devices that normalize, and justify war itself. While these memorials do not obliterate soldier dead — whose names are listed on memorial walls and engraved in memorial pavers — they do conceal the harsh histories of why and how they died within an abiding national narrative of blood sacrifice.

In fact, with occasional exceptions like the dead GI on the beach in the National D-Day Memorial, and the disfigured corpse in Munster, Indiana's all-war theme park, most of today's war memorials are utterly bloodless. Few show the abject soldier body; most feature strong physical types who are celebrated as normal, natural, and national bodies. Even those memorials that do depict vulnerable soldiers do so on inspirational terms: as Susan Sontag observed, in the "current political mood" of patriotism and war porn, "pictures of wretched hollow-eyed GI's that once seemed subversive of militarism and imperialism" are re-viewed and revised as images of "ordinary American young men doing their unpleasant, ennobling duty."[25] Whether or not they are "heroes," these memorial bodies are certainly embraced on heroic terms: as stoic soldier subjects who perform to social and political expectations, for which the nation gratefully receives and accepts "dividends." They may not raise flags on remote Asian islands, but they do conform to popular modern assumptions about a strong body politic and an able-bodied masculinity that, as David Serlin argues, helps to articulate a heroizing and consensual "rhetoric of Americanism."[26]

Images of abject soldiers are largely prohibited today anyway: the U.S. Department of Defense has banned media images of U.S. soldier dead — images of their bodies, coffins, and funerals — since 1991, ostensibly to honor and protect their privacy, and that of their families. In 2006, President George

W. Bush signed into law the "Respect for America's Fallen Heroes Act," barring protests and demonstrators at military funerals for the same reasons.[27] Wrenching images of wounded soldiers are more problematic: when a lead character lost his leg in the syndicated cartoon *Doonesbury*, columnist Garry Trudeau (who draws George W. Bush as an empty Roman helmet) was commended by the Pentagon for drawing public attention to the grim injuries of U.S. soldiers in Iraq, where "limb-loss has occurred twice as often as in any other conflict of the past century."[28] However, when Trudeau began listing the names of U.S. soldiers killed in Iraq, many newspapers dropped his column.[29] Shielding the public from the facts of American militarism took an especially ridiculous turn in early 2003, when a tapestry copy of Picasso's *Guernica* (a 1937 painting depicting the horrors of the Spanish Civil War), which had been on display at United Nations headquarters in New York since 1985, was covered up by a blue cloth during press conferences given by Secretary of State Colin Powell and other government officials announcing U.S. military intentions in Iraq. As newspaper columnist Maureen Dowd observed, "Mr. Powell can't very well seduce the world into bombing Iraq surrounded on camera by shrieking and mutilated women, men, children, bulls and horses."[30]

Images of war's effects may be banned, but Powell, for one, avidly embraces war memorials. "Paying homage to the fallen holds a deeply personal meaning for me and for anyone who ever wore a uniform," Powell stated in a 2004 article titled "Why Memorials Matter," published by *USA Weekend Magazine* and marketed to coincide with the dedication of the National World War II Memorial. Reminiscing about visiting the graves of family members on Memorial Day as a child, and later touring Washington's memorials with foreign dignitaries, Powell observed: "Our monuments and memorials tell us a great deal about America's commitment to life, liberty and the pursuit of happiness for all." He added: "They can teach us much about the ideas that unite us in our diversity, the values that sustain us in times of trial, and the dream that inspires generation after generation of ordinary Americans to perform extraordinary acts of service."[31]

Indeed, multiple generations are recalled in America's many war memorials, testifying to the nation's relentless, repetitious, and seemingly endless militarism. As a significant — and expanding — body of war porn, war memorials cue Americans to concepts of citizenship, patriotism, and unity as they simultaneously whet national appetites for further martial adventures. The "awesome power" referenced in the National World War II Memorial's mission statement equates American militarism with the sublime, with similarly awesome and all-powerful forces of destruction and disaster like hurricanes, tsunamis, and volcanic eruptions. American militarism is thus naturalized as an inevitable authority, and the nation's super-abundance of war memorials is the prominent bearer of an American military sublime.

Notes

1. Kate Zernike, "D-Day Memorial is Clouded By Scandal, Debt and Doubts," *New York Times* (April 27, 2003): A-1, A-25.
2. "Remarks by the President at the Dedication of the National D-Day Memorial," 6 June 2001, accessed from http://www.whitehouse.gov/news/releases/2001/06/20010606-2.html on January 8, 2007).
3. War games are the top money makers in the online computer industry: the World of Warcraft series, marketed by Blizzard Entertainment and featuring games like Burning *Crusade* (released 2007), has more than eight million subscribers who pay $15 a month to play. See Seth Schiesel, "O Brave New World That Has Such Gamers In it," *New York Times* (January 19, 2007): 13.
4. See "Purpose," National World War II Memorial, accessed from http://www.wwiimemorial.com/default.asp?page=facts.asp&subpage=intro on December 26, 2006.
5. Emily S. Rosenberg, *A Date Which Will Live: Pearl Harbor in American Memory* (Durham, NC: Duke University Press, 2003), 66–67, 130, 188. John Bodnar similarly argues that films such as *Saving Private Ryan* preserve "the World War II image of American soldiers as inherently averse to bloodshed and cruelty"; see his "*Saving Private Ryan* and Postwar Memory in America," *American Historical Review* 106, no. 3 (June 2001): 805.
6. On the *Enola Gay* controversy see Edward T. Linenthal and Tom Engelhardt, eds., *History Wars: The Enola Gay and Other Battles for the American Past* (New York: Metropolitan Books/Henry Holt and Company, 1996).
7. David Hoogland Noon, "Operation Enduring Analogy: World War II, The War on Terror, and the Uses of Historical Memory," *Rhetoric & Public Affairs* 7, no. 3 (2004): 339; Dan Balz and Bob Woodward, "America's Chaotic Road to War," *Washington Post* (January 27, 2002): A-1; Christopher Hayes, "The Good War on Terror," *In These Times* (September 8, 2006): 7.
8. Michael Sherry, *In the Shadow of War: The United States Since the 1930s* (New Haven, CT: Yale University Press, 1995), 460–461.
9. Jean Baudrillard, "Pornographie de la guerre," *Liberation* (May 19, 2004), reprinted as "War Porn" in *The Conspiracy of Art: Manifestos, Texts, Interviews* (Cambridge, MA: MIT Press, 2005), 205–212; "A Slap in the Face: War Porn," *Adbusters* 52 (March-April 2004), accessed from http://adbusters.org/the_magazine/52/War_Porn.html on January 10, 2007.
10. Andrew J. Bacevich, *The New American Militarism: How Americans Are Seduced by War* (New York: Oxford University Press, 2005), 2.
11. Lears discusses the role of the "martial ideal" in turn-of-the [20th]-century America in *No Place of Grace: Antimodernism and the Transformation of American Culture, 1880–1920* (New York: Pantheon, 1983), 97–102, and Hansen discusses the reduction of patriotism to militarism in the same era in *The Lost Promise of Patriotism: Debating American Identity, 1890–1920* (Chicago: University of Chicago Press, 2003); see also Amy Kaplan, *The Anarchy of Empire in the Making of U.S. Culture* (Cambridge, MA: Harvard University Press, 2002).
12. Patrick Hagopian, "The Commemorative Landscape of the Vietnam War," in Joachim Wolschke-Bulmahn, ed., *Places of Commemoration: Search for Identity and Land-*

scape Design (Washington, D.C.: Dumbarton Oaks, 2001), 312–313, n. 1; see also Jerry L. Strait and Sandra S. Strait, *Vietnam War Memorials: An Illustrated Reference Guide to Veterans Tributes Throughout the United States* (Jefferson, NC: McFarland, 1988).

13. Author e-mail correspondence with Richard Rist, March 21, 2007.

14. Although apparently during the conflict in Kosovo, a number of Bronze Stars were awarded to soldiers in the Air Force and the Navy who never actually saw combat. This drew complaints from the Army, and astute analysis from the members of Critical Art Ensemble about the future of the military body; see "Reimagining the War Machine," *Body & Society* 9, no.4 (2003): 89–91.

15. Julie Rotblatt, "War Memorial, The Fine Art Studio of Rotblatt-Amrany," accessed from http://www.rotblattamrany.com/commissions_part03.htm#War on January 13, 2007.

16. Visitor quoted on the segment "Indiana War Memorial," produced by Jenny Lawton for "Hello Beautiful!! The Sunday Morning Arts Show," on Chicago Public Library, October 17, 2004, accessed from http://www.chicagopublicradio.org/audio_library/hb_oct 04.asp on January 15, 2007; Rumsfeld quoted in U.S. Department of Defense briefing, August 9, 2005, accessed from http://www.defenselink.mil/transcripts/transcript.aspx?Tran scriptID=3082 on January 20, 2007.

17. "Monument Honors African Americans," *Mississippi History Newsletter, Online Edition*, vol. 46, no. 2 (February 2004), accessed from http://www.mdah.state.ms.us/pubs/mhn/feb04index.html on January 15, 2007.

18. On women and Civil War memory see Cynthia Mills and Pamela H. Simpson, eds., *Monuments to the Lost Cause: Women, Art, and the Landscapes of Southern Memory* (Knoxville: University of Tennessee Press, 2003), and David W. Blight, *Race and Reunion: The Civil War in American Memory* (Cambridge, MA: Harvard University Press, 2001), 255–299 and passim; on women and the recovery of soldier dead see G. Kurt Piehler, "The War Dead and the Gold Star: American Commemoration of the First World War," in John R. Gillis, ed., *Commemorations: The Politics of National Identity* (Princeton: Princeton University Press, 1994), 168–185, and Michael Sledge, *Soldier Dead: How We Recover, Identify, Bury, and Honor Our Military Fallen* (New York: Columbia University Press, 2005), 136 and passim.

19. "West Virginia: Less G.I. Joe, More Barbie?" *New York Times* (March 3, 2005): A-21; Jennifer Lunden, "Women Vets Say Memorial Statue Too Masculine," National Public Radio, All Things Considered (March 5, 2005), accessed from http://www.npr.org/templates/story/story.php?storyId=4524261 on January 17, 2007; Heather J. Höpfl, "Becoming a (Virile) Member: Women and the Military Body," *Body & Society* 9, no. 4 (2003): 26; see also Cynthia Nantais and Martha F. Lee, "Women in the United States Military: Protectors or Protected? The Case of Prisoner of War Melisa Rathbun–Nealy," *Journal of Gender Studies* 8, no. 2 (1999): 181–191.

20. Bryan Turner, "Warrior Charisma and Spiritualization of Violence," *Body & Society* 9, no. 4 (2003): 105.

21. Judith Butler, *Gender Trouble: Feminism and the Subversion of Identity* (New York: Routledge, 1990).

22. Joe Vargo, "Lest We Forget: Homage and Monuments to Veterans Are Popular Again," *Press Enterprise.com* (30 December 2006), accessed from http://www.pe.com/local news/inland/stories/PE_News_Local_S ... on January 16, 2007; John Hunneman, "'Letters Home' Tells War Stories in the Words of Those Who Served," *North County Times* (November 7, 2004), accessed from http://www.nctimes.com/articles/2004/11/08/news/californian/11 ... on January 16, 2007). The Vietnam Veterans Memorial in New York City (1985) similarly incorporates excerpts from soldier's letters on its glass blocks; see Bernard Edelman, ed. *Dear America: Letters Homes from Vietnam* (New York: W. W. Norton, 1985).

23. Carroll quoted in Vargo, "Lest We Forget," Naggar quoted in Hunneman, "'Let-

ters Home' Tells War Stories." On Carroll's book see Andrew Carroll, *War Letters: Extraordinary Correspondence from American Wars* (New York: Simon and Schuster, 2001).

24. Jay Winter, *Sites of Memory, Sites of Mourning: The Great War in European Cultural History* (Cambridge, MA: Cambridge University Press, 1995), 2–5 and passim.

25. Susan Sontag, *Regarding the Pain of Others* (New York: Farrar, Straus, and Giroux, 2003), 38.

26. David Serlin, *Replaceable You: Engineering the Body in Postwar America* (Chicago: University of Chicago Press, 2004), 2 and passim.

27. The bill, HR 5037, bans demonstrations within 300 feet of a military cemetery and 150 feet from any military funeral (including those at non-federal sites) within an hour of the memorial service.

28. Michael Weisskopf, "A Grim Milestone: 500 Amputees," *Time* (January 18, 2007): 27.

29. Gene Weingarten, "Doonesbury's War," *Washington Post* (October 22, 2006): W-14.

30. Maureen Dowd, "Powell Without Picasso," *New York Times* (February 5, 2003): A-31.

31. Colin Powell, "Why Memorials Matter," *USA Weekend Magazine* (April 30–May 2, 2004), accessed from http://www.usaweekend.com/partners/mktpromo/040502articles/04 on April 26, 2004.

2

Sporting Aces and the Military
Performance, Discipline, and Nationalism in the Fields of Honor

FABIAN VIRCHOW

Introduction

Physical fitness has always been an important demand on soldiers. Therefore, sporting activities rank high in military training all over the world. However, there are additional dimensions of the relationship between sports and the military. So-called *sport-soldiers* figure prominently as role models and serve recruitment and promotion purposes of the armed forces. Drawing on theoretical considerations from sports sociology, cultural studies, and military sociology and taking contemporary Germany as an example, this article investigates the growing cooperation between the German Federal Armed Forces and several German sports associations and the marketing of successful sport-soldiers under the vision of "performance," "discipline," and "iron will." Against this background, the use of sport as a recruitment tool might be seen as an attempt to get young people into the armed forces that are not only physically fit but also dedicated to their hobby and used to ideas of obligation, discipline, and sacrifices.

The 2006 Baltic Sea–Triathlon took place in the small North German city of Glücksburg. More than a hundred soldiers of the German Federal Armed Forces, the Bundeswehr, had been among the 800 participants. One of the servicemen who had entered the Hawaiian Ironman competition several times ranked fourth in the end. The German Navy acted as the co-organizer of this sporting event.[1] In the summer of 2007 the Bundeswehr ran its BW-Beachen-event, a beach volley tournament, which since 2002 was organized for the second time together with the BW-Olympix.[2] Both these events target young people and try to make them interested in doing military service.

Armed forces have always paid attention to the mental and physical fitness of their soldiers. A complex relationship between sports on the one hand and military or battle training on the other hand can be traced back through the centuries historically.[3] Sports — just like any other sphere of social interaction — is shaped according to the cultural and social context in which it takes place and, at the same time, reproduces societal conditions as these are expressed by it. This is quite obvious in American football, a game that demonstrates several dimensions of belligerent behavior: "The aim of this scaled down artificial war is not the death of the enemy but the capture of his territory.... The poles that mark the position of the ball between separate actions can also be seen as an analogy to war; the poles which are called *flags* are equivalent to the pins and pennants on a military operation map: 'Here are we, there is the enemy.'"[4] Literally, this has been expressed particularly impressively by Don DeLillo's football novel *End Zone*.[5]

Surveying the mosaic relationship between war, military, and sports leads to a broad range of different ways in which they are connected: the use of war metaphor in linguistic usage when covering political and sports events, analogies between sporting games and war, and the media's portrayal and communication of war with terms from sport events. The latter ones probably lead to the impression that warlike events in far away regions are quite familiar.[6] Yet, there are also quite direct interactions between protagonists of the military and the field of sports respectively. As far as Germany is concerned, the orientation of sports to the interests of the monarchist military, the relevance of paramilitary training in the interwar period and the militarizing of sports after the Nazi seizure of power, amongst other issues, have been investigated in full.[7] Other dimensions are still under-researched. Therefore, this essay investigates the fact that the attention provided by the German Federal Armed Forces to sports is not so much about the physical fitness of the soldiers as it is about recruiting new soldiers. This rationality finds its expression in bilateral agreements of cooperation with several German sports associations and in the marketing of successful sport-soldiers under the vision of "performance," "discipline," and "iron will."

Sports as a Publicity and Recruitment Tool

With regard to the fulfillment of its tasks and compared to other societal actors like political parties or the media, the Bundeswehr has a good reputation in the German population and public opinion.[8] However, this does not correspond with the willingness of young people to do military service or enlist for a longer period of time. In light of the fact that refusal to do military service is easy in contemporary Germany and regarding the heightened probability to be deployed abroad and, in that case, be exposed to serious risks and burdens, the German Federal Armed Forces has had to intensify its recruiting activities considerably. In addition to existing efforts like posters and flyers with military motifs, exhibitions of military equipment and "Open-Ship"–functions, which offers the general public the opportunity to visit a warship, the Bundeswehr offers special entertainment activities addressed at young people. These events are organized around music and football, two issues which are of great relevance for many youths.

In 2002 the Bundeswehr started its BW-Olympics. More than 1,000 young men and women were invited to the army's sport school in the small town Warendorf where they not only took part in sport competitions but also were "informed about the attractive career opportunities the army has to offer as an employer" as the army's web page stated.[9] Attending this event included military-like behavior such as lining up like a platoon or decreed bed rest at a certain time. Over the weekend, the competitions in soccer, swimming, beach volleyball, track and field athletics, and cross-country running were completed by the presentation of weapon systems. The idea to make young people — at least on a basic level — familiar with and interested in the soldiery profession comes down to the prizes too: winners were offered visits to military units deployed as far away as Sardinia. Just like the biennial BW-beachen which is held in several bathing resorts of Northern Germany during the summer, these events tell nothing about the reality of war that includes battle, destruction, being wounded, and death.

Often top class athletes show up at such sport events. They are so called sport-soldiers because they are soldiers of the Bundeswehr but devote most of their time to sport training. The system of sport-soldiering has a firm root in the political bloc confrontation and competition between the western and the eastern bloc.[10] In the German Democratic Republic (GDR) the systematic use of sports for military and political purposes began as early as 1956 when the *Armeesportvereinigung Vorwärts* had been founded. As the GDR athletes performed successfully at the Olympics, the West German parliament decided in May 1968 to boost the centralized support structure for top class athletes that was closely linked to the armed forces.[11] The deepening of cooperation between the military and the Deutscher Sportbund (DSB, a German Sports Association) and the unification of the East and West German military sport support facilities after the uniting of the two German states led to an increase in the percentage of soldiers in the cadres nominated for international sport competitions. In the early twenty-first century there are some

740 sportsmen and women in the German armed forces exercising sixty to seventy different kinds of sport ranging from soccer, rowing, swimming, and boxing to rugby, chess, and crazy golf. Becoming a sport-soldier depends on top performance, the vote of the respective sport association and the willingness to enlist. If the performance does not match the set objectives the sport-soldier has to return back from the sport-training unit to his or her military unit.

In the German case, military support of top class athletes has resulted in a high percentage of medal winners at the Olympics.[12] In Nagano (1998) 55 percent of German medal winners had been sport-soldiers, in Salt Lake City (2002) 71 percent, in Sydney (2000) 43 percent, and in Athens (2004) 50 percent.[13] The German weightlifter team in Athens consisted of sport-soldiers completely; in bobsleighing German sport-soldiers have dominated in international competitions for years.

A close symbiosis has developed between the Bundeswehr and the German sports associations over the last decades. Already in the mid–1970s it had been noted that the growing costs of training top class athletes could not be matched by the clubs alone, but only through nation-wide training centers, centralized training communities and support groups financed by the police and the armed forces.[14] This development has been reinforced and grown into a high-grade dependency of top sports from military support. This is acknowledged by representatives of sports associations and leads to the public commitment of sporting aces to the Bundeswehr on many occasions.[15]

Sports and Integration Into the Military

The achievements of the sport-soldiers are communicated and celebrated widely inside the Bundeswehr. Competitions like the biathlon World Championship where a significant number of sport-soldiers fight for medals are transmitted live by the army's radio station. Medal winners are presented in the army's own papers and their performance is presented on the web page of the Bundeswehr. While the sport-soldiers are used as advertising and recruiting medium, their existence is also relevant for the cohesion and the morale of the soldiers. This is what former German Minister of Defense Manfred Wörner noted when he praised the sport-soldiers not only in regard to their animating role concerning sport activities of the youth in general but also because of the pride produced inside the Bundeswehr in case of medal winning sport-soldiers.[16] As sport sociologist Detlef Grieswelle has noted, sympathy with sport events contributes to the emergence and stabilization of a feeling of common bond; large groups like the nation-state or the military as an institution need such symbolic events, as they can hardly be experienced in real and concrete terms by the individual.[17] Indeed, the successes of the sport-soldiers have been celebrated by one of the leading German daily newspapers as a relevant contribution to the process of "nation-making" in a country that had been divided over decades.[18]

Sport can count as the paradigmatic form of the (re)construction of (nation)states as can be seen from international sport events. Opening ceremonies of the Olympic Games are "elaborately staged and commercialized narratives of nation"; they "dramatize national myths, experiences, and values, focusing on such themes as the antiquity of the nation and the struggles, triumphs, courage, and character of its people."[19] Thus, the team captain of the U.S. gold-medal winning ice hockey team of 1980 that beat its Soviet competitor in the golden age of the arms race between the two countries, participated in the opening ceremony in Salt Lake City, just a few months after the terrorist attacks of 9/11. Such elements, whose connotations to foreign and military policy were obvious ("Let's beat the present enemy the same way"), made the ceremony "another front in the U.S. 'war on terror.'"[20]

The performance of the respective national teams, which are regularly measured according to the number of medals and easily readable in tabular rankings, is widely read as an indicator of the national prestige of a country. Heads of state comment on the bad performance of their country's Olympic team as the "deterioration of our once admired national strength" (John F. Kennedy) or as a "national disgrace" (Charles de Gaulle).[21] Accordingly, reaching the final or even winning it gives presidents a frequently used opportunity to represent the nation-state and to stage the national collective.

The societal importance of sports as a phenomena of mass culture is especially big with World Championships and Olympic Games. Remembering them is as significant to the construction of "national identity" as wars are. When, in 1954, the German soccer team won the World Championship, many German sport officials celebrated this as an expression of "true Germanness": In a large number of media and amongst widespread parts of the German population, this success was seen as an important step to overcome the pariah status in the system of international politics.[22] Quite many international soccer matches like England vs. Germany, England vs. Argentina, or U.S. vs. Iran offer mediated opportunities to refer to "sleeping memories" of international conflicts and appeal to nationalist(ic) undertones.[23] In this way, sport may "reinforce antagonisms bred on battlefields, keep alive memories of 'battles long ago,' defeats deep in the past, and victories recorded in history books, and as such exacerbate antipathy, fuel hostility, and extend dislike."[24]

When, in 2005, the German tabloid *BILD* celebrated the successful performance of a German racing cyclist at the Tour de France with the headline "At last, a German hero again," this is just another example of the relevance that a nationalist use of language has for the (re-)construction of national identity.²⁵ Nations as symbolic constructions are in a steady need to be reproduced in countless and mostly non-spectacular day-to-day routines and interactions.²⁶ Sport fits these demands well because, on the one hand, a huge number of people is associated to it either by presence in the stadiums or via the mass media, and because of its "narrative contributions" on the other hand that are easier to connect for cultural and nationalist stereotyping than other societal phenomena.²⁷ Also, in sports, realization of nationalist sentiments is more tolerated: "The sportsfield and battlefield are linked as locations for the demonstration of legitimate patriotic aggression."²⁸

In light of the fact that there is a broad interest towards top sports which is a relevant part of popular culture of male adolescents and therefore makes sport a wide-spread issue of everyday conversation, the significance of sporting aces as a point of reference for a national "We" can hardly be overestimated.²⁹ Therefore, we can conclude reasonably that in cases where the sportsmen and women converges with the soldier who has been constructed historically as a "national figure" and a "protagonist of national interest" too — and this convergence may be the case prototypically in the figure of the sport-soldier — not only the everyday reconstruction of the nation but of the military as well takes place.³⁰

It is not always the case that the different ways to "serve" the nation can be combined without contradictions. Aside from the integration of both roles in one person (sport-soldier) and the complementary appearance of the "representatives of the nation" (soldier and sportsman) as it has found expression in a German tabloid that ran the headline "Our boys meet our soldiers," there is the option of a sportsman becoming a "real soldier."³¹ This dissociation (sportsman *or* soldier) has been the (prominent) case with the well-known NFL player Pat Tillman. He turned down a $ 3.6 million offer in professional football and instead joined the army in May 2002. His decision, which had been influenced by 9/11, was praised by many statements of sport officials and in media reports as heroic and exemplary. When he was shot in 2004 fighting in Afghanistan he was awarded the Silver Star posthumously and the funeral was aired nation-wide. Obituaries written by NFL officials valued Tillman's decision to join the military as a vocation and emphasized that he had put his country over his personal interest.³² However, attempts to use Tillman for political reasons failed. When still alive he rejected approaches by the Pentagon that wanted to use him for advertising purposes such as recruitment posters for the U.S. armed forces. When he was shot to death an extensive instrumentalization by the U.S. government was made impossible by the critique of his parents that he was killed by friendly fire and that the U.S. army showed no interest investigating the incident.[33]

The construction of the nation through the public production of representatives of the nation like heroes of war or sport aces gives plenty opportunities to (re)produce a collective "We." In doing so, international sports as well as the military fall back upon living or dead representations that range from representatives of the state to flags, anthems and medals. As German sport sociologist Horst Geyer has put it: "The symbolism of national superiority on the basis of an earlier crossing of the finishing line is already understood by kids in early age. Since we have radio and television we do not even need to be literate to be involved in this experience. Due to its general intelligibility, participation in the we-experience of sports is not tied to intellectual abilities; therefore, integration includes all. And it so also for the members of a nation because sport for all is a matter of physics that seems to be value-free. Therefore, integration through sports also takes place with national groups that might be disintegrated politically, socially, or ideologically."[34]

Performance and Discipline

Sport as a cultural institution is controlled by fixed rules by which time, space, equipment, and handling of an activity is given norms. This leads to highly standardized configurations of social acts which are, however, not the same in all areas of sports. They have to be differentiated according to different variables. The area of top sport is standardized to a high degree; the same is true for the military. Becoming successful in competitive sport requires strict discipline, partial isolation from the social environment, the extensive integration into a structure of officials, medics, and trainers, and to be subjected to a scientific training program. This situation has some parallel to the situation of soldiers where it is also important to improve the physical fitness in connection with the ability to make an efficient decision under pressure.

Officials of the Bundeswehr assess sport positively because "the idea of competition, competitiveness, hierarchy, discipline, and group cohesion inherent in the society and the armed forces is expressed by it."[35] The usefulness of these dimensions for competitive sports and for military service are clear; this is especially true for the willingness to perform and behave in a disciplined manner in the sense of internalizing compulsion. This self-discipline may not be experienced as heteronymous but top performance in sport demands a "rigorous physical and psychic disciplining of the top athletes.... Sports as competitive sports needs the alignment of the whole person with the sporting aims; the athlete has to adjust his behavior towards these aims in the professional sphere too.... Often this leads to conflicts between the expectations of school, parental home, job, and family on the one hand and the demands of the sport training on the other hand; for the most part it is difficult to meet the sporting and the non-sporting roles equally and simultaneously."[36] Thus, staff sergeant Jörg Dallmann, who is a speed skating ace, states that training is time consuming: "We do not have holidays, most of the time is devoted to training."[37]

Self-discipline is also directed towards one's own body, seen as an adversary that has to be subjugated.[38] This is true for top class athletes who demand best performances from their bodies again and again; it is also true for soldiers who are expected to conquer their weaker self, for example in case of prolonged field exercises. Neither the "discipline and hardness against oneself," as former MoD Manfred Wörner puts it, nor the standardized procedures of motion that are trained in the military have much to do with a human desire to move one's body.[39]

After the German Federal Armed Forces have become an army engaged in military action abroad, two further developments related to sports can be observed. One is the militarization of the popular sport inside the armed forces and the other is the celebration of extreme sports by the military.

From its beginning, popular sports inside the Bundeswehr saw itself as non-militaristic. Viewed as a fundamental distinction to sports in the Nazi period, popular sport now was not used as a direct contribution to combat training but became part of general training exercises and soldierly duties. The underlying distinction was explained in an army magazine devoted to sport issues in particular: "The sportsmen will also admit that there is a difference between covering a longer distance on an even track wearing perfectly comfortable sportswear ... or to manage an equally long passage in difficult terrain being clothed in battle dress and boots as part of a mission.... The latter one is not sports but combat training."[40] However, in 1994 the inspector general of the army issued a decree according to which the traditional sporting activities inside the army should be supplemented by a military fitness training that has to be done in uniform. This military fitness training consisted of exercises like a military relay race in which a rucksack or a box of ammunition functions as the relay. Even if this is no return to the grotesque situation of the imperial German Army, where soldiers had to perform a circle at the horizontal bar in full military outfit, it marks a definite shift away from the principled distinction between sports and military training.

In recent times, soldiers engaged in extreme sports are celebrated by army journals. Whether downhill mountain-biking or mountain climbing, the soldiers go as far as they can because they are "motivated to the end of the hair."[41] Some are marathon runners, others devote much of their time to prepare for the conquering of the Himalayas.[42] Extreme sports are not so much about beating a competitor but mainly "through a radical one-to-one contest, to test their strength of character, their courage and their personal resources." It is "a commitment to reinforcing personal will-power and overcoming suffering by going right to the limit of a personally imposed demand."[43] Extreme sport aims at controlling the dangers, surpassing one's limits, and staying in control in situations of stress. There is an increased risk of mortality in extreme sports and many sportsmen engaged in this kind of sports suffer serious injuries.[44]

Sport and Banal Militarization

Sportsmen and soldiers alike are expected to be fit; they must both train hard and expose themselves to mortal dangers. Even if they care about their own lives, the idea to train and exercise toughness in relation to their own physique and engage in battle without self-pity dominates their actions.

Modern top-class sport cannot be done by everyone because it is organized under special conditions.[45] Only this special status made it possible that a performance by which a sportsman or woman was world champion twenty years ago might be sufficient for today's national championships only. Sporting aces stand out from popular sports; it is just this non-ordinariness that allows their economic, media, and political commercialization. Modern competitive sport offers the opportunity to identify with the biography, charisma, and prominence of sportsmen and women und sport idols. The Bundeswehr makes use of this by supporting top class athletes and by establishing contacts, face-to-face or via the media, between them and youngsters practicing sport themselves. Although, in general, the idolization of sporting aces is accompanied by a growing distance to the audience, this may be reduced in case of the sport-soldiers when they meet young persons who are also devoted to bodily fitness, commitment, discipline, stamina training, the idea of competition, motivation of success, readiness to take risks, and the willingness of putting off rewards. Sport — which is associated with "team spirit," "discipline," and "enthusiasm for action" — is used to recruit young people for the armed forces. While many may be enthusiastic about the seemingly great status sport has in the Bundeswehr, some may even dream of a career as a sport-soldier.

Sport communicates the antagonistic idea of victory and defeat, which is also constitutive for the core task of the military. Sport provides an offer of interpretation patterns relevant for the acceptance of the normative foundations of a given social and political order.[46] As it does so without administrative decrees or moralizing linguistic discourses, the attitudes and orientations acquire their quasi-legitimized status as by-products of behavior. Sport, therefore, is obtaining legitimation latently.[47]

Sport holds a great attraction and has a prominent and profitable effect for other societal systems. Sport heroes are clearly promoted by the media as a source of national pride and function to represent national qualities, traditions, and distinctions. Where sporting activities and the military sphere converge, the legitimation created by sport as a latent legitimizing factor not only refers to principles that are at the center of the social type "top sport athlete" but also give credit to the military because the performance is adduced as a sport-soldier and it is made possible by the support of the armed forces. Giving legitimation to the armed forces does not mean that a specific policy gets support or pronounced approval. Rather, it is the military as such that gains credibility and legitimation. Thus, sport-soldiers and sport events organized by the military contribute to the idea that armed forces are an everyday and ordinary matter.

Social scientist Michael Billig has coined the term *banal nationalism* for the "whole complex of beliefs, assumptions, habits, representations and practices" by which established nations are reproduced as nations in "a banally mundane way."[48] The sport activities investigated in this article have been interpreted as an element of *banal militarism* to point to mechanisms and procedures which are parallel and by which the military, its necessity, and its demands for financial assets are (re)produced in society.[49] This perspective opens up new frontiers of research dealing with the multiple ways the military as an institution as well as military attitudes and belief systems are embedded in societies.

Notes

1. See PIZ Marine, "Ironman am Ostseestrand," *Die Bundeswehr,* September (2006): 29.
2. *BW* is an abbreviation for Bundeswehr.
3. See James A. Mangan (ed.), *Militarism, Sport, Europe. War Without Weapons* (London & Portland, OR: Frank Cass, 2003).
4. Allen Guttmann, *Vom Ritual zum Rekord. Das Wesen des Modernen Sports* (Schorndorf: Verlag Karl Hofmann, 1979), 116–117, author's translation. Unless otherwise noted, all translations from German are by the author. For the widespread understanding of Aus-

tralian football as war see Pamm Kellett, "Football-as-War, Coach-as-General: Analogy, Metaphor and Management Implications," *Football Studies* 5, no. 1 (2002): 60–76.
  5. Don DeLillo, *End Zone* (Boston: Houghton Mifflin, 1972).
  6. In the British press, for example, connections are frequently drawn between sport stars and past military war heroes. See R. Holt, "Champions, Heroes and Celebrities: Sporting Greatness and the British Public," in *The Book of British Sporting Heroes*, ed. J. Huntington-Whiteley, 10–25 (London: National Portrait Gallery, 1999); and Gill Lines, "Villains, Fools or Heroes? Sports Stars as Role Models for Young People," *Leisure Studies* 20 (2001): 285–303. For analogies between sporting games and war see Michael J. Shapiro, "Representing World Politics: The Sport/War Intertext," in *International/Intertextual Relations*, ed. James Der Derian and Michael J. Shapiro, 69–96 (Lexington: Lexington Books, 1989); Andreas Musolff, "Zur Analyse von Kriegsmetaphorik im öffentlichen Sprachgebrauch," *Sprache und Literatur in Wissenschaft und Unterricht* 21, no. 2 (1990): 62–80; J. McKay, "Hawk(e)s, Doves and Super Bowl XXV," *Social Alternatives* 10, no. 1 (1991): 58–60; N. Trujillo, "Machines, Missiles, and Men: Images of the Male Body on ABC's *Monday Night Football*," *Sociology of Sport Journal* 12, no. 4 (1995): 403–423. The following articles for the issues of portrayal of war with sporting terms: James Aulich, "Wildlife in the South Atlantic: Graphic Satire, Patriotism and the Fourth Estate," in *Framing the Falklands War: Nationhood, Culture and Identity*, ed. James Aulich (Milton Keynes: Open University Press, 1992); Stanley D. Rosenberg, "The Threshold of Thrill: Life Stories in the Skies over South-East Asia," in *Gendering War Talk*, ed. Miriam Cooke and Angela Woollacott, 43–66 (Princeton: Princeton University Press, 1993).
  7. After the Nazi seizure of power, sport was reorganized according to the needs of public health and racial selection excluding Jews from sport associations; sports were militarized as a preparation for the wars of aggression conducted in order to control Europe. For the different periods see Klaus Cachay, *Sport und Gesellschaft* (Schorndorf: Verlag Klaus Hofmann, 1988), 200–232; Berit Elisabeth Dencker, "Popular Gymnastics and the Military Spirit in Germany, 1848/1871," *Central European History* 34, no. 4 (2001): 503–530; Hermann Bach, "Volks- und Wehrsport in der Weimarer Republik," *Sportwissenschaft* 11, no. 3 (1981): 273–294; Hajo Bernett, "Wehrsport — ein Pseudosport. Stellungnahme zu Hermann Bach," *Sportwissenschaft* 11, no. 3 (1981): 295–308; Michael Krüger, "'Das Turnen als reaktionäres Mittel' — Wilhelm Angerstein und die Disziplinierung des Turnens," *Sportwissenschaft* 23, no. 1 (1993): 9–34; Lorenz Pfeiffer, *Turnunterricht im III. Reich. Erziehung für den Krieg?* (Köln: Pahl-Rugenstein, 1987); Mario Leis, *Sport in der Literatur. Einblicke in das 20. Jahrhundert* (Frankfurt/Main: Peter Lang, 2000), 45–67.
  8. Johannes M. Becker, "Aspekte psychologischer Kriegsvorbereitung — Der Wandel der Legitimationsbasis für Militär in der Bundesrepublik Deutschland," in *Dem Krieg widerstehen. Beiträge zur Zivilisierung der Politik*, ed. Ralph-M. Luedtke and Peter Strutynski, 118–138 (Kassel: Jenior, 2001); Heiko Biehl, "Armee im Einsatz. Meinungsbild der Bevölkerung zu Aufgaben und Einsätzen der Bundeswehr," *Information für die Truppe* 49, no. 1 (2005): 47–49.
  9. "Rückblick 2002" accessed from http://www.bw-olympix.de/kap_1_4.htm on August 20, 2006.
  10. For further details see Uta Andrea Balbier, *Kalter Krieg auf der Aschenbahn: Der deutsch-deutsche Sport 1950–1972* (Paderborn: Schöningh, 2006).
  11. Sportschule der Bundeswehr, *Sportschule der Bundeswehr. Porträt einer Schule* (Koblenz: Mönch, 1993), 53; Klaus Karteusch, "Der Hardthöhen-Kurier berichtet hautnah über Sport in der Bundeswehr," *Hardthöhenkurier* 19, no. 2 (2003): 48–49.
  12. For the U.S. see http://www.defenselink.mil/armedforcessports/ accessed on November 15, 2007. For the sports career of General George S. Patton, Jr. see Harold E. Wilson, Jr., "A Legend In His Own Mind: The Olympic Experience of General George S. Patton, Jr.," *Olympika* 6 (1997): 99–114. The broader perspective is outlined by Steven W. Pope,

"An Army of Athletes: Playing Fields, Battlefields, and the American Military Sporting Experience, 1890–1920," *Journal of Military History* 59, no. 3 (July 1995): 435–456.

13. Bundesministerium der Verteidigung, *Sport* (Bonn: BMVg 1998), 6; also Dietmar Buse, "Konzentration," *BW-aktuell* 39, no. 8 (2004), 3; also Sandra Gliem, "Schaffen Vorbilder," *BW-aktuell* 39, no. 41 (2004), 1.

14. Detlef Grieswelle, *Sportsoziologie* (Stuttgart: Kohlhammer, 1978), 73.

15. Gerd Kebschull, "Heimspiel alpin," *Y. Das Magazin der Bundeswehr* 4/2005: 90–92, 92.

16. Manfred Wörner, "Breite mit Spitzen," *Truppenpraxis — Sonderheft: Sport in der Bundeswehr* 1984: 1.

17. Grieswelle, "Sportsoziologie," 91.

18. Michael Reinsch, "Medaillen auf Befehl," *Frankfurter Allgemeine Zeitung*, January 14, 2004.

19. Jackie Hogan, "Staging the Nation: Gendered and Ethnicized Discourses of National Identity in Olympic Opening Ceremonies," *Journal of Sport and Social Issues* 27, no. 2 (2003): 100–123, 104, 102.

20. Ibid., 117.

21. Sepp Binder, "Nun siegt man schön. Sportpolitik zwischen Milliarden und Medaillen," in *Die vertrimmte Nation oder Sport in rechter Gesellschaft*, ed. Jörg Richter (Reinbek bei Hamburg: Rowohlt 1972), 87.

22. Arthur Heinrich, "The 1954 Soccer World Cup and the Federal Republic of Germany's Self-Discovery," *American Behavorial Scientist* 46, no. 11 (2003): 1491–1505.

23. Joseph Maguire and Emma Poulton and Catherine Possamai, "Weltkrieg III. Media Coverage of England Versus Germany in Euro 96," *Journal of Sport and Social Issues* 23, no. 4 (1999): 439–454; also Pablo Alabarces and Alan Tomlinson and Christopher Young, "Argentina versus England at the France '98 World Cup: narratives of nation and the mythologizing of the popular," *Media, Culture & Society* 23 (2001): 547–566; Fernando Delgado, "The Fusing of Sport and Politics. Media Constructions of U.S. Versus Iran at France '98," *Journal of Sport and Social Issues* 27, no. 3 (2003): 293–307,

24. Mangan, *Militarism, Sport, Europe*, 4.

25. *BILD-Zeitung*, July 11, 2005: 1.

26. Etienne Balibar and Immanuel Wallerstein, *Rasse, Klasse, Nation: Ambivalente Identitäten* (Hamburg: Argument 1990), 96; see also Michael Billig, *Banal Nationalism* (Thousand Oaks: Sage, 1995); David Miller, *On Nationality* (Oxford: Clarendon Press, 1995); Tanja Thomas, *Deutsch-Stunden. Zur Konstruktion nationaler Identität im Fernsehtalk* (Frankfurt am Main: Campus, 2003).

27. William J. Morgan, "Patriotic Sports and the Moral Making of Nations," *Journal of the Philosophy of Sport* 26 (1999): 50–67, 51. Hugh O'Donnell, "Mapping the Mythical: A Geopolitics of National Sporting Stereotypes," *Discourse & Society* 5 (1994): 345–380.

28. James A. Mangan, "Foreward," in *Shaping the Superman: Fascist Body as Political Icon*, ed. James A. Mangan (London: Frank Cass, 1999): xii.

29. For an Austrian example see Matthias Marschik, "Österreich und Europa — Österreich im Sport. Anmerkungen zum Beitrag des Sportes zur nationalen Identität," *Medienimpulse* 6 (1998): 19–26.

30. Ruth Seifert, "Militär, Nation und Geschlecht: Analyse einer kulturellen Konstruktion," in *Krieg/War. Eine philosophische Auseinandersetzung aus feministischer Sicht*, ed. Wiener Philosophinnen Club, 45 (München: Fink, 1997).

31. *Bild-Zeitung*, November 11, 2002.

32. *USA Today*, April 23, 2004.

33. Josh White, "Tillman's Parents Are Critical of Army," *Washington Post*, May 23, 2005; also "Soldier Blames Officer for Tale of Star's Death," *International Herald Tribune*, April 25, 2007.

34. Horst Geyer, "Stellvertreter der Nation. Repräsentation und Integration durch Sport," in *Die vertrimmte Nation oder Sport in rechter Gesellschaft*, ed. Jörg Richter (Reinbek bei Hamburg: Rowohlt 1972): 75–87, 79.

35. Jörg Udo Keck, "Die Sportschule der Bundeswehr in Warendorf," *Hardthöhenkurier* 2/2003: 50–54, 52.

36. Grieswelle, *Sportsoziologie*, 39.

37. Dallmann quoted in Sascha Plischke, "Agenda 2010," *BW-aktuell* 39, no. 48 (2004): 13.

38. Dirk Steinbach, "Der Körper als Gegner," *BW-aktuell* 39, no. 24 (2004): 13.

39. Wörner, "Breite mit Spitzen," 1; see also Ulrich Bröckling, *Disziplin. Soziologie und Geschichte militärischer Gehorsamsproduktion* (München: Fink, 1997).

40. Reinhardt Geermann, "'Knobelbechersport' im Heer?" *Truppenpraxis — Sonderheft: Sport in der Bundeswehr* (1984): 67–68, 68.

41. Heike Hasselbach, "Immer bis ans Limit," *BW-aktuell* 41, no. 41 (2006): 8–9.

42. Marco Seliger, "Süchtig nach Laufen," *Maz & More* no. 155 (May 8, 2002): 5; also Heike Hasselbach, "Nie auf der Strecke geblieben," *BW-aktuell* 42, no. 28 (2007): 14; also Heike Hasselbach, "Besessener Himmelsstürmer," *BW-aktuell* 41, no. 42 (2006): 12.

43. David le Breton, "Playing Symbolically with Death in Extreme Sports," *Body & Society* 6, no. 1 (2000): 1–11, 1.

44. Ibid., 2.

45. Karl-Heint Bette, *Körperspuren. Zur Semantik und Paradoxie moderner Körperlichkeit* (Bielefeld: transcript, 2005).

46. Peter Becker, "Latente politische Sozialisation durch Sport," in *Die Politisierung des Menschen. Instanzen der politischen Sozialisation*, ed. Bernhard Claußen and Rainer Geißler, 263–273 (Opalden: Leske+Budrich, 1996), 270.

47. Ibid., 271. It needs further empirical work to find out if the (illegal) use of drugs in elite sport will fundamentally undermine or alter this mechanism.

48. Billig, *Banal Nationalism*, 6.

49. See Tanja Thomas and Fabian Virchow, *Banal Militarism* (Bielefeld: transcript, 2006).

3

The Camera at War
When Soldiers Become War Photographers
METTE MORTENSEN

Lyrics from the song "Conflict," by the heavy metal band Disturbed, blast out of the speakers accompanying a video recorded, edited, and distributed to a global audience by Danish soldiers.[1] Lyrics refer to a people's enemy, and the enemy referred to is the Taliban forces fought by Danish troops in Afghanistan as part of NATO's alliance ISAF, International Security Assistance Force. Tens of thousands worldwide have watched the video on internet sites such as YouTube and LiveLeak. Like an action-packed Hollywood war movie, it focuses on combat, explosions, and weapons. Details catch the viewer's attention, as when soldiers laugh after a target is hit, or the handwritten word "Joy!" on a TMG machine gun, or the Latin inscription, "Dulce et decorum est pro patria mori" on a soldier's helmet, meaning "It is gratifying and an honor to die for your country." After nearly five minutes, the video reaches its grand finale with an image of a luminous Afghan desert sunset. Danish soldiers stand beneath the waving red and white flag in a pose resembling Joe Rosenthal's famous Second World War photo of United States marines raising the Stars and Stripes on Mount Suribachi, Iwo Jima in February, 1945. Against the desert background, a scrolling text states: "Many Taliban were either wounded or killed during the making of this film. It's fantastic!"

What are we to make of this film? Does it belong to popular culture or politics? Is it entertainment? War propaganda? A political document offering new knowledge about war, as seen through the viewfinder of its closest eyewitness, the soldier? Evidence of what it is like to be a Danish soldier fighting in a war far away from home? Taking a look at the context for viewing the film does not make us any wiser. When watching the clip on LiveLeak on a random Wednesday morning we see advertising from the sponsors of the site for "Meet Sexy Ladies," "See Funny Videos," and "Paris Hilton Videos." At the bottom, LiveLeak promotes its most popular videos with headlines which fuel the curiosity of the viewer, such as "Man Changes into Tree because of Giant Warts," "Ghost caught on security tape at gas station," and "U.S. Soldiers engage Taliban in the mountains of Afghanistan." In short, the commercial blend of celebrities, sensationalism, sex, war, and violence, characteristic of the internet, serves as the framework for watching. What the impact of this and thousands of similar representations might be is an open question. However, one thing is certain. They *do* have an impact. An impact on popular culture and on the democratic debate. And not least on the public support for the war and political decision-making.

Left: Screen shot from a private video which Danish soldiers stationed in Afghanistan uploaded on YouTube in 2007 (under pseudonym) of their own recordings of war edited with music and titles, *http://www.youtube.com/watch?v=8FtSEq27cfU.*
Right: End titles of the Danish video.

In this article, I wish to reflect on what the framework of popular culture means for how the new representations of war can and will influence the democratic debate. On the one hand, these images reach a huge audience possibly enriched by powerful counternarratives to those provided by official sources. On the other hand, one should not forget the security risks involved with soldiers becoming war photographers. Using the video produced by the Danish soldiers in Afghanistan as my example, I will focus on what knowledge, information, and options of identification this type of material offers a viewer. This involves looking into how the video functions as a source for war with its blurred boundaries between photographer and soldier, between documentary and performance, and between the representation of war and war itself.

The New Eyewitness

War tends to advance the development and propagation of new technologies, both in the weapons industry and in the realm of information technologies. The wars of the new millennium are no exception. The Vietnam War was the first living room war which broadcasted the atrocities of the front line into Western homes, and the Gulf War was the first war to be transmitted live on TV. Now, Afghanistan and Iraq are becoming the first internet wars. Global and digital visual culture makes the production and circulation of images cheap and easy enough for any participant in the war may take on the role of war photographer with a world-wide audience. The result of this is well known. Time and again, the images which turn into "breaking news" in the international media have not been taken by professional photographers but rather by soldiers or others active in the war.[2] *The new eyewitness*, as I call this powerful figure, has entered the global arena of politics and the media.

As the most prominent example, the pictures from Abu Ghraib instantly come to mind. The photographs documenting the abuse of Iraqi prisoners by American soldiers spurred international debate about the legitimacy of the Iraq war and led to violent reactions. However, even before the Abu Ghraib scandal broke in late April, 2004, the American government was well aware of the security threats posed by the troops producing images. Earlier that month, the *Seattle Times* showed pictures of coffins, draped with the American flag, being returned to the United States, taken by a cargo worker employed by a U.S. military contractor. This publication violated the prohibition enacted by the Pentagon in 1991 to prevent the media taking and showing pictures of American losses. After the release of the photos, the Secretary of Defense, Donald Rumsfeld, promptly banned all U.S. army personnel from bringing cell phone cameras to Iraq; a ban which was doomed to failure. Other well-known examples of the new eyewitness include the two security officers, working for the Iraqi Department of Justice, who illegally filmed the hanging of Saddam Hussein with their cell phones, as well as the many videos and stills produced by hostage-takers, displaying theatrical set-ups that we have by now become all too familiar with. Nicholas Mirzoeff estimates that more pictures have been produced during the war in Iraq alone than during any previous period in history.[3] Without doubt, the new eyewitness has contributed significantly to this flood of images.

Taking into account how these images saturate the media, they have been the subject of surprisingly little academic scrutiny. Of course, numerous articles and books have been written about Abu Ghraib, yet they tend to explore the political implications of the case or outline the pictures' references to visual culture such as pornography and depictions of lynching.[4] Consequently, it has been largely overlooked that the photos from Abu Ghraib do not represent an isolated instance, but rather forecast a radical shift in war imagery, and so the vital question of how this will change public access to information about war remains unanswered.

A Battlefield of Pictures

Digital visual culture is a growing risk strategically as well as operationally, demanding a balancing act of the military and those in power between censorship and respect for the freedom of expression. As such, there is nothing new about a battle over the use of images as part of warfare. This has been the case ever since photographers first stepped into the combat zone of the Crimean War (1853–1856). What is new is how the camera is no longer just a tool for recording war. It has itself become an integrated and determining part of warfare, affecting it on all levels, from the everyday lives of soldiers to global politics; a powerful weapon in its own right.

Progressively, the production and distribution of images, along with the political management and mobilization of them, play an extensive and complex role in modern war. In recent years, we have seen numerous examples of how the global media circulation of images from war zones not only leads to local instability and violence, but also has a bearing on public opinion and political debate. In the early days of global visual culture, the hope was uttered that it would evolve into a "new visual Esperanto."[5] Today, that hope has faded. Although images cross national and linguistic borders, it is evident that they are interpreted and produce political consequences in local contexts. As a result, visual culture is now inevitably incorporated into security policy in order to create a defense against potentially damaging images and provide the media with affirmative and assenting images of the war. Look at the new war representations for instance: On the one hand, we see soldiers using fast-speed technologies to disseminate their pictures worldwide, and on the other, there are continuous attempts to regulate this looming digital anarchy. This point can be exemplified by the debate in Denmark about the video from Afghanistan.

After being available online for several months, an unknown Danish soldier's video made during his service in Afghanistan became the eye of the media storm in August 2007, along with similar videos from Iraq. Military sociologist, Claus Kold, pointed out the risk of the videos causing danger to the Danish troops if used by the Taliban or Al Qaeda for propaganda purposes.⁶ Other words of warning came from the defense spokesman for the opposition party SF, the Socialist People's Party, Holger K. Nielsen, who was concerned about the influence the video would have on future recruitment: "We don't want people ... who think it would be cool to go to Afghanistan, having watched a war movie on YouTube."⁷ He was troubled by the film showing the Danish commitment in Afghanistan as a war against the Taliban, rather than participation in the NATO alliance. However, the Danish army did not feel compelled to remove this or other videos from the public domain. A press release from the Army's Operational Command made it clear that, owing to freedom of speech, "the army can not, and will not, censor private footage placed on the internet."⁸ The army is only going to interfere if videos contain clips that are illegal or jeopardize personal or operational safety. Even though the Secretary of Defense, Søren Gade, found the pictures "distasteful" in their "glorification of war," he supported the army's policy.⁹

That this liberal Danish strategy differs from the more restrictive American policy was already evident when Pentagon forced the CBS television network to hold back the Abu Ghraib pictures for two weeks. Since then, the U.S. administration has tried in different ways to prevent soldiers from taking on the role of do-it-yourself war photographers. To name but one example of the U.S. administration acting on the offensive, access to YouTube, MySpace, and eleven other sites were blocked on all the army's computers in May 2007. The U.S. Defense Department justified this move by claiming that the pictures represented "a significant operational security challenge."¹⁰ In other words, they might reveal classified information, undermine the support for the war or misrepresent American warfare. As Lt. Col. Christopher Garver, a spokesman for the U.S. military in Iraq, states: "It has been frustrating. There are 150,000 troops out here doing great work every day, but what you see is the one knucklehead who shot the three-legged dog and put it up on YouTube."¹¹ Moreover, as a strategic counter-strike the U.S. army has launched its own YouTube channel. Garver explains that "it is a battle space in which we have not been active, and ... a media we can use to get our story told."¹²

From an historical point of view, the security risks posed by the digital exchange of images are ironic since the internet was originally conceived by the U.S. Defense Department during the Cold War to ensure communication in the eventuality of nuclear conflict. Today, when Secretaries of Defense publicly address the new possibilities of picture taking and sharing, it is a strong indication of their perceived security threat. In order to comprehend that threat, it is useful to look into the new war representations as sources of information.

No User's Manual

In Saigon in 1968, the chief of the South Vietnamese national police, General Nguyen Ngoc Loan, escorts a suspected Vietcong leader out to the street where journalists and photographers have gathered. Without hesitation he shoots the prisoner at point blank. We know the scene from Eddie Adams' Pulitzer Prize winning photo, taken precisely at the moment the bullet hits. The prisoner grimaces. He has not yet started to fall. According to Susan Sontag, General Loan would not have carried out this summary execution had the press not been present.[13] The lesson taught by this forty-year-old photo is that the camera does not merely frame and capture reality in war zones. What goes on in front of the lens might not have happened in that way and sometimes might not have happened at all, if the camera had been turned the other way. Lately, this development has taken a decisive step further. Not only are soldiers performing for the camera. They are also performing for their own cameras. War representations follow the current tendency for deploying digital technologies as tools for staging, exposing, and exhibiting the self.

When war representations tend towards visual performance, where does this leave the public with respect to gaining access to information about war? One way of answering that question is to sketch how the new war imagery breaks with tradition.

Hungarian born photographer and co-founder of the legendary photo agency Magnum, Robert Capa (1913–1954), incarnated the classical ideal of the war photographer as independent, humanistic, and heroic. With the motto "If your pictures aren't good enough, you're not close enough," Capa bared the authentic, brutal realities of war to the home front. The new representations deviate from the classic ideals, established by Capa and his generation of war photographers, in three respects: No auteur has his name in the byline, they avoid censorship, and they are distributed on a massive scale.[14]

First of all, the new image makers are mostly amateurs who take on the double role of documenting combat and being part of it themselves. As a rule, the photographer is either subjective and biased or anonymous and without obvious motives for picture making. Moreover, it is seldom possible to track a picture's origin or route in the global information systems. For example, the video from Afghanistan was placed on LiveLeak by the alias Gulogulo, and on YouTube by the alias Hornet1985. The identities behind these assumed names are unknown to us, preventing us from establishing any authorship. Paradoxically, the images come across as authentic even though they are difficult to authenticate. Whereas the aesthetically refined pictures of professional photographers are often accused of being staged, amateur eyewitness accounts are perceived as more genuine and credible. That appears to be the case even today, in spite of most spectators being familiar with the art of digital manipulation. The pictures' apparent authenticity makes them more unsafe and unpredictable in relation to arousing violent reactions because people tend to respond to them emotionally rather than analytically. Furthermore, no editor, organization, or administration has made decisions about whether to release the pictures or not, based on a risk calculation of the probable responses from different groups. On the contrary, their intent is often vague and their contents messy and incoherent. As a result, they are vulnerable to radical readings that may be as motivated by the spectators' private lives and ethnic, religious, geo-political, and cultural background as by the pictures themselves. To sum up, the lack of a stable and identifiable figure or institution responsible for the images has wide-ranging consequences, from security policies to lack of transparency when it comes to the interests invested in them.

Secondly, the new representations also depart from tradition in their ability to slip through censorship. So far, no method has been developed to efficiently prevent unwanted digital communication.[15] The new representations typically circulate independently of governmental or military press supervision.

Thirdly, there is a break from tradition with regard to distribution. The material reaches a vast audience on platforms such as YouTube and LiveLeak, on war blogs, and in the traditional media. Viewers are to be counted in tens or even hundreds of millions when controversial cases such as the Abu Ghraib pictures or the bootleg recordings of Saddam Hussein's execution make worldwide headline news. The immense appeal can partly be explained by how the new representations put forward an alternative to the mainstream media war coverage which is often criticized for being both too loyal to governmental and military interests and restricted by its own conventions.[16] A less politically correct reason for their popularity is the voyeurism sparked by the dramatic, sensational, or violent nature of the content.

In short, we know neither the creator, nor the targeted audience, nor how we are supposed to react to or gain knowledge from the new war representations. They come without a user's manual, and this is more than just a challenge to the individual viewer. Much more is at stake. In order to grasp not only the security political issues, but also the democratic potentials and shortcomings of the pictures as unique sources of war, we need to examine the ways in which meaning is conveyed by them and how they function as communicative acts. We need to outline a new method for understanding and analyzing war imagery.

Visual Performance as Evidence

With the camera embedded in warfare, we have moved beyond the point where it makes sense to judge war representations solely on whether they are true in the impartial and objective meaning of that word. This traditional criterion depended on the idea of a trustworthy individual behind the camera with no hidden agendas and an untarnished moral codex. Clearly, this is not the case with contemporary war representations.

Instead, I suggest we see war imagery as *performative sources*. A quote from Thomas Keenan's article "Mobilizing Shame" (2004) will allow me to pursue this line of reasoning: "What would it mean to come to terms with the fact that there are things which happen in front of cameras that are not simply true or false, not simply representations and references, but rather opportunities, events, performances, things that are done and done for the camera, which come into being in a space beyond truth and falsity that is created in view of mediation and transmission?"[17] Although I agree with Keenan — that war depictions are often influencing or creating reality rather than merely reproducing it — I oppose to his definition of them as simply "opportunities, events, performances" because it does not seem to recognize the reality in, behind, and beyond the pictures. As Susan Sontag indignantly observes: "To speak of reality becoming a spectacle is a breath-taking provincialism. It universalizes the viewing habits of a small, educated population living in the rich part of the world, where news has been converted into entertainment."[18] The viewpoints of Keenan and Sontag need not be conflicting. Taking a perhaps controversial stance, I would like to argue that there is not necessarily a contradiction between war imagery as documentary and performance. Indeed, insisting that war visuals must be strictly documentary practically rules out the whole genre. Likewise, performed or not, it would be the end of war pictures if one were to deny them the ability to pass on insights.

It is difficult, not to say impossible, to grasp the manifold wartime interactions between image and reality in their complex chains of causes and effects. The pictures from Abu Ghraib demonstrate this point. They were obviously staged and highly performative in their quotation of familiar pictorial traditions such as pornography, sadomasochism, photographs of lynchings, and colonial depictions of "primitive" people as inferior, sexualized bodies rather than individuals with rights. In spite of the scenes being acted out in front of the camera, and conceivably even *for* the camera, they proved themselves to be valuable sources for revealing the conditions of the detainees, and the blatant disregard for the Geneva conventions by the prison's guards and officials.

Even performed pictures may serve as visual evidence. Bearing this in mind, I suggest that war representations should be judged on their effect on the audience: on the effect they actually have and the effect they might have. In a positive sense, this includes heightening the viewer's consciousness, understanding, and knowledge of the war, thereby enabling him or her to take a stand. In a negative sense, one has to consider the hazards of the pictures leading to augmented hostility between the opposing sides with all the implied security risks and diplomatic challenges. Judging war imagery on their effect permits us to move beyond the opposition between "true" and "false" which has stagnated the debate for so long. Additionally, it has the advantage of not only focusing on the (often unidentifiable) maker and original context, but also on distribution and the role of the spectator. Crucial in estimating the material's effect is the options of identification and non-identification it offers.

National Identities at War

Watching almost any war movie may convince us of the close connection between war, popular culture, and national identity. Albeit non-fictional, the video from Afghanistan is in continuance of this convention. Dramatic scenes from the battlefield intersect with constructions of identity. As part of psychological warfare, negotiations of identities take place within the realm of visual popular culture. It is an essential function of wartime visuals to create stable, easily recognizable pictures of "us" versus "the enemy." Working within this logic, the video collides with the official Danish narrative of the military engagement in Afghanistan as part of the NATO effort to secure peace and democracy. When comparing the film's violent, triumphant, and patriotic iconography with the military reception of it, a divide manifests itself between the military maintenance of its private nature and the soldiers' display of themselves as representative of the nation and the national armed forces in particular.

The Danish army is in line with official American policy by dismissing the video as "private." After the Abu Ghraib photos, President George W. Bush regretted the "disgraceful conduct by a few American troops who dishonored our country and disregarded our values."[19] In addition, he stressed that they did "not represent America."[20] It may be true that soldiers do not represent the army in a strictly legal sense when making pictures, yet this issue can not be isolated to a matter of law, as was indicated by the prevailing opinion voiced after the scandal, that the photos did in effect represent America. First, the interrogation methods deployed in Abu Ghraib were in accordance with those used in other American-run prisons throughout the world, and with the Defense Department's bending of the Geneva Conventions under Donald Rumsfeld. Second, the pictures were representative of America's visual culture. The employees at Abu Ghraib were no different to other amateur photographers, by taking pictures of scenes and themes they knew from their cultural heritage and thereby creating "an American family album of racist, pornographic iconography" as Max Gordon puts it.[21] The same goes for the Danish video. While not representing Denmark or the Danish army legally, the iconography discloses how the soldiers in the film see themselves as agents of precisely that.

Calling the video repetitive would be an understatement. In less than five minutes we see twenty something video sequences or stills of Danish soldiers firing various weapons. Another recurring motif is explosions. And the waving Danish flag makes an appearance in three scenes. But we scarcely see the "enemy," a word repeated like a mantra by the heavy metal music on the soundtrack and alluded to in the scrolling text's counting of "60–70 affirmed kills." Alleged Taliban fighters only show in one scene; three men clad in traditional Arab garments sit on the ground, perhaps in prayer. In the next frame an explosion goes off. Regardless of whether the two clips were filmed in sequence, or whether the scene is the result of subsequent editing, the image presented of the "enemy" is indistinct. Filmed from the back, the distant figures project a generalized vision of the enemy as primitive, fundamentalist, and non–Europeans, rather than Taliban specifically. The film's rationale seems to be that the less discernable the enemy, the more the Danish soldiers are represented as being soldiers and as being Danish.

Without a clear and unequivocal image of the enemy, the film decontextualizes itself from the actual conflict and turns to the myth of soldiers united in their fight for each other and for their nation as featured in countless Hollywood war movies such as *Saving Private Ryan* (1998) by Steven Spielberg and even in anti-war films such as Sam Mendes' *Jarhead* (2005). The most distinct example is the previously mentioned closing photo of Danish soldiers imitating Rosenthal's 1945 photo of U.S. marines planting the American flag on Iwo Jima. This iconic shot is culturally recycled as a symbol of victory, patriotism, and fellowship. To mention the most famous instances, the scene was recreated in the Washington, D. C., monument, the Marine Corps Memorial erected in 1954, and in the renowned image taken after 9/11 of three fire fighters raising the American flag on the ruins of the World Trade Center. Lastly, Rosenthal's photo, and the story behind it, inspired Clint Eastwood's *Flags of Our Fathers* (2006). Given that the small country of Denmark is in alliance with the world's only remaining superpower, the inspiration from American popular culture hardly comes as a surprise. Since Denmark does not have a long tradition of troops engaged in combat outside Europe, no national frames of understanding can be applied to the soldiers' service in Afghanistan. The visual legacy of American Second World War history fills that void.

Planting the national flag on foreign soil is a powerful demonstration of conquest. The glowing sunset suggests a tourist gaze at the Afghan landscape, as if this was a colonial narrative of winning conquering exotic land. While the American marines in Rosenthal's original photo were unified in raising the flag, the Danish soldiers are past that moment. They are now prepared to protect this new Danish territory from enemies outside the picture frame, under the protection of the flag, and with a machine gun pointing in each direction. Apart from this reference to impending combat, the flat, empty landscape shows no signs of history, no signs of prior inhabitants. The scrolling text, "Many Taliban were either wounded or killed ..." is a further clue that Taliban fighters, standing in the way of the Danish take-over of this land, have been exterminated.

Seeing the soldiers only as dark silhouettes, their individual traits are erased and they become symbolic of "the Danish Soldier" as such. The three bodies are united in an almost symmetrical figure signaling harmony and fellowship. This is contrary to the only glimpse of the "enemy." As mentioned before, "the enemy" is also shown as three men in a desert landscape, but with the significant difference that they are sitting separately with their heads turned in the same direction so as to circumvent communication between them. So, the narrative proposed by this photo, is one of Danish soldiers joined in a heroic, patriotic mission. A mission accomplished.

The final shot allows the viewer to take a breath after having experienced the video's rapid exposure of one fragmented war scene after the other. It has the key function of summarizing and unifying the film. For a "private" video, as the Army's Operational Command claimed it to be in the press release, American war memorial is a remarkably official discourse to rely on for inspiration and authorization. Especially if we consider the source of the photo is none other than the website of the Army's Operational Command. Here, we see the photo in a gallery of out-posted soldiers' own war snapshots from Kosovo, Iraq, and Afghanistan, which the Army's Operational Command have found suitable for online publication. Surely, the Army's Operational Command cannot be made responsible for the re-contextualization of the photo within the video from Afghanistan. And surely, it alters the photo's meaning to appear in the video. It is nevertheless striking that the soldier behind this "private" video found the patriotic and heroic picture for his spectacular climax on an official Danish army website. Just as it is striking, that the soldier who uploaded the video on YouTube provides a link to the website of the Danish Department of Defense in the category "About this video." Once again, it underscores the conflict between on the one hand the new eyewitness positioning himself as an ambassador of national interests and values and, on the other hand, the military regarding this as a "private" enterprise.

This representational crisis is deeply rooted in questions of identity and politics. If the video signifies how soldiers stationed in Afghanistan would like to present themselves to the public, is this a "private" matter? Or should it be taken seriously by the army and the general public as a political testimony? Are soldiers turning to American popular culture obtained in part from the army's own online resources in lack of any other appropriate and attractive model for the role they play in the Afghan war? The video shows the ongoing struggle of identities.

Since wartime communication increasingly takes place within the visual domain, this also becomes a battle space for soldiers. We may as well get used to videos like the one from Afghanistan as sources of information about war. It borrows from popular culture's generous repertoire of *war as entertainment*, and bears little resemblance with the authentic realism conventionally associated with eyewitness accounts. It is selective and subjective. Staged and performed. But it is also a unique insight into the frame of mind of soldiers and the experience of war. We need only the proper tools to approach it. For there is no denying that the footage demands a great deal of the spectator.

From Seeing to Experiencing War

Like many other contemporary forms of culture and entertainment, the new representations of war leave much work to the viewer. This applies to art works within the tradition termed *relational aesthetics* by French curator and critic Nicolas Bourriard. It applies to interactive theatre inviting the audience to participate in the play. It applies to reality TV asking viewers to vote via sms. It applies to newspapers urging the readers to post digital recordings on their webpage. And it applies to the internet in its overall user-generated structure as well as in many of the individual sites. Without the user's or spectator's active and engaged participation, the art work, play, television program, or site is not complete. This tendency also manifests itself in the new war representations, no longer allowing the viewer to simply see war. We are now experiencing war through them.

In *Virtuous War: Mapping the Military-Industrial-Media-Entertainment*

Network (2001), James Der Derian writes: "The new wars are fought in the same manner as they are represented, by military simulations and public dissimulation, by real-time surveillance and TV live-feeds. Virtuality collapses distance between here and there, near and far, fact and fiction. It widens the distance between those who have and those who have not. Representing the most penetrating and sharpest (to the point of invisibility) edge of globalization, it disappears the local and the particular. It leaves little space for the detached observer."[22] Der Derian's argument enables us to clarify the position for viewing contemporary war representations. He stresses that war is fought in the same way as it is represented, and further that this collapse of the boundaries between war itself and representations of war does not leave much space for the detached observer.

Returning our attention to the video, we see that it draws the viewer into warfare in different ways. Firstly, several of the pictures featured in the film originate from surveillance devices such as night cameras, aerial surveillance, and measuring optics. Inserted into the narrative of the video, they close the gap between war and representations of war completely. Secondly, most of the scenes are shot with a handheld camera and, additionally, many of them are filmed while in motion. This makes the video chaotic, unsteady, and shaky, pulling the viewer into the action. Thirdly, it is inherent of the internet as an interactive medium that it is the viewer's own choice to watch the video and to decide when to press the stop bottom.

In view of the advanced spectator participation, the important issue is what messages and meanings are conveyed by the video or, to put it another way, how it acts as a source of war. While experiencing the bodily sensation of war — the adrenalin rush, the excitement, the anxiety — the video makes the spectator draw his or her own line for the physical engagement. A decisive factor in this is its monotony. Witnessing the succession of explosions and weapons being fired is like asking the viewer: How much more are you going to see? Why are you watching this? And, crucially, the question of identification is raised. The video invites us to identify with the soldiers or, alternatively, position ourselves in relation to their self-exposure. Can we relate to how they present themselves? What would be the alternative? How might a viewer from the opposing side read the pictures? Perhaps we go on to consider the legitimacy of the video and the larger issues at stake concerning the Danish engagement in Afghanistan: What is Denmark's role as part of NATO? Is the cause worth fighting and losing soldiers' lives for? As noted by Judith Butler in another context, these issues do not solely stem from the spectator's autonomy. They also lie inherent in the material itself.[23]

The important question is not only what the pictures show but also who chooses to look at them. As James Elkins writes in his book, *The Object Stares Back: On the Nature of Seeing* (1996): "seeing is self-definition. Objects look back, and their incoming gaze tells me what I am. Our sense of ourselves is like a television station always going out of focus, and we tune and clarify ourselves by seeing."[24] While watching the video from Afghanistan, it defines the spectator in new ways, just as the footage itself is defined in new ways. The spectator is actively involved in generating new knowledge, experience, and awareness, which did not exist in that particular form before.

Taking part in the writing of the video's story, spectators get a responsibility for what they see and how they see it. It is one of the hazards (and thrills) of the internet, that global interaction can take place in the privacy of your home. However, the idea of this private zone is just as much an illusion as the idea of being a passive spectator. Interacting with different publics means becoming part of them yourself. In other words, while watching for example the video from Afghanistan on the internet, you engage in a public exchange of opinions and, hence, you also gain a responsibility for this exchange. After all, the new eyewitness would soon lose his power if a huge audience did not look for, look at, and circulate his pictures. Spectators become part of visual warfare and hold a considerable power over the interpretations and consequences of the new representations of war.

The Internet as Combat Zone

The reception of pictures is influenced by the medium through which they are transmitted. At this point in history, the new war representations raise more questions than they give answers about the internet as a source for war. Is it the same inquisitive urge which drives internet surfers to download Paris Hilton's sex video and soldiers' war movies? Do they nourish popular culture's obsession with sex and violence that goes hand in hand with the commercialism of the internet? Or can the staggering interest be explained by their ability to reveal the non-photogenic aspects of war which usually take place when the cameras are turned off? Allow me to finish with outlining the potentials and limitations of contemporary online representations of war in order to foresee how they might influence the democratic debate.

On the one hand, the security risk must be taken seriously. There is a delicate balance between safety concerns and the public's demand for free, uncensored and nuanced media coverage of the war. Already, the new war representations have had fatal results which can not be justified just because they facilitate more in depth knowledge. Furthermore, the pictures make heavy demands on the viewer because they both document warfare and take part in it themselves. This double role is mostly at the expense of their documentary value since they tend to be vague and unfocused and thereby more susceptible to radical reactions.

On the other hand, the new war imagery can enlighten us about aspects of war we normally would not see or hear about. This enlightenment can sometimes prove successful in revealing the principles behind the traditional media's framing, selection, and editing of news from combat zones, as well as war faring nations' agendas regarding visual representations of war. One example is the execution of Saddam Hussein. Without touching on the discussion of whether it is desirable that recordings of his or any other person's death should be available on the internet, the bootleg recordings disclosed, to a global public, that the hanging did not take place in the controlled and orderly manner as first claimed in the Iraqi government's official video of the event. So, the new eyewitness is capable of enriching the public with a more informed and differentiated background for forming an opinion.

A central point is the significance of the quantity of images. To many skeptics, the vast number of images in global circulation and "the pictorial turn" announced by art historian W. J. T. Mitchell in 1994 have resulted in a general lack of trust in the individual image as able to make a difference.[25] The argument is that the mass of pictures weakens our critical apparatus and reduces us to uncritical visual consumers, for whom one single picture can hardly make a difference any longer. Predictably, the quantity of images will reduce the number of icons with symbolic value uniting spectators in shared opinions and emotions which photo history is full of, from Robert Capa's falling Republican soldier from the Spanish Civil War to Huyng Cong Ut's young napalm-burnt girl running away during the Vietnam War. Perhaps this is not only to be regretted. Photographic icons can provide a visual entrance to war and block that very same entrance with one-dimensional, schematic or clichéd depictions creating, in the words of Susan Sontag, an "illusion of consensus."[26] Whereas icons confirm and strengthen the predominant feelings and views about a given war, one could, optimistically perhaps, say that the bulk of the new representations are closer to the complexity of war with their messy, disconnected, and disconnecting contents.

All things considered, the individual war picture's loss of significance is hardly sufficient reason to write the genre's epitaph. In my opinion, the opposite standpoint seems more reasonable; that representations of war play a greater role than ever before. Political communication is becoming more and more tied up with images and we constantly see them activated and mobilized in new ways. Instead of iconoclasm, the rapidly changing conditions for making and distributing pictures call for a theoretical and methodological rethinking and redefinition of war representations as genre.

Global digital visual culture is tearing down the walls that have up till now protected and defined the genre of war representations. A number of consequences can already be seen and there are undoubtedly more to come. Soldiers have become war photographers. The user-generated media force the viewer to take a greater responsibility. War visuals tend to be more performative and security politics have to deal with visual culture in new ways. It is easy to point at the lurking dangers and challenges that this development might give rise to. Nevertheless, one should not overlook the democratic potentials of the easy access to producing, distributing, and receiving images from combat zones.

Notes

1. The video can be viewed online at YouTube http://www.youtube.com/watch?v=8FtSEq27cfU and LiveLeak http://www.liveleak.com/view?i=77e_1174526783 (Links active on December 21, 2007).
2. It should be noted that soldiers taking photos is not a new phenomenon. An earlier documented example is German soldiers on the Eastern Front during the Second World War. Hannes Heer and Klaus Naumann (eds.), *Vernichtungskrieg: Verbrechen der Wehrmacht 1941–1944* (Hamburg: Hamburger Edition HIS Verlag, 1995).
3. Nicholas Mirzoeff, *Watching Babylon: The War in Iraq and Global Visual Culture* (London: Routledge, 2005), 67.
4. The most important studies of the political aspects of Abu Ghraib include Mark Danner, *Torture and Truth: America, Abu Ghraib and the War on Terror* (New York: New York Review Books, 2004) and Seymour Hersh, *Chain of Command: The Road from 9/11 to Abu Ghraib* (New York: Allen Lane, 2005). For interpretations of Abu Ghraib within a cultural framework see Susan Sontag, "Regarding the Torture of Others," *New York Times Magazine*, May 23, 2004; Luc Sante, "Torturers and Terrorists," *New York Times*, May 11, 2004; and Abigail Solomon-Godeau, "Remote Control: Dispatches from the Image Wars," *Artforum* 10, vol. 62 (summer 2004), 61–64.
5. Mirzoeff, *Watching Babylon*, 2.
6. Laust Farver, "Flere krigsfilm med danske soldater" (More War Movies With Danish Soldiers) *Jyllands-Posten*, August 29, 2007.
7. "Forsvaret vil ikke censurere voldsvideoer fra Afghanistan" (The Army Will Not Censor Violent Videos from Afghanistan), *Urban*, August 24, 2007.
8. Press release of August 23, 2007, from the Army's Operational Command.
9. Lars Igum Rasmussen, "Nettet bugner med videoer af danske soldater i krig" (The Internet is Full of Videos with Danish Soldiers at War), *Avisen.dk*, accessed on August 23, 2007.
10. Alex Spillius, "Website ban on U.S. troops," *The Daily Telegraph*, May 15, 2007.
11. Alexandra Zavis, "Military takes battle for Iraq to the Internet," *Los Angeles Times*, May 2, 2007.
12. Ibid.
13. Susan Sontag, *Regarding the Pain of Others* (London: Penguin Books, 2003), 53.

14. It is beyond the scope of this article to go further into the tradition of war photography. For a critical historical account see Caroline Brothers, *War and Photography: A Cultural History* (London: Routledge, 1997).

15. Gabriel Weimann, *Terror on the Internet: The New Arena, the New Challenges* (Washington D.C.: United States Institute of Peace Press, 2006), 173–202.

16. Naila Hamdy and Radwa Mobarack, "Iraq War Ushers in Web-based Era," in *Global Media go to War: Role of News and Entertainment Media During the 2003 Iraq War*, 246, ed. Ralph D. Berenger (Spokane, Wa: Marquerette Books, 2004).

17. Thomas Keenan, "Mobilizing Shame," *The South Atlantic Quarterly* 103 (nr. 2/3 2004): 435.

18. Sontag, *Pain of Others*, 98–99.

19. "President Outlines Steps to Help Iraq Achieve Democracy and Freedom," speech at the United States Army War College, Carlisle, Pennsylvania on May 24, 2004, accessed from http://www.whitehouse.gov/news/releases/2004/05/20040524-10.html on December 21, 2007.

20. Danner, *Torture and Truth*, 5.

21. Max Gordon, "Abu Ghraib: Postcards from The Edge," *Open Democracy*, October 12, 2004, accessed from http://www.opendemocracy.net/media-abu_ghraib/article_2146.jsp on December 21, 2007.

22. James Der Derian, *Virtuous War: Mapping the Military-Industrial-Media-Entertainment Network* (Boulder Colorado: Westview Press, 2001), xviii.

23. Judith Butler, *Precarious Life: The Powers of Mourning and Violence* (London: Verso, 2004), 130.

24. James Elkins, *The Object Stares Back: On the Nature of Seeing* (New York: Hartcourt Brace, 1997), 86.

25. See among others Mirzoeff, *Watching Babylon*, 67.

26. Sontag, *Pain of Others*, 5.

4

Getting the Story Right
Myth, Meaning, and Gendered War Mythology in the Case of Jessica Lynch

RIKKE SCHUBART

> Pfc. Jessica Lynch, rescued Tuesday from an Iraqi hospital, fought fiercely and shot several enemy soldiers after Iraqi forces ambushed the Army's 507th Ordnance Maintenance Company, firing her weapon until she ran out of ammunition, U.S. Officials said.
> Lynch, a 19-year-old supply clerk, continued firing at the Iraqis even after she sustained multiple gunshot wounds and watched several other soldiers in her unit die around her in fighting March 23.... "She was fighting to the death," the official said. "She did not want to be taken alive."
> —*The Washington Post*, April 3, 2003

> I don't think it happened quite like that....
> —Jessica Lynch, November 12, 2003

Once a story is forged in the shape of myth it becomes unbreakable. Why? Because myths are rooted in society's old experiences, old emotions, and old narratives. Myths are the stories society tells to itself, about itself, drawn from its own historical past.[1] We need myths to make sense of the world, to turn random events into comprehensible stories, and to supply such stories with a recognizable narrative structure, familiar emotions and an already-known content. Once an event has been turned into a mythic story, we experience it as true and meaningful. And only then can we use it to guide us in future actions. Not any event, however, may become a story of mythic proportions. The narrator is not free to change the plot as he or she pleases, or replace old mythic characters with new ones. Only a story that respects the rules of myth is accepted by an audience. If not, things will end as did the story of Jessica Lynch.

Viewed in a short perspective, the story of how a nineteen-year-old female soldier was taken prisoner by Iraqi soldiers and nine days later freed by American elite soldiers served its purpose: it strengthened morale at a time when American soldiers were discouraged by relentless storms and unexpected resistance in Saddam Hussein's desert. Later, however, critical listeners disputed the story: Were the narrators — the U.S. military — true to facts? Was "the Jessica Lynch incident" really an event of mythic proportions or was this an example of what Roland Barthes in *Mythologies* (1973) describes as the bourgeoisie's cynical use of myth?

Let me place my cards on the table: I am not interested in any "truth" whatsoever about Jessica Lynch. My business is not to reveal her story as an example of media spin. If I do so nonetheless, this is merely because such exposure demonstrates the consequences of manipulating myth. Jessica's story was not exposed because it was "false" or because it mythologized her capture and rescue. It was exposed because its narrators failed to recognize *what myth* they were handling. Their untruthfulness was not towards factuality, but towards myth itself. This chapter will look at the nature of myth, the constructed mythic story of Jessica Lynch as a war hero, and at what Richard Slotkin calls one of the first myths of the white Americans, the "captivity narrative." We shall see how the three clash over Jessica's white, innocent, mutilated soldier-body.

Jessica — an American Hero?

This chapter will divide the story of Jessica into four chapters: "Capture," "Rescue," "Exposure," and "Captivity Victim."[2] The first two attempt to create the mythic story of Jessica as hero, the third chapter disputes this, and the fourth chapter reinterprets Jessica as captivity victim.

"The Capture" is straightforward: On March 20, 2003, the U.S. invades Iraq in a war which according to president George W. Bush will last only a week. It is called Operation Iraqi Freedom. The Americans expect to be greeted by cheering Iraqis, grateful to be rid of a dictator. But a week has passed and Baghdad has not been taken, Saddam not found, and the harsh climate discourages the soldiers. Critique coming from France and Germany and within the Coalition Forces (as active war participants counting the U.S., Great Britain, Australia, Denmark, and Spain) increases.[3] This will turn into another Vietnam, the warning goes. On top of this are the missing weapons of mass destruction which had been the central argument for invading Iraq.

The Gulf War in 1991 had had no media visibility of victims: Iraqi losses didn't make it into Western media and the U.S. had no losses.[4] But in 2003 the media of the opposite side had gained visibility. On March 24 the Arab newspaper *ShiaNews* brings photographs of dead and wounded Iraqi children, also shown by the Arab television station Al-Jazeera. An Arab television station brings pictures of executed American soldiers and of American soldiers shaking in fear of interrogation.[5] The Allies need moral support. And on March 30 the story of the missing Jessica Lynch, a supply clerk in the maintenance troops, circulates in the worldwide media. Her convoy had fallen behind, taken a wrong turn, and was attacked March 23 in Nasiriyah. Of 33 soldiers, seventeen were missing,[6] one of them blond, a teenager, a woman.

"Missing" is the headline on the front of Danish newspaper *Berlingske*'s second section on March 30 with a large prom photo of Jessica, smiling, innocent, delicate.[7] In the left corner is her small military photo with the American flag as background and Jessica looking "like a child who had sneaked into her daddy's closet and tried on his uniform to play soldier."[8] The compassionate and riveting article—written in the same tone as articles in other national media appearing at the same time—describes how her hometown Palestine is decorated with yellow ribbons in the American tradition while its population prays for a miracle. Jessica's family could not finance the children's education. The army was her ticket to travel the world, to leave the U.S. for the first time, serve the country and save up enough money for an education as a kindergarten teacher. "She lived her life at the end of a small road, in a little town in a ravine in West Virginia," the article states and ends with the words: "But she got to see the sun set in a foreign country, she heard the wind carry a foreign language, and if hope can perform miracles, one day she will be home and tell them all about it."[9]

The second chapter, "The Rescue," follows April 1, nine days after the attack, in the form of a rescue mission with Black Hawk helicopters landing in front of Saddam Hussein General Hospital in Nasiriyah, while a simultaneous attack with tanks on the town diverts attention. A special forces unit composed of U.S. Army Rangers, Navy SEALS, marines and Air Force combat controllers[10] storms the hospital, kicks in the doors, rescues Jessica, digs up the bodies of eleven American soldiers with their bare hands and leaves the hospital, all of it recorded by a film photographer whose footage is edited by the military and sent to news stations.

It feels like divine salvation. Jessica's parents had prayed to God and with them Palestine, the U.S. and the entire Western world prayed. As time passed, rescue became less probable, but faith and hope grew. Greg, Jessica's father, wore a bracelet with her name and the date of her capture, another American tradition. A stranger had given him his bracelet with the name of a son MIA in Vietnam. Greg wore both bracelets. But not since the Second World War had an American rescue mission succeeded. In 1980 a mission failed in

Iran with a helicopter and a plane colliding and resulting in eight causalities. In 1993 a mission in Somalia failed (not a rescue mission but a capture mission, portrayed in Ridley Scott's *Black Hawk Down*, 2001). Film recordings of dead American soldiers dragged in the streets of Mogadishu made the U.S. withdraw its troops from Somalia. A lot is at stake. And for the first time in half a century a rescue succeeds. Military footage shows Jessica smiling from a stretcher covered with the American flag while soldiers load her into the helicopter.

The military informs the public that Jessica was a hero. She had shot and killed an unknown number of Iraqi soldiers, suffered shot and knife wounds, and was only captured because her ammunition ran out. "She was fighting to the death," a spokesman is quoted April 3 in the *Washington Post*, "she did not want to be taken alive."[11] The myth of a young female soldier fighting bravely, being captured and miraculously saved, is complete, with testimonies to support the story, among them one from Mohammed Odeh Al Rehaief, who had informed the Americans he had seen a blond prisoner in the hospital and "had seen one of Saddam's Fedayeen, dressed all in black, slap the young woman across the face."[12] The wounded, waif-like woman, weighing just a hundred pounds and only five-foot-three, was maltreated on her sickbed by dark men.

The Iraqi hospital performed surgery on Jessica; later she was taken to a German military hospital where she was operated on; and on April 12 she was taken to Walter Reed Army Medical Center in Washington. She was awarded three medals while in the American hospital: a Purple Heart for being wounded in combat, a Prisoner of War Medal for her capture, and a Bronze Star for distinction in active combat.[13]

War Spin

In Barry Levinson's satirical drama *Wag the Dog* (1997) about spin doctors, war, and politics, an unfortunate affair with a girl scout threatens the president's election campaign. His public relations manager (Robert De Niro) hires a Hollywood producer (Dustin Hoffman) to create a war. "How close are you to this thing?" the producer asks. De Niro grabs his cell phone and calls the president's spokesman who is giving a statement on live television. "What do you want the kid to say?" The producer dictates: "I know we're all concerned for the President. I'm sure our hopes and prayers are with him." The spokesman repeats the exact words. The film producer is impressed — but disappointed with the performance: "He didn't *sell* the line."

In the third chapter of Jessica Lynch's story, "Exposure," the spin doctors enter the scene. They have been pulling strings and selling lines in the previous chapters, but are now forced into the limelight by critical media coverage, one being BBC's program *War Spin*, aired on May 18. In the days before, both American and European news media had written about BBC's "real story behind a modern American war myth": Jessica hadn't killed any Iraqi soldiers or released a single shot — because her rifle had jammed. She was not wounded; her injuries were the result of RTA — Road Traffic Accident — and her body had neither gun nor knife wounds. She was not maltreated in sickbed. Having been given asylum in the U.S., the Iraqi witness maintained his statement although the slapping was denied by Jessica. She had been a prisoner, yes, but before her rescue the Iraqi doctors had tried to turn her over to the Americans, who fired at the ambulance, which therefore had to turn back. She was treated in the best possible manner: She had the only special hospital bed, she was assigned one of the floor's two nurses and she was the only patient having orthopedic surgery. "You could not help but feeling sorry for her. A young girl. An American. A prisoner. We did our best. Believe me, she was the only orthopedic surgery I performed," doctor Mahdi Khafaji told the *Washington Post*.[14]

And was the rescue really as dramatic as it appeared? Or was it an act? Iraqi soldiers had left the hospital before the rescue, so the firefight in the film shootings came only from the American soldier's weapons. The doctors offered the soldiers the keys to the hospital but they preferred to kick down the doors instead, maybe to create more action for the later replay of events in the media. "It was like a Hollywood film. They cried, 'Go, go, go,' with guns and blanks and the sound of explosions. They made a show — an action movie like Sylvester Stallone or Jackie Chan, with jumping and shouting, breaking down doors," doctor Anmar Uday told *The Guardian*.[15] Rumors went that the Pentagon had been inspired by Scott's *Black Hawk Down* to "script" Jessica's rescue. The producer of *Black Hawk Down*, Jerry Bruckheimer, and producer Bertram van Munster, who was behind the reality show *Cops*, had visited the Pentagon in 2001 to suggest a reality show, *Profiles from the Front Line*, which would portray American soldiers in Afghanistan. *Profiles from the Front Line* aired February 27, before the war in Iraq, and Pentagon was enthusiastic. Unconfirmed rumors asserted that the photographer filming the rescue of Jessica Lynch had been Scott's assistant during the shooting of *Black Hawk Down*.[16]

The Pentagon denied the accusations put forward in the BBC program *War Spin*. Although the British and the Americans were allied, the British had not had access to the unedited shootings or to Jessica's medical journal. The

Americans had played their cards close to the vest. "In reality we had two different styles of news media management," said spokesman for the British army, captain Al Lockwood. "I feel fortunate to have been part of the UK one."[17] Where the European news media demanded documentation, the American news media wanted visuals: "The American strategy was to concentrate on the visuals and to get a broad message out. Details — where helpful — followed behind. The key was to ensure the right television footage. The embedded reporters could do some of that. On other missions, the military used their own cameras, editing the film themselves and presenting it to broadcasters as ready-to-go-packages."[18]

A Captivity Victim: "Oh God Help Us"

The fourth chapter is Jessica's biography *I Am a Soldier, Too: The Jessica Lynch Story* (May 2003) written by journalist Rick Bragg.[19] The book paints the picture of a neat and quiet girl from an ordinary working class family in the little town of Palestine, more occupied with clothes than sports, and giving up being a cheerleader when shorts replaced the prettier skirts. Her muster was as big a surprise to herself as to her family and she was content to be in the maintenance troops where she was responsible for supply of things like toilet paper. When her Humvee was attacked she put her forehead on her knees and prayed: "Oh God help us. Oh God, get us out of here. Oh God, please."[20]

Three hours passed between the time Jessica was attacked and when she was turned in at an Iraqi military hospital. In this period of time, the biography asserts, she was raped and tortured:

> The records also show that she was a victim of anal sexual assault. The records do not tell whether her captors assaulted her almost lifeless, broken body after she was lifted from the wreckage, or if they assaulted her and then broke her bones into splinters until she was almost dead.
>
> *
>
> Jessi's body armor and her bloody uniform were found in a house near the ambush site, the place that some military intelligence sources said she was taken to be tortured.
> But Jessi remembers none of this. When she awoke in the military hospital, it was during treatment, not torture. When she came to, the cruelties were over.[21]

At the time of publication Jessica is on the cover of *Time Magazine*. "The *real* story of Jessica Lynch" is the tagline, echoing *The Guardian*, May 15: "The truth about Jessica." "I'm not a hero," it says in the bottom right corner of her portrait on the cover. The article is illustrated with photographs of Jessica's rehabilitation training.[22] Her visual mise-en-scène with braids, shorts, and sneakers underlines innocence and sufferings, she looks like a child next to the enormous physical therapist who towers over her white body. Not a hero, but an *all–American girl*. Blond, petite, miss congeniality from a town where no one can afford their children's education. To the Americans it makes no difference if she fired shots or not; being captured and returning home is a miracle in itself.

Female Gender and War Mythology

The fight over the "right" version of the story does not end here. Iraqi doctors denied accusations of rape. They cut Jessica's uniform from her body before she received blood transfusions, was washed and had surgery, and her clothes could therefore not have been found in another building. There were no signs of rape, five doctors took part in the surgery, and the staff donated their own blood. "It was war, but we cared about her and we did everything we could for her," said the hospital director, Dr. Khudair al–Hazbar. "I know she is grateful."[23]

As stated in the beginning I am not interested in the "truth." Let us therefore leave this media circus and fly up where the open air allows a view from where the pieces of the puzzle form a motive. Because there *is* a motive. A mythological motive, older than the foundation of the United States. When the Pentagon choose Lynch as front-page material, they were both wrong and right. They were right that her story is mythic. But they were wrong about *what* myth. Not recognizing the myth that beautifully frames Jessica's experiences, they tried instead to invent a myth of Jessica as female action hero. But they ignored two essential things: First, a woman cannot represent a nation as a hero of war.[24] And second, Jessica was not a hero of war but a victim of captivity.

According to Richard Slotkin in *Regeneration Through Violence: The Mythology of the American Frontier, 1600–1860* (1996) a captivity narrative was the first myth Americans formed about their encounter with the Indians and the frontier. The captivity narrative is the story of a white woman abducted by Indians and rescued by Americans: "the New England Indian captivity narrative functioned as a myth, reducing the Puritan state of mind and world view, along with the events of colonization and settlement, into archetypal drama. In it a single individual, usually a woman, stands passively under the strokes of evil, awaiting rescue by the grace of God. The sufferer represents the whole, chastened body of Puritan society."[25]

We know the plot from John Ford's western *The Searchers* from 1956 where Ethan (John Wayne) spends five years tracking down the Indians that massacred his relatives and abducted his two nieces. The oldest niece was raped, scalped and killed. The youngest became Chief Scar's bride and refused to return with Ethan, but was finally saved.

Abductions were common during the Indian wars. Most known is the minister wife Mrs. Rowlandson's account of her abduction and captivity, which became the archetype of the captivity narrative: *The Sovereignty and Goodness of God, Together with the Faithfulness of His Promises Displayed: Being a Narrative of the Captivity and Restauration of Mrs. Mary Rowlandson* (1682). Captivity narratives were read in their time as being both real and symbolic: The war between immigrants and Indians was interpreted as an allegory of the battle between Christianity and demonic chaos, civilization and savagery. Mrs. Rowlandson thus understood events as a test of her faith, and captivity narratives were often used in sermons. Testing belonged to what Americans should expect. "It just so happens that we be Texicans," says Mrs. Jörgensen in *The Searchers*. "A Texican is nothing but a human man way out on a limb."

Historian Richard Slotkin, semiotic theorist Roland Barthes, and literary scholar Northrop Frye agree that myths do not adhere to criteria of "truth." Myths are neither true nor false, they are metaphorical narratives whose narrative form are emptied of historical facts and filled with mythic content.[26] "A mythology is a complex of narratives that dramatizes the world vision and historical sense of a people or culture, reducing centuries of experience into a constellation of compelling metaphors," says Slotkin.[27] The captured woman represents Christian faith, ideals of civilization, democracy, innocence, and martyrdom. The white female flesh becomes like that of the Virgin Mary, thus changing events from the extermination of the Indians to the immigrants' experience of faith, testing, and retribution. In Slotkin's words, "The captivity narrative ... reduced a complex of religious beliefs, philosophical concepts, and historical experiences to a single, compelling, symbolic ritual-drama."[28]

The dramatic structure and clear-cut protagonists made the captivity narrative an obvious point of identification for a vulnerable frontier society: most clearly drawn was the victim, then the demonized savages and finally the liberators. The narrative provided the immigrants with a figure onto which they could project a Christian enemy — the Devil. "The heroine-victim" represented the yet immature democracy, not as a heroic male figure, but as a female martyr calling out for freedom and liberation. The narrative had a therapeutic function: It raised hope, united and strengthened society, and lent its myth-structures as a narrative frame to the mission of the American immigrants.[29]

The analogy is striking: The military chooses Jessica to enter media mythology because she embodies the female victim of the captivity narrative — young, Anglo-Saxon, blond, with the innocent features of an angel in her soft teenage face. The military does not choose Lori Piestewa, a 22-years-old woman in Jessica's unit, who was also captured by the Iraqis. Lori would have been a wrong choice: Hopi Indian, separated, a mother of two, heavily built, without Jessica's waiflike appearance (Lori turns out to be one of the soldiers dug up by the rescue team). Neither does the military choose Shoshana Johnson who was captured in the same attack, shot in both legs and rescued on April 13, twelve days after Jessica.[30] Shoshana is black, a single mother, thirty. No good. The soldier Patrick Miller, whom the press later announces to be the "real" hero and who has since been on the *Jay Leno* show, is no good neither. He was caught in a crossfire as he drove up to Jessica's Humvee to check for survivors. Patrick found cover and killed seven soldiers firing on them with mortars. "And he did an amazing thing," a survivor told, "he saved our lives. If that mortar had hit that vehicle we were underneath, we'd be gone. And so would Jessica, because it would have been a chain reaction. It had all that fuel, we'd be dead."[31] Miller is unsuitable as protagonist in the captivity narrative because he is a hero and, of course, because he is a man.

The captivity narrative is complete with Jessica as abducted victim, the Iraqis as "demonic savages" and the American rescue team as heroes. But the Pentagon's public relations people do not see this. They are obsessed with creating a hero who can provide the war with a human face. A female American soldier. And this is where they make a mistake. Later attacks on the story of Jessica as hero strike at exactly this action-heroine figure. We know combative women from the historical Jeanne d'Arc and the mythic Marianne, the last leading the people in Eugène Delacroix's painting *La Liberté Guidant le Peuple* from 1830. But these are two exceptions in an otherwise gender-conservative war mythology. Jeanne was so controversial that it took her half a millennium to become a saint. And the other woman, Marianne, "contradicted the 'feminine' values of respectability and rootedness, and was quickly domesticated or dethroned,"[32] states historian George L. Mosse in *Nationalism and Sexuality* (1985). Almost all other female war symbols, such as the English Britannica and the German Germania, combined a maternal appearance with a beautiful and passive aesthetic taken from the sculptures of antiquity and the Pietà-figure of Catholicism. With sword in her hand Philipp Veit's *Germania* (1848) resembles a Pietà rather than a soldier. As a symbol of war, woman symbolized society's foundation, the survival of her people, and the body of the nation. "Woman was the embodiment of respectability; even as defender and protector of her people she was assimilated to her traditional role as woman and mother, the custodian of tradition, who kept nostalgia alive in the active world of men." In war, women symbolize "not war or military action," but "virtue fighting against vice."[33] They are not action heroes but represent virtue, tradition, and the nation state.

Two images are repressed from both mythic versions of the Lynch story: One is that of *the male soldier* symbolizing traditional dominant masculinity, power, and strength. Think of the picture of the American soldiers inside Hussein's palace circulating newspapers in Western media on April 8, 2003, in Denmark under the headline "U.S.A. into Saddam's palaces."[34] The soldier in the center of the group leans back in a rococo armchair inside a devastated palace, spreading his legs and relaxing with a smoke. It is an alarming image invoking themes of rape and imperialism with the palace as a "feminine" space being molested and conquered, quite a different image from that of a smiling Jessica.

The other repressed image is that of *the female soldier with "masculine" traits*. Such an image would also be unsettling, and until May 2004 this image had not appeared in the press. July 2003 the English magazine *Glamour* interviewed three women stationed in Iraq: a journalist, a corporal, and a doctor, visually presented as beautiful, caring, and unarmed.[35] If aggressive female soldiers were portrayed, they came from outside of Western civilization. Thus, images of a young black colonel in Liberia calling herself Black Diamond is an example of a non–Western exotic female aggression: In tight jeans, red beret, red top with bare back, gold earrings, long nails and a wig she appeared in Western news media under the headline "Colonel with Long Nails."[36] With her anger and her AK–47 she demonstrated exactly what Western war mythology cannot contain: A rape victim obsessed with revenge and anger, and with a daughter in a refugee camp. The demonic opposite to white Jessica, useless for raising sympathy and empathy. As a mixture of victim and hero, savage and soldier, Black Diamond confounded the gendered war mythology of the West: women as victims and men as angry avengers. Black Diamond was both.

In the past, Americans were preoccupied with what the Indians did to prisoners: rape, torture, and cannibalism. According to Slotkin all three took place, often, however, for a "reason": Cannibalism was religiously motivated; torture was an integrated part of the Indians' own masculinity rites, and even if they were first tortured many prisoners were later adopted by tribes; and rape happened, but not as often as Americans raped Indians: "[T]he eastern Indians almost never committed rape. In this, as the court records show, they differed from their white counterparts."[37] Today's Americans are also preoccupied with what the Iraqis — the "savages" — had done to Jessica. The Pentagon reported "multiple gunshot wounds" and knife wounds. The Iraqi informant told of black-clad soldiers slapping Jessica in her sickbed. The biography claimed Jessica's injuries were the result of Iraqi soldiers hammering their rifles into her body. And the American doctors found evidence of rape when Jessica returned to the United States — 21 days after her capture. These sufferings are not confirmed by Jessica. But they *feel* true because they fit the myth.[38]

War is a complex action founded on political and national — if not always democratic — decisions. War is not about individuals, but about nations. Even dictators can only wage war as a national and not an individual action. This action is dressed in a gendered mythology where men and women play archetypical roles. *Historically* the roles can change — the American military has thus since 1973 witnessed a rising number of female soldiers — but *mythologically* war is conservative. The story of Jessica Lynch thus demonstrates that the relation between war, gender, and myth is not open for mythic negotiations.

The Therapeutic Function of Myth

Before we return to the ground where the battle over the meaning of myth is fought as fiercely as war itself, we need to rise even higher up again. Up where the air is so thin that our wings can hardly carry us, but the view is truly panoramic: Myth is now one piece in a yet again larger image of our existence. The simple pattern from before disappears and gives way to a non-figurative piece of art open to interpretations.

Events happen. But sense does not. It is created. We can say that myth lives in the space between events and our interpretation of them. We can compare this mythic domain to the space between a psychologist and his or her patient. "A domain that only comes alive within the analytic situation," writes psychologist Donald P. Spence in *Narrative Truth and Historical Truth* (1982).[39] Within this space an explanation arises, uniting past and present and leading the patient into a future. Such an explanation — the therapeutic narrative — is usually understood as a *reconstruction* of the past. But, argues Spence, we are dealing rather with a *construction*. Past events (the patient's past, recollections, fantasies) are not available in their original and inaccessible form, untouched by words and linguistic structure. Only through *verbalization* do events acquire coherence, form and intentionality. To verbalize events is to interpret, to give them an intention they did not have originally. The next step is finding their "narrative home" or "narrative fit." We understand things by comparing them to other things, and a good story is not necessarily the one containing "historical truth" but the one letting us experience "narrative truth": "An interpretation satisfies because we are able to contain an unfinished piece of reality in a meaningful sentence; that is part of what we mean by finding its narrative home. The sentence acquires additional meaning when it meshes with other parts of the patient's life; it acquires narrative force by virtue of these connections, and adds narrative understanding to what is already known and understood. *The power of language is such that simply putting something into words gives it a certain kind of authenticity; finding a narrative home for these words amplifies and expands this truth*" (my emphasis).[40]

Myth is such a narrative home. Here, events are given dramatic structure, people become archetypes, the story receives an aesthetic touch that makes it more convincing. A "real" story feels true, is experienced as explanatory and is of therapeutic value to the patient. Not because it *is* true, but because it activates the patient's past experiences in a useful story — that is, it *transforms* the patient's past into a useful story — that can affect change. Myths function similarly in our culture. Not as historical truths, but as narrative and therapeutic truths: "The use of captivity narratives in revival sermons was the most typical form of ritual-therapeutic use of the captivity mythology," writes Slotkin.[41]

The first story about Jessica as a female soldier hero found a wrong home — that of the hero soldier and the female action hero. Here it crashed with traditional gender mythology and with American national mythology. It had to be renegotiated until it found a new narrative home where it could resonate. Resonance is crucial. Only when it is resonated by its surroundings (that is, when it is accepted by the patient) will a story be turned into an explanation. Likewise myths, retold continuously by society to make sense of itself. Myths are used to express "the community's sense of the meaning of its experience, to rationalize its actions, and to move its people to new actions."[42] Like therapy, myths can only "prove" their "truth" by captivating the audience.

Playing the Game of Myth

An ironic twist about Jessica's story is thus that underneath the constructed myth of a heroic female soldier was the material for a much better myth: the American captivity narrative. The Pentagon probably holds a different opinion of Jessica Lynch, but one thing is certain: her story demonstrates that a narrator alone cannot turn an event into a myth. *The transfor-*

mation from event over story to myth must take place in collaboration with an audience. The meaning of myth arises from this shared space, and not from the narrator.

Jessica's fate also demonstrates that myth-telling is a game with several political agents: We have the *myth-constructors* (which are both the people who naively believe in the myth as well as the people who cynically construct and manipulate myth), and we have the *myth-deconstructors* (those who deconstruct myth and prefer historical facts). "The savages" have wisely joined the last group, and now accuse the *myth-constructors* of being cynical tacticians. "The savages" refuse to play their part and, instead, demand recognition for civilized behavior. Jessica's nurse massaged her back and sang to calm her down, acts that are a nuisance because they contradict the American version of the story. Iraqi doctors rejected accusations of rape: "She was fighting for her life, her body was broken. What sort of an animal would even think of that?" said the hospital director.[43] The Americans were unable to answer and stuck to their version: "A doctor who treated Lynch (at a U.S. military base) and who was privy to all her medical records has reported that some of her injuries are consistent with an assault. What more verification do you need?" replied the military spokesman.[44] Yes, what verification is proof in the war about the meaning of myth?

The answer is simple, yet complex: resonance and faith. If an audience is to find a myth meaningful they need not know whether it is factually true. They do, however, need to recognize its form and content as true to myth itself. Narrative agents in political communication cannot freely construct new myths out of events. If such new myths do not resonate with audiences, they do not create faith, and then — factually true or not — they will be rejected.

Notes

1. I regard myth as a metaphorical and meaningful language drawn from a society's history and retold by that society to itself, placing myself in line with a cultural and semiotic approach to myth. In this cultural approach there is no difference between religious myths and secular myths. Myths exist because they are essential to society; they provide us a social and cultural identity by placing us in a larger narrative; they create culture through their narration in various forms; they influence the development of history; and we use myths to guide us in our actions.

Myth is a narrative and poetic form; it is neither true nor untrue. Literary critic Northrop Frye describes myth thus: "Myth has two parallel aspects: as a story, it is poetic and is re-created in literature; as a story with a specific social function, it is a program of action for a specific society. In both aspects it relates not to the actual but to the possible." Northrop Frye, *The Great Code: The Bible and Literature* (New York: Harvest, 1983), 49.

2. This article was presented at the Crossroads in Cultural Studies Conference held at the University of Illinois at Urbana-Champaign, Illinois, the United States, June 25–28, 2004, on the panel "War Isn't Hell, It's Entertainment," organized by the author. The Jessica Lynch incident has become widely known in the field of media studies and political studies. See for instance Stacy Takacs, "Jessica Lynch and the Regeneration of American Identity and Power Post-9/11," *Feminist Media Studies* 5, no. 3 (2005): 297–310 and Bruce Tucker and Priscilla L. Walton, "From General's Daughter to Coal Miner's Daughter: Spinning and Counter-Spinning Jessica Lynch," *The Canadian Review of American Studies*, vol. 36, no. 3 (2006): 311–30. It was made into a television movie by NBC, *Saving Jessica Lynch* (2003, Peter Markel). Documentaries include *Saving Jessica Lynch* (A&E, April 18, 2003); *War Spin* (BBC, May 18, 2003); *Primetime* interview special *Private Jessica Lynch: An American Story* (ABC, November 11, 2003); *Saving POW Lynch* (Discovery, November 12, 2003).

3. A list of participants in the Coalition Forces can be found on http://en.wikipedia.org/wiki/Multinational_force_in_Iraq, accesssed on June 14, 2008. On this date, 23 countries were active participants, among them Denmark, while 16 had withdrawn since 2004. Some of the withdrawing countries were never active combatants to begin with, as some of them did not have standing armies (like the Marshall Islands). Others, like Spain, withdrew out of political reasons.

4. The most famous massacre by Americans of tens of thousands of retreating Iraqi soldiers withdrawing on two roadways from Kuwait on February 26, 1991— known as "The Highway of Death"— was made public later, in March 1991.

5. According to a Danish news story, an Arabic TV channel aired images of living and dead American soldiers and according to Lynch's biographer Rick Bragg the TV station Al-Jazeera aired images of dead soldiers. From the description in the two sources it seems to be the same footage. Poul Høi, "Savnet" [Missing], *Berlingske Tidende*, Magasinet, March 30, 2003, 1–2; Rick Bragg, *I Am a Soldier, Too: The Jessica Lynch Story* (New York: Alfred A. Knopf, 2003); 101.

6. The number varies. *Politiken* claims 15 missing (Høi, "Savnet"), later *BBC News* mentions 11 dead and 7 missing ("Jessica Lynch 'raped' in Iraq," November 6, 2003), in all 18 from Jessica's regiment. Most sources say 11 dead and 6, among them Jessica, captured, in all 17.

7. Høi, "Savnet," 1. All translations from Danish into English by the author.

8. Bragg, *I Am a Soldier*, 37.

9. Høi, "Savnet," 2.

10. *Army Rangers* is a special forces unit established in 1670 when a team of Rangers was assembled by Captain Benjamin Church to fight Indians. The famous motto "Rangers lead the way" comes from the attack on Omaha Beach June 6, 1944. *Navy SEALS* (Sea, Air, Land) was developed in 1943 from a former special forces unit, *the Naval Construction Battalions* (*SeaBees*). The American *Marine Corps* was founded in 1775 during the War of Independence against Great Britain. *Marines* are special forces operating on land, water and in the air like *SEALS*. Their motto is "honor, courage, commitment." *Combat controllers* are a special unit in the American airforce whose task is to show and secure the way for later troops. Their motto is "first there, last out." The unit started as *Pathfinders* in 1943, where they were used in Italy during the World War II. In 1947 they were renamed *combat controllers*.

11. Bragg, *I Am a Soldier*, 157.

12. Ibid., 123.

13. A Purple Heart and a Prisoner of War Medal are routinely given to soldiers wounded and captured in battle.

14. Dana Priest, William Booth and Susan Schmidt, "A Broken Body, a Broken Story, Pieced Together," *Washington Post*, June 17, 2003, accessed from http://www.washington

post.com/ac2/wp-dyn?pagename=article&node=&contentId=A2760-2003Jun16& notFound=true on November 18, 2003.
  15. John Kampfner, "The Truth About Jessica," *The Guardian*, May 15, 2003, accessed from http://www.guardian.co.uk/Iraq/Story/0,2763,956255,00.html on November 12, 2003.
  16. This information is hinted to by many sources, all referring to the single same source where the information is alleged: "State-sponsored Lies," Ignacio Ramonet, *Le Monde diplomatique*, July 2003, accessed from http://mondediplo.com/2003/07/01ramonet on December 5, 2003.
  17. Kampfner, "Truth About Jessica."
  18. Ibid.
  19. Ironically, Pulitzer-winning journalist Rick Bragg had just resigned from *Times* in May 2003, after it was revealed that some of his stories were based on notes from freelance journalists without crediting them in the byline.
  20. Bragg, *I Am a Soldier*, 78.
  21. Ibid., 96.
  22. Nancy Gibbs, "The Private Jessica Lynch," *Time Magazine*, November 17, 2003, 26–35.
  23. Rosalind Russell, "Iraqi Doctors Deny Jessica Lynch Raped," *The Age.com.au*, November 11, 2003, accessed from http://www.theage.com.au/articles/2003/11/11/1068329536658.html on November 26, 2003.
  24. On the subject of female soldiers, myth, and their representation in popular film see my chapter 10, "Disturbing Creature: The Female Soldier in the War Film," in Rikke Schubart, *Super Bitches and Action Babes: The Female Hero in Popular Cinema, 1970–2006* (Jefferson, NC: McFarland, 2007), 249–70.
  25. Richard Slotkin, *Regeneration Through Violence: The Mythology of the American Frontier, 1600–1860* (New York: Wesleyan University Press, 1996, 1973), 94.
  26. American historian Richard Slotkin, Canadian literary critic Northrop Frye and French semiotic Roland Barthes differ in their valuation of myth: To Barthes myth is a political lie; to Frye it contains a deeper cultural and social truth; and to Slotkin myth can be put to truthful as well as untruthful use. Barthes' opinion on myth as "false" metaphorical language is expressed by an often-used quote from *Mythologies*: "The function of myth is to empty reality: it is, literally, a ceaseless flowing out, a haemorrhage, or perhaps an evaporation, in short a perceptible absence." Roland Barthes, *Mythologies* (London: Paladin, 1973, original 1957), 155. Frye defends the opposite view in *The Great Code*, in which he sees the Bible as the great code to contemporary society and culture: "History makes particular statements, and is therefore subject to external criteria of truth and falsehood ... the universal in the history is what is conveyed by the *mythos*, the shape of the historical narrative. A myth is designed not to describe a specific situation but to contain it in a way that does not restrict its significance to that one situation. *Its truth is inside its structure*, not outside" (my emphasis), Frye, *The Great Code*, 46.
  27. Slotkin, *Regeneration Through Violence*, 6.
  28. Ibid., 101.
  29. Ibid.
  30. Lee Hockstader, "Insult to Injury: Raw deal for Jessica Lynch's black comrade-in-arms," *Washington Post*, October 25, 2003, accessed from http://www.smh.com.au/articles/2003/10/24/1066974315046.html#top on November 27, 2003.
  31. Mike Wallace, "Pfc Patrick Miller — Jessica Lynch's Hero," *CBSNews.Com*, November 6, 2003, accessed from http://www.rense.com/general44/hereo.htm on November 27, 2003.
  32. George L. Mosse, *Nationalism and Sexuality: Respectability and Abnormal Sexuality in Modern Europe* (New York: Howard Fertig, 1985), 97.

33. Mosse, *Nationalism and Sexuality*, 97, 98.

34. Jens Holsøe, "USA ind i Saddams paladser" [U.S.A. Into Saddam's palaces], *Politiken*, frontpage, April 8, 2003.

35. Cordelia Kretzschmar and Rachel Pask, "Women in the Line of Fire," *Glamour* no. 28, July (2003): 66–74.

36. Rory Carroll, "Oberst med lange negle" [Colonel With Long Nails], *Politiken*, August 31, 2003.

37. Slotkin, *Regeneration Through Violence*, 125.

38. The same myth that sees rape as done by savages violating the innocence of a pure woman is unable to see rape as a systematic weapon of terror used by soldiers. Rape is part of war across the world and used in for example Africa to turn children into sex slaves and female soldiers. In Denmark fugitive female child soldier China Keitetsi has published her biography *Mit liv som barnesoldat i Uganda* [My Life as a Child Soldier in Uganda] (Copenhagen: Ekstra Bladets Forlag, 2002).

39. Donald P. Spence, *Narrative Truth and Historical Truth: Meaning and Interpretation in Psychoanalysis* (New York: W.W. Norton & Company, 1982), 292.

40. Spence, *Narrative Truth*, 137–8.

41. Slotkin, *Regeneration Through Violence*, 112.

42. Ibid., 96.

43. Russell, "Iraqi Doctors."

44. Ibid.

5

Celebrities and 9/11
"A Simple Show of Unity"
SUE COLLINS

> Those of us here tonight are not heroes. We are not healers, nor protectors of this great nation. We are merely artists and entertainers here to raise spirits and we hope a great deal of money. We appear tonight as a simple show of unity to honor the real heroes and to do whatever we can to ensure that all their families are supported by our larger American family. This is a moment to pause and reflect, to heal, and to rededicate ourselves to the American Spirit of one nation indivisible.
> —Tom Hanks, America: A Tribute to the Heroes

Introduction

Within hours of the fallout from the September 11 terrorist attacks, shell-shocked New York City residents organized food and supply drives for displaced New Yorkers and relief workers at ground zero. Nationwide, Americans by the hundreds of thousands inundated Red Cross blood banks and other relief organizations with phone calls asking what they could do to help. At the same time, Muslims and Arab-Americans across the United States braced themselves for vigilantist retaliation by angry Americans. That night, President Bush announced that the United States "would make no distinction between the terrorists who committed these acts and those who harbor them."[1] The next day, after President Bush declared the attacks "acts of war" on the United States, premonitions of the bombing of Afghanistan began to surface on the news networks.[2] On September 13, Bush vowed that "now that war had been declared on us," the country would "lead the world to victory."[3] On September 14, the President authorized the mobilization of 50,000 military reservists, while Congress swiftly passed a resolution approving the use of force in response to the attacks. Todd Purdum of the *New York Times* reported the following day that early polls indicated that Americans were gearing up for the nation to go to war, overwhelmingly supporting retaliation even at the expense of innocent lives.[4] At a Pentagon briefing on September 17, Bush summoned the Western frontier edict "Wanted: Dead or Alive" in an off-the-cuff response to questions on the capture of Osama bin Laden, then later that day visited an Islamic center in Washington, D.C., where he issued a statement of condemnation regarding the attacks on Arab-Americans and Muslims living in the United States. By September 21, ten days after the World Trade Center and Pentagon attacks and the downing of United Airlines Flight 93, the United States was poised to bomb Afghanistan, its B–52 and B–1 bombers mobilized for the imminent departure of what would be referred to two weeks later as "Operation Enduring Freedom."

That same night, the U.S.-dominated entertainment industry hosted a two-hour A-list all-star global telethon to raise money for the families of 9/11's victims. By any definition, *America: A Tribute to the Heroes* was a media event. Entirely underwritten by the big four networks, the telethon was simulcast during the 9:00 to 11:00 P.M. Friday prime time slot without commercial interruption, as well as on most cable or broadcast outlets invited to participate.[5] It reached an estimated 89 million viewers for at least some portion of the show, and surpassed the ratings for President Bush's first speech addressing the attacks.[6] Airing on over 30 network channels and some 8,000 radio stations, streamlined through the Internet, and seen in two hundred and ten countries, the telethon flooded the spectrum leaving little else as entertainment. The unprecedented nature of media collaboration in the production of the telethon and the magnitude of the tragedy inspiring it suggests that the simulcast would have been a success despite its recruitment of celebrity capital. Indeed, the telethon, combined with CD and DVD sales, raised $129.5 million, making it one of the most lucrative fundraisers to date.[7]

The question I wish to raise is less about the efficacy of celebrity activism, or more accurately in this case, celebrity philanthropy, and more about the naturalized logic of the invocation of entertainment celebrity to house affect and to persuade people to donate money. This is not a new logic, but it is one that is often charged with cultural hegemony in the service of consumer capitalism. Today's proliferation of celebrities aligned with socio-political causes is indicative of a symbiotic relationship that no doubt does some good, but that is also met with skepticism by audiences who understand how the Hollywood machine works. Television critic Matt Roush, for example, framed the telethon this way: "Two weeks ago, we might have called this a publicity stunt, the idea that celebrities are doing this.... But everybody's dropped their cynicism in the wake of this."[8]

In this chapter I discuss stardom or entertainment celebrity in terms of its productivity as a mechanism of neo-liberal governance. This is not to say that celebrity eludes being categorized as a modern form of hegemony's "functuaries," that is, the individuals of a society whose moral and intellectual leadership act on and across various sites such as education, religion, and high and popular culture to sustain a system of meaning that expresses a particular class interest and that works to "cement" a collective will into forms of consent. Indeed, as Jackson Lears observes, the "who" of the ruling class includes not just statesmen, soldiers, and business leaders, but also "parents, preachers, teachers, journalists, literati, 'experts' of all sorts, as well as advertising executives, entertainment promoters, popular musicians, sports figures, and 'celebrities'— all of whom are involved (albeit often unwittingly) in shaping the values and attitudes of a society."[9] Hegemony widened the reach of ideology to include the entirety of lived experience so that all spheres of social life, the economic and political, as well as the cultural, would be "common sense" reality to the "masses." Despite the recognition of various modes of expressing power, hegemony's theoretical underpinnings suggest constant struggle and negotiation, which secures the essential relationship of dominant over dominated continually. For Tony Bennett it is precisely the problem of hegemony's totalizing processes that warrant its reconsideration as a theory of power. Moreover, says Bennett, hegemony is incapable of addressing the specifics of institutional and discursive conditions under which certain agents can influence practices of culture; nor can it assess the specifics of the deployment of particular cultural technologies. Bennett argues that hegemony "commits us to too automatic a politics, one which — since it contends that all cultural activities are bound into a struggle for hegemony — is essentially the same no matter what the region of its application. It has paid insufficient attention to those considerations which, in differentiating cultural technologies from one another, give rise to specific sets of political relations and forms of calculation."[10]

In light of this critique, I examine *America: Tribute to the Heroes* with respect to its implications as an ancillary to cultural policy. In Bennett's formulation culture is defined predominately by its historical relationship to government as both "object and instrument," as opposed to an aesthetic notion having to do with the arts or by a broader anthropological conception involving whole ways of life. Cultural policy can be understood as the deployment of the "stuff" of culture (its art forms, communication systems, customs and rituals) by governments and organizations in the production of cultural citizenship. I treat celebrity, then, as a site upon which to constitute the virtuous citizen, an ethical "well-tempered self" whose uses of culture produce a better, and better yet, self-governing citizen.[11] Celebrity is a cultural technology or a mechanism of neo-liberal governance acting in concert with cultural policy, whether explicitly or implicitly, to influence collective cultural behavior.

Cultural Citizenship, Governmentality and Celebrity

Following Bennett's lead, Toby Miller offers closely related genealogies of the terms "culture" and "policy" to argue that citizenship has a long history as a site upon which the state inscribes instructions for virtuous living associated with the modern city. Cultural policy operates to "find, serve, and nurture a sense of belonging through educational and other cultural regimens that are the means of governance, of the orderly formation of public collective subjectivity."[12] It is in this sense that citizenship, for Miller, is conceived of as an "open technology," that is, a discursive formation through which the state informs its subjects on how citizenship is to be defined, and how it is to be dispersed through various sites of culture or modes of expression.

To produce a cultural citizen is to produce a social subject whose sense of belonging is connected to his cultural ancestry and to the common cultural practices that maintain and develop that ancestry. But the production of cultural citizenship is also a moral question, for citizenship denotes not only rights (legal and otherwise), but also obligations. An objective of cultural policy is the constitution of the virtuous, self-governing citizen. For Miller, the citizen does not exist outside of the knowledges deployed to govern the subject; he comes to recognize himself as a part of the public, and then learns to scrutinize and improve upon his conduct: "[Citizenship] is a technology that produces a 'disposition' on [the subjects'] part not to accept the imposition of a particular form of government passively, but to embrace it actively as a collective expression of themselves (even though this expression itself derives from preconditions for knowledge set by the state)."[13] Citizenship is accomplished through the inscription of "ethical indeterminacy" onto the cultural subject through technologies of governance such that the subject is encouraged to embrace moral conduct in a continuous effort to render him or herself complete, and thus manage one's own conduct. Miller's argument is influenced by Foucault's ideas on the nature of subjectivity as self-governance, which for Miller provides the essential link between government and culture.

Famously referred to as "the conduct of conduct," Foucault sees government as not only the actions of the state, but more critically, as the actions of the population in governing itself. Governing is a set of practices or techniques of power with multiple ends, exercised by different authorities through various agencies, and aimed at the population within a given state or society such that it comes to be "the subject of needs, of aspirations, but it is also the object in the hands of government, aware, vis-à-vis the government of what it wants, but ignorant of what is being done to it."[14] This is distinct from sovereignty because the devices under the domain of government move beyond the imposition of laws to the deployment of "multiform tactics" in the disposition of things — and in the development of "a whole complex of knowledges."[15] Government resides in the "contact point" where techniques of domination and techniques of the self intermingle and co-exist: "techniques of domination of individuals over one another have recourse to processes by which the individual acts upon himself and, conversely ... where techniques of the self are integrated into structures of coercion."[16] In this way, governmentality represents a theoretical move away from determinist calculations of the relations of the state to the mode of production and toward an emphasis on multiple sites for "technologies of rule" in the management of populations. It is in these multiple sites, principally, that Foucault conceptualizes the exercise of power by government as generative: power "doesn't only weigh on us as a force that says no; it also traverses and produces things, it induces pleasure, forms of knowledge, produces discourses."[17]

In his advancement of Foucauldian governmentality, Nicolas Rose argues that governing in an advance liberal state involves a "technology of rule" that resituates the authority of expertise from various systems of formal political rule into a consumer based market subject to the pressures and instrumental rationalities of competition and accountability. In this scheme, individuals, "now construed as subjects of choice and aspiration to self-actualization and self-fulfillment," are governed through their own regulated choices. Governed through their freedom, they become "members of heterogeneous communities of allegiance, as 'community' emerges as a new ways of conceptualizing and administering moral relations among persons."[18]

Characteristic of this type of governing within the spaces of civil society and community are nation-forming devices such as common language and customs, and crucially, the regulating function of mass media. While the logics of such technologies as soap operas, opinion polls, advertising, and the "experts of subjectivity" do not originate in the state, they nevertheless provide a "plethora of indirect mechanisms that can translate the goals of political, social, and economic authorities into the choices and commitments of individuals locating them into actual or virtual networks of identification through which they may be governed."[19] In the United States such indirect mechanisms are located in a public sphere constituted by the private commercial media system, whose interests in deregulation and protection of property depend vitally on the state's adherence to market logic.[20] The government defends certain corporate interests by allocating spectrum and by providing legal protection of private property, while denying its import of cultural policy in these relationships. Yet, Miller and Lewis argue, the U.S. "has the largest and most powerful set of private culture industries, and while their heritage in commerce is well-known, they have equally important links to the state," despite claims to the contrary.[21]

In returning to thinking about celebrity as a mechanism of governance, David Marshall's work is suggestive because he defines celebrity fundamentally in terms of its capacity to function both as a means of representing and celebrating conceptions of individualism as part of democratic capitalism, and as a site to house the affective power of the crowd. For Marshall, the historical materialization and ascendancy of celebrity at the turn of the twentieth century is related to strains of irrationality emerging from the modern mass, an entity that was seen as threatening and as requiring strategies to contain its irrational sentiment and proclivity toward civil disruption. In the contemporary mediascape, celebrity is at once a celebrated public individual, a commodity of the cultural industries, and embodiment of audience subjectivities. Marshall's cultural studies approach to celebrity emphasizes the ways in which audiences negotiate meaning within the binary tension of conceptions of celebrity as authentically meaningful, and representations of celebrity as pure exchange or false value. While the cultural industries position celebrity to articulate "the transformation of types of cultural value into the rationalizing system of the commodity,"[22] the celebrity sign houses meaning and affect that positions audiences into categorical existence, that is, it acts on audiences to constitute them. At the same time, celebrity's power comes from the audience's configurations of meaning given to celebrity, as celebrity represents "subject positions that audiences can adopt or adapt in the formation of their social identities."[23] In explaining celebrity's political function in terms of governmentality, Chris Rojek paraphrases Marshall to say that celebrity's containment of the mass is best understood as a discursive power in which celebrities "present preferred models of subjectivity with which audiences are encouraged to identify. They are, so to speak, 'the star police' of modern democracies."[24] Both Rojek and Marshall focus their attention primarily on celebrity's ideological functions; for Rojek, this is most salient in the metaphors associated with religion; for Marshall, it is inherent in celebrity's continual rationalization of consumer capitalism.

In considering *America: Tribute to the Heroes* as a space of civil action, I problematize celebrity for the contradictions of its "show of unity" as it works to contain affect through vicarious performance, while at the same time, to substantiate the obligations of the virtuous citizen in concert with neo-liberal objectives of the state in governing through self-care. Although telethons are not new, *Tribute* represents an unprecedented moment of industry-wide cultural collaboration, poised on the precipice of what would presently become a divisive climate of war-torn controversy and the systematic dissuading of dissent. *Tribute* was not intended to be a space for Hollywood artists, star musicians, the invisible crew of below-the-line labor, nor the producers or powerful assemblage of broadcast and cable executives to argue for or against the Bush administration's military response to the terrorist attacks. By doing neither, by imploring instead for Americans to give money to Americans, *Tribute* effectively channeled the irrational, emotional, and affective into the charity economy, where sentiment is productively contained, yet ambiguously positioned, and susceptible to other modes of nationalist inscription through cultural practice.

An Affective Public Sphere of Media Friends

For several days following September 11, U.S. networks grappled with when to reinstate commercial interruptions into their news coverage and when to restore scheduled programming, while the late night talk shows struggled with when and how to bring comedy and irony back into their daily fare. Though the critics had predicted the demise of irony, the death of celebrity, and the end of popular culture as we had known it, the President told a confused and restless nation to "go shopping," and the commercial imperative of the U.S. media system augmented the President's message by beginning its retreat to its essential programming logic. Calling it "event TV," Lynn Spigel argues that *Tribute* was one among several of television's programs functioning to bring the nation back to normalcy or at least, as she puts it, back "to the normal flows of television and consumer culture."[25] *Tribute* effectively worked to reestablish the present both spiritually and materially through its use of live feeds and unadorned sets, producing a sense of unrehearsed spontaneity and para-social intimacy. At the same time, *Tribute* served as a platform for the stars to "enact the role of patriotic publics," standing in for ordinary people as the stars performed what Spigel calls "celebrity citizenship." The "live" presence of dozens of the cultural industries' most visible elite — its star actors and musicians — assembled to signify an unswerving sense of nationalist unity. This display sought to effectively stave off terrorist-induced fear by means of deeply heartfelt heroic tales of the survivors and the fallen, resolved calls for the public to stand up to the terrorists by pledging, and poignant musical performances rich in intertextual nostalgia.

Notwithstanding the logistical difficulties of collaboration in a matter of a few days among network sponsors, production personnel, and star performers, the audience saw no such complexity or spectacle that we might imagine would showcase such star display. Telecast from undisclosed studios in New York, Los Angeles, and London, the preparation for *Tribute* was a clandestine operation, in part to protect the stars from fans and paparazzi (and perhaps terrorists), but more so to mark it symbolically, as an intimate and solemn memorial. Said one anonymous insider, "There will be no audience, no commercials, and no press.... It's a very special thing, dedicated for a very special reason, and not to be commercialized."[26] The telethon was publicized solely by press release, sparing publicity expenses. All technical support was donated, including all space and equipment, telephone lines, food supplies, and labor. Production assistants, stage crews and, of course, the screen and musical artists all worked for free. According to producer Joel Gallen, no one received compensation of any kind: "People said, 'I can't get there, can you get me a flight?' I said no. We sent no cars. There was no hair and makeup. Well, there were if people wanted a touch up — but they donated their time too."[27]

Despite its spectacular star-studded line-up, *Tribute* denied itself the trappings of visual spectacle that would have accompanied such a feat in any other context — a denial which contributed significantly to the construction of its authenticity. "While certainly designed to be a global media event," Spigel notes, "this was a deliberately understated spectacle, achieved through a deliberate display of 'star capital' minus the visual glitz and ego."[28] Indeed, the sets were modest, decorated simply with pale yellow candles displayed on cast iron candelabras and tiered shelves scattered across the set, bathing it with a warm and solemn hue mixed with variable red, blue and gold effects from stage lights cast onto plain backdrops. The stars for the most part were remarkable in their ordinariness, most donned in plain black gowns or suits, or unpretentious street clothes, without adornment, and manifestly humbled in their demeanor. Musical segments were punctuated with a dark candlelit stage and slow rise and drop soft spotlights. There were no announcers, no credits, not a single star was named. All performance segments were live, despite Celine Dion's request to pre-record "God Bless America." Only the music tracks laid onto three of the four short film segments were pre-recorded. The verbal stumblings of George Clooney, Jim Carrey, Robin Williams, Tom Cruise, and Clint Eastwood were not edited. Although there were numerous phone banks set-up across the country, between segments camera shots featured stars working the phones from a central location, inviting pledgers to chat with the real person — Jack Nicholson, Al Pacino, Sylvester Stallone, Brad Pitt, Meg Ryan, Ben Stiller, or Whoopi Goldberg to name a few. For a brief two hours, audiences were privy to the "real" behind Hollywood's machinations and hype. These were individuals, Americans, using their visibility to "give back," expressing their mourning through their art, persuading the public to do as they do and give money, enacting an affective public sphere of nationalist unity through artistic expression of grief for the dead and hope for the living.

Tribute's purposeful diminution of spectacle in its production processes functioned nevertheless to valorize celebrity as a site of power. Among his observations on the nature and function of spectacle, Guy Debord argues that spectacle works to reproduce relations of domination by separating out non-dominant spectator-subjects from vehicles of display such that they can be acted upon by dominant interests.[29] In the contemporary mass-mediated landscape, celebrity is both constitutive of and constituted by the mechanisms of spectacle, so that the ordinary watch the extraordinary do what the ordinary cannot, for celebrity, ostensibly at least, has earned access to spectacle as a site to reproduce its visibility and status as cultural value. Yet, for Debord, the social relationship that is invoked by spectacle between the spectators and spectacle itself is a false one, for "[a]t the root of the spectacle lies the oldest of all social divisions of labor, the specialization of *power*."[30] Celebrities in this capacity are "spectacular representations of living human beings" who renounce their autonomy in order to "identify with the general law of obedience to the course of things."[31] Despite contemporary examples of celebrity's crossover to the elected polity, for the most part, celebrities within the field of cultural production, more aptly put in Bourdieu's terms, "occupy a dominated position in the dominant class"[32] But this is not to say that stars do not have some sort of power; rather, the question is best problematized with cultural and historical specificity.

Although the stars of *Tribute* present themselves to us as ordinary Americans, it matters greatly who these Americans are. It is unlikely that such a non-news event collaboration across broadcast and cable networks would have been proposed, let alone materialized, without the star cache to front the project. But more significantly, I wish to discuss the deployment of celebrity as an audience-gathering mechanism which invokes particular meanings to function in particular ways. Key to discerning the telethon's significance is an understanding of the discursive management of the "star image" across all of its sites of production. Originally the crown jewel of star studies, a sub-genre of cinema studies, the star image can be theoretically deployed as an explanatory factor of the broader conceptual category of entertainment celebrity. It refers to the confluence of media texts that house the star whether in textual performance (film, television, music video, etc.) or in extra-textual moments such as celebrity journalism. The critical mechanism of the star image involves the collapsing of distinctions between the star-as-performer and the star-as-person, which operates to confound authenticating processes while continually inviting audiences to re-establish the authentic. In other words, the star image, while incoherent and ordinary in extra-textual discourses, offers the promise of its "completeness" in textual performance, which re-constitutes the image as extraordinary.[33] This paradox — the star as extraordinary as performer and ordinary as person — continually renews both the star image and the audience's pleasure in their consumption of stars, as they continually attempt to locate the "real" behind the star's performance.

In concert with this paradox's ideological objectives, cultural intermediaries circulate star meaning among these sites of cultural production in an attempt to manage the star's symbolic and economic value. Barry King explains the star performance in terms of creating and sustaining a "persona," the site where these discourses come together to suggest a coherent subjectivity, or unique star personality. In the case of film stars, King argues that they are bound to particular typecasts and become "committed in their on and off screen life to personification in the hope that by stabilizing the relationship between person and image on the screen they may seem to be the proprietors of a marketable person."[34] In this way, King defines stardom as a "strategy of performance that is an adaptive response to the limits and pressures exerted upon acting as a discursive practice in mainstream cinema."[35] While King is referring to a sort of performance that takes place in extra-textual discourses of celebrity journalism, the implications of his argument are important for understanding why celebrity's import into the political sphere tends to shift a social movement's claims toward consensual contentions, as Myer and Gamson[36] argue, or to redirect media focus upon the celebrity him or herself and off of the movement's actors and issues, as Meg McLagan[37] has shown. There are limits to what audiences will accept in terms of celebrity's political activity, just as there are limits to celebrity scandal. Celebrities know this, of course, and so they tend to choose more benign associations with respect to socio-political activism.[38]

As Marshall tells us, the star image is constructed differently across distinct sectors of the cultural industries, which functions to establish a kind of vicarious identification and to produce particular affect in the subjectivities of audiences. The cinematic apparatus of film, for example, produces aura and distance from the audience in order to invite the dissolution of aura through extra-filmic discourses, as fans turn to texts of celebrity journalism to get at the ostensible "real" behind the enigmatic star. Marshall argues that the "play" between how the star appears to us across all of her screen texts and the personality revealed in celebrity journalism is the essential mechanism of celebrity's reproduction. Television, on the other hand, initiates forms of para-social interaction with audiences by collapsing distance through televisual properties of production, performance codes of intimacy and familiarity, and the audience's conditions of attendance. Television's stars are our "media friends," accessible to us as their performances are regularly scheduled, direct in their address to us as hosts of show, or longitudinally developed as characters, and delivered to us in our domestic space.[39] Arguably, the distinctions between film's star image and television's personality, between the building and management of celebrity's on-screen as performer and off-screen as person dichotomy, are blurred as celebrity journalism discriminates little to fill its expansive appetite for coverage.[40] To be sure, however, the performer-citizens on *Tribute* were Hollywood's most successfully circulated stars, but here they were answering the phones to speak directly with us and to "personally" take our pledges and to remind us of our responsibility to our "larger American family," as Hanks had put it. They were at once the same as us, yet different, our adored stars, our media friends, just individuals, Americans, modeling for us appropriate behavior in our time of disconcertion and loss, enacting citizenship on the assumption that so many did not know what to do or think. The stars were, in effect, positioning audiences into existence as ethical and moral subjects whose work in this moment of indeterminacy was to recognize the self as a selfless and active, benevolent citizen.

Accordingly, Dennis Franz, *NYPD Blue* cop, and former partner cop and more recent *West Wing* U.S. President Jimmy Smits told the story of Officer Leahey and the hundreds of New York City cops just like him, who "are willing to risk their lives in an instant for people they do not know." *Late Night*'s Conan O'Brian and *Sex and the City*'s Sarah Jessica Parker stood together in representation of a "city that never sleeps" to debunk the mythological New York as "a town of strangers," and to announce that "on every street corner in every neighborhood people are helping one another." In the aftermath of anti–Muslim backlash across the United States, and despite the professions of New Yorker munificence entertained by O'Brien and Parker, non-white celebrities stood in to represent race and to appease racial relations. Will Smith appeared with Muhammad Ali, the only participant in *Tribute*'s assembly to be identified when Smith cued him to speak with the title, "Champ?" One of America's greatest heroes was a Muslim, Smith told us, and so it was "hate not religion that motivated the horrible acts of September 11" and that "nothing could be more un–American than to respond to mindless hatred with blind vengeance." Ali insisted that all Muslims are against killing, and "that people should know the real truth about Islam." Professing an ideal and mythic nation embracing global unity, Lucy Liu declared that the hundreds of citizens from around the world sharing in America's lost would "always be our brother and sisters, just like all the people who walk America's streets." In a few words of reassurance, Liu negated a history spanning centuries of racial injustice and conflict by calling on Americans to heed the "true" spirit of America. "And in our pain and anguish," she pronounced, "we must remember that American's greatest enemy is hatred itself. Judging people by the way they look, that's not America."

In contradiction to Liu's claim that "tolerance goes hand in hand with freedom" was the equivocal speech delivered by Kelsey Grammer, well known as a quirky but erudite and lovable Anglophile on the popular sitcom *Frasier*. Suggesting that Americans could find comfort in the words of past heroes, Grammer quoted from John F. Kennedy's book *Profiles in Courage*: "A man does what he must in spite of personal consequences, in spite of obstacles and dangers and pressures, and that is the basis of all human morality." This message valorizing opposition to popular judgment was negated by his second quote, from Kennedy's inaugural address, and Grammer's conclusion: "'Let every nation know whether it wishes us well or ill that we shall pay any price, bear any burden met any hardship, support any friend, oppose any foe, in order to assure the survival and the success of liberty.' That is the challenge President Kennedy put before us forty years ago and now, confronted by evil, we must rise to the occasion. Please do your part"—positioning audiences within a double-bind of resisting the incantation of blind nationalism or supporting the imminent military retaliation. More disconcerting was the intertexual invocation of Inspector "Dirty Harry" Callahan, SFPD cop who characteristically takes things into his own hands. Squinting as he read the teleprompter, Eastwood boldly issued *Tribute's* final decree: "The terrorists who wanted three hundred million victims instead are going to get three hundred million heroes, three hundred million Americans with broken hearts, but unbreakable hopes for our country and our future. In the conflict that's come upon us we're determined as our parents and our grandparents were before us to win through the ultimate triumph so help us God." Just what Eastwood meant by "the ultimate triumph" was left unanchored to any specific unified political stand. Grammer's insistence that "we must rise to the occasion," however, was also articulated by Tom Petty's visibly stern facial expression during the refrain of "I Won't Back Down," the only contextually defiant selection out of an impressive array of classic rock and popular musical performances.

While consonance among on-screen performances and *Tribute*'s offscreen appearance worked to authenticate a right to speak to and for the American public, the musical artists appearing on *Tribute* served a different kind of proxy as they eulogized the dead for us through songs of love, remembrance, and peace. Here, the performance codes of the popular music industry work to position celebrity much closer to the audiences through the live and earnest display of emotional sincerity channeled through song. As Marshall argues, recording artists are constructed differently from other forms of celebrity, relying fundamentally on "the conveyance of both commitment and difference" to authenticate themselves through their music.[41] The popular musician expresses sentiment through the song's lyrics and in the construction of a direct and personal relationship between the performer and audience. In the construction of authenticity, musicians enact performance codes that signify solidarity with an audience. Calling "rock authenticity" a "matter of culturally determined convention, not an expression of essence," Philip Auslander reminds us that the "semiotic markers of authenticity" are constructed differently within musical genres at different times.[42] *Tribute*'s musicians, if not born out of the political strife and consequent civil gains of the 1960s, share the cultural values emanating out of the era, many of whom reputably express their politics at least implicitly through their art. Although a range of musical genres was performed on *Tribute*, symbolically dominant were the longstanding social activist and politically minded musicians such as Neil Young, U2, Sting, Bruce Springsteen, Paul Simon, Stevie Wonder, and Willie Nelson.

In liveness, authenticity is all the more ratified, not only for the "evidence" that the sound production confirms the musicians as the legitimate makers of the song, but in this case also for the bareness of some of the performances. This is part of the logic of live television operating under intensive time constraints, but it also signifies a collapsing of the star image as performer with the person, to reveal the expression of a real person, standing in for us, whether in anguish and profound sorrow or in love and hope. Both sound and sight operate to authenticate a particular historical and culturally specific relationship between the performer and audience. I am arguing that with respect to *Tribute*, a significant part of the musical artist's cultural power is derived from his or her access to the site of collective mourning, for mourning's sake, and from the conscious choice to adapt the performance codes of the "unplugged" concert to diminish the distance between performer and audience. As the stage sets appropriated the solemnity of sacred places of worship, the musicians shared in collective and ecumenical expressions of "prayer," solidarity, love, and peace for the world, while we watched. Now, positioned less as spectators and more as members of a culture, audiences partook in the memorial and in the vicarious release of complicated emotions.

And so it was the baby boomers' biggest living "rock-and-roll hero"[43] in the New York metropolitan area, Bruce Springsteen, who opened the telethon by performing a deeply moving acoustic and harmonica solo rendition of "My City of Ruin." Seldom articulating his politics publicly, Springsteen introduced his song and the telethon with, "Here's a prayer for our fallen brothers and sisters." Backed by a chorus of seven, including Steven Van Zandt, holding raised hands and singing in crescendo the refrain, "With these hands," Springsteen's anguished voice rang out "We pray for your love Lord, we pray for the lost Lord, we pray for this world Lord." Illuminated by the soft glow of lights accenting the stage backdrop to resemble stained glass, Stevie Wonder bequeathed a prayer for humanity with "Love's In Need of Love Today," prefacing in soft voice, "When you say that you kill in the name of God or in the name of Allah, you are truly cursing God, for that is not of God.... Let us pray that we see the light." Accompanied by the spiritual reverberation of organ chords, Eddie Vedder's tender "Long Road" comforted audiences with the calm of life after death, while in rhythmic uplift an impressive African American gospel chorus energized Faith Hill's hymn "There Will Come a Day," Enrique Inglesias's "Hero," and Celine Dion's "God Bless America."

Symbolically charged were the messages of peace characterizing most of the musical performances such as U2's "Walk On," broadcast from London in black and white filtered camera. U2's lyrics of unity through nonviolence resonant in their song "One" underscored a powerful montage of ground zero wreckage, fire fighters in search and rescue, a city confronting chaos, chains of people passing supplies, people embracing each other, flags at half mask, missing posters, candlelit memorials, and the Statue of Liberty. Extending its reach to wider audiences, *Tribute* combined rock classics with popular performers such as Limp Bizkit and John Rzeznik of the Goo Goo Dolls who sang in purposeful unison Pink Floyd's "Wish You Were Here," substituting with poetic license: "So do you think we change, everybody that hates before its too late, so proud to be free, but who can we blame, don't be ashamed, do you think we can change." And, appropriately standing in for deceased cultural icons were Wyclef Jean's patriotic rendition of Bob Marley's "Redemption Song," and Neil Young's earnest performance of John Lennon's "Imagine."

Conclusion

To be sure, many of us at home, paralyzed by a lack of proximity, unable to give of ourselves at the physical sites where help seemed needed, unable to understand what had happened or how to express grief, took relief from watching celebrity citizens eulogize the dead. But where were people to go from here? What would be the right and moral course of action? Should the American public support or not support the President's war cry? These unresolved policy questions residing in *Tribute*'s subtext revealed the inevitable contradictions in the presentation of Hollywood as a unified front, and presaged the nation's complacent response to the Bush Administration's commandeering of the congressional power to declare war. Without either an overt endorsement of a military response to the terrorist attacks or a direct and unequivocal call against war, *Tribute*'s ambiguous and contradictory messages sustained a climate of indecision and irresolution. We could, however, realize our citizenship under "the sign of community," wherein our "bonds of obligations and responsibilities for conduct"[44] assemble around the moral and cultural lead of stars enacting a charity community on behalf of, as Springstein put it, "our fallen brothers and sisters." In this way, celebrity as a cultural technology serves a social function in that it effectively valorizes the emotional as a part of citizenship in the public sphere, commonly discussed as detrimental to good citizenship,[45] and a political function in that it contains emotion by redirecting it toward an ethos of self-responsibility, that is, to participatory community of civil action, governed at a distance.

Notes

1. "George W. Bush Addresses the Nation," FDCHeMedia, Political Transcripts, September 11, 2001, accessed from http://www.lexis-nexis.com/.
2. "The O'Reilly Factor," *Fox News Network*, 9/12/01, transcript # 091202cb.256, accessed from http://www.lexis-nexis.com/.
3. "Excerpts from President's Remarks on Investigation into Attack," *New York Times*, September 14, 2001, accessed from http://www.lexis-nexis.com/.
4. Todd Purdum, "After the Attacks: The Strategy," *New York Times*, September 15, 2001, accessed from http://www.lexis-nexis.com/.
5. Because the sponsors wanted *Tribute* to air as a primetime simulcast on both coasts, cable networks without dual feeds were not permitted to participate. "Cable Operator Complain that Networks Shut Them Out of Telethon," *Communication's Daily*, September 21, 2001, accessed from http://www.lexis-nexis/.
6. David Bauder, "Nearly 60 Million Watch the Stars in Television Pitch for Terrorist Attack Victims," *The Associated Press*, September 22, 2001; Scott Vernon, "Scott's World," *Hollywood Reporter*, September 24, 2001, accessed from http://www.lexis-nexis.com/.

7. The September 11 Telethon Fund, http://www.september11fund.org/faq.php#2. It is also noteworthy that five major music companies (Bertelsmann Music Group, EMI, Sony Music Entertainment, Universal Music Group and Warner Music Group) cooperated in CD and DVD not-for-profit release of *America: Tribute to the Heroes* by suspending all of their rights and fees in its distribution, along with the all the artists who participated in the telethon's production; accessed from www.prnewswire.com/cgi-bin/stories.pl?ACCT= 104&STORY=/www/story/11-07-2001/0001610343&EDATE= on February 9, 2007.

8. Don Aucoin, "Stars of Every Strip Join Show of Patriotism," *The Boston Globe*, September 21, 2001, accessed from http://www.lexis-nexis.com/.

9. T. J Jackson Lears, "The Concept of Cultural Hegemony: Problems and Possibilities," *The American Historical Review* 90, no. 3 (June 1985): 572.

10. Tony Bennett, "Putting Policy into Cultural Studies," in *Cultural Studies*, ed. Lawrence Grossberg, Gary Nelson, and Paul Treichler (New York: Routledge, 1992), 29.

11. Toby Miller, *The Well-Tempered Self: Citizenship, Culture, and the Postmodern Subject* (Baltimore: John Hopkins University Press, 1993).

12. Ibid., 26.

13. Miller, *Well-Tempered Self,* 12.

14. Michel Foucault, "Governmentality," in *Michel Foucault: Power*, ed. James D. Faubion (New York: The New Press, 1994), 217.

15. Foucault, "Governmentality," 211, 220.

16. Michel Foucault, "Truth and Subjectivity," The Howison Lecture, Berkeley, mimeo, quoted in Graham Burchell, "Liberal Government and Techniques of the Self," in *Foucault and Political Reason: Liberalism, Neo-liberalism and Rationalities of Government*, ed. Andrew Barry, Thomas Osborne, and Nickolas Rose (Chicago: University of Chicago Press, 1996), 20.

17. Michel Foucault, "Truth and Power," in *Michel Foucault: Power*, ed. James D. Faubion (New York: The New Press, 1994), 120.

18. Nickolas Rose, "Governing 'Advanced' Liberal Democracies," in *Foucault and Political Reason: Liberalism, Neo-liberalism and Rationalities of Government*, ed. Andrew Barry, Thomas Osborne, and Nickolas Rose (Chicago: University of Chicago Press, 1996), 41.

19. Ibid., 58.

20. Justin Lewis, "Introduction to Part II," in *Critical Cultural Policy Studies: A Reader*, eds. Justin Lewis and Toby Miller (Malden, MA: Blackwell Publishing, 2003), 46.

21. Lewis and Miller, *Critical Cultural Policy Studies*, 8; also see, Toby Miller and George Yúdice, *Cultural Policy* (London: Sage Publications, 2002).

22. David Marshall, *Celebrity and Power: Fame in Contemporary Culture* (Minneapolis: University of Minnesota Press, 1997), 55.

23. Ibid., 65.

24. Chris Rojek, *Celebrity* (London: Reaktion, 2001), 38.

25. Lynn Spigel, "Entertainment War: Television Culture After 9/11," *American Quarterly* 56, no. 2 (June 2004): 239.

26. Leah Garchik, "Telethon a Closely Guarded Secret," *San Francisco Chronicle*, Daily Datebook, C1, September 21, 2001. Retrieved from Lexis-Nexus(r) Academic.

27. Amy Oldenburg, "Cause Celeb," *USA Today*, LIFE, 1D, December 18, 2001. Retrieved from Lexis-Nexus® Academic.

28. Spigel, "Entertainment War," 251.

29. Guy Debord, *Society of the Spectacle* (Detroit: Black and Red, 1977).

30. Debord, *Spectacle*, 18.

31. Ibid., 38–39.

32. Pierre Bourdieu, *The Field of Cultural Production: Essays on Art and Literature* (New York: Columbia University Press, 1993), 164.

33. Richard Dyer, *Stars* (London: BFI, 1979); Richard Dyer, *Heavenly Bodies: Film Stars and Society* (New York: St. Martin's Press, 1986).
34. Barry King, "Articulating Stardom," in *Star Texts: Image and Performance in Film and Television*, ed. Jeremy G. Butler (Detroit: Wayne State University, 1991), 144.
35. King, "Articulating Stardom," 127.
36. David Meyer and Joshua Gamson, "The Challenge of Cultural Elites: Celebrities and Social Movements." *Sociological Inquiry* 65 (1995): 181–206.
37. Meg McLagan, "Spectacles of Difference: Cultural Activism and the Mass Mediation of Tibet," in *Media Worlds: Anthropology on New Terrain*, ed. Faye Ginsburg, Lilia Abu-Lughod, Brain Larkin (Berkeley: University of California Press, 2002).
38. I expand on this argument in "Traversing Authenticities: *The West Wing* President and the Activist Sheen," in *Politico-Entertainment: Television's Take on the Real*, ed. Kristina Riegert (New York: Peter Lang Press, 2007), 181–212.
39. Joshua Meyrowitz, *No Sense of Place: The Impact of Electronic Media on Social Interaction* (New York: Oxford University Press, 1985).
40. Sue Holmes, "Reality Goes Pop! Reality TV, Popular Music, and Narratives of Stardom in Pop Idol." *Television & New Media* 5, no. 2 (2004): 147–172.
41. Marshall, *Celebrity and Power*, 163.
42. Philip Auslander, *Liveness: Performance in a Mediatized Culture* (New York: Routledge, 1999), 70.
43. Thomas Gencarelli, "Trying to Learn How to Walk Like the Heroes: Bruce Springsteen, Popular Music, and the Hero/Celebrity," in *American Heroes in a Media Age*, ed. Susan J. Drucker and Robert S. Cathcart (Cresskill: Hampton Press, 1994).
44. Nickolas Rose, "The Death of the Social? Re-figuring the Territory of Government." *Economy and Society* 25, no. 3 (August 1996): 334.
45. Mervi Pantti and Liesbet van Zoonen, "Do Crying Citizens Make Good Citizens?" *Social Semiotics* 16, no. 2 (June 2006): 205–224.

Part Two
War and Entertainment

6

Gender Management, Popular Culture, and the Military

Tanja Thomas

The armed forces are a gendered institution. Their structures, practices, values, rites, and rituals reflect conventionalized and widely accepted images of masculinity and femininity.[1] Based on selected studies on military and gender, this chapter will argue for a shift in interest from the military institution as an "agency to produce hierarchic gender-dualism"[2] to the relations between the military and gender hierarchies in seemingly non-military areas of the social production of meaning.

This summarizes the results of a cooperative research project on "banal militarism" conducted with conflict researcher Fabian Virchow.[3] Following the term "banal nationalism," used by Michael Billig[4] to describe the daily and ordinary routines which reproduce the nation-state and the "nation," we created the term "banal militarism." Banal militarism includes the wide range of public discourses, media activities and political courses of events, which imply the existence of armed forces, their visibility in public, the spending of relevant amounts of money for military purposes, and the acceptance of war as a means to resolve conflict.

This chapter consists of four parts: The first part reflects on military science from a gender perspective and introduces the military as a site of gender management. Based on empirical studies, the second part focuses on the construction of gender stereotypes in mediated discourses produced by the military institution itself. Then I will turn to texts that, firstly, reveal "the military" as a cultural system, displaying gendered perspectives, horizons, and strategies of interpretation,[5] and, secondly, are commonly presented and appropriated in German media and everyday culture. An analysis of these texts reveal how military gender hierarchies are embedded in civilian gender hierarchies. Understanding masculinities and femininities as cultural constructs which are produced by a symbolic system and conveyed by the media, the third part of the article looks at mediated entertainment offerings. These support the circulation and construction of available "truths" and constructions of reality. In addition, they popularize social knowledge and therefore play a central role in supporting dominant discourses and maintaining hegemonic structures.[6] This part of the article looks at the representation of young female soldiers in TV shows like *Die Rettungsflieger* (The Rescue Pilots) and the repeatedly aired TV documentary *Feldtagebuch — Allein unter Männern* (Field Journal — Alone Amongst Men).

Finally, the fourth part analyzes forms of female morale, recreation and welfare activities, which are not only common in U.S. deployment areas, but are also becoming a reality on Bundeswehr posts: A young radio host from Leipzig, for instance, who entertained the troops in Kosovo and was involved in processes of "militainment," broadcasts messages from soldiers on her radio station and considers this her "service for the audience." Accordingly, national newspapers praise the effort of young women to keep up the troops' morale. This reveals that media contents as symbolic forms and cultural practices are reality-producing productions, which — in the tradition of Cultural Studies — shall be considered integrated in an ongoing struggle for social meaning: Together with power and culture, media contents constitute a triangle.[7]

The armed forces know about the identification potential of famous female singers. Thus, Jeanette Biedermann is a welcome guest at the Schooldays, a pop culture event staged to recruit future soldiers. In addition to Schooldays, talent shows of the Bundeswehr Big Band, BW Musix Contests, Adventure Games or BW Beachen '05 — The great Bundeswehr-Beachvolleyball-Tour are used to introduce young women to the military institution.

Gendered bodies produce power constellations and power techniques, which then become power impacts and in turn affect social processes. If we are to analyze this process, we need to pay special attention to the representations of the military in the media and everyday life as well as to the ordinary occurrences of military cultural practices. The key focus should be on involved actors and groups of actors and on the interactions of military facilities with other social/cultural actors and environments. Finally, we need to study the impact of these phenomena on domains which are not primarily shaped by the military.

To describe "militainment" as a means of improving the image of the armed forces and of recruitment does not suffice. It is important to relate these phenomena, their interwoven gender constructions and social functions to changes in the political culture of a country.

In my opinion, civilian approval of the existence and mission of the military are established via forms of everyday media communication. The same is true for the normalization of military force as state-organized and politically legitimized approach to conflicts. On the one hand, the persisting dual conception of information and entertainment is already gender-coded.[8] On the other hand, media discourses as "technologies of gender"[9] always have to be considered in their connection with gender discourses and social practices, which influence each other and are perpetually constructed in society. Therefore, the central task is to study processes of gendering in media and everyday representations and in performances of the popularized military.

Military and Gender: Background and Research Focus

Due to historical reasons concerning the Second World War, German scholars have been reluctant to engage in research about the social and political functions of the military.[10] Furthermore, military science is called a "men's science" for two reasons: Women have been virtually excluded from social practices in the military and men are paramount in military science.[11] Yet, several publications have been emerging in German-speaking countries, which open the research field "military and gender": socio-scientific monographs, interdisciplinary anthologies, special editions of *L'Homme*, the European journal for feminist science of history, annotated bibliographies, and summarizing articles.

Current research provides two major threads of argumentation.[12] I will outline them in the following, as needed for the scope of this article. From a historical point of view, the question of female involvement in wars has been researched thoroughly. In reference to the present question of the social embedding of military gender hierarchies, it is noteworthy that women in the past have been more integrated in military organizations than commonly assumed. Female participation in war only became scandalous after the military revolution of the sixteenth and seventeenth centuries. And the reason was not outrage about the gruesomeness of war, but outrage about the armed woman, who assumes a social position not conceded to her according to differentiated gender relations. Nira Yuval-Davis points out that "military and warfare have never been exclusively 'male domains.' Women have always been in charge of specific and important duties."[13] According to Klein, women have supported both world wars — not only by war economic employment, but also through propaganda.[14]

In Germany, armed forces and civilian army administration are constitutionally separated. This has always enabled the Bundeswehr to employ women in spite of the ban of armed duty for women. Therefore, "they fulfill different functions as civilians, which are carried out by soldiers in other armies."[15] Moreover, Astrid Albrecht-Heide refers to the active entanglement and partaking in the military of not only female soldiers, but also mothers, spouses and partners of soldiers.[16] She emphasizes that the military would not function without (female) civilian employees and their providing and assisting collaboration. However, producing and reproducing soldierly work force perfectly fits in with traditional female roles. And she calls attention to another important fact: "Women function, at the very least ideologically, as a defense motive. As part of the civilian population, they are employers of what is called defense and military mission for as long as they do not irrevocably object."[17]

According to Apelt the second thread of argumentation comprises the relation of military and masculinity, the importance of armed duty for the construction of masculinity, the importance of masculinity for military organization and culture, and the differentiation of masculinities within and outside the institution.[18] For instance, there are studies on masculine-military identity formation which has relied on the exclusion of women for a long time. The reason is that in addition to disciplinary and de-individualization practices, military training often consists of submission and fear strategies associated with the negative isolation and devaluation of the "feminine": The soldier has to clean, keep his possessions orderly, check his clothing, subordinate et cetera. According to Albrecht-Heide the military systematically utilizes fear of feminization by frequently demonstrating toughness.[19] Based on Connell's conception of hegemonic masculinity, several empirical studies have emerged focusing on different masculinities.[20] In Germany, these studies are discussed in view of acceptance and convertibility of masculinity constructions, since the integration of female soldiers and the potential change from mandatory military service to a professional army have been dominating recent debates.

The entanglement of masculinity and war also becomes apparent in the importance of militarized masculinity. Militarized masculinity is not only applied to warfare, but also to definitions of politics, security, and the theory and practice of international relations.[21]

Authors refer differently to the "construction of a pacifist women" as a complement to the male fighter: Some analyze functions and consequences of this dichotomous construction; others study women as combatants or deduce political demands in view of peace missions. Debates and studies about the functions and consequences of opening the military to women and integrating them into the military are closely connected to this thread of argumentation. In light of changing gender hierarchies, these studies are currently emphasized in scholarly and mediated discourses in Germany.[22] Several recent contributions deal with this issue: The recent anthology *Frauen im Militär* (Women in the Military) understands the absolute opening of the Bundeswehr as an "expression of a thorough change of orientation, redefining the relation of the genders to each other."[23] However, the motives for the inclusion of women are discussed critically: Recruiting problems, assumed or real war and crises dangers, the goal of improving troop morale and discipline, the need for legitimation resources, the introduction of new war technology, the increasing importance of operations behind the front (administration, logistics, infrastructure) and the, in her opinion overrated, desire of women to participate. Nira Yuval-Davis analyzed the functions of including women into the armed forces and studied processes of female integration into the U.S. Army, when it was opened to women in 1973.[24] She shows that opening the American armed forces to women followed strategic (and partly racist) considerations. She points out that one reason was the prevention of Vietnam-like mass mobilizations in the future and another was to prevent the "flooding of the armed forces by blacks." Plus, women were allowed in the military at the same time when mandatory military service was done away with. This solved an argument for women's rights, which had been used repeatedly in different historical contexts and drew on the symbolic connection of military service and civil rights. Seifert argues that relations between military and gendered society are generally useful in analyzing discursive movements within the entanglement of military service, national state and citizenship. Looking at the development of the military profession, she claims: "One common perspective of the otherwise different approaches is that the construction of the military profession in the formation phase of the modern civic state overlaps the fundamental social hierarchy criterion "gender" with the power structure of the national state and individual masculine identity. Within this construction and on the level of symbolic representation, men are systematically positioned on the side of military, war and violence while women find themselves on the side of the civilian, peace and peacefulness."[25]

Comparative studies on current military gender politics in different national contexts can be found in an anthology by Ruth Seifert and Christine Eifler.[26] The Bundeswehr Institute of Social Sciences provides quantitative and qualitative studies which focus less on the motives and more on the process of the integration of women into the German armed forces and try to understand that process.[27] Carefully, Kümmel and Werkner point out that a quota of 15 percent is too low to speak of a successful integration of women into the military.[28] They emphasize that current studies of the integration of women will have to be repeated, since women who join the military later might not be as motivated as the first cohort and will also enter the military environment with more previous knowledge. Additionally, the organization presently pays close attention to the integration process; the media interest in female soldiers is high and functions as a control mechanism. By comparison, Uta Klein's statement during the international women's peace conference "Womanoeuvres — Feminist Debates on Peace and Security" in summer 2003 reveals a more resolute positioning: "... integration of women does not exist. That means, the current inclusion might provoke and confuse some people in their gender stereotypes, but it does not whatsoever challenge the gender dichotomy and the masculinity of the military."[29]

The participation of women in the military — in May 2005 about 11,380 women served in the Bundeswehr (that is equivalent to six percent of all regular soldiers) — did not change anything about the persisting reproduction of established gender roles within the Bundeswehr, as Klein emphasizes in further studies.[30] On the contrary, some even argue that the presence of women optimizes the reproduction of the sexist basic structure of the military.[31]

All these studies show a certain continuity of including women into warfare and the military. They reveal the central importance of femininity in historical and present construction processes of (military) masculinity and how femininity is used to legitimate the military and warfare. Based on these insights, it seems safe to say that opening the military for women as soldiers does not per se disrupt traditional, patriarchic gender relations. The results of my tentative considerations, which will be elaborated on in the following, point in the same direction: Strategies and representations of the inclusion of women as soldiers, morale, recreation and welfare personnel, and recruitment aides cement traditional gender relations rather that change them.

Female Soldiers: Media Invocations and Representations

Sylvia Schießer's main interest is *how* "the 'gender-hierarchy problem' caused by female military members is symbolically solved in the print media of the Bundeswehr."[32] These media are conceived by the information and press department of the German Department of Defense and by the leaders of the joint forces. Thus, her problem definition ties up to the studies outlined in the first part of my article. It is based on the fact that the 'social figure woman' touches two symbolic levels, which are coded masculine: "the public-collective level on the one hand, by representing the state monopoly on legitimate use of force and the idea of nation, and on the other hand the individual-emotional level of masculinity, which is the core area of masculine-soldierly gender identity."[33] The results of the study speak for themselves: The gender images are based on patriarchal projection and are supposed to symbolically exclude the female from the military. Schießer puts the representations of female soldiers into the categories "mother/wife," "seductress," "soldierly comrade" and "gun moll." However, examples for the first two categories outweigh the others quantitatively. The "soldierly comrade" is presented in a desexualized way and the "gun moll" is either a concept of enemy or neutralized by an assumed, but allegedly obvious wish for marriage and motherhood.

Jörg Keller also analyzes the construction of female stereotypes in print media and recruiting brochures of the Bundeswehr.[34] His basic finding is that "the core mission of the military, combat, arms, death and destruction, to be experts on violence"[35] play no role whatsoever in recruitment brochures. The young man is shown in combat gear, but never fighting, yet busy with his work. Young women, however, even though also presented with combat helmets, are consistently shown facing the reader, suggesting eye contact. The monthly Bundeswehr magazine *Y. Magazin der Bundeswehr*, which has a circulation of 72,000 and is used for internal as well as external communication, portrays men as dominant, purposeful, confident, ready and endows them with regalia of power. Women in pictures seem unprofessional and relation oriented. Thus, women become a "foil for masculinity, because the male symbolic system can stand out from it."[36]

The German soldier was a rare sight on German TV until the early 1990s. The famous German actor Til Schweiger, for instance, played a recruit in *Die Lindenstraße*. At the beginning of the 90s, the career fields of non-commissioned officers and troops in the medical and military music service just began to open for the voluntary service of women.[37] In 1994, the public channel ARD started *Nicht von schlechten Eltern* (Not From Bad Parents; the second and third seasons were broadcast in 1995 and 1998), a family show about marine members, with Ulrich Pleitgen playing marine officer Wolfgang Schefer. In the show's third season, daughter Jenny is grown up and unemployed after earning a medical degree. Thus, she becomes a marine doctor on her father's post. Conflicts follow since the admiral generally accepts women in uniform, yet not with the marines and even less his daughter. Episode 34 shows Jenny Schefer as a dentist and the only woman amongst men on a frigate on the way to England: When they enter Plymouth harbor, not the German flag, but Jenny's bra is hoisted. In this image, her bra is symbolically charged and can be read as an imagination of fear that a sexualized female threat might destroy the male collective's combat readiness and authority.

The show *Die Rettungsflieger* has been broadcast on ZDF since 1997; the twelfth season is currently in production. The Bundeswehr provides helicopters, pilots, and advice for the use of weapons and helps train the actors. "The close cooperation with the Bundeswehr and especially Dr. Thomas Samek's advice — an experienced rescue pilot — enabled ZDF to assure a very high degree of authenticity," the show's website informs, which also displays the Bundeswehr logo. The website also describes basic features of the female soldier's characters: Surgeon major emergency doctor Dr. Ilona Müller (Julia Heinemann) "is very attached to her profession. She is courageous and always there for her patients. But the doctor also listens to the problems of her colleagues." Chief staff surgeon emergency doctor Dr. Sabine Petersen (Marlene Marlow) is described as follows: "She is a brilliant and empathetic doctor despite her young looks and often turns a guy's head." Yet information is scarce on Dr. Maren Maibach (Gerit Kling), playing the first emergency doctor from 1995 to 1997.

From February 1999 to April 1999 the private TV channel Pro7 broadcast eleven episodes of *Jets — Leben am Limit* (Life at the Limit). The new TV protagonists were supposed to be Bundeswehr soldiers who risk their lives all over the world fighting for human rights. The Bundeswehr provided — for a fee, as they insisted — shooting locations and expensive technology. The broadcast of the first episode on February 21, 1999 coincided with the debate about the Bundeswehr deployment in Kosovo and the Bundesluftwaffe (German air force) providing 14 tornado jets for that mission. Soldier virtues, hard training, loyal male comradeship and the "erotic significance" of a combat jet were accompanied by lusty sound bites from the young combat pilots: "Excuse me, but I thought about making love to you 3,000 meters above ground." The episodes covered the broad and different missions of German soldiers: They fight against flooding, trace illegal troops of mercenaries, and discover illegal gun trades. An example of a female soldier is chief staff surgeon Michaela von Stetten: As soon as first lieutenant Stein is introduced, she develops a crush on him. When combat pilot Robin fears that Stein endangers his promotion to assistant staff officer, they decide to take their rivalry to a mountain climbing duel in the Alps. After eleven episodes the show was stopped due to bad TV ratings. Two already produced episodes were broadcast on a Sunday morning in September 2001.

Yet, the Bundeswehr considers itself "presentable" in the media. The five episode docusoap *Frauen am Ruder* (Women to the Fore, WDR) showed the first training year of four female officer candidates on board of the training ship *Gorch Fock*.[38] According to the Bundesmarine (German marines), the show was "truthful and realistic." However, the SWR production *Feldtagebuch — Allein unter Männern* caused controversy with the Bundeswehr: The film documented "misconduct in tone" of instructors and "inappropriate leader conduct" of supervisors.[39] Consequently, it was altered with new material and broadcast under the title *Attacke! Frauen ans Gewehr* (Attack! Women to Arms). The documentary shows the training of four women in an armored infantry battalion and was last broadcast in August 2005.

Despite the controversy, rookie director Aelrun Goette received the Juliane-Bartel-Prize[40] in 2002 for the first version of *Feldtagebuch*. The award was justified as follows: "The film observes four of the first female Bundeswehr soldiers for several weeks. It documents basic training without comment, yet sharply. It unmasks the authoritative and destructive structures of a man's world, which plays war in the middle of Germany in a way that is scandalous and subtly violent. The introduction of the female into that man's world shows two strange worlds inexpiably crashing into each other. In the end, the performance and comradeship invoking harassment is exposed as what it really is: A breeding ground for violence, frustration, humiliation."

Finally, there is *Soldatenglück und Gottes Segen* (Soldier's Luck and God's Blessing) by Ulrike Franke and Michael Loeken (subtitle: About the Life in Deployment). It has been broadcast on German TV several times. The feature-length documentary shows soldiers in Kosovo shining their shoes, cutting their hair, standing at attention or receiving mail. It also observes their free time activities: as local radio hosts, playing cards, or listening to singer Gunter Gabriel, who is active in morale, recreation and welfare activities and plays his guitar for the soldiers. The central message of the film is the extensive simulation of an everyday normality which conveys a calculable risk to the ones left behind. The inclusion of women follows a certain pattern in the program: For example, it refers to the better organized morale, recreation and welfare activities for American soldiers: It shows a female band, whose front singer sits on the laps of several soldiers. When interviewed, the soldiers underline the special relevance of this "moral support."

As we see in the film, Gunter Gabriel sings for the German soldiers. To the tune of "House of the Rising Sun," he intones a song written exclusively for the troops. The first and fourth verse of "Es steht ein Haus im Kosovo" (There is a House in Kosovo) are as follows:

> There is a house in Kosovo
> It is bombed and vacant,
> But the boys from good old Germany,
> They make it whole again.

> ...
> Only at night, they have time to dream
> About their home and their pretty woman,
> But if she remained faithful all this time,
> They never know for sure.

Gabriel highlights the questions "Will my wife be faithful?," "Will everything be like before, when I come home?" in his lyrics, but also in an interview conducted by the author of this article and Fabian Virchow within the framework of their research project on banal militarism.[41]

These examples show how popular culture is bound to an immanent gender hierarchy, for which the military is an integral part. The TV shows and documentaries, but also Gunter Gabriel's lyrics, reproduce the antagonism between the military and the feminine. In addition, they condition military functioning during war and social functioning in established gender hierarchies beyond war. The cementation of this antagonism is not only obvious in the mediated stereotypes of female characters as empathetic, caring doctor, as seductress, and as the object of male competition and sexual fantasies. It also reveals itself in discourses meant to be critical of society, constructing "two strange worlds" of the male and the female. This construction is based on an essentialist understanding of women and men having certain skills, which is neither theoretically nor politically tenable. An example of this discourse is the jury's statement about the Juliane-Bartel-Prize.

"Militainment": Women for Morale, Welfare, and Recreation

Mediated gender representations and performances, which this article examines with Germany and the United States as examples, are sometimes called "militainment," but without specifying the term or clarifying its dimensions. I use the term militainment to describe the cooperation of software companies and the military to produce simulations, war movies and so-called "military soaps" as well as the morale, recreation and welfare activities of artists and media protagonists. Due to changing foreign affairs and military paradigms, this cooperation phenomenon is currently gaining importance in Germany. However, militainment does not refer to crisis-related efforts of the military (and their political leadership) to control images and information, and to direct, disperse or censor them. It means cooperation between the military and the media and culture industry on an everyday basis that goes beyond war and crises.

6. Gender Management, Popular Culture... (Thomas)

Many areas of militainment could be analyzed with focus on gender. Nevertheless, this part will spotlight morale, recreation and welfare activities, which can be called an established, even genuine form of militainment. Therefore, I shall concentrate on singing and performing protagonists, who have supported and lobbied for the troops at the front and at home in Germany.

Expanding the military missions of the Bundeswehr also brought new missions for morale, recreation and welfare activities. Ever since the formation of the Bundeswehr in 1956, it has been connected with culture. An example is the Bundeswehr orchestra, which has played nationally and abroad in military and non-military contexts in order to establish new acceptance for the German military after 1945.[42] There is also a Big Band, which I will talk about later. Another example are various dance and amusement events organized by Bundeswehr units. They usually include music performances and female dancing partners are invited, often via newspaper advertisement.

The growing number of foreign deployments changes cultural-military cooperation in a way that has long been familiar to American armed forces: Cultural services take place at the front and outside national territory. Visits to the front have been common for U.S. troops since both world wars. After September 11 these activities have gained significant importance: Julia Roberts, Brad Pitt, George Clooney, Andy Garcia and Matt Damon, for instance, traveled to Incirlik Air Base in South Turkey, which serves as a main hub for missions in support for U.S. military operations in Afghanistan. American pop stars Jennifer Lopez and Mariah Carey sang at Ramstein Air Base and in military gear for U.S. soldiers in Kosovo respectively and ex–Spice Girl Geri Halliwell visited British troops in Oman.

Until the early 1980s, morale, recreation and welfare activities in Germany predominantly meant attractive leisure activities on Bundeswehr posts. But since more German troops are sent to foreign and combat missions, the Bundeswehr is becoming more active in this area. The first Bundeswehr UN-deployment in Somalia from June 1993 to March 1994 for the UNOSOM II-Operation of the United Nations commenced a visible changing process: Since then the number of German soldiers outside Germany have been increasing as have tour durations in areas of deployment and crisis. This brings new challenges for the Bundeswehr, because troop morale amongst other factors depends on leisure and entertainment offers.

Morale, recreation and welfare activities in deployment and war comprise permanent offers like satellite TV, movie theaters, workout equipment and contact to loved ones via phone as well as additional activities, one of them being cultural services: These could be a performance by DJ Bobo, an almost week-long stay by rock group Asshole in April, 2000 in Bosnia, a dance performance of the Berlin Thunder Cheerleaders on New Year's Eve 2001/2002 in Macedonia, or guest performances by country singer Gunter Gabriel, or the German band Blues Guys with front singer Juli. Next to fameless cover bands like the Heart & Soul Blues Brother Cover Band,[43] the popular German girl group No Angels sang and danced for 1,000 soldiers in Prizren in January 2002. The concert had been organized by the BILD tabloid; who reported about the "hottest cargo" ever transported in a Transall military aircraft in its print edition and videos on the Internet.

Newspapers reflect the quantitative imbalance of genders and the deficit:[44] Pictures of beaming No Angels in front of upheld soldier arms present a uniform male collective compared to the erotic spectacle. It has always been and still is a male perspective which artists at the front reflect in most morale, recreation and welfare activities.

But not only stars and models are approached by military personnel. The young radio host Friederike Lippold (Freddy) for instance, still working for Radio Energy in Leipzig, was invited to host a party for the soldiers at the front. I visited and interviewed her in Leipzig and asked her to describe her impressions from her stage appearance in Raijlovac: "Well, I saw what mood the boys were in and that they were very, very, very happy about any kind of female distraction. Yes, I think that's good, I mean, they really don't have anything but their four kitchen ladies that they can look at for a half year, and if it's really just dancers then I think it's ok. Yes, I mean, even if it's more, they do have a lot of work over there, the boys, and I don't think it's bad. I wouldn't do it, because I saw it, how it was when I was on stage ... oh, well, manly, well, very brute [laughs]" (my translation).

Sexual drives and potent masculinity as core areas of male-military masculinity — in Lippold's statement as well as her performance — are not only anticipated, but also reproduced and reinforced. This confirms Hartmut Winkler's hypothesis of politics not against, but with sexuality.[45]

Friederike Lippold considers her stage appearance in Raijlovac as "service for the audience." After her return to Leipzig, she started a radio program which transmitted greetings for and from soldiers. According to Lippold, this is her "service for the woman." Radio Energy pays for sending stuffed animals across the country. Freddy responds to emails from admirers at the front and, when invited, attends the "bundeswehrish festivities in Leipzig."

The military leadership appreciates the benefit of these cultural offers. Bundeswehr media for soldiers (magazines *Bundeswehr Aktuell, Informationen für die Truppe, Keiler* etc.; broadcasts on Radio Andernach and several online services) frequently run reports on cultural events at the front, narrations and comments from the soldiers' points of view and interviews with cultural protagonists.

While each performance is a special event within the armed forces, the entanglements of cultural protagonists and the military have gone almost unnoticed by the public so far. Yet the Bundeswehr is interested in continuing cooperation for two reasons. Firstly, cultural events show appreciation for the troops and function as a means of solidarity via identification figures. And secondly, they improve the military's image in society and banalize the military by presenting concentrated interactions between the military and cultural protagonists in the media. The alleged historically established situation of women at the home front is inscribed in the inclusion of young women and in the gender performances, which are partly staged for the media: their position as protection-worthy "cultural treasure" and as customers of male combat readiness.

About "Schooldays" and Talent Shows: Popularizing the Military

The Bundeswehr is working to intensify their contacts with famous female artists: Recently, female singers have not only been involved in morale, recreation and welfare activities, but also in recruitment efforts. The German pop singer Jeanette Biedermann, for instance, sang and danced for "Schooldays." These are Bundeswehr-organized events to approach and recruit male and female students. In a short film produced for the Bundeswehr, Jeanette Biedermann is asked about her relation to the military before her show. This is the intro and a short interview sequence (my translation): "[OFF] The pop princess mainly attracts younger fans; she's in the front line, in a manner of speaking. Being a native of Berlin, she doesn't have any reservations about the military — quite on the contrary — and told us before the show that she gets excited by men in uniform: [JB] 'oh I don't know, it's a special charisma, there's like, something strong, something powerful about it, well, just men' [OFF] In her usual sexy outfit, she performs at full throttle for an hour and heats up the Messeplatz in Karlsruhe by several degrees."

The Bundeswehr tries to increase the attractiveness of the military by such events. Yet the reproduction of established gender roles is cemented at the same time.

In 2005, their fiftieth year, the Bundeswehr tried to be particularly present. Therefore, they were pleased to promise support for the Catholic World Youth Day and Bundeswehr posts around Cologne were involved in the organization. The units provided accommodation for pilgrims, soldiers as aides, support with transportation and room on their premises. Yet the Bundeswehr was not only aide, but also an active protagonist in shaping the event: When Pope Benedikt XVI arrived at the Köln-Bonn airport, he was greeted with military honors by the guard battalion and the Staff Music Corps.[46] The Catholic military miter hat invited about 300 soldiers from thirteen nations to the World Youth Day. Three hundred and sixty German soldiers from over a hundred locations took part. After the final church service of the World Youth Day, the Bundeswehr Big Band with twenty-year-old soloist Christina Maria Brenner opened the afternoon music festival Building One World. Serving as opening band for Cliff Richards was a huge success, as one press officer put it. Weeks before that, the Bundeswehr had announced a talent show in cooperation with an advertising agency. The goal was to find musical accompaniment for the tour of the new anniversary exhibition *Unsere Bundeswehr*. "Forty-five Sänger" (using the male version of the German word for singers) were invited to castings, where the jury picked "16 young ladies." They went through a week-long workshop with vocal coaches in Euskirchen. One of them was Christina Maria Brenner who was "greatly honored" by playing for so many people with the Bundeswehr. The exhibition *Unsere Bundeswehr* toured four cities in September 2005. In each city, four male and female singers performed for the visitors.[47]

The Bundeswehr has experience with talent shows: From September 19 to 21, 2003, they had already experimented with youth marketing. The BW-Musix '03 event was modeled after talent shows like *Deutschland sucht den Superstar* (*German Idol*, RTL) or *Star Search* (Sat1) and targeted young people aged 14 to 24. There were five categories in which participants could "meet and compete": In the categories orchestra, corps and ensembles, the contestants were judged by officers of the music corps. Disc jockeys and student bands performed in front of famous experts of the DJ and band world. Prizes were a CD production, live-performances with the Bundeswehr Big Band and training workshops with the Bundeswehr music corps. The mayor even declared the event location Dillingen "music capital of Germany" for one weekend. Institutional goals like image improvement, recruitment and the promise of low-priced personnel might have been motives for the organizers.

Military Gender Management

The military, which presented itself as "school" of the male nation and considered "masculinity" an essential goal in the nineteenth century, has always massively protruded into civilian space, viewed from a gender historical point of view: It socializes all men liable to military service into the role of the Fatherland defender, it claims to transform all other masculinities and puts them into hierarchies, it provides men with additional means of power and therefore further strengthens the social inequality of the genders.[48]

In summary, this inequality is depicted by less resources and power opportunities; it is expressed and simultaneously caused by the routine practices of its reproduction on different levels: On a structural level, e.g., by segmentation and segregation in employment, education paths, occupational areas, tasks, duties, income etc.; on a symbolic level in form of discourses, which include stereotyping, classification and hence hierarchies and differences in status and value. In view of established gender constructions and the politic-economic foundation of military gender management described in the first part of the article, it remains doubtful whether opening an army like the Bundeswehr for women will achieve a reduction of power asymmetries between genders. Also, the military institution is not the only place of military gender management. Rather, it is important to scrutinize practices framed by the military, which are often embedded in a pop cultural reproduction of gender hierarchies and express themselves in gender definitions, representations, invocations and performances of corresponding meanings. This article demonstrates that the banalization of the military via entertainment includes representations of women as soldiers. Yet this inclusion is often tied to traditional, stereotypical representations and performances of women and normalizes the manner of the military man, while affirming cliché-prone ideas of women.

The embedding of military practices in entertainment offerings does not only derive from long-term strategies of indoctrination, but from the interrelated references of military and cultural protagonists to each other. This confirms the banalization hypothesis, which points to mechanisms and procedures by which the military, its necessity and its demands for financial assets are (re)produced in society. Thus the performances and exercises of military gender constructions find their way into every day life and, agreeing to the before-mentioned quote of Uta Klein, do not at all disrupt the gender dichotomy, the masculinity of the military and corresponding patriarchic gender inequalities.[49] Some scholars argue that in view of the worldwide institutionalization of equality norms, the reproduction of asymmetric gender inequality ceases to be automatic and routine. However, the processes of banalizing the military in the civilian sphere do not promote this process.

Notes

1. Frank J. Barrett, "Die Konstruktion hegemonialer Männlichkeit in Organisationen: Das Beispiel U.S.–Marine," in *Soziale Konstruktionen. Militär und Geschlechterverhältnis*, ed. Christine Eifler and Ruth Seifert (Münster: Westfälisches Dampfboot, 1999), 88.
2. Astrid Albrecht-Heide, "Militär und Patriarchat," in *Die Zukunft des Militärs in Industriegesellschaften*, ed. Wilfried Karl and Thomas Nielebock (Baden-Baden: Nomos, 1991), 115.
3. Tanja Thomas and Fabian Virchow (ed.), *Banal Militarism. Zur Veralltäglichung des Militärischen im Zivilen* (Bielefeld: transcript, 2006).
4. Billig, Michael, *Banal Nationalism* (London: Sage, 1995).
5. Ute Frevert (ed.), *Militär und Gesellschaft im 19. und 20. Jahrhundert* (Stuttgart: Klett-Cotta, 1997), 10.
6. Johanna Dorer, "Diskurs, Medien und Identität. Neue Perspektiven in der feministischen Kommunikations-und Medienwissenschaft," in *Feministische Kommunikations- und Medienwissenschaft*, ed. Johanna Dorer and Brigitte Geiger (Wiesbaden: Westdeutscher Verlag, 2002), 54.
7. Elisabeth Klaus, "Ein Zimmer mit Ausblick? Perspektiven kommunikations-wissenschaftlicher Geschlechterforschung," in *Kommunikationswissenschaft und Gender Studies*, ed. Elisabeth Klaus, Jutta Röser and Ulla Wischermann (Wiesbaden: Westdeutscher Verlag, 2001), 15.
8. Elisabeth Klaus and Jutta Röser, "Fernsehen und Geschlecht. Geschlechtsgebundene Kommunikationsstile in der Medienrezeption und-produktion," in *Blick Richtung Frauen. Theorien und Methoden geschlechtsspezifischer Rezeptionsforschung*, ed. Gudrun Marci-Boehnke, Petra Werner and Ulla Wischermann (Weinheim: Deutscher Studien Verlag, 1996), 37–60.
9. Dorer, "Diskurs, Medien und Identität," 63.
10. See for instance Paul Klein and Peter-Michael Kozielski, "Das Militär und die Sozialwissenschaften in Deutschland," in *Militär und Wissenschaft in Europa –Kritische Distanz oder hilfreiche Ergänzung?*, ed. Paul Klein and Andreas Prüfert (Baden-Baden: Nomos, 1998), 27.
11. Maja Apelt, "Geschlecht und Militär—Grundzüge einer neueren Diskussion," in *Frauen im Militär. Empirische Befunde und Perspektiven zur Integration von Frauen in die Streitkräfte*, ed. Jens-Rainer Ahrens, Maja Apelt and Christiane Bender (Wiesbaden: VS, 2005), 13.
12. Apelt, "Geschlecht und Militär."
13. Nira Yuval-Davis, *Geschlecht und Nation* (Emmendingen: Verlag die Brotsuppe, 1997), 154.
14. Uta Klein,"Womanoeuvres: Männlichkeit und Militarisierung," (2003:3), accessed from http://www.soziale-arbeit-und-gesundheit.fh.kiel.de/lehrende/hauptamtliche/daten.u.klein/womanoeuvres.pdf on April 25, 2007.

The fact that the Wehrmacht was not an exclusively male domain is often overlooked: a half million female "Wehrmacht aides" supported the male soldiers. For further information see: Gudrun Schwarz and Gaby Zipfel, "Die halbierte Gesellschaft. Anmerkungen zu einem soziologischen Problem," *Mittelweg 36, Zeitschrift des Hamburger Instituts für Sozialforschung*, no. 7 (Feb/March 1998): 78–88.

15. Anne Mangold and Sylka Scholz, "Können Frauen nicht Kampfschwimmen? Die Konstruktion von Männlichkeiten und Weiblichkeiten in der Bundeswehr," *Perspektive 21, Brandenburgische Hefte für Wissenschaft und Politik*, no. 12 (2000): 45, my translation from German. Unless otherwise noted, all translations from German are my own. According to Bender, Christiane, approximately 49,700 women in civilian positions are employed by the Bundeswehr administration (almost 35 percent of all employees).

16. Astrid Albrecht-Heide, "Krieger wollen nicht weiblich sein. Sexismus und Bundeswehr," *Illoyal—Journal für Antimilitarismus* no.7 (1999:6), accessed from http://www.illoyal.kampagne.de/nr7/seite5.htm on April 4, 2007.

17. On women's rights as legitimation of war in the media, refer to Elisabeth Klaus and Susanne Kassel, "Frauenrechte als Kriegslegitimation in den Medien," in *Männerkrieg und Frauenfrieden. Geschlechterdimensionen in kriegerischen Konflikten*, ed. Julia Neissl, Kirstin Eckstein, Elisabeth Anker and Silvia Arzt (Wien: Promedia, 2003), 13–30.

18. Apelt, "Geschlecht und Militär," 16.

19. Albrecht-Heide, "Krieger wollen nicht weiblich sein," 4.

20. Robert Connell, *Der gemachte Mann. Konstruktion und Krise von Männlichkeiten* (Opladen: Leske + Budrich, 1999). See for instance Barrett's study of images of masculinity in the U.S. Marines: Barrett, "Die Konstruktion hegemonialer Männlichkeit in Organisationen: Das Beispiel U.S.–Marine" (1999), 71–91.

21. Cynthia Enloe, "Männlichkeit als außenpolitisches Problem," *Ruberta*, no. 8 (2003): 32–35.

22. On October 27, 2000, the German Bundestag approved changing Article 12a of the Grundgesetz (German consitution). Thus, voluntary armed duty in the Bundeswehr became possible for women.

23. Ahrens, Apelt and Bender, *Frauen im Militär*, 7.

24. Yuval-Davis, *Geschlecht und Nation*, 161.

25. Seifert, "Militär und Geschlechterverhältnisse. Entwicklungslinien einer ambivalenten Debatte" (1999), 46.

26. Ruth Seifert, Christine Eifler and Heinrich-Böll-Stiftung (ed.), *Gender und Militär. Internationale Erfahrungen mit Männern und Frauen in den Streitkräften* (Ulrike Helmer Publisher, 2003).

27. Stastistics, interviews, and journals, e.g., Gerhard Kümmel and Ines-Jaqueline Werkner, *Soldat, weiblich, Jahrgang 2001. Berichte*, vol. 72 (Strausberg: Sozialwissenschaftliches Institut der Bundeswehr, 2003).

28. Ibid., 17.

29. Klein, "Womanoeuvres," 3.

30. Ibid.

31. Samira Fansa, "Soldatinnen und nun? Die Präsenz von Frauen optimiert die sexistische Grundstruktur des Militärs," (2001), accessed from http://www.nadir.org/nadir/periodika/jungle_world/_2001/02/05b.htm on October 5, 2007.

32. Sylvia Schießer, "Gender, Medien und Militär: Zur Konstruktion weiblicher Stereotype in der Darstellung von Soldatinnen in den Printmedien der Bundeswehr," *Beiträge zur feministischen Theorie und Praxis. Themenheft Frauen in den Medien*, no. 61 (2002): 47.

33. Ibid., 48.

34. Jörg Keller, "Soldat und Soldatin — Die Konstruktion von Männlichkeit und Weiblichkeit am Beispiel von Printmedien der Bundeswehr," in Ahrens, Apelt and Bender, *Frauen im Militär*, 79–107.

35. Emphasis in original, ibid., 86.

36. Ibid., 105.

37. In 1975 the first women were employed in the medical service of the Bundeswehr as registered doctors or pharmacists as medical officers. In 1989 the first female medical cadets followed.

38. Ute Lange, "Auf Augenhöhe," *Y. Magazin der Bundeswehr*, no. 11 (2002): 12–15.

39. The annual report 2002 of the military ombudsman of the German Bundestag states that the case was thoroughly discussed by the troops, under participation of the army leadership. Accessed from http://sicherheitspolitik.bundeswehr.de/10/23A.php on August 5, 2007.

40. For further information about the Juliane-Bartel-Prize, who was awarded by the federal state Niedersachsen, see http://www.ms.niedersachsen.de/master/ C1203681_N2309400_L20_D0_I674.html, accessed on September 20, 2007.

41. Gabriel was interviewed by the author and Fabian Virchow on September 3, 2003, in Hamburg-Harburg.

42. Fritz Masuhr, *Die Militärmusik in der Bundeswehr: Militärmusikgeschichte 1955–1975* (Bonn: Bundesminister der Verteidigung, 1977).

43. Then Minister of Defense Peter Struck's performance as lead singer became not only "picture of the week" in the *Stern magazine* but also provoked several smug comments, e.g., *Frankfurter Allgemeine Sonntagszeitung*, April 27, 2003.

44. Corresponding photos recall the photos of Marilyn Monroe's performances in Korea; refer to the D.W. article's illustration: "No Angels singen im Kosovo für die Bundeswehr," *Die Welt*, January 25, 2002.

45. Hartmut Winkler, "Der weibliche Star als Kriegsbraut," *Augenblick*, no. 12 (1992): 35–55.

46. For the importance of these ceremonies as instruments of power see Markus Euskirchen, *Militärrituale. Analyse und Kritik eines Herrschaftsinstruments* (Köln: Papyrossa, 2005).

47. All quotes concerning the Big Band appearance during the World Youth Day are from http://www.streitkraeftebasis.de/C1256C290043532F/vwContentFrame/F25F5DBE7E22F2BDC125705F002805C8, accessed on September 15, 2007.

48. Frevert, *Militär und Gesellschaft*, 13.

49. Klein, "Womanoeuvres," 3.

7

"Tell Me That Wasn't Fun"
Watching the Battle Scenes in Master and Commander *with a Smile on Your Face*

Anne Gjelsvik

> What do we want from war films? Entertainment, mostly, a few hours' escape to other lands and times, as well as something excitingly different, something reassuringly familiar.[1]

The first fifteen minutes of Peter Weir's epic *Master and Commander: The Far Side of the World* (2003) make for a powerful experience.[2] Starting with the sound and motion of the ship and the sea, the sense of the power of the ocean and the loneliness of the ship immediately engage the spectator. Life on board is briefly depicted before the threat of war is introduced. The young officer on watch, Mr. Hollum, believes he sees a ship in the distant fog. The camera gives the spectator a peek through the watchman's binoculars but leaves us — like him — uncertain. Is there a ship in the fog, and if so, is it the enemy? The uneasiness of the young man spills over onto us — what should he do? What if he wakes the captain and the crew in the middle of the night and it's only a false alarm? We are actually led to hope, for his sake, that the shape in the distance is in fact "a man o'war," and that the men will face a battle.

The drums beat and the men prepare the ship for battle. The doctor places his instruments on the table ready for surgery and the captain puts on his belt and uniform. The ship is struck by enemy fire and struck again. The chaotic situation is rendered through close-ups of fire, blood, and damaged wood, mixed with panoramic shots of the two beautiful ships and the movements and actions of the crew members. Wounded men are dragged across the deck floor by their legs and dead men are hanging in the mast ropes. After several damaging hits, water pours into the ship, the steering is damaged, and the ship's sick-bay is full of bleeding and screaming men. There is blood everywhere, leading the doctor to yell: "More sand on the floor" in order to prevent the men from slipping and sliding in the greasy pools of blood.

Even the captain himself falls once, but Captain Aubrey (Russell Crowe) rises to the occasion, settling on an escape into the fog. He succeeds. In calm water, the repair of men and ship can begin. "The butcher's bill" counts nine dead men and twenty-seven wounded. As in the case of *Saving Private Ryan* (1998), the spectator finds herself thrown into the middle of a war scene. But still, the captain goes to war with a smile on his face and the spectator can feel engaged and excited. Aubrey wants more fighting and we will follow him. How can this be? Why do we want to follow the captain into a war zone?

This article discusses some of the reasons why war movies can serve as exciting entertainment for spectators. Using Peter Weir's *Master and Commander* as my subject of scrutiny, I will discuss some of the different emotions experienced by moviegoers when they watch war movies. The most attention will be paid to mixed emotional responses towards battle scenes. After watching the first ten minutes of the movie the spectator has already experienced a wide range of emotions of which some are quite contradictive, for instance both excitement and fear. Drawing on a philosophical framework I will discuss this contradiction and argue that it is crucial to understand the reasons for these different emotions in order to understand the pleasure of watching war movies in order to show how emotional ambivalence may be produced in viewers, and how we can distinguish between different levels of emotions which are derived from different elements in the fiction film. Such distinctions can be fruitful in making sense of apparently problematic pleasures, such as appreciating painful depictions of war, and in this line of argument I will foreground the importance of representation and the role of fiction. In sum, this analysis will shed some light on what this kind of pleasure tells us about our moral condition, as it also could be argued that it is repugnant taking pleasure in watching someone's suffering.[3]

The paradox in question is not a new one, and in discussing it may draw up on theoretical and philosophical perspectives using examples from both classical tragedy as well as contemporary cognitive film theory's discussions of horror films.[4] In his article, "Emotion in response to Art," philosopher Jerrold Levinson identifies several challenging questions with respect to spectators' emotional reactions towards works of art.[5] In discussing the battle scenes in *Master and Commander*, at least two of these questions are relevant: What kind of emotions are experienced in response to works of art and how can we make sense of the interest that spectators "have in empathetically experiencing art that expresses negative emotions," the so-called "paradox of tragedy."[6]

The paradox of negative emotions in art is related to the contradiction embodied in the following: if works of art are likely to cause negative emotional responses such as sadness, fear or disgust, why don't spectators or readers avoid them? Why and how would anybody want to see a theatrical tragedy or a horror movie or depictions of war?

The first to elaborate on the classical problem about the spectator's response to tragic art was Aristotle in his discussion on the tragedy. In the *Poetics*, he claims that the purpose of the tragedy is to give the spectator a specific sort of pleasure, "that which comes from pity and fear through imitation."[7] How can feeling pain be considered a pleasure? This is our point of departure, but the main concern will be the ambivalence of mixed feelings, that is to say how can we feel pain and pleasure at the same time. These issues have been much debated in art criticism, but are no less relevant in relation to cinema, this being either horror film, action film or the war movie. In the public debate, if not in film studies, such questions have been frequently asked and in contemporary cinema most concern has been given to the question of violence in fiction film. Representations of violence in the movies are always considered problematic, particularly when the depiction of violence is used as entertainment.[8] This being a question of much concern in the public, I will use this area as an empirical supplement to my overall theoretical approach. I will mostly use examples from film reviews to illuminate differing attitudes towards the depiction of violence in films, and the challenges raised by different emotional responses among reviewers, whom will serve as examples of different spectator responses.

During the 1990s, debate over the morality of violence in the movies reached a peak in the Norwegian public (as in other countries). This climate led Norwegian film critics to write extensively about the purpose and experience of violence in their newspaper reviews, in particular in regard to popular American cinema. These reviewers struggled with a critical public discourse on media violence and their own mixed feelings regarding depictions of explicit violence. The questions the reviewers repeatedly asked were: Do we need this? And do we need this much, or in such minute detail?[9] The answers to these questions formed the distinction between acceptable and problematic depictions of violence in the reviews. When regarded as necessary or important in relation to the movie's theme, the use of violence was considered acceptable. However, when violence was seen as being "just for fun," the movie tended to receive bad reviews.

From this perspective, a movie like Spielberg's *Saving Private Ryan* would be considered an important piece of filmmaking, requiring the use of violent scenes in order to allow moviegoers to fully understand the horror of the Second World War battle scenes at Omaha Beach. The graphic depiction of the allied invasion of Normandy was accepted and acclaimed for several reasons. Roger Ebert of the *Chicago Sun-Times* states two of the main arguments quite clearly in his review. First and foremost was the notion that this was what the war actually looked and felt like: "For the individual soldier on the beach, the landing was a chaos of noise, mud, blood, vomit and death." Secondly, the experience of the movie leaves the spectator with appropriate feelings and moral afterthoughts: "But weeping is an incomplete response, letting the audience off the hook. This film embodies ideas. After the immediate experience begins to fade, the implications remain and grow."[10]

The experience of the battle scenes in *Master and Commander* must be considered something quite different. Most likely you won't cry and many of the feelings provoked by the movie could be considered inappropriate if seen from the perspective of the public discourse on media violence. Like Captain Aubrey on the screen in front of you, you might find yourself going to war with a smile on your face.

The Attractions of Accuracy and the Excitement of Adventure

One of the attractions of a movie like *Master and Commander* is the historical setting and the accuracy of the details. Set during the Napoleonic War in 1805 the story introduces us to the British tall ship HMS *Surprise* with its 197 souls and 28 guns off of the northern coast of Brazil, and with orders from the admiral to "intercept the French Privateer *Acheron* en route to the Pacific and to Sink, Burn or take her a Prize."[11] HMS *Surprise* is Great Britain's representative at the far side of the world, or, as the Captain states: "This is England."

The movie is based on Patrick O'Brian's novels — and most directly on the novel *The Far Side of the World*— which have been acclaimed as "the best historical novels ever written."[12] The novels, twenty in all, starting with *Master and Commander* published in 1969, portray the British navy during the Napoleonic War, and in particular the relationship between Captain Jack Aubrey and Doctor Stephen Maturin. In the movie, Captain Aubrey, who is also known as Lucky Jack due to his seamanship and victories in earlier battles, faces a challenge greater than ever before. The French ship he is up against has twice the crew and twice the gun power as his HMS *Surprise*. With his own ship badly damaged and much of his crew injured, he puts his ship, his luck and his friendship with Maturin at risk when he changes his mind and chooses battle instead of escape. During most of the movie's two hours and ten minutes we follow the preparations for battle in combination with tactical considerations and moral discussions between the captain and his friend and confidant, Stephen Maturin (Paul Bettany). Maturin is a well-educated man who plays the cello and speaks several languages, but he is also an accomplished surgeon and scientist. When Aubrey wants to pursue the *Acheron*, Maturin sees this as an act of hubris, and he himself is much more eager to undertake scientific research on the Galapagos Islands than to risk battle yet again. It is therefore possible to argue that *Master and Commander* first and foremost is a "buddy movie," and a story about friendship between two men who represent different views of the world and different attitudes towards war?

Patrick O' Brian (1914–2000) was an acclaimed translator who also had written several other novels before his success with the Aubrey-Maturin series. O'Brian's strong position as a historical novelist is first and foremost related to his accuracy in historical details, whether regarding food, dialogue, navy routines, weapons, or the construction of ships.[13] Evidence of the importance of the historical setting for his readers can be found in numerous web pages dedicated to the discussion of his work.[14] Another example of this interest can be found in the existence of books such as *Patrick O'Brian's Navy: The Illustrated Companion to Jack Aubrey's World*, which contains a wealth of details about the navy, ships and weapons. This coffee table book contains details about every aspect of navy life, with the following as an illustrative example: "In a strict sense, it should be noted, a ship is a vessel with a bowsprit and three masts, each carrying a topmast and a topgallant mast, and yards on each of these masts."[15] It is also curious that this book at times has been narrated as if Jack Aubrey was an historical person, and as if his ships did in fact exist, which thereby adds to the feeling of historical truth.[16]

Like O'Brian and the authors who wrote about his works, the Australian director Peter Weir and his film producers were meticulous with historical details in the film's production.[17] As an article in *The Guardian* points out, absolutely nothing was left to chance, whether it was the accents spoken or the sound of the wind: "Peter Weir's maritime epic pays fanatical attention to acoustic detail. The wind racing through the rigging is in reality the wind racing through 1,000 feet of rope strapped to a lorry driving through the Mojave desert at 70 mph."[18] 20th Century-Fox bought *The Rose*, a reproduction tall ship built in 1970, and made several alterations to the ship in order to achieve the 1802 design of the HMS *Surprise*. The miniatures of both HMS *Surprise* and the *Acheron* were built by WETA workshops in New Zealand, the workshop made famous for its model work for *The Lord of the Rings* trilogy.[19] They made miles of original rope for the ships, and Paul Bettany studied the use of 18th century surgical instruments, and on and on and on.[20]

Of course, the reason behind these efforts is an attempt to create an aura of authenticity and historical truth. This is a potential tool for involving the spectator in the actions and the experience of being at war. What was it like to draw a sword against another man and what kind of injuries were you likely to face if stabbed yourself? What were the consequences if a ship were to be hit by a cannon ball? The historical setting is likely to tie the spectator closer to events and thereby create strong emotional reactions to the representations of violence on the screen. Historical accuracy creates an impression of "this is what it must have been like" and works against a distant viewing position where the spectator can comfort herself by thinking "it's only fiction." (And indeed there is no comfort, because it was even worse in real life). Works of fiction belongs to a different world where we — the spectators — play no part, and this can in some circumstances create a distant viewing position. The Danish film researcher Anne Jerslev has shown how adolescent viewers use this divide to create a distance between themselves and violent depictions. The movies are something different than reality, tellingly summarized in statements like: "It's only a movie!"[21]

And the movie *is* just fiction and even more so due to the fact that *Master and Commander* is an action adventure movie more than anything else (this said, as a hybrid genre film, it contains elements of the buddy movie, historical film *and* the war movie). As Brian Taves has pointed out, the adventure movie's style of storytelling is dependent on physical movement, violence and suspense, and is consequently linked to the action film genre. Another characteristic element is the apparently invulnerable hero overcoming obstacles and narrowly escaping catastrophes.[22] The moral framework is usually based on a Manichean moral where the hero serves as a moral agent and where the hero's violent actions seem both necessary and legitimate to vanquish villains.[23] The film also draws on the tradition of the swashbuckler movie, with its focus on brave and adventurous men fighting with swords in fine costumes.[24] Two scenes showing Captain Aubrey clinging to the mast while chasing the enemy at high speed create an overall feeling of being on an adventurous voyage in exotic corners of the world.

A minor change in the adaptation process adds to the fictionalization of the story.[25] While the book *The Far Side of the World* is set during the American-British War of 1812, both the time and setting have been changed in the movie. In the novel, Captain Aubrey sails around Cape Horn and into the Pacific Ocean to defend British whalers against an American frigate, the USS *Norfolk*. By changing the setting to the Napoleonic War in 1805 and the enemy to France, the filmmakers create, if not an ocean, at least some distance between the story and the American audience. This approach also kept moviegoers' associations with the ongoing war in Iraq at a safe distance (the movie was screened in theaters during the winter of 2003), as well as the traumas of the Second World war or the Vietnam War.

Because it is both fictional and true, *Master and Commander* can at the same time be educational and entertaining, and the spectators can expect different emotional experiences during their cinematic journey.

War: The Lesser of Two Evils

Being on board the HMS *Surprise* through storms, battles and surgery takes the spectators on a trip through a range of emotions from suspense to physical pains, but not necessarily in the way one might think. The fact is that the battles scenes are not the most dangerous or painful incidences during the voyage; instead, that role belongs to the battle against nature and the illnesses afflicting several crew members. In fact, far more sailors lost their lives during the Napoleonic War from illness than from war wounds. According to statistics listing fatal casualties in the British Royal Navy during in the period 1793–1815, only 6.3 percent of the seamen died due to enemy action. Of the 103,000 navy deaths in the period, more than 84,000 died as a result of diseases or personal accidents, and 12 percent died of catastrophes such as shipwrecks or fire.[26] As the writers of *Patrick O'Brian's Navy* comment, "death in battle was almost the last of a sailor's worries."[27] And the risk of going down with the ship was mostly related to bad weather or navigational error, and rarely would a wooden ship sink in battle.

In *Master and Commander* these dangers come through to the spectators, particularly in the most dramatic scene where the men's lives are at risk from a storm. When chasing the *Anchoron* around Cape Horn, the HMS *Surprise* encounters a terrible storm and the sea threatens to wash the crew overboard and even to drag the ship down into the dark water. The sound of the sea and the cries of the men come together as sounds of mourning from the deep, serving as a warning of the danger of disappearing into the roaring ocean. As Maturin points out in some sort of a meta-comment in the movie, "The deaths in battle are the easiest to bear, for my own part those who die under my knife, or from some subsequent infection [are most difficult]." The two most painful scenes to watch are the scene where the thirteen-year-old Lord Blakeney has to have his arm amputated after getting splints from the damaged mast in his arm during the attack, and the one where Maturin performs surgery on himself after a shooting accident. Although the amputation scene is quite short and not particularly explicit, focusing more on the child's feverish face than his arm and the doctor's actions, it is a tough scene to watch. According to the students in my film class, this is the most difficult scene to endure, and even so for professional doctors, as this comment in a newsletter for anesthesiologists illustrates: "Even though I knew it was only a movie, I really felt uncomfortable during the amputation scene. I wondered if the nonanesthesiologists in the theater had any concept of what an arm amputation without anesthesia would be like. Then the realization struck me — this was real life before the 1840s and Crawford W. Long, Horace Wells and William T.G. Morton. I left the theater with a renewed appreciation of what anesthesia is and what a gift the relief from surgical pain is for humankind."[28]

My reason for dwelling on these details is to foreground the fact that the two operation scenes are by far the most painful for the spectator to watch. Aside from the events themselves — operations performed without any relief from pain — the reason for this discomfort is connected to the length of the scenes and the fact that the victims are personalized. But the movie also depicts surgery as entertainment for sailors of the day. In one scene, half of the crew is gathered around to watch the doctor perform an open skull surgery on a sailor, in which the doctor replaces a bullet in the man's head with a coin. From this perspective, the movie itself foregrounds the ambiguity of people watching others experience bodily pain; the surgery attracts a crowd that watches with ambivalent reactions.

As the saying in the movie goes, you have to choose between evils, and in this movie, war is not the worst thing that can happen to you.[29] After losing his arm, little Lord Blakeney is disappointed when his young friend Mr. Calamy is made acting third lieutenant and placed on the front line during the boarding of the enemy ship, while he has to stay behind on the quarterdeck. As reviewer Peter Bradshaw describes in his assessment of the meaning of this scene, the movie plays on the image of war as an exciting experience: "And the same lad gets the Boy's own fantasy of commanding the ship for some euphoric minutes."[30] That is not to say that this is a war without casualties or without pain, but compared to other battles on board, war is the lesser of two evils.

There are several reasons why the movie is able to create an expectant atmosphere before the final battle, the two most important being the structure of the movie and the other the role of the captain. First, as already described, the movie does not contain many actual war scenes. As film genre theoretician Steve Neale has pointed out, the battle scene is a requisite ingredient in the war film genre.[31] With only two battle scenes, one might even argue that *Master and Commander* does not belong to the genre at all. But I will argue that the two scenes are the most important in the movie's dramatic structure, a fact that makes for another main genre characteristic of the war movie. After the opening battle scene, one hour and forty minutes have elapsed before we face actual battle again. During this time HMS *Surprise* has escaped the enemy twice (once into the fog and once into the darkness of night) and they have been obstructed in their own pursuit of the enemy because of the storm, a shooting accident, and finally by being becalmed in dead water. By this time, both the men and the spectators are in a somewhat combative mood. As reviewer Philip French in *The Guardian* puts it: "Until finally there's another magnificently staged battle."[32] We are led to believe that this is going to be a positive experience, not the least because we are tired of waiting, or as the reviewer Peter Bradshaw puts it: "It may sag a bit in the middle."[33] The Captain does his share of preparing us for battle. After the long wait, he proclaims: "I know you are as anxious as I am to get into close action." And the captain keeps smiling. If we are worried his smile will chase the worries away.

Mixed Emotions

How can it be that my emotional response towards the battle scenes in *Master and Commander* is as much excitement and admiration as pity or fear? First of all, it is by no means fair to state that the war scenes are totally without the sense of the horror of war; they are in fact overwhelming, brutal, and chaotic — but at the same time beautiful and exciting. In this movie, as in many spectacular war movies such as *The Lord of the Rings* trilogy (2001–2003), *King Arthur* (2004), or *Kingdom of Heaven* (2004), the spectator experiences different feelings while watching battle scenes. These kinds of battle scenes create what correctly could be termed "mixed aesthetic emotions" (Freeland 2003).

This topic is related to some of the most central philosophical questions concerning the relationship between art and emotions, such as the "paradox of fiction" (how can we be moved by something that we know is fictional?) and "the paradox of tragedy" (why do we want to feel negative emotions?). Aesthetical theory has offered a range of explanations for the answers to these questions and drawing on Levinson and Freeland's categorizations of the explanations, I will summarize the current thinking on the subject.

American philosopher Cynthia Freeland distinguishes between two traditional categories of explanations for this paradox, either a "no-pain" or a "pain-pleasure" solution.[34] The first category, the "no-pain solution" is a combination of different views. Some will argue the depictions of painful events neither intend to nor do evoke painful emotions in audiences; although events are painful, the spectator feels something else.[35] Others might argue that despite appearances, viewers do not experience real emotions in response to fiction; these emotions are merely simulations or make-believe emotions.[36] Both positions share the view that the pain shown on the screen is *not* shared by the audience.

The "pain-pleasure" category also consists of different views, but these explanations take into consideration the fact that the artworks in question do actually raise real feelings of both pain and pleasure in an audience. The reasons why we endure these experiences are that the pain caused by the movie or book is in fact being outweighed by the pleasure (two arguments are that either the pain is changed into pleasure, or the overall experience is a mixture of pain and pleasure).[37]

Finally, Freeland proposes a third category she terms "pleasure as Metaemotion." This explanation is particularly provocative in relation to watching violent representations in the movies in general and useful in relation to the battle scenes in *Master and Commander*. Pleasure as a meta-emotion solution acknowledges that we do indeed feel both pleasure and pain. However, the pleasure is distinct from the pain, and can be felt as something different. The pleasure can be caused by something other than the elements causing the pain, and Freeland suggests that aesthetic elements, such as the plot, the construction, special effects or the acting, can fill this role. While the events in the diegesis can create painful emotions, the construction of the artwork can create joy or admiration. A good example is the scene where the doctor Maturin has to perform critical surgery on himself after a shooting accident. While we are likely to feel both admiration and pity for Maturin, we can at the same time enjoy the nuanced performance from Russell Crowe as he portrays a strong man trying to hide his feelings of distress while witnessing the operation.

Freeland's concept can be combined with a useful distinction put forward by Dutch film researcher Ed Tan.[38] In his theory on the psychology of film and emotion, Tan proposes that the spectator does in fact experience genuine emotions and that these emotions can be separated into two categories. Tan distinguishes between what he calls "Fiction emotions" (or F-emotions) and "Artefact emotions" (or A-emotions).[39] Fiction emotions are responses to the action and the characters within the film's diegesis and these feelings consist largely of witness feelings. The spectator's emotions correspond with effects in daily life, such as empathic emotions towards a child losing his arm or towards the suicide of a troubled officer on board, with the distinction that we cannot act upon the emotions; we are merely onlookers or witnesses. Artefact emotions, which are *aesthetically* motivated emotions on the other hand, are emotions in the viewer evoked by the film "as manmade artefact" or as "an admiration of the film as a film."[40] These emotions are caused by the cinematography, sound editing, and music, exemplified by the image of beautiful ships or the authenticity of the imitation of the sounds of a ship in a storm. The first category accordingly consists of emotions like hope, fear, anxiety, pity, relief, admiration, and terror in relation to the fictional world. The second category can include enjoyment, admiration and astonishment related to the fiction as fiction.[41]

For some movies, the first category of emotions is dominant, and Tan follows the common assertion that the traditional feature film (typically, classical Hollywood cinema) places the spectator in a position where she is primarily interested in fictional events and less concerned with the artefact characteristics.[42] I will argue that the artefact emotions are far more important than Tan suggests, and will illustrate this in relation to the final battle in *Master and Commander.* Although I will foreground the role of artefact emotions more than Tan does, I believe his distinctions are useful in relation to the discussion of battle scenes in war movies. This theoretical framework enables us to distinguish between emotions towards "the events in the fictional world" and the "enjoyment and admiration for the film as film."[43] The first can cause pain and the other pleasure, but the different feelings can be felt at the same time.

Between the Horror and Beauty of War

The experience of watching the movie can be evoked using one of the scenes in the movie itself. The second time the *Acheron* catches up with the *Surprise,* Aubrey sets up a trap to enable his ship's escape. He has the crew build a raft with masts and lanterns, and when night falls, young Mister Calamy is lowered to the raft and set out onto the open sea to light the raft's lanterns while at the same time all the ship's lights are extinguished. The constant firing from the enemy ship on the raft's lights makes Calamy's task an extremely dangerous one, and the young man's life is at risk the whole time. As the raft floats away and the enemy takes the bait, the crew is able to pull the thirteen-year-old officer aboard the ship again. The captain greets him with a joyful and excited cry: "Now, tell me that wasn't fun!"

Before the final battle Aubrey disguises his ship as a whaler to gain the advantage of surprise and as the French are ready to board they find themselves attacked by the *Surprise*'s guns instead. This scene is the movie's most important battle scene, the movie's climax and a scene that make an impressive impression. Peter Bradshaw describes it in this way: "Weir constructs a thrilling, forthright adventure, and the realer-than-real battle effects are simply breathtaking."[44]

Several elements work together to create this breathtaking experience along with what I have described as a combination of pain and pleasure. These elements can be identified partly as witness-emotions, but to a great degree they can also be identified as emotions towards the movie as art. Following Tan's model, I will assert that it is the so-called "fiction-emotions" which create the spectators' painful experiences. The fictional events evoke both fear and pity for the characters, particularly the child-soldiers. While we never fear for Jack Aubrey throughout the entire voyage we are painfully aware of Calamy and Blakeney's fragility as teenaged soldiers.

The most painful scene takes place after the battle when the dead men are prepared for their funeral. Little Lord Blakeney offers to stitch up the bag containing his young dead friend Calamy but because he has lost his arm he needs a helping hand. The captain reads the names of all the dead before they are all buried in the deep. Several members of the crew die during the battle, among them three of the men that we have come to know. Allen was the first to fall during the boarding as he was struck by a bullet to the forehead and Nagel is shot at close range. But the actual death of Calamy is not shown on screen, and overall there is actually little visual depiction of wounds or deaths.

The battle scene is less than ten minutes long, counting from the first gunshot until everything is over (whereas the opening battle scene in *Saving Private Ryan* lasts approximately thirty minutes). The first part focuses on the firing of the guns, but it keeps everything at a distance and focuses on the damage to the ship. While soldiers move to close action as they board the enemy ship, the filmmakers continue to keep their distance, showing more fire and smoke than blood. Although the sword battles are fought face-to-face with swords and axes, the war is not depicted as a war between men, but as a war between nations. The enemy is faceless; in fact the enemy is a ship. No man on the other side is identified by name or appearance and the captain on *Acheron* makes only a very short appearance at the end of the movie (and even then under cover, disguised as a doctor).

The fast movement of the camera and the rapid changes between scenes leave little room for brutal details. There is no time to dwell on wounded men crying or dying and we see no details of bodies shattered by cannonballs or slashed by sword cuts. The impression of the battle is a collective chaos, more than individuals facing death, through more focus on shouting and confusion than on wounds and pain.

Compared to other war movies, *Master and Commander* is beautiful, mainly because of the maritime setting. The exterior shots during the fight resemble the beauty of Joseph M.W. Turner's classical paintings. The great British romantic painter is most famous for his pictures of landscapes and marine themes. Turner is known as "the painter of light" and his paintings, like the famous *The Battle of Trafalgar, as Seen from the Mizzen Starboard Shrouds of the Victory* and *Snow Storm — Steam-Boat off a Harbour's Mouth* seem to have influenced the cinematography in several of the scenes.[45]

My description of the battle scenes in *Master and Commander* might suggest that the filmmakers in this circumstance have been trapped into an ethical misjudgment, celebrating the war. I will argue otherwise, because the spectators experience an entirely different set of emotions when watching movies like this. Even during the final battle, the spectator can find herself admiring the cinematography or the choreography of the battle scenes, or, to use Tan's terminology, they can have positive emotions towards the "film as film." Time and time again, the pleasures created by great movie-making are felt alongside the pains created by the fictional events. Admiration for the craftsmanship of the director or the actors (above all Russell Crowe) is an important part of experiencing a fiction film. In my opinion, this doesn't count as an inappropriate response towards fictional violence. This pleasure functions as a meta-emotion, where the pleasure is distinct from the pain.

Confronted with a beautiful depiction of unpleasant events, the spectator may experience ambivalence; how can she admire such a movie? To under-

Ships at sea in Peter Weir's war drama *Master and Commander: The Far Side of the World* from 2003 (Twentieth Century–Fox), whose aesthetics were inspired by Joseph M.W. Turner's paintings.

Painting by Joseph M.W. Turner, *Peace — Burial at the Sea* from 1842 (image ©Tate, London 2008).

stand ambivalent or complex emotional responses, such as the pain-pleasure mixture, our theoretical approach needs to take into consideration the important role of fictional representation. When admiring a battle scene, we are not admiring the battle but the representation of the battle. The spectator can keep a certain distance where she reflects on the staging and editing of the battle, at the same time she can feel the revulsion of children being killed by war. Spectators' reaction towards the visual or spectacular elements doesn't have to create an emotional distance, because the spectator is capable of having two emotions in her head at once.

Again, the ambiguity depicted in the movie itself can function as a reflection of this duplicity. Although the HMS *Surprise* barely survives a dangerous voyage, the story ends with the sound of Aubrey and Maturin playing Boccherini's duet "La Musica Notturna Delle Strade Di Madrid No. 6, Op. 30" on violin and cello. The two of them are celebrating the victory when they discover that the French captain has fooled them by disguising himself as a doctor. Fearing a new battle onboard the French ship which is now on its way to imprison the French hostages under Mr. Pulling's command, Captain Aubrey once again sets sail towards the enemy ship. As the crew prepares for battle once again, he and his friend return to the music. The sound of the drums of battle is drowned out by the light strains of the music — but the drums are still there.

Notes

1. Manohla Dargis, "A Ghastly Conflagration, a Tormented Aftermath," *New York Times*, October 6, 2006, accessed from http://movies2.nytimes.com/2006/10/20/movies/20flag.html?8mu&emc=mu on November 20, 2006.
2. From here on I will use *Master and Commander* as the title of the movie.
3. Alex Neill, "Tragedy," in *The Routledge Companion to Aesthetics*, ed. Berys Gaut and Dominic McIver Lopes (London and New York: Routledge, 2002), 363. This was Nietzsche's position in *The Birth of Tragedy*.
4. For a general discussion of fiction and emotions see Alex Neill's introduction "Fiction and emotions," Alex Neill and Aaron Ridley, *Arguing About Art* (London and New York: Routledge, 2003).
5. Jerrold Levinson, "Emotion in Response to Art: A Survey of the Terrain," in *Emotion and the Arts*, ed. Mette Hjort and Sue Laver (London: Oxford University Press, 2001), 20–37. Because these are theories on art, there are several challenges involved when applying them to popular cinema. I will not take these issue into consideration here.
6. Levinson, "Emotion in Response to Art," 20–21.
7. Aristotle, *The Poetics of Aristotle*, trans. S. Halliwell, 1453b.10 (Chapel Hill: University of North Carolina Press, 1987).
8. See for instance Martin Barker and Petley Julian, *Ill Effects* (London and New York: Routledge, 1997).
9. In my doctoral dissertation I have conducted a survey of Norwegian reviewers' reception of American movies containing explicit violence from 1990–1999 (among the movies discussed are *Fight Club*, *Pulp Fiction*, and *Natural Born Killers*). Anne Gjelsvik, *Fiksjonsvoldens etiske betydninger* [*The significations of fictional violence*], Dr.Art thesis at Norwegian University of Science and Technology, Trondheim, 2004. Edited and published in bookform as *Vondt og vakker. Vold i audiovisuelle medier.* [*Bad and Beautiful. Violence in Audio Visual Media*], Kristiansand: Høyskoleforlaget 2007.
10. Roger Ebert, "Saving Private Ryan," July 24, 1998, accessed from http://rogerebert.suntimes.com/apps/pbcs.dll/article?AID=/19980724/REVIEWS/807240304/1023 on October 19, 2006.
11. Quoted from the film's opening text. A Privateer was a private ship with an authorization from the government to hunt down ships from other nations and take their cargo. Patrick O'Brian, *The Far Side of the World* (London: Harper Collins Publishers, 1997).
12. Review by Robert Snow in *The New York Times*, January 6, 1991. The quote from the review is accessed from O'Brian's publisher W.W. Norton's home page accessed from http://www2.wwnorton.com/pob/bio.htm on June 10, 2008.

13. His popularity is due to other factors as well. Fans refer to the friendship between men, his way with dialogue, etc.
14. See for instance http://206.26.213.70/forums/POB/POBforum.htm or http://www.hmssurprise.org/.
15. Richard O'Neill, *Patrick O'Brian's Navy: The Illustrated Companion to Jack Aubrey's World* (Philadelphia: Salamander Press, 2003), 50.
16. The following is an example of this approach: "The *Surprise* was built at Le Havre and completed in 1794 with a displacement of 579 tons and a gun deck length of 126 ft, and she carried an armament of 32 32-pounder carronades and two long 6-pounder guns." O'Neill, *O'Brian's Navy*, 50.
17. After a career as an important art house director in Australian national cinema during the 1970s and 1980s with movies like *The Last Wave* (1977) and *Picnic at Hanging Rock* (1975), Weir continued to work in Hollywood making several acclaimed movies in different genres. Among these are *Witness* (1985), *Dead Poets Society* (1989), *Fearless* (1993), and *The Truman Show* (1998). For a short introduction to his work see for instance Romy Schumacher. "Commanding Waves: The Films of Peter Weir," *Senses of Cinema*, January 2004, accessed from http://www.sensesofcinema.com/contents/directors/05/weir.html on October 11, 2006.
18. Erlend Clouston, "Read My Lip Flaps," *Guardian,* Wednesday, December 10, 2003, accessed from http://film.guardian.co.uk/features/featurepages/0,,1103937,00.html on October 16, 2006.
19. The third movie in *The Lord of the Rings* trilogy, *The Return of the King,* spoiled a potentially great night for *Master and Commander* at the Academy Awards (The Oscars). *Master and Commander* was nominated for ten Oscars, among them best picture, best director, best art direction and best visual effects. *The Lord of the Rings* (*The Return of the King*) won every award it was nominated for and *Master and Commander* won only for best cinematography and sound effects, categories in which the *Lord of the Rings* trilogy was not nominated.
20. http://www.imdb.com/title/tt0311113/trivia.
21. Anne Jerslev, *Det er bare film* (Copenhagen: Gyldendal, 1999).
22. Brian Taves, *The Romance of Adventure: The Genre of Historical Adventure Movies* (Jackson: University Press of Mississippi, 1993), 4–5.
23. Thomas Leitch, "Aristotle v. the action film," in *New Hollywood Violence*, ed. Steven Jay Schneider (Manchester & New York, Manchester University Press, 2004), 103–125.
24. Steve Neale, *Genre and Hollywood* (London & New York: Routledge, 2000).
25. Since the series as a whole is set during the Napoleonic War this change can be considered minor.
26. O'Neill, *O'Brian's Navy*, 92.
27. Ibid., 117.
28. Orin F. Guidry, "A lesson from the movies," Newsletter April 2004, *The American Society of Anesthesiologists*, vol. 68, accessed from http://www.asahq.org/Newsletters/2004/04_04/admin04_04.html on June 10, 2008.
29. Or as the joke in the movie goes: "The lesser of two weevils."
30. Peter Bradshaw, "Master and Commander: At the Far Side of the World," *Guardian,* November 21, 2003, accessed from http://film.guardian.co.uk/News_Story/Critic_Review/Guardian_review/0,,1089474,00.html on November 16, 2006.
31. Neale, *Genre*, 125.
32. Philip French, "Command Performance," *Guardian,* November 23, 2003, accessed from http://film.guardian.co.uk/News_Story/Critic_Review/Observer_Film_of_the_week/0,,1091222,00.html on November 16, 2006.
33. Bradshaw, "Master and Commander."
34. Cynthia Freeland, "Negative Aesthetics," paper presented at the conference "Ethics

and Negative Aesthetics," Norwegian University of Science and Technology, Trondheim, October 21—24, 2003. Freeland refers to Malcolm Budd's *Values of Art* for this distinction.

35. Freeland, "Negative Aesthetics."

36. Levinson, "Emotion in Response to Art," 29–30; Freeland "Negative Aesthetics." The term make-believe emotions draws on Kendall Walton's theory of fiction and imagination. It should be noted, however, that Walton considers emotions in relation to fiction-as-emotions, but these "quasi-emotions" are of a specific kind and differ from real-life-emotions. For differentiations between theorists see Levinson, "Emotion in Response to Art," 29–30.

37. The most important work in this line of argument is David Hume's "Of Tragedy," where he distinguishes between emotions caused by the manner of representation and of what is represented. Malcolm Budd, *Values of Art: Pictures, Poetry and Music* (Allen Lane Penguin Press: Middlesex, 1995), 112–113.

38. This distinction is also used in his work with Nico Friidja.

39. Ed Tan, *Emotion and the Structure of Narrative Film: Film as an Emotion Machine* (Mahwah: Lawrence Erlbaum, 1996), 81–83; Ed Tan and Nico Friidja, "Sentiment in Film Viewing" in *Passionate Views*, ed. Carl Plantinga and Greg Smith Baltimore (Baltimore: John Hopkins University Press, 1999), 51-2.

40. Tan and Friidja, "Sentiment," 52.

41. Tan, *Emotion and Structure*, 82.

42. Ibid., 81.

43. Tan and Friidja, "Sentiment," 52.

44. Bradshaw, "Master and Commander."

45. Compare, for instance, *Master and Commander* to Joseph M.W. Turner's *Burial at Sea* (1842) or *Battle at Trafalgar* (1822).

8

Comic Situations/Endless War
M*A*S*H and War as Entertainment
YVONNE TASKER

In a post-network era viewers in the west experience war as a spectacle of inconsequential imagery, as Nicholas Mirzoeff writes: "There is no longer anything spectacular about this updated society of the spectacle."¹ Here I explore war as entertainment in a rather different moment and manner, that of 1970s American network television and the ongoing success of the Korean War–set situation/service comedy, M*A*S*H (CBS, 1972–1983).² Why return to M*A*S*H now? After all, while it remains alive in syndication the final (feature length) episode was first aired more than 25 years ago.³ In its day M*A*S*H was not only one of the most commercially successful network series, but was widely regarded as a benchmark of quality liberal programming. In his 1989 study of television sitcom, David Marc characterized M*A*S*H as one of three 1970s shows that constituted "the sitcom at literate peak during the last days of three-network hegemony."⁴ At around the same time, however, critics began to question the series' anti-war credentials, drawing attention to its individualist, masculinist aura and (somewhat less often) its casual racism.⁵ My interest in the series — and I am not primarily concerned here with the Altman film that generated it — has to do with its innovative evocation of war, an experience associated more often with melodrama or tragedy, through the conventions of situation comedy. The central comic irony of the series is that of heroic white American men (and to a lesser extent women) whose agency is bounded by perverse historical circumstances; war is presented as a sort of limbo in which the characters battle the combined forces of boredom and military mundanity, a tedium punctuated by intense bouts of activity when the numbers of wounded suddenly increase. Thus, sitcom's defining return to the same, the restitution of the comedy generating situation on which the form is premised, is here the continuation of war, the arrival of wounded and the peace talks that produce only talk. In this context it is in part the very *longevity* of *M*A*S*H* that interests me; the series ran for longer than the UN police action which it ostensibly depicts, and outlasted the U.S. involvement in Vietnam, which provided a more immediate military and ideological context for its initial audience. In the current war on terror, one which lacks clear temporal or spatial definition, the ways in which *M*A*S*H* enacted a process of living with war, and with moral outrage, via television are perhaps instructive.

War as Comic Situation

The comic potential of the military had been mined before *M*A*S*H* in shows such as *The Phil Silvers Show* (CBS, 1955–1959) or *McHale's Navy* (ABC, 1962–1966). Built around the central character of scheming Master Sergeant Ernest Bilko, and based, far from the distractions of the city at Fort Baxter, Kansas, *The Phil Silvers Show* sent up peacetime army life (and the character of large institutions more generally). Bilko is a career soldier and con artist, a gambler perpetually in search of funds; constantly setting up elaborate schemes that almost (but never quite) come off, Bilko is an unofficial authority figure, an NCO who is comically opposed to, but more evidently in charge than, the post's commanding officer. The military represents a system to be played for Bilko, who charms and deceives to provide himself with a life of leisure and comfort. The comic situation, which sets the scene for Silvers' performance, is essentially one of role reversal; it is Bilko who runs Fort Baxter, rather than the ostensible commander, Colonel Hall. In their celebration of the series, David Thompson and Ian Irvine characterize the relationship between Sergeant and Colonel (as exemplified in the second episode, "Empty Store," September 27, 1955) in precisely these terms: "the colonel looks on in amazement at the rewards of wheeler-dealing versus his own blameless and hard-working career."[6] And yet the wheeler-dealing never quite achieves for Bilko what he desires, maintaining the precarious relationship of mutual dependence between the two and the continuance of the underlying comic situation.

In *M*A*S*H*, by contrast, it is the military machine/bureaucracy in wartime mode that provides the recurring situation for comedy. Although there were other wartime comedies, *M*A*S*H*'s humor was distinctive in its bleakness, each episode's comedy typically interleaved with more serious/dramatic themes and storylines. Indeed it was the weaving together of distinct narrative elements, each quite different in tone that was the series team's central formal innovation. In Carl Freedman's words, *M*A*S*H* was "a landmark as the first weekly show successfully to mix comic with serious drama." He describes the series format in more detail thus: "Most episodes contain three (or sometimes two) story lines, and of these one tends to be tragic or (more often) pathetic; one tends to be farcical; and the third is a wild card, usually humorous with some serious leavening."⁷ *M*A*S*H* employs a familiar work-family format, centering on the work of doctors and nurses in an army surgical hospital in Korea. The drama concerns the impact of war on those who enact it: soldiers, mostly U.S. though occasionally Korean or other UN nationalities, injured in combat; individuals (especially, indeed primarily the core group) separated from loved ones and familiar surroundings; and sometimes (though far less often) the civilians whose lives are disrupted by the war. The doctors exercise their morbid humor amidst the vivid blood stains of the operating theatre, while both doctors and nurses find themselves involved in the physical and emotional suffering of their patients. The evidence of blood and death, though relatively unremarkable by comparison with the visceral display of contemporary crime and medical dramas, was a controversial aspect of the show, a marker of *M*A*S*H*'s riskiness in network terms. If bodies and blood assert the presence of death in war, the series' humor stemmed primarily from wordplay (slapstick and physical comedy certainly featured in *M*A*S*H* however, particularly in the early years).⁸ War as setting and a wry commentary on its material consequences thus coexist in the operating theatre that, together with the "Swamp" and the mess tent, forms one of *M*A*S*H*'s basic sets.

While war itself is not played for laughs in *M*A*S*H*, the absurdity of the military at war is frequently a source of comedy. The unit, and most particularly Captain "Hawkeye" Pierce's (Alan Alda) ironic, occasionally angry, response to death and corruption fuels an anti-authority feeling to the series, even as the moral authority of the medics remains (more or less) sacrosanct. American film scholar William Paul situates the Altman film *M*A*S*H* (1970), on which the show was based, as a key precursor of the 1980s films he groups under the label "Animal Comedy." For Paul, a defining characteristic of this group of films is: "An us versus them mentality" that provides "the only real forward dynamic in the loose plot structure." Within these terms, he notes "[T]he central group generally defines itself by values inimical to its opponents, who are often the ruling power structure."⁹ This dynamic is also in evidence within the series *M*A*S*H*, with the good doctors/soldiers opposed to corrupt, inept or militaristic figures who stand in for the "problem" of the war and the military as an institution. As the run continued, *M*A*S*H*'s comedy became less evidently "animal" in character. Instead a bitter resignation and introspection sets in with, as various critics have noted, a turn to themes of personal crisis. Thus Mike Budd and Clay Steinman write of the changing character of *M*A*S*H*, that "[P]lot resolutions center increasingly on characters helping one another and getting in touch with their feelings," a move they regard as firmly in line with the program's desire for "quality audiences."[10] As well-intentioned men and women play their part in the perpetuation of war, the comic situation continues and the long-term effects of that situation become an explicit narrative concern.

M*A*S*H certainly foregrounds some of the brutal consequences of war, yet the wounded (like Korea itself) more often serve as an ongoing background to the unit's work, their stories only occasionally emerging in poignant, tragic or comic fashion. More typically, the absurdity of war is signaled by the smaller absurdities of army life, generating storylines in which the characters must deal with the black market or make elaborate trades with other units to acquire basic provisions. "For the Want of a Boot" (January 12, 1974) follows Hawkeye's elaborate schemes to secure new boots by bartering through unofficial channels. The complex chain of favors he constructs, each dependent on the other, ultimately falls apart in generic fashion. Amidst howling winds the episode begins with Radar taking delivery of 5,000 diapers and 5,000 pairs of rubber pants, an ironic counterpoint to Hawkeye's quest for functioning boots; it ends with a defeated Hawkeye wearing a golf club case on one leg, a perverse image of middle class masculine leisure turned into an absurd utility. Similarly, "The Light That Failed" (October 25, 1977) has the *M*A*S*H* unit struggling with freezing winter weather; running out of basic general and medical supplies (light bulbs, bandages), they receive a shipment of salt tablets and an ice cream churn. This comical error is one that the driver can only shrug off and put down to the army way (the episode's coda sees the correct supplies delivered however, suggesting a partial restoration of order). What can be had rapidly by bribery, theft, or corruption is not readily available by honest means, as the show repeatedly reminds us. As in *The Phil Silvers Show*, honesty and rationality are not compatible with advancement in the military bureaucracy; we see numerous instances of senior officers enjoying privilege (luxury food items, expensive liquor, the best movies) denied to the ordinary soldiers. A good company clerk knows how to play the system as Corporal Klinger demonstrates in "Cementing Relationships" (December 1, 1980) when he persuades the army to supply the unit with cement by claiming that they need to build a barbeque for a visiting dignitary.

In *M*A*S*H* authority clearly lies with the army, the institution which enforces the presence of the doctors in Korea; however much they may rail against military authority, they can only leave when permitted to do so. Such restriction is at odds with the free-wheeling masculinity associated with the doctor heroes in the early years of the series. Through costume, behavior and language Pierce, McIntyre (Wayne Rogers) and later BJ (Mike Farrell) reject and resist military life, even as they continue to work on the bodies of soldiers damaged in the fighting, thus contributing to the work of war. This is of course the chief irony structuring both film and television series: the pursuit of healing against the background of war. The brilliance of the rebellious surgeons, Pierce in particular, accords them a certain license (albeit within limits). This tension between medics and war/death bubbles to the surface on numerous occasions, for instance when the comically masculine military figure of Colonel Flagg (Edward Winter) orders Pierce and McIntyre to perform a life-saving operation on a Korean prisoner so that he can be taken to Seoul for execution ("Officer of the Day," September 24, 1974). The pair outwits Flagg by substituting the North Korean with the cross-dressing Klinger, who has been frustrated in his attempts to secure a pass to Seoul throughout the episode. A small victory is secured at Flagg's expense, yet the ultimate fate of the North Korean remains unresolved (and presumably insignificant). Such scenarios point to a carnivalesque logic of inversion by which the doctors subvert the authority of those that keeps them in place.[11]

Symptomatically, Hawkeye rails against his "helpless" situation and drives for miles, evading witless security checks, to intervene in the stalled peace talks ("Peace On Us," September 25, 1978). His manic efforts to get the negotiators to communicate underline the futility of his actions, although they raise the spirits of the unit and secure the unofficial admiration of a General afflicted with gastritis. Such small victories, which change nothing, allow a feeling of triumph, a perverse feel good factor expressed in carnivalesque activities (the party that ends "Peace On Us" sees the unit's uniforms and hair dyed red in a symbolic, if temporary, rejection of the military uniform so evocatively termed "olive drab.") Similarly perverse, "Depressing News" (February 9, 1981) has Pierce build a memorial to the dead and wounded from a shipment of tongue depressors, blowing it up in front of a mystified army reporter who has come to document the achievement.

The blinkered perspective and careerist goals of militaristic characters are repeatedly exposed/satirized from the pilot episode in which Margaret Houlihan fumes over Pierce and McIntyre's irreverence: "These two, they're ruining this war — for all of us!" Houlihan's perverse pleasure in the war as career opportunity is echoed by numerous generals indifferent to causalities or officials who insist on protocols even when they are clearly irrational. Under fire from both Chinese and U.S. forces in "C*A*V*E" (February 5, 1979), the unit must evacuate wounded to a nearby cave since Potter, having failed to locate the up to date codes needed to "prove" their identity, cannot convince his own "side" to redirect fire. Just as perverse, when Pierce is wrongly listed as dead in "The Late Captain Pierce" (October 3, 1975) he is unable to receive pay or reach his father to reassure him. Occasionally, the doctor heroes make a more direct intervention. A season one episode, "The Ringbanger" (January 21, 1973), has Hawkeye and McIntyre conspire to delay the return to action of a Colonel with a high casualty rate ("some real estate doesn't come cheap," their target blithely observes). Pierce repeats the intervention solo in season seven, when he drugs another colonel indifferent to casualties amongst his men; having simulated the effects of appendicitis he performs an unnecessary operation to keep the Colonel off the line ("Preventive Medicine," February 19, 1979). Hawkeye's action serves as a small, temporary respite although casualties keep coming in waves. As such action suggests, military leaders are stubborn, ineffective and, crucially, ageing.

Those characters who align themselves with either the military or anti-communism are two-dimensional buffoons: Frank Burns (Larry Linville), Margaret Houlihan (Loretta Swit) and the occasional character of Colonel Flagg all serve in this capacity. "Rally Round the Flagg, Boys" (February 14, 1979) has Hawkeye treat an injured North Korean ahead of an American soldier, thus emphasizing his identity as a compassionate physician over his role as army surgeon. Both the pompous Winchester and the U.S. soldier's buddy are enraged at Hawkeye's actions. The comic figure of Colonel Flagg, who has long suspected Hawkeye to be a communist sympathizer/homosexual, rebukes the show's protagonist: "you took a yellow red before a white American which is pretty pinko." Such satire at the expense of the anti-communism of the cold war period runs through the show; in "A Smattering of Intelligence" (March 2, 1974) two competing, though equally inept, intelligence agencies spy on each other and the M*A*S*H unit. Pierce and McIntyre turn the potentially nightmarish scenario into a practical joke, casting suspicion on arch-patriot Frank Burns, leading Flagg to believe that Burns is a communist and another agent to believe that he is a fascist before revealing the joke at the expense of all three. Such a scenario is quite typical of both the show's political humor and the parameters of sit-com, involving an anarchic mockery of authority framed by a broad acceptance of the impossibility of overturning the surreal situation of war.

The show's sole female protagonist, Major Margaret "Hot Lips" Houlihan, is, as I discuss in more detail below, a figure of fun. Importantly, the definition of Houlihan as a *military* woman renders her comic since the anarchic humor and carnivalesque qualities of the *M*A*S*H* world is achieved very much at the expense of military (or indeed any) authority.[12] The only regular male character who is defined as career military — Col. Sherman Potter, a World War I veteran who joined the cast in season four — shares the general feelings of disillusion with the ongoing war. Though he may be career army, the aging Potter redeems himself by his intolerance for the war, paternal demeanor, and love of animals; having served and lived through other (implicitly better) conflicts his judgment appears valuable. For Freedman this character "represents *M*A*S*H* at its least anti-institutional."[13] Absorbed as a welcome patriarch, Potter facilitates Houlihan's emergence as a more human character and a more familiar inscription of the television work family.

The constant exposure to injured bodies on the one hand and the peculiarities of army life on the other, generate a distinctive mix of humanist outrage and adolescent behavior (drinking, practical jokes). Anarchy aside, a recognition of the medical unit's complicity in the war forms the focus of one of the narrative strands in "Letters" (November 24, 1980) in which the camp receives letters from U.S. schoolchildren: here we see Pierce struggling with a letter from a young boy whose soldier brother has been "saved" by doctors, sent back to the line and killed. Pierce's liberalism and his limited capacity for action are directly confronted here, amidst a series of stories that reveal the care, compassion, and good humor with which the unit typically operates. The letter poses a question that the series cannot effectively answer since its comic, and indeed its dramatic rationale lies in the continuation of war and of the suspension of its characters in limbo. The repetitive format of the sitcom is distinct from the sort of narrative arcs culminating in tragedy or loss that we associate with tragic or melodramatic modes. Indignities small and large do not trigger breakdown or refusal but are instead met (and to some extent resisted) with comedy. "Letters" is indicative of the more personal inflection given to the themes of war as madness in later series' of *M*A*S*H*. As David Marc notes, the show shifted towards a therapeutic discourse with respect to the experience of war: "Psychological introspection established itself as *M*A*S*H*'s primary text during the late seventies." In this process "Personal madness replaced the insanity of the bureaucracy as the main villain, though the former was still often spurred by the latter."[14] Meaning within the show's surreal war-torn world has to do with the core cast's experience of trauma and the personal growth that this produces. This development, while quite in keeping with the evolution of *M*A*S*H*'s core characters, underlines the show's preoccupation with a U.S. experience of war and the general disinterest in the specificities of Korea, an issue to which I return in the final section of this essay.

Despite *M*A*S*H*'s association with liberal television (it was launched, as Todd Gitlin notes, "on a wave of anti-war sentiment,")[15] from the late 1980s onwards scholars have called into question the show's liberalism. For critics such as Freedman both film and series work to center and champion the heroic individualism of the central male protagonists. Yet as Gitlin notes, *M*A*S*H*'s availability for radically different interpretative positions works both to secure its status as a hit and to shore up the association of quality television with ambiguity, depth and complex/evolving characters. The grim comedy of living in/with the military forms the substance of *M*A*S*H*: from mix-ups in supply, through the martial dreams of ridiculous, borderline insane officers (and the youthful death that results from those dreams), the show depicts both absurd regulation and anarchic rebellion, each sustaining the other in carnivalesque fashion.

Sitcom, War, and Sex Comedy

Sex comedy underpins much of *M*A*S*H*'s humor, with Pierce and McIntryre's bawdy pursuit of nurses and the sexual humiliation of Houlihan a staple of the early years. At the most basic level *M*A*S*H* concerns itself primarily with male characters. Its core group of disaffected army surgeons are all drafted; most define themselves in opposition to, rather than seeing themselves as part of the military in which they reluctantly find themselves. Their constraint is, it seems, an intolerable passivity one implicitly experienced as feminizing. Misogyny is no stranger to either the family based sitcom or service comedy of course, though the two pull in somewhat different directions. While *The Phil Silvers Show*'s Bilko is always eager to make money, he is just as determined to avoid the commitments of conventional heterosexuality. Women, whether military or civilian the show seems to suggest, have marriage as their goal; it is the soldier's job (implicitly a man's job) to avoid being outwitted by the "opposite" sex, such that married men are typically presented as foolish, miserably restricted or "henpecked." Thus the situation on which the comedy is premised is continuous (peacetime) military service, ensuring ease and comfort and limiting male exposure to women. The dangers of suburban domesticity, as showcased in that key site of 1950s situation comedy, the white family home, are best avoided. In *M*A*S*H*, with endless war as comic premise, the lures of domesticity and of "home" are very much desirable, present but distant, returning to the characters in the form of letters, home movies, phone calls and memories recounted at length with colleagues. The companionship and friendship emphasized through the M*A*S*H "gang," and a key element of audience affection for the series, is premised on absence and loss. The U.S. is thus constructed in sentimental terms of family, domesticity, and community, all defined by more or less traditionalist gender norms.

If *M*A*S*H* is centered on male doctors it nonetheless features a roster of female characters, a consequence of its roots in service and medical comedies. Indeed my initial interest in the series related to its visible inclusion of women within the U.S. military, the acknowledgement (though hardly central to the series dynamic) that military women form a fundamental part of the waging of war, even as the gendered codes of both narrative form and military culture work to construct the military woman as oxymoronic. The gradual incorporation of Houlihan's military woman into the boys club that is the *M*A*S*H* unit was one of the series' most remarked-on changes. Various critics have comments on the show's engagement with U.S. feminism, linking this engagement to star Alan Alda's star status, his increased involvement in the production after the departure of Larry Gelbart and his high profile advocacy for the Equal Rights Amendment (ERA).[16] Here I'd like to address these connections and to consider the ways in which they relate to broader questions of war, nation, gender, and citizenship. Specifically, what kind of feminism is enacted here? How does it relate to the longevity of *M*A*S*H* as a series and war as (comic) situation? In this section I also raise questions to which I return below as to the limits of a feminism that typically excludes civilian/Korean women. This exclusion is actually fundamental since *M*A*S*H*'s commitment to feminism is worked out primarily in relation to the evolution of Hawkeye Pierce as a character and secondarily through the integration of Margaret Houlihan. In the process, and somewhat ironically, the conservative values that Margaret represents become more acceptable, even rational.

In a context in which chaos reigns, with the Korean war presented as an absurd oscillation between intense boredom and intensive slaughter, Houlihan's commitment to the minutiae of military life seems surreal and out of place, in the process generating comedy. Houlihan began and was to remain the butt of the joke for some time. Much of the humor sustained at Houlihan's expense centers quite precisely on her over-investment in military procedures and protocol, an over-investment belied by her nature as a sexual being and as a woman. There is something humorous, it seems, about a conventionally attractive white woman so invested in an implicitly masculine military authority. Houlihan's character is framed by questions (why would she want to be a soldier or an officer? Does her military status trouble her gender identity?) which comedy serves to resolve. Unsurprisingly it is through Houlihan's relationships with men that many of these issues are worked out. The open secret of her sexual relationship with the inept, selfish and cowardly Frank Burns works to make Houlihan a ridiculous figure in seasons one through four. Comedy stems not only from the relationship itself, but also from the pair's attempt to keep it secret (and thus their hypocrisy). While the two are seen to share the same values, Burns' conservative patriotism is not backed by courage; moreover his limitations as a surgeon are repeatedly referred to. Houlihan by contrast, though officious, is clearly a good nurse, hardworking, and brave. These qualities occasionally show through her alliance with Burns in the first four seasons, coming to the fore in those later seasons in which she is a more central, and a more compassionate character. For example, in "Preventative Medicine," mentioned above, Houlihan is initially welcoming towards the visiting Colonel but is later repelled by his cavalier attitudes towards casualties in pursuit of military goals.

Through her relationship with Frank Burns, Houlihan's investment in military masculinity is rendered comic; he so clearly falls short of the mark that her attentions towards him seem overstated, ridiculous. A similar dynamic is at work in her various comic encounters with senior male officers: visiting dignitaries allude to past sexual encounters; she fawns over a variety of military men, whether for their seniority or their shoulders. Houlihan and Burns are overcome with passion as they sit together on the bed intended for use during General MacArthur's visit ("Big Mac" February 25, 1975); in "Quo Vadis, Captain Chandler" (November 7, 1975) she swoons over the ludicrous Flagg, telling him "you're some guy"; in "Margaret's Engagement" (September 28, 1976) she announces her ill-fated engagement to Lt. Col. Donald Penobscott with the comic line "I couldn't love someone who didn't outrank me." Although Houlihan's professional capabilities are never questioned, her sexual and emotional impulses are repeatedly played for comedy, laying the ground for an undercurrent of suggestion that she has used her sexual attractiveness in order to secure advancement. Such a suggestion was quite in line with the political contours of early 1970s popular culture, one reacting in ambivalent fashion to contemporary feminism and the searching questions the women's movement posed around male privilege. Later episodes begin to evidence an emergent postfeminist sensibility, one that emphasizes women's individual choices rather than the institutional hierarchies against which they might find themselves pitted.

The underlying tension between Margaret Houlihan's masculine and womanly characteristics is played out comically through rapid alternations between tough and tender personas. Houlihan's military demeanor regularly slips in episodes which show her not only nagging, hysterical, sexually demanding, furious, sad and, significantly, drunk. One notable and oft-used device in playing out the comedy of sex is Houlihan's fascination with weaponry. She swoons not only over medals and muscles, but tanks and guns. Through the series run, although less so towards the end, we see a recurrent suggestion that Houlihan finds military equipment and rank sexually alluring. In "Hey, Doc" (October 10, 1975) for instance, Margaret is delighted with the appearance of a tank commander in camp, enthusing, "Oh it must be very exciting riding around in one of those *massive* machines, with that big cannon just going through everything in front of you." (Later Frank will try to impress her by driving the tank, with predictably destructive results). An unsuccessful season eight relationship between Margaret and a Sergeant (Scully) suggests that by this point rank is of less importance to her. As the series progressed through its run, and Houlihan's character became more complex, these elements of back story and the different facets of her personality play into the construction of Margaret as a contradiction rather than simply a joke: by the season eight episode "Stars and Stripe" she describes herself explicitly in these terms: "I'm me. Sometimes a nurse; sometimes a Major; sometimes a woman in love; sometimes all three at once." Her capacity for an almost hysterical femininity — the moments when she is more or less explicitly characterized as a nagging, excessively shrill woman — and her capacity for physical violence, come to function as endearing character flaws when framed by an emphasis on her humanity rather than her militarism. Effectively, Houlihan's career ambitions and sexual desires are given increasing legitimacy as her character becomes more central to the show. Hence, in large part, the wider perception of *M*A*S*H* as an instance of liberal feminism. The challenge posed by the military woman, her associations with modernity and liberalism are relevant to the presentation of war (a traditional site for male rites of passage) as a *positive site of transformation*, invigorating as much as deathly; such "progress" is intimately bound into *M*A*S*H*'s longevity as a series. The legitimacy accorded Margaret's desires is not extended to Korean women, however. In a season four episode, "Of Moose and Men" (21 November, 1975) BJ draws attention to the hypocrisy of Sergeant Zale, who maintains a Korean mistress/servant while mourning his wife's confession of sexual infidelity via a letter from home. Zale's mistress speaks neither Korean nor English in the episode (thus receiving no credit); wryly amused, BJ does not condemn Zale for his exploitation of a Korean woman but for his refusal to extend privileges of sexual freedom to his wife. Defined in familiar terms of peasant dependability, sexual availability, demure femininity and so on, Korean women are not seen to experience war as transformative in the way that U.S. servicewomen so clearly do.

Mobility and Stasis: California and Korea

M*A*S*H is named for an innovation of military medicine associated with the Korean war in the form of the mobile surgical units which treated battlefield casualties and improved survival rates. As we might expect of situation comedy however, the *M*A*S*H* set was to become both fixed and familiar, characterized by its immobility as a feature on the "Korean"/Californian and televisual landscape. Indeed movement of the unit is unusual and even remarkable, forming a central narrative element of those episodes in which it does occur (such as "Bug-Out," the double episode which opens season 5). In its lack of mobility, the M*A*S*H unit serves as an occupying force both benign and malignant, temporary and permanent. Larry Gelbart acknowledges something of this in interview, noting that: "by routinizing an acceptance of war, year in and year out, it essentially defeats the original purpose of the series. I would almost hope that there would be a way to be even blacker about what war does to people, rather than just to say — and I'm afraid it does, as it always did, but in the tenth year much more than in the first — that listen: Given the right buddies, and the right CO, and the right kind of sense of humor, you can muddle through."[17] What is perhaps most striking about Gelbart's comments, here and elsewhere, is that *M*A*S*H* has little or no interest in Korea or Korean people; its concern is with the effect of war on U.S. citizen-soldiers ("We wanted to say that war was futile," he remarks).[18] As we have seen, various commentators have noted the ways in which the show evolved over time, shifting from adolescent male misogyny to a more complex rendition of men and masculinity via an emergent therapeutic discourse. For many the show was "really" about Vietnam, changing in character following the end of the U.S. involvement in 1975. The view that these two conflicts/Asian nations are essentially interchangeable for western audiences is telling. Indeed, I would argue that the show's true subject is only ever the U.S. and the ways in which its citizens might become accustomed to living with war. As in our contemporary context, with the ongoing conflicts in Iraq and Afghanistan, that familiarity is not to do with the absence of dissent but with a persistent military presence which unfolds for U.S. and UK viewers via its media presence.

Along these lines, Korea itself is rendered as empty space: as the show portrays it there is literally nothing there that the U.S. might want (not then oil-rich Iraq).[19] While Burns attempts to sell the camp's garbage to the locals he treats with ignorance and contempt ("Some 38th Parallels," January 20, 1976), the U.S. soldiers trade primarily in trinkets and souvenirs.[20] The suggestion that Korea holds nothing of value for the U.S. reinforces the possibility of an altruistic interpretation of their presence, most evidently in the camp's (and the padre in particular) relationship to the nearby orphanage. "Hey, Doc" (October 10, 1975) is an interesting episode in this context. The narrative is triggered by the theft of the unit's microscope and Sergeant Kimble's desire to return home via sea rather than air, a passage that will allow him to transport a ton of loot. Pierce and BJ agree to falsify medical papers if Kimble will secure them a replacement microscope. Kimble, whose trickery is humorously represented, represents himself as an entrepreneur in the making: "I'm only taking enough to open a restaurant back in Philly. Kimble's Korean Cafe — three K's, you get it?" Kimble's Korean loot will be recycled stateside into a theme restaurant. By contrast, the local people are typically peasants who struggle to make a living through farming, trading, and small-scale commercial engagements with the camp itself. Occupying crude huts, Koreans are typically passive figures eager for western patronage; occasionally dignified, but more often primitive, superstitious or simply ruthless, Korean characters are resolutely stereotypical. In this context we can note that while the crude conditions against which the doctors find themselves operating are partly a result of the army's inefficiency, they are also figured as an effect of Korea itself, the country drawn as an inhospitable environment defined by primitive conditions and intemperate extremes of weather. In its absence the U.S. is figured as a site of leisure, ease and abundance.

In line with sitcom conventions, Korea functions as a site for interactions amongst the core group. Thus, no Koreans ever serve as central characters, although they may feature as guest stars within selected storylines. As Hye Seung Chung writes, *M*A*S*H* worked to perpetuate "inauthentic, imaginary images of Korea" circulating in American media more widely: "Korea was depicted as nondescript, mountainous rural backdrops occasionally peopled with pidgin English-speaking farmers, orphans, profiteers, and "business girls" adorned in Vietnamese hats and Chinese garb."[21] The interchangeability of Asian characters, culture (and performers) identified here enacts precisely the sort of racism regularly satirized in the series' dialogue. Frank Burns is frequently heard holding forth on the duplicity and generally ungrateful attitudes of Korean people. In "Of Moose and Men" for instance, Frank talks of the deceitful cleverness of "these people." His racist observation that "they don't all look alike by accident y'know," is followed by a series of cuts showing silent rebuke from Nurse Kellye (who describes her ethnicity as Chinese/Hawaiian) and his responding embarrassment. Yet *M*A*S*H* replicates this attitude of interchangeable Asian ethnicity through its casting practices, employing performers of Korean, Chinese and Japanese ethnicity to play Korean characters.[22] On one occasion, Flagg is mocked for shouting at a

Korean who does not understand English, yet Hawkeye does the same to a North Korean soldier (played by well-known Japanese performer Mako) in season nine opener, "The Best of Enemies" (November 17, 1980). Thus both "well-intentioned" Americans and evident buffoons/comic butts show similar traits in their dealings with Korean people.

In this context, consider the affectionate terms in which the local economy of alcohol and prostitution (notably within the space of Rosie's bar) is presented. The sexualized treatment of civilian and military women is something of a contradiction for *M*A*S*H*, not least in the way it skirts around the subject of prostitution. As Cynthia Enloe's work emphasizes, prostitution is taken for granted as a basic component of military life: "Prostitution can seem comforting to some. They imagine it to be 'the oldest profession.' Around a military camp prostitutes connote tradition, not rupture; leisure, not horror; ordinariness, not mayhem. To many, militarized prostitution thus becomes *un*newsworthy."[23] Raucous visits to Seoul or Tokyo are a series staple in *M*A*S*H*; rarely portrayed in any detail, but suggestively referred to by the male personnel (Houlihan even has one such visit in "Der Tag," January 6, 1975). Yet as early as season one, members of the core group object to the more ruthless exploitation of Korean women. In "The Moose" (October 15, 1972) Pierce, McIntyre, and Spearchucker (the black surgeon played by Timothy Jones in season one) object to Sergeant Baker's purchase of a young Korean woman, Yung Hi (Virginia Lee). Though Baker is roundly condemned, it is made clear that his relationship to Yung Hi is not sexual (she tells an amused Pierce and McIntyre that there is no "monkey business"), perhaps facilitating the somewhat comic presentation of the group's attempts to free her from servitude. Having won Yung Hi in a card game, Pierce sets about educating her as to her rights to freedom and self-determination (giving her "person lessons" in McIntyre's words), a process that finally results in her refusal to be re-sold by her brother Benny (Craig Jue) and commencing an education in a Seoul convent.[24] Yung Hi's pidgin English and naïve attitude function as sources of comedy within the episode, while Pierce and McIntyre's paternalist concern for her welfare confirms U.S. decency against a corrupt military which condones the kind of servitude into which the young woman has been sold.

As this instance suggests, the exploitative relationship between the U.S. military and the Korean population is one from which the show attempts to place the central characters at a distance. Pierce is openly hostile towards a nurse who he has been romancing when she expresses racist views in "LIP (Local Indigenous Personnel)" (October 27, 1973), an episode centering on Pierce's efforts to facilitate the marriage between a white U.S. soldier and his

Korean girlfriend. When Pierce becomes romantically involved with a Korean woman, it is with the dedicated Kyung Soon (Kieu Chinh), an aristocrat fallen on hard times, heroically caring for her mother and a number of orphaned children in what remains of their property ("In Love and War," November 1, 1977). The couple is drawn as evident equals in class terms, an equivalence that frames their interracial romance. For all the distance placed between Pierce and the U.S. military, Kyung Soon leaves following the death of her mother, reminding him that a war zone is no place to raise children. "In another two years," she tells Hawkeye, "the boys would learn to be thieves; and the girls — what do you think will happen to the girls?" Her implicit reference to the problems faced by women and young girls seeking to eke out a living in a war zone serves, however briefly, to render visible the effects of the military presence on local women.[25]

The distancing effect is perhaps most nuanced when the sexual exploitation of Korean women is portrayed for either comic or tragic narrative effect. These themes are once more worked out in overtly comic fashion in the season eight episode "Private Finance" (November 5, 1979) which opens in Rosie's bar with the tentative steps of a young woman making her first foray into prostitution; youthful appearance and awkward phrases set against her garish dress suggests inexperience rather than the worldly wisdom usually associated with military prostitution. Klinger recognizes Oksun Li (Denice Kumagai), a camp "laundry girl," and intervenes with the drunken Crosetti to prevent the imminent sexual/financial exchange. Outside, Klinger is caught offering money to the girl, with her peasant mother Mrs. Li (Shizuko Hoshi) mistaking a gesture designed to *preserve* her implicitly virginal body as an enactment of prostitution. Both Oksun Li's faltering steps on her unfamiliar high heels and the mother's assault on Klinger with a broomstick (she serves here as a composite of earthy peasant and fearful witch) are played for laughs, underlined by the show's laugh track.

The conflagration is disrupted by the episode's serious narrative thread, the arrival of wounded and the death of youthful soldier Eddie Hastings despite Hawkeye's best efforts in the OR. Almost $9,000 of ill-gotten currency and a subsequent investigation reveals that Hastings' character belies his Norman Rockwell appearance. Meanwhile, despite Oksun Li's efforts to reassure her mother that Klinger did not "shame" her, the Corporal comes under (comic) threat with a pitchfork and invective. (Klinger's increasing desperation leads him back to women's clothing, a ruse his character had employed for some years in fruitless attempts to secure a discharge on the grounds of insanity).[26] As a response to this intrusive femininity, Potter and Houlihan undertake to visit the mother and resolve the conflict. Amidst the primitive surroundings of her village we learn that Oksun Li's father is dead and her brother missing; the farm has been repeatedly destroyed by soldiers of different nationalities (U.S., Chinese, North Korean, South Korean) signaling the families' status as generalized victims of war. Oksun Li asserts that sex work was her only option to raise the money needed to take her mother away from the fighting to family in Pusan. This narrative problem is neatly resolved when Hastings' god-fearing family return the money he has corruptly earned, requesting that Hawkeye put it to good use. An undisclosed portion of it is donated to Oksun Li and her mother, ensuring that the latter retains her honor and allowing a comic reconciliation between Klinger and Mrs. Li. Oksun Li and her mother are thus the *beneficiaries* of U.S. military patronage, one soldier's corruption producing unexpected value. In presenting the Korean mother/daughter's story as primarily *comic*, the light relief against the narrative thread of a young soldier's corruption and death, the episode works to foreground the economy of "Private Finance" while minimizing its implications. Thus the show transforms a narrative of sexual exploitation into one of charity and gratitude. The good soldiers (the M*A*S*H unit) more than compensate for the bad soldiers (Hastings, Crosetti) whose exploitative relationship to their military colleagues and to Korean women allude to the more extensive consequences of war.

Although rarely discussed directly, the Korean War (technically a UN-sponsored police action) itself is typically presented as a mistaken exercise. Like the American military involvement in Vietnam the war is constituted as meaningless, though it was hardly so for the Korean people who are once more rendered invisible through such formulations. These themes are articulated alongside the show's humanist rejection of violence in "Guerilla My Dreams" (October 1, 1979) in which, unseen by military personnel, a wounded Korean guerrilla (Haunani Minn) attempts to kill another patient in post-op. The bulk of the episode concerns Pierce and BJ's attempts to keep the woman away from Lt. Park (Mako) who is intent on questioning her. The medics regard her as a victim rather than a combatant, despite Park's assertion that she is "as dedicated to killing as any uniformed soldier." When the woman's murderous intent is finally revealed, Pierce's humanist faith is punctured. Significantly in terms of the more general inscription of Korean women within the series, her defiant words are not available directly to us. Translated by Park, these words serve as a weapon in his final confrontation with Pierce ("this woman's life is more important to you than it is to her"); Pierce's contempt for Park ("you son of a bitch") sidesteps somewhat his problematic relationship to an enemy combatant who is clearly depicted as ruthless, simultaneously erasing the "other" female's subjectivity.

Conclusion

I began by suggesting that a consideration of *M*A*S*H* might be instructive for thinking war as entertainment within contemporary culture. The show's ongoing presence on television screens, a presence that continues via syndication, is suggestive in itself of a certain resignation to war and the effects of war, as Larry Gelbart acknowledges in the comments cited above. It is the privileging of the white male U.S. soldier/surgeon's experience of war, the act of making this the story that matters over all others, which is perhaps most significant in this context. Over the years the show's masculinist ethos did indeed adapt in response to contemporary U.S. feminism. Yet ironically, this process served to underline the peculiar invisibility of Korean women (and men), and a general indifference to the historical, geographic and cultural context of the show's setting. Requiring cash, culture or tuition in self-assertion, Korean women typically occupy the margins of *M*A*S*H*, speaking to assumptions of U.S. superiority which are only occasionally punctured within the series and which remain a ready resource within contemporary political/journalistic discourse. From the vantage point of its U.S. protagonists, Korea is pictured as empty space, a brutal and primitive void which sucks life from U.S. (and occasionally Korean) soldiers. While war and Korea are interchangeable for *M*A*S*H*, it is the largely unseen U.S. that serves to give meaning to this void: an idealized site of freedom, dreams — and, of course, television.

Notes

1. Nicholas Mirzoeff, *Watching Babylon: The War in Iraq and Global Visual Culture* (New York: Routledge, 2005), 67.
2. The series title refers to the mobile army surgical hospitals or M*A*S*H units associated with the Korean war.
3. Todd Gitlin describes *M*A*S*H* as "one of the most widely syndicated shows in TV history." *Inside Prime Time* (New York: Pantheon Books, 1985), 216.
4. David Marc, *Comic Visions*, second edition (Oxford: Blackwell, 1997), 137.
5. Mike Budd and Clay Steinman emphasise *M*A*S*H*'s function as a commercial property designed to deliver quality audiences to advertisers in "*M*A*S*H* Mystified: Capitalization, Dematerialization, Idealization," *Cultural Critique* no. 10, Fall (1988): 59–75. A somewhat more detailed, though no less critical, exposition of the novel, film, and series is given in Carl Freedman's "History, Fiction, Film, Television, Myth: The Ideology of *M*A*S*H*," *The Southern Review* vol. 26 (1990): 89–106,
6. David Thomas and Ian Irvine, *Bilko, The Fort Baxter Story* (London: Hutchinson, 1985), 8.
7. Freedman, "History, Fiction, Film," 98.
8. On language and comedy in *M*A*S*H* see Corrine Holt Sawyer, "'If I Could Walk

That Way, I Wouldn't Need the Talcum Powder': Word Play Humor in *M*A*S*H*," *Journal of Popular Film and Television* vol. 11, no. 1, Spring 1983: 42–52.

9. William Paul, *Laughing Screaming: Modern Hollywood Horror and Comedy* (New York: Columbia UP, 1994), 112.

10. Budd and Steinman, "*M*A*S*H* Mystified," 72.

11. Bakhtin conceptualises the carnivalesque as a ritualised site within which social hierarchies are playfully and temporarily inverted. For a useful discussion of contemporary applications of Bakhtin's work to culture see Sue Vice, *Introducing Bakhtin* (Manchester: Manchester University Press, 1997). As Anne Karpf writes, British traditions of medical comedy also poke fun at the hospital as rule-bound institution. Thus, "medical comedies invariably end in medical mayhem.... The institution is finally subverted and disrupted by its wayward patients or staff, who've refused to confirm to its unbending routines. Anarchy triumphs over bureaucracy, and the enforced compliance of most real-life hospitalised patients inverted." *Doctoring the Media: The Reporting of Health and Medicine* (London: Routledge, 1988), 216.

12. See Yvonne Tasker, *Soldier's Stories: Military Women in Cinema and Television since World War II* (Durham, NC: Duke University Press, forthcoming).

13. Freedman, "History, Fiction, Film," 100.

14. Marc, *Comic Visions*, 164.

15. Gitlin, *Inside Prime Time*, 216–7.

16. See Freedman for a discussion of this, particularly 102–4.

17. Gitlin, *Inside Prime Time*, 217.

18. Ibid.

19. This is not to say that enemy countries are typically drawn with complexity in U.S. media (that would be untrue), but to point to the way in which *M*A*S*H* specifically visually emphasises Korea as a barren, worthless territory.

20. Burns is in turn tricked by Pierce and McIntyre into believing that he has discovered gold, a comic error premised on his overvaluation of Korea ("Major Fred C. Dobbs," March 11, 1973).

21. Hye Seung Chung, "Portrait of a Patriot's Son: Philip Ahn and Korean Diasporic Identities in Hollywood," *Cinema Journal* 45, no. 2 (2006): 43–67.

22. Hye Seung Chung comments on recent contestations over casting and costuming in her "From *Die Another Day* to 'Another Day': The South Korean Anti-007 Movement and Regional Nationalism in Post–Cold War Asia," in the forthcoming special issue of *positions,* "What's Left of Asia?" (Durham, NC: Duke University Press).

23. Cynthia Enloe, *Maneuvers: The International Politics of Militarizing Women's Lives* (Berkeley: University of California Press, 2000), 108.

24. Four years earlier Craig Jue had served as the symbol of "why we fight" in John Wayne's Vietnam war propaganda picture *The Green Berets* (1968).

25. For a recent discussion of the impact of war on civilian women see H. Patricia Hynes, "On the Battlefield of Women's Bodies: An Overview of the Harm of War to Women," *Women's Studies International Forum* 27 (2004): 431–445.

26. In the feature-length finale, Klinger's character marries a Korean woman, Soon-Lee Hahn (played by Chinese American Rosalind Chao). Both appeared in the short lived spin-off, *After M*A*S*H* (CBS, 1983–5).

9

Lavishing the Body Politic
The Manchurian Candidate
DEBRA WHITE-STANLEY

Just after the release of Jonathan Demme's 2004 remake of *The Manchurian Candidate,* former American Sergeant Charles Robert Jenkins rematerialized like a ghost from the Korean War. Jenkins, as if he were a stray member of the Lost Patrol of John Frankenheimer's 1962 film *The Manchurian Candidate,* claimed he had been abducted by the North Korean military in 1965. After surrendering to American military authorities, he pled guilty to desertion and aiding the enemy and was imprisoned for one month.[1]

Media coverage of Jenkins' continuing presence in the news is just one way that, far from being the "forgotten war," the Korean War seemed to be more present than ever during the perverse unfolding of the Iraq War. In summer 2007 the Bush Administration tried to take control of this undesired affinity between the two conflicts, and President Bush claimed the Korean War as a model for the War in Iraq. He argued that, like South Korea, Iraq could be transformed into an American ally, and that the public should prepare itself for a long-term presence in Iraq.[2] These words, far from winning public support for the war, only inspired more determined resistance.

Jonathan Demme's remake of *The Manchurian Candidate* in 2004 intervenes in the presence of elements of the Forgotten War within the Iraq conflict. The 1962 film version of Richard Condon's political novel *The Manchurian Candidate* from 1959, which imagines the Cold War communist brainwashing of American soldiers, reflects the traumatically high number of American soldiers held as prisoners in Korea. While American soldiers have sustained nowhere near the level of casualties and imprisonment of the Korean War, a series of POW-related news events hailed the 2004 release of *The Manchurian Candidate.* For instance, Daniel Pearl had been imprisoned and beheaded by Arab militants in February 2002. November 2003 saw the release of a Jessica

Lynch biography and the made-for-television film. And the events surrounding the scandal at Abu Ghraib prison were revealed to the American public in the summer of 2004. In a conflict that, like the Korean War, is marked by the gross violation of Geneva Convention standards, *The Manchurian Candidate* is a significant bridge between these two eras. The 1962 version of the film has been exhaustively analyzed for its treatment of gender, Orientalism, and anti-communism.[3] This essay argues that the 2004 remake of *The Manchurian Candidate* creates a political conspiracy that links the corruption of private war contractors with a commentary on the continuing inequality of African American soldiers and citizens.

From Korea to Operation Desert Storm

In the 2004 *Manchurian Candidate* actor Denzel Washington follows in the footsteps of his predecessor James Edwards, the African-American star of *The Manchurian Candidate* (1962), who starred in a number of 1940s and 50s war films directed by the likes of Samuel Fuller, Douglas Sirk, Anthony Mann, and Lewis Milestone.[4] Availing himself of a range of roles far more extensive than those available to James Edwards, Washington has starred in war films such as *Glory* (1989), *Courage Under Fire* (1996), and *Antwone Fisher* (2002). The typical Denzel Washington character becomes enmeshed in a political scandal that results in his expulsion from the military; after this initial disgrace the Washington character seeks a restoration of status and honor within the military. Such fictionalized threats to Denzel Washington's honor reflect the disenchantment of African-Americans with the military since 9/11. As official figures indicate, the numbers of African-American soldiers in the U.S. military have decreased since 2001, with the Army realizing the largest decrease of black representation.[5] According to Defense Department figures, the number of black enlistees has fallen by over 58 percent since fiscal year 2000.[6] While many African-Americans are opposed to the War in Iraq, especially after the Bush Administration's Hurricane Katrina fiasco, the press has prominently featured stories about African-Americans in the military. African-American officers, a population on the rise even as enlisted African-Americans continue to decline, have been a particular focus of that coverage.[7] In *The Manchurian Candidate*, Denzel Washington is cast in the lead role as Major Ben Marcos, a character played by Frank Sinatra in the 1962 version. Additionally, the character of Private Al Melvin, the lone black character in the 1962 film, is played by the African-American actor Jeffrey Wright.

The remake is centrally concerned with racial representation, not only through casting but also in the way it infuses the idea of "brainwashing" with racial significance. The director of the film, Jonathan Demme, is not a director whose body of work is known for his attention to problems of race. However, he did direct *Beloved* (1998), an adaptation of Toni Morrison's 1987 Pulitzer Prize–winning novel, and directed and wrote a television special, *Haiti Dreams of Democracy* (1988). A powder keg of racial tension erupts in the 2004 *The Manchurian Candidate*. In the 1962 version, the idea of brainwashing was conceived as an Orientalist Communist threat poised to corrupt white American soldiers. In the 2004 version, the real threat to the body politic emerges from within American's racial and class inequality. The brainwasher, no longer an Asian Communist, is now a rogue scientist from South Africa named Atticus Noyle (Simon McBurney) who has been accused of experimenting on political prisoners there. The film strongly implies Noyle has immorally practiced his science on helpless prisoners during the years of Apartheid, a South African political and economic system of racial segregation dismantled between 1990 and 1993. Noyles' affiliation with Apartheid in a film that so prominently features African-American characters and stars becomes an unacknowledged foundation upon which rest all the other links: the multinational corporation Manchurian Global and it's ruthless quest to control the American political system; the meaningless rhetoric of American politicians who do not want to admit the racial and class inequities that are so evident in the film; and, ultimately, the neocolonialist tenor of the war in the desert.

Many of the changes made to the remake's plot and characters involve changes in racial identity of characters and of national settings. For instance, the remake updates the setting of the action from the Korean War (1950–53) to Operation Desert Storm (1991). Manchurian Global Corporation, a large multinational like Halliburton (the American multinational firm whose profitable contracts to support the Iraq War have attracted great controversy) replaces the Manchurians as the brainwashers. Ben Marcos' military unit is composed of both African-Americans and whites, allowing for the recasting of the Orientalism of the 1962 brainwashing scene in terms that evoke black/white violence. The investigation into the brainwashing sessions is then led by a female African-American FBI agent rather than a white military general. The two soldiers who experience flashbacks of the brainwashing sessions are African-American males. In a complicated string of cause-and-effect, Gulf War Syndrome sends them seeking refuge in a depressed inner-city neighborhood in which urban poverty is clearly connected with government neglect. A close analysis of the film reveals how these changes in race and national affiliation redirect the 2004 version of *The Manchurian*

Candidate to address failed rhetoric and persistent inequalities within the United States.

Racial Tension, Torture, and Terror

From its very beginning, the 2004 *Manchurian Candidate* presents the viewer with an image of the military marked by racial tension and guided by powerful myths of white military heroism. Racial tension erupts in the credit sequence during which a group of primarily African-American soldiers play cards in the back of a military vehicle in Iraq while listening to rap music. When the white Sergeant Shaw (Lev Shreiber) calls the African-American soldiers to duty, they mock him. As in the 1962 film, Shaw is the star of a false narrative created by the brainwashers, in which he single-handedly rescues an entire squad of primarily African-American soldiers. Major Marcos (Denzel Washington) recounts this tale of white military heroism for a rapt audience of African-American Boy Scouts. "Sergeant Shaw, he took command," Marcos brags. We later learn that it was Marcos, the African-American officer, who took the risks and acted heroically that night in the desert.

This submerged history of African-American military excellence will haunt the film, lending a different spin to the exploration of the awarding of the Medal of Honor. At the high point of his speech, Marcos stresses the Medal's value as a signifier of military merit and conveys his hope that one of the Boy Scouts in the audience — they are mostly African-American — will some day win the Medal of Honor. Afterwards, Al Melvin (Jeffrey Wright), an African-American soldier whose costume and acting style suggest battle fatigue, desperation, and poverty, approaches Marcos. Their awkward and mysterious conversation is depicted in a shot-reverse shot sequence that captures each character in close-ups from a straight-on angle. The absence of over-the-shoulder anchoring shots lends an uncanny quality to the mirror framings of these two characters. Melvin questions Marcos' narrative of white salvation: "I'm just a little stuck, sir. Because I remember, okay, Shaw, Shaw, okay, Shaw saving us, right, but that doesn't make sense, because that should've been you."

These words have much larger implications given that out of over 3,400 total Medals of Honor only 88 Medals have ever been awarded to African-Americans. The issue of the Medal of Honor is so racially loaded that in 1992, when the Army realized that no African-Americans had been awarded the Medal of Honor in the Second World War, a special study was commissioned "to determine if there was a racial disparity in the way Medal of Honor recipients were selected." As a result, eight medals were posthumously awarded to African-American recipients.[8]

The character of Al Melvin articulates fears of white control and counter narratives of Black resistance that will emerge full-blown within the film. One is reminded of Sigmund Freud's observation that the "uncanny element is actually nothing new or strange, but something that was long familiar to the psyche and was estranged from it only through being repressed."[9] Melvin, as Marcos' uncanny double, brings to the surface repressed truths that will play out over the course of the film and eventually be contained in a new way. The remake follows patterns articulated by Mladen Dolar, who argued that stories that feature the double repeat a predictable pattern: the subject encounters his double, producing terrible anxiety; only the subject can see his double; the double turns up at the most inappropriate moments; the double realizes and acts out the subject's repressed desires. In a final showdown the subject kills his double; in killing his double he kills himself.[10] As in the pattern outlined by Dolar, soon after Marcos — an officer in a position to listen to Al Melvin and offer help — encounters Melvin, Melvin is found floating face down in the Potomac River. With Melvin gone, Marcos is left with his inner conflict between the brainwashing narrative and his dawning awareness that he and the rest of the Lost Patrol have been brainwashed.

The dawning awareness that breaks through into Marcos' conscious awareness is no less than the emergence of a buried historical narrative of lynching and racist conquest photographs, released just as the scandal at Abu Ghraib came to public awareness. Al Melvin's notebook is a repository of graphic torture imagery whose images haunt us in a slow montage of the bodies of African-American soldiers being strangled and violated. These images parallel both the most troubling episodes of American racial history and the Abu Ghraib torture scandal. As Susan Sontag suggests, "if there is something comparable to what these pictures show it would be some of the photographs of black victims of lynching taken between the 1880's and 1930's ... souvenirs of a collective action whose participants felt perfectly justified in what they had done."[11] Others have argued that Sontag's discussion of the torture photographs does not go far enough in drawing parallels between the Abu Ghraib photographs and the history of African-American oppression. For instance, Marxist-Feminist critic Hazel Carby argues that "the importance of spectacles of abuse, the taking of photographs and videos, the preservation and the circulation of the visual image of the tortured/lynched body, the erotic sexual exploitation which produced pleasure in the torturers — all these practices are continuities in the history of American racism."[12] The film's narration, images, and sound all support Carby's observations.

The film also highlights the inability of political figures to address such buried realities of American history and the violent resurgence of our racist history through the Iraq War. For instance, crosscutting and the use of the television screen as a visual and aural prop emphasizes the chasm separating the social plight of many Americans and the false and overblown political rhetoric used by Senator Raymond Shaw's (Schreiber) political campaign for the vice presidency. As Ben Marcos sits in his humble and dark apartment eating Ramen noodles, Shaw eats gourmet food in his luxurious hotel room. Both characters watch the same television news program, as the liberal vice-presidential candidate Tom Jordan (Jon Voight) urges viewers that, "We need to attend to our own house" while responding to the War on Terror. Medium shots emphasize Ben Marcos' brainwashed state as coverage shifts to Raymond Prentiss Shaw's recently announced vice-presidential candidacy and his inherited wealth. Marco's meager surroundings and blank affect politicizes the plight of Gulf War veterans in a way that recalls Thomas Elsaesser's discussion of melodrama's ability to represent "the patterns of domination and exploitation existing in a given society" through characters "helplessly struggling inside their emotional prisons with no hope of realizing to what degree they are the victims of their society."[13] Melodrama — far from being politically irrelevant — has historically served as an outlet for the emotional and cultural legacy of racial oppression in America.[14] This racial oppression is clearly suggested by the disparity between the two hotel rooms — one luxurious and the other squalid — and the two meals — one gourmet and the other Ramen noodles.

And yet, even though the disparity between the white politician Shaw (recipient of an unearned Medal of Honor) and the African-American war hero Marcos is clear to us, the members of the Lost Patrol display a brainwashed obliviousness to these disparities of wealth and power. Melvin, appearing on the television news in an interview done for the profile of Shaw, repeats the refrain, "Raymond Shaw is the probably the kindest, bravest, warmest, most selfless human being I've ever known" and Marcos silently mouths these words and passes out on the sofa under the spell of his first flashback of the brainwashing experience. As cross-cultural violence, this flashback portrays the white Raymond Shaw suffocating Private Baker — an African-American — with plastic. This is a noteworthy change from the 1962 film, in which the white Raymond Shaw murders two white soldiers in the infamous brainwashing scene. To extend the film's depiction of cross-cultural violence, the bodies of several other African-American soldiers are shown, bloodily invaded by metal machinery and tentacles. These images of pain at the hands of a doctor we later discover to be in exile from Apartheid South Africa suggest a black/white racial dimension to this violence that is simply absent from the 1962 film. At the same time, these melodramatic images of the pain and inequality suffered by African-Americans in the United States offer a racial perspective that remains overtly unacknowledged, in a noteworthy example of melodrama's ability to encode and render complex social dynamics in ways that are suggestive — there because they are embedded in the subtext of the film.

Brainwashing: The Multinational Corporate Horror

The remake also reworks the infamous Ladies' Garden Club scene from John Frankenheimer's 1962 *The Manchurian Candidate*, in which an extraordinary 360 degree pan reveals the illusion suffered by the brainwashed soldiers who misidentify their communist brainwashers as middle-aged gardening enthusiasts.

In the reinterpretation of this scene, its Cold War gender dynamics are transformed into a commentary on racial and class conflict that is also expressed through camera movement and point of view editing. Instead of the Victorian Garden Club ladies at the Garden Club meeting, the remake aptly situates Ben Marcos at a gathering for wealthy political supporters of Raymond Shaw, an event held in an outdoor garden. This setting emphasizes the economic disparities between white American politicians and their constituencies. Marcos, who is the only African-American present, listens as Shaw poses the rhetorical question, "I mean, isn't that supposed to be the point of this great country of ours, that everybody matters, not just the people at this party, but perhaps more importantly, those who can't afford to be here?" Shaw's rhetoric of inclusion is belied by a tracking shot that briefly adopts Shaw's point of view as he avoids Marcos. Later Shaw angrily tells Marcos not to touch him, as he gravitates toward the richest men in the room. Shaw's rhetoric obfuscates the racial disparities that are featured so prominently in shots of Marcos approaching Melvin's cheap hotel room on the wrong side of town, shots crosscut with images of Shaw in his resplendent and brightly lit hotel room.

The remake's brainwashing sequences create a central and incredibly resonant opposition in the film between a "white zone" of whitewashing, brainwashing, and denial, and a "black zone" of repressed outcry, rebellion and historical truth. The "white zone" is established from the first brainwashing scene in which Raymond Shaw picks up the telephone receiver and a disembodied voice with an English accent — later recognizable as belonging to Apartheid doctor Atticus Noyle — asks the question: "Is this Raymond Shaw?" "Raymond Prentiss Shaw?" The repetition of Shaw's full name triggers an altered state of consciousness in which the room's lighting is gradually increased, creating a state of whiteness that Raymond Shaw has been conditioned to enjoy. Shaw is led down a light-bathed hallway, and the wall of a room is pushed aside by militants dressed in black to reveal an interior room equipped as a medical clinic. As an updating of 1962 scene, in which Shaw's conditioning links are tested by Communist Party doctors, this scene emphasizes the white light that suffuses the hidden room and the doctor's white gloves as they update the mechanical implant which allows them to control Shaw's thoughts.

As Shaw is swallowed up by this "white zone" of brainwashing, Marcos penetrates Melvin's hotel room, a "black zone" filled with memories of the "Lost Patrol." The walls of this "black zone" are covered with Melvin's pen and ink drawings of images from the nightmarish memories of the brainwashing that have haunted the nightmares of Melvin and Marcos. Crosscutting emphasizes the contrast between the "flawless working condition" of Shaw's brain implant and the destruction of Marcos' conditioning. Additional imagery explores the explosive racial knowledge uncovered by the African-American soldiers; for instance, in one of Melvin's drawings a Nazi swastika has been etched on Shaw's forehead. This external knowledge is relocated within Marcos' body when he — without anesthesia or expert medical assistance — discovers and removes his own mechanical implant with a bowie knife. The comparison between Shaw's operation, conducted by doctors in white gloves in a sanitized "white" room, and Marcos' bowie-knife triage conducted in a bathroom, illustrates the complexities of Susan Jeffords' assertion that white masculinity is "defined in and through the white male body and against the racially marked male body."[15] Raymond Shaw's white body is pampered, clothed and respected while Ben Marcos' black body is put under surveillance, targeted and disrespected.

When Marcos retreats into the "black zone" — a nightmare state suffused with brainwashing images that have a kind of historical significance in the wake of black history as well as the most recent Abu Ghraib scandal — he is dismissed from active military service and thrown back onto his own resources. A global perspective on the brainwashing conspiracy can be achieved but only by connecting the knowledge he can harvest from his own body to objective clues. As a kind of savant he desperately describes the chip he has extracted from his back to unsympathetic policemen who dismiss him as a veteran suffering from Gulf War syndrome. Key reaction shots of an unnamed white woman in the rear of the interrogation room indicate that there may be some higher-level governmental interest in Marcos' theories. This sense is confirmed when Raymond Shaw reads surveillance reports on Ben Marcos which indicate that Marcos has indeed been under FBI surveillance.

The foreign body of the microchip provides clues to the moving parts of the brainwashing conspiracy. Under the microscope, the microchip that Marcos bit out of Shaw's back appears to be a series of white crystals surrounding black chips, and white diagrams over a black background. These geometric patterns of black and white shapes in formation cleverly illustrate the themes of white dominance and black resistance that are the true subject of this film. A scientist friend believes the chips to originate with a project funded by Manchurian Global to develop "scary implantables — a goddamn geopolitical extension of policy for every president since Nixon." With these words the scientist administers electroshock to re-induce the brainwashing montage in Raymond. This brainwashing montage, through which Shaw is able to recover the events of the brainwashing as a chronological narrative, begins and ends with a suffusion of bright light — the "white zone" — that recalls the one that Shaw experienced earlier in the film. This chronological narrative reassembles the individual images and sounds Marcos has already encountered with new stimuli, most notably images of animated United States Army style training videos.

As Marcos uncovers the brainwashing conspiracy, a number of thematically significant props depict the layers of racial imagery contained within the "black zone," linking the Manchurian Global plot, the historical struggle of African-Americans for political equality, and the Iraq War torture scandal. During the scene in which he slices open his shoulder to locate and remove the mechanical implant from his body, a poster of American actor, singer, writer, and activist Paul Robeson is visible in the background, hanging on the bathroom wall. Paul Robeson was, like Ben Marcos, an African-American who made controversial statements and conflicted with the American government. In 1949, Robeson controversially promised "We shall not make war on anyone. We shall not make war on the Soviet Union" at the Paris Congress of the World Partisans of Peace. These and other statements by Robeson drew criticism by public figures as diverse as Eleanor Roosevelt and Jackie Robinson, and resulted in the revocation of Robeson's passport until 1958.[16]

Marcos discovers a second resonant prop while researching Manchurian Global: an art exhibit in the library's lobby that appears to be a replica and enlargement of the black and white mechanical implant seen earlier under the microscope. While the Robeson poster linked the implant to the Federal

Bureau of Investigation's historical surveillance of African-Americans such as Martin Luther King, the art exhibit adds more layers to the conspiracy. In his research Marcos discovers that the mechanical implant was created by Atticus Noyle, a South African doctor accused of violating human rights during the Apartheid era, and additionally that Noyle has been working with Manchurian Global to implant Gulf War soldiers with microchips.

Manchurian Global, like the multinational corporation Halliburton, is haunted by corruption in its servicing of Gulf War military contracts.[17] In fact, Demme has stated, "I was taken with Dan's idea [Dan Pyne, scriptwriter] of replacing communism as the great global threat to mankind with what is arguably the biggest threat to humanity today: the multinational corporations who profit from war."[18] The conspiracy uncovered by Marcos fuses the cost inflation charges made against Halliburton with the military medical charges levied against the military and the Red Cross in the Abu Ghraib scandal. A voice-over on the radio intones: "Pentagon watchdogs today accused the private equity fund Manchurian Global of grossly overpricing plasma and other critical medical supplies during the recent Indonesian excursion even as the company secured a half-billion-dollar no-bid contract to provide combat support services to American soldiers preparing to mobilize in Sri Lanka." Later a female television announcer reports: "... private equity fund Manchurian Global confirmed today it is continuing with plans to finance privately owned combat units to beleaguered U.S. troop deployments worldwide. It is a move that could save the Defense Department billions of dollars." The resultant Manchurian Global scandal consequently comes to involve not only race but also abuses of medical authority and wealth. As in the torture scandal at Abu Ghraib, the lines of authority and accountability are blurred and the laws regulating the treatment of soldiers during wartime have collapsed.[19]

Gender Dynamics

The multiple levels of conspiracy in the 2004 *Manchurian Candidate* are rendered even more complex by the dynamics of gender and sexuality that feed into the issues of race, class and wartime corruption. In the 1962 version of the film, the character of Raymond Shaw was torn between his love for the innocent Jocelyn Jordan (Leslie Parrish) and the dictates of his mother, Eleanor Shaw/Mrs Iselin (Angela Lansbury), ultimately revealed to be a communist agent and shot. The character of Eugenie Rose Chaney (Janet Leigh) falls in love with Ben Marcos although a number of clues suggest the possibility that she is also an enemy agent. In the 1962 version, not only does Mrs. Iselin exert control over her son Shaw but other visual cues are offered to suggest the extent to which women are in control. Shaw's "trigger card"— the playing card used by his mother to send him into a brainwashed susceptibility to her will — is the Queen of Diamonds. In the Garden Party scene, the prisoners misrecognize their captors as Garden Party ladies. As Tony Jackson argues, the 1962 *Manchurian Candidate* "imagines masculinized women and feminized men to be the real source of cultural failure."[20] Jackson's analysis rightly emphasizes the way that the film locates the white nuclear family as the site from which the Cold War political threat menaces the American way of life.

In the 2004 remake, the gender dynamics originally introduced in the 1962 original are complicated considerably by each male lead's pairing with a female character along racial lines. In the "white zone," Raymond Shaw is controlled by Eleanor Shaw (Meryl Streep) and in the "black zone" Ben Marcos is controlled by Eugenie Rose (Kimberly Elise). Both of these female characters are spies — Eleanor Shaw for the multinational corporation Manchurian Global and Eugenie Rose for the FBI. Each female spy attempts to manage her racially defined realm of political intrigue through surveillance and control techniques that bring about the ultimate confrontation between the FBI and private corporations that occurs at the end of the film. This confrontation is defined in the 2004 remake through the collapse of the distinctions between the "white zone" and the "black zone."

The 2004 remake transforms the character of Marcos, making him both African-American and in many ways a less powerful character than the 1962 character played by Frank Sinatra. For instance, while the remake strips Marcos of all his military authority, the 1962 film had Marcos leading the military investigation into Raymond Shaw and the brainwashing of the Lost Patrol. Rather than assuming control of the military's investigation into the brainwashing of the Lost Patrol, Denzel Washington's character is placed under government surveillance himself for much of the film. The character of Eugenie Rose, played by Janet Leigh in the 1962 version, is transformed into a female action hero in the 2004 version and played by Kimberly Elise. This character revision is significant because it adds to the perception of Ben Marcos' disempowerment; whereas Janet Leigh's Eugenie Rose assumes a role of wifely support for Frank Sinatra's Marcos as he leads his investigation, in the 2004 version it is Eugenie Rose who can, as an FBI agent, place Denzel Washington's character under government surveillance as part of the agency's investigation into the fate of the members of the Lost Patrol.

As a former military officer doggedly pursuing an investigation through which he hopes to purge the government of dishonest individuals, Denzel Washington's role in the 2004 *Manchurian Candidate* recalls his role as Lt.

Colonel Nate Serling in Edward Zwick's *Courage Under Fire* (1996). Here, Denzel Washington plays Lt. Colonel Nathaniel Serling, a military officer who suffers from alcoholism and emotional problems as he pursues — against the wishes of the military — an investigation into the cause of the death of Captain Karen Emma Walden (Meg Ryan). In both *Courage Under Fire* and *The Manchurian Candidate*, Denzel Washington's characters are drawn into unpopular investigations that are framed around the awarding of the Medal of Honor — in the case of the earlier film, to establish a woman's heroism and in the later film to show the fictional narrative surrounding the awarding of the Medal to a white man. In the course of these investigations, both characters are fired from their military posts and later reinstated. Both characters are town between the influences of two powerful female characters. In *The Manchurian Candidate*, Marcos is torn between Eugenie Rose and Eleanor Shaw, played by Meryl Streep. In *Courage Under Fire*, Nate Serling conducts an investigation to purge military corruption, parrying between his wife, played by Regina Taylor, and his own reconstruction of the persona of Captain Karen Emma Walden, played by Meg Ryan. Each of Washington's characters seeks to expose the Washington politics surrounding the Medal of Honor, and to set the record straight in terms of who deserves this honor, whether this deserving person is a woman, a white man, or an African-American. Feminist critic Susan Linville argues that restoring the Medal of Honor to Walden allows the film to ultimately uphold an idea of the army as a "great equalizer": "It unites black and white, wealthy and less wealthy, and male and female, transcending historical divisions while focalizing events through the heroic African American's purview."[21] In solving the mystery of what happened to the Lost Patrol, the 2004 *Manchurian Candidate* implies that the military is no longer able to purge itself of corrupt influences and needs the intervention of the FBI as a "great equalizer," a democratic structure in which black women can attain positions of authority. Since the resources of powerful Halliburton-like private corporations are powering the War in Iraq, the special expanded powers of the FBI to place ordinary citizens under surveillance are validated by the film and shown to effectively police corporate attempts to gain control over the American government, namely, the presidency.

This hazardous political terrain fosters conflict within the "white zone" and the "black zone" as the female and male characters within each zone battle for control. In the "black zone," Marcos, after discovering that Rose has placed him under surveillance from the beginning of their relationship, breaks into her apartment and attacks her in the dark. The mise-en-scene of this set is blue and black; a sequence of sequentially tighter close-ups on Ben approximate Rose's point of view as she lay in her bed. Because the tight framings do not capture the lower half of Ben's torso, the shots mimic those of an attempted rape, until Rose uses her gun to force him off her. Marcos wins Rosie over to his side when he stands up to her imposing weapon and says, "Help me or shoot me; make a decision." These two African-American characters join forces to battle white characters — including Eleanor Shaw, Raymond Shaw, and the directors of the Manchurian Global corporation — who work at cross-purposes and are unable to align their common interests.

Even as the forces of the white zone are unable to unite, Raymond Shaw and Ben Marcos form a bond of military brotherhood that allows them to transcend the barriers of race. In a scene set at a schoolhouse, Marcos states, "We are connected and that's somebody that nobody can take from us." Their connection of military brotherhood runs so deep that even though he is ensconced in the "white zone" of brainwashing, Raymond feels compelled to warn Ben of the threat posed by his mother, Eleanor Shaw, and the Manchurian Global corporate figures: "You don't think they saw this coming? You don't think they factored you in? I am the enemy, Ben." When he hands Marcos his cell phone, Eleanor Shaw utters Ben Marcos' full name, triggering the pleasurable high-key lighting that accompanies the onset of her brainwashing control over a character. This scene is crosscut with news coverage of Shaw's anticipated nomination as vice-president, as he shakes the hands of black voters.

Maternal Panic

The film's narrative attributes both the strength and the weakness of the white zone to the complex consequences of Eleanor Shaw's incestual lust for her son. This incestual desire is what has motivated Eleanor Shaw to go to such extraordinary lengths to secure a powerful position for her son in the world, but at the same time her lust sets into motion the machinations through which the Manchurian Global executives choose Raymond Shaw as the target for their brainwashing scheme. The novel spells out the extent to which Eleanor Shaw herself has been, in a sense, also brainwashed by her own incestual abuse at the hands of her father, with whom she had shared a "bond so secret, so deep, and so thrilling that it surpassed into eternity the drab feelings of other people."[22] While Eleanor Shaw's incestual relationship with her father is elided from the novel, a version of this line is uttered by Meryl Streep's character: "When you smile, Raymond dearest, for that instant I am a little girl again and the miracle of love begins all over again."[23] This incestual desire becomes, for Eleanor Shaw, an Achilles' heel that proves to be her undoing in all versions of the narrative. In a perverse scheme to secure a powerful position for her son, and to thereby ensure the continuation of her total sexual control over him, Eleanor has herself been tricked into complicity with the brainwashing scheme, only to later discover that her son is the individual who has been selected as the front man for the brainwashers.[24] The vestiges of this incestual back-story are present in the 2004 film when Eleanor confronts the Manchurian Global executives and compares them unfavorably to her father, Tyler Prentiss Shaw. Vowing to usurp their power, she lavishes the body of her son and in doing so, seeks to exert her control over the body politic with her unwelcome incestual interest. Her kiss with its incestual freight defines the perversity of the white zone.

In addition to the incestual root of Eleanor Shaw's unwelcome overtures, the white zone demonstrates its reliance on gender stereotypes through gendered rhetorical figures that obfuscate its true agenda of class and race superiority. For example, as in his stump speech, Raymond Shaw exploits the effectiveness of the rhetorical use of gender to win the election: "Somewhere, right now, an American in the War on Terror is worried about his family back home. Somewhere right now, in some small American town, his grandmother is standing in her kitchen. She's got her medicine bottle in one hand, she's opening the refrigerator with the other and she's thinking, I can pay for my medicine or I can pay for my dinner, but I can't do both. I don't believe our mothers and grandmothers should have to face that kind of decision ... not in this country."

Shaw's rhetoric imagines the homeland to be protected as a grandmother who is white, female, domestic, and mythological; indeed, as Jean Bethke Elshtain has written, "the nation is home and home is mother."[25] The quotation above links the War on Terror with the need to protect this imaginary grandmother by helping her to afford both health care and food, as if, somehow, winning the War on Terror will somehow, magically, improve this grandmother's quality of life. Such war rhetoric fits in with the idea that war is a means through which gender roles are established in the modern nation state: "Wars destroy and bring into being men and women as particular identities by canalizing energy and giving permission to narrate. Societies are, in some sense, the sum total of their 'war stories.'"[26] So, in addition to recreating the Cold War image of perverse maternity, the 2004 *Manchurian Candidate* renders visible a certain resurgence of rigidly stereotypical gender roles — a protective American masculinity and a vulnerable femininity in need of all kinds of assistance — that structure political discourse during the "War on Terror" (and even the utility of the phrase "War on Terror" itself).

The conclusion of the 2004 *Manchurian Candidate* celebrates the formation of an interracial bond of military masculinity between Marcos and Shaw that cancels the power of the overweening and incestuous mother and protects the body politic from the corporate threat that she promotes. In *The Remasculinization of America* (1989), Susan Jeffords describes such patterns as they recur in the war films of the 1990s — cultural texts in which the unified purity of the soldier male is juxtaposed against a shifting and simultaneous female multiplicity: "The ability to occupy contradictory positions simultaneously is the greatest threat to the singular masculine."[27] The character of Eleanor Shaw elegantly embodies this shifting and simultaneous female threat. She is incestuous mother, she is front person for corrupt corporate interests, she is Raymond Shaw's most vocal advocate, she is an effective female politician who is unmistakeably styled to invoke the image of Hillary Clinton, a high profile politician whose presidential candidacy four years later was also bound up with problems of race, class and gender. This assassination of the shifting and simultaneous female threat eradicates the film's white zone — its space of incest and corruption — while aligning the film's black zone with America's rule of law. And yet, even though the assistance of the FBI has apparently restored law and order by the end of the film, the viewer is again reminded of the illicit pleasures manufactured by *The Manchurian Candidate* for our ready consumption. In reference to the many deaths sustained in the Iraq War by civilians and military personnel, Marcos' therapeutic flashbacks are accompanied by an aural flashback of Atticus Noyle repeating the line, "There are always casualties in war." He remembers these words while walking on the island where he was held prisoner — an island replete with Middle Eastern desert imagery. Marcos, overcome with emotion, submerges a photograph of the military unit he once commanded in the ocean water. This Ophelia imagery — and the use of yet another uncanny and unanchored reverse shot to reveal what Marcos face looks like from the perspective of the — mostly African-American — dead soldiers — again turns the tables on the apparent victory of the black zone. Within the wider frame of history and of war, the high-key lighting is again increased, bathing Denzel Washington's face in whiteness and again pointing to the viewer as the true consumer of the hypocrisy and contradictions underlying the War on Terror that resurge like the uncanny itself.

Notes

1. James Brooke, "G.I., 64, Pleads Guilty to Desertion From Duty in Korea in '65," *New York Times*, November 3, 2004, accessed from http://query.nytimes.com/gst/

fullpage.html?res=9D03E7DC163CF930A35752C1A9629C8B63 on August 10, 2007. For Jenkins' narrative of his forty year absence see also Charles Robert Jenkins and Jim Frederick, *The Reluctant Communist: My Desertion, Court-Martial, and Forty-Year Imprisonment in North Korea* (Berkeley and Los Angeles: University of California Press, 2008).

2. See for instance David E. Sanger, "With Korea as Model, Bush Team Ponders Long Support Role in Iraq," *New York Times*, June 3, 2007, accessed from http://www.nytimes.com/2007/06/03/washington/03assess.html on June 10, 2007; Fred Kaplan, "Bush's Appalling Iraq-Korea Comparison," *Slate*, May 31, 2007, accessed from http://www.slate.com/id/2167362/ on June 10, 2007; Bill Powells, "Why Iraq Isn't Korea," *Time*, June 5, 2007, accessed from http://www.time.com/time/world/article/0,8599,1628185,00.html on June 10, 2007.

3. See Greil Marcus, *The Manchurian Candidate* (London: British Film Institute, 2004), Matthew Frye Jacobson and Gaspar González, *What Have They Built You To Do? The Manchurian Candidate and Cold War America* (Minneapolis: University of Minnesota Press, 2006), and Tony Jackson, "The Manchurian Candidate and the Gender of the Cold War," *Literature/Film Quarterly* 28, no. 1, January (2000): 34–40.

4. Edwards starred in many well-known American war films from the 1940s and '50s including *Home of the Brave* (Mark Robson, 1949), *The Steel Helmet* (Samuel Fuller, 1951), *Battle Hymn* (Douglas Sirk, 1957), *Men in War* (Anthony Mann, 1957), and *Pork Chop Hill* (Lewis Milestone, 1959).

5. The Research Directorate, "Twenty-Seven Year Demographic Trends: Active Duty Forces, 1977–2004." Defense Equal Opportunity Management Institute Pamphlet, no year.

6. Joseph Williams and Kevin Baron, "Military Sees Big Decline in Black Enlistees," *The Boston Globe*, October 7, 2007, accessed from http://www.boston.com/news/nation/articles/2007/10/07/military_sees_big_decline_in_black_enlistees/ on June 20, 2007.

7. For instance, one story celebrates the role of the historically African-American First Squadron in securing the Iraq/Iran border: "Lt. Col.: Buffalo Soldiers Serve Proudly in Iraq," *CNN*, accessed from http://www.cnn.com/2004/WORLD/meast/01/08/cnna.allen/ on January 9, 2004.

8. "Medal of Honor," accessed from http://www.army.mil/cmh/moh.html on August 10, 2007.

9. Sigmund Freud, *The Uncanny*, trans. David McLintock (New York: Penguin Books, 2003), 148–149.

10. Mladen Dolar, "'I Shall Be with You on Your Wedding-Night': Lacan and the Uncanny," *October*, Fall (1991): 11.

11. Susan Sontag, "Regarding the Torture of Others," *New York Times*, 2, May 23, 2004, accessed from http://query.nytimes.com/gst/fullpage.html?res=9503E5D7153FF930A15756C0A9629C8B63&sec=&spon=&pagewanted=1 on August 10, 2007.

12. Hazel Carby, "A Strange and Bitter Crop: the Spectacle of Torture," *Open Democracy*, October 10, 2004, accesssed from http://www.opendemocracy.net/media-abu_ghraib/article_2149.jsp on November 14, 2007.

13. Thomas Elsaesser, "Tales of Sound and Fury: Observations on the Family Melodrama," *Home is Where the Heart is: Studies in Melodrama and the Women's Film*, ed. Christine Gledhill (London: BFI, 1987), 64, 66.

14. Linda Williams, *Playing the Race Card: Melodramas of Black and White from Uncle Tom to O.J. Simpson* (Princeton and Oxford: Princeton University Press, 2001), 44.

15. Susan Jeffords, *The Remasculinization of America: Gender and the Vietnam War* (Bloomington and Indianapolis: Indiana University Press, 1989), 148.

16. Gail Buckley, *American Patriots: The Story of Blacks in the Military from the Revolution to Desert Storm* (New York: Random House, 2001), 346. Robeson's biographer, Martin Bauml Duberman, claims another statement attributed to Robeson is false, in which

Robeson claimed it was "'unthinkable that American Negroes would go to war on behalf of those who have oppressed us for generations against a country [the Soviet Union] which in one generation has raised our people to the full dignity of mankind'" (Buckley, 345).

17. In June 2007 the Pentagon announced it was splitting military contracts for the Iraq War between three different companies in response to charges that Halliburton inflated costs for the war and cost taxpayers over $200 million in padded costs. See "Pentagon Splits War-Support Contract 3 Ways," *New York Times*, June 28, 2007, accessed from http://query.nytimes.com/gst/fullpage.html?res=9802EEDC163EF93BA15755C0A9619C8B63 on August 10, 2007. For details on the charges see Farhad Manjoo, "Halliburton's Iraq Gravy Train," *Salon*, February 27, 2004, accessed from http://dir.salon.com/story/tech/feature/2004/02/27/halliburton_whistleblower/index.html?pn=1 on June 15, 2007.

18. David Thompson, "Mind Control," *Sight and Sound* 14, no. 12, December (2004): 15.

19. University of Minnesota Bioethicist Steven Miles argues that the stage was set for the human rights abuses at Abu Ghraib by administrative policies and medical procedures that were inattentive to human rights, and that medical personnel were complicit in these procedures and policies and failed to report the abuses. Steven H. Miles, "Abu Ghraib: Its Legacy for Military Medicine," *Lancet* 364: 9435, July 21 (2004): 727.

20. Jackson, "The Manchurian Candidate," 39.

21. Susan E. Linville, "'The Mother of All Battles': *Courage Under Fire* and the Gender-Integrated Military," *Cinema Journal* 39, no. 2 (2000): 112.

22. Richard Condon, *The Manchurian Candidate* (New York: Signet Books, 1959), 84.

23. Condon, *Manchurian Candidate*, 326.

24. This is spelled out in the novel on page 325 and in each of the two film adaptations.

25. Jean Bethke Elshtain, "Sovereignty, Identity and Sacrifice," in *Reimagining the Nation*, ed. Marjorie Ringrose and Adam J. Lerner, 164 (Buckingham and Philadelphia: Open University Press, 1993).

26. Jean Bethke Elshtain, *Women and War* (New York: Basic Books, 1987), 166.

27. Jeffords, *Remasculinization*, 154.

10

Hiroshima and Nagasaki
Image and Reality
LAWRENCE H. SUID

"It happened in an instant. The television sets went blank, the radios — silent. The cities were gone, the future abandoned. And the only thing they had left to hold onto, is the people they love." Thus goes the tagline for the 1983 film *Testament* (Lynne Littman), another in a long line of Hollywood's portrayals of the result of dropping the atomic bombs on Japan in 1945. Also in 1983, the television movie *The Day After* (Nicholas Meyer), set in Kansas, contained the same post-apocalyptic images. The recent, critically panned, but audience-rescued television series *Jericho* (2006–2008) follows the same script. From Jericho, a small Kansas town, residents watch as a mushroom-shaped cloud rises in the distance over Denver. Other cities across the country suffer the same fate.

Hollywood, however, did not always portray the bomb in such negative terms. In this essay I shall look at the bomb in a number of feature films, television fiction, and documentaries produced between 1947 and 2005. Some are heavily critical of the United States' use of the bomb while others are less critical or even positive.

The Beginning or the End (1947)

MGM's *The Beginning or the End* (1947) alleged that it represented the building and use of the first atomic bomb with historical accuracy. The producer, Sam Marx, even went so far as to meet President Harry Truman in the White House to discuss the project and the decision to use the bomb. The producer later recounted how the President told him to tell the whole story because the bomb represented the "beginning or the end" of civilization.[1]

Marx later solicited and received permission to use Truman's comment as the title of the movie as long as the filmmakers did not attribute the phrase to the President. However, despite Truman's input and Sam Marx's stated intention of creating an accurate portrayal of the building of the atomic bomb, the film failed to produce much veracity. The film did not provide viewers with neither an understanding of the building nor of the use of the bomb. And it immediately raised the question of the limits of dramatic license in a film, feature or documentary, which claims to portray a historical event.

Anticipating criticism from historians or people with firsthand knowledge of the Manhattan Project, Marx opened the film with a disclaimer: "This is a true story. However, for dramatic license and security purposes, some rearrangement of chronology and fictionalization was necessary." *The Beginning or the End*, which today might come closer to a docudrama, did provide a newsreel-like portrayal of how the U.S. Army Corps of Engineers acquired the land and built the Manhattan Project facilities. The film also use the actual names of many of the scientists as well as that of General Leslie Groves, the head of the project. However, Colonel K.D. Nichols, the Manhattan District Engineer and actual builder of the facilities at Oak Ridge, Hanford, and Los Alamos, appeared only as part of a composite figure.

In an apparent effort to hold the story line together, the filmmakers also created a fictional scientist who appeared at all key events until he radiated himself to death on the island Tinian as he made one last inspection of the bomb the night before the mission to Hiroshima. This never happened. But the story, which appeared again in Roland Joffé's *Fat Man and Little Boy* (1989), became part of the mythology surrounding the building of the bomb and clearly intended to serve as a cautionary tale of the dangers of radiation emanating from nuclear weapons.

There were other historical obfuscations in *The Beginning or the End* apart from the radiated scientist: Despite the radioactive emission seeping from the heart of the bomb as a result of the scientist's tinkering, the technicians loaded the bomb onto the *Enola Gay* that night without, apparently, checking for damage. The film then shows the B–29 taking off in daylight even though it actually took off at 2:45 A.M. Since the tarmac on Tinian was actually brightly lit for the many cameras recording the event for posterity, the filmmakers would have, in fact, had sufficient light to recreate the historical takeoff accurately. Moreover, in most cinematic portrayals of the event, the B–29 representing the *Enola Gay* had turrets, which the actual plane did not have. Tibbets had directed that the bomber not have weaponry except for the tail gun to save weight and increase weight. Perhaps a nitpick but nevertheless inaccurate. Worse, the cinematic *Enola Gay* had its name on the right side of the fuselage instead of the left side. Are these errors significant? At a minimum, it shows a lack of concern for accuracy by the filmmakers — a lack of accuracy also reflected in the film's overall portrayal of the bombing of Hiroshima and Nagasaki.

On his part, General Groves found a few relatively minor problems in how the script portrayed him. He noted: "Incidentally, all attempts to make me demonstrate emotion, such as getting mad or excited or pacing the floor which appears from time to time [in the film], are entirely untrue to life. The less emotion, the more true to life it will be."[2] He also pointed out that contrary to the written scene, no one at the Trinity test wore goggles or covered themselves with suntan lotion. Far more serious, he questioned where the screenwriters had learned that, "I infrequently eat a chocolate or two. I would suggest that one of the two references ... be eliminated. Mrs. Groves might remember the incident less if the earlier reference were the one left in."[3]

In this instance, of course, Groves manifested more concern with his personal image than historical reality since he remained a chocoholic his entire life. Of course, his primary concern with the script focused on security matters and he concluded, "No classified information has been given away nor would any individual or group be assisted in guessing at classified information by means of this script."[4] More important, he concluded that the depictions of the Army and people, real and imagined, did "not in any way reflect discredit on the Army" and for this reason he felt that the filmmakers had "done their job well."[5]

Perhaps the filmmakers had done their job well from Groves' perspective. However, in addition to the glowing scientist, the film contained two crucial historical errors. *The Beginning or the End* portrayed then-Colonel Paul Tibbets as being guilt-stricken at having to drop the atomic bomb on Hiroshima. Admiral William Parsons, who had armed the weapon aboard the *Enola Gay*, found the completed film "dangerously *untrue*" because it portrayed key people as emotionally unbalanced, which he emphatically denied. He wrote, "Any story or film that shows us mixed up is distorting and sugar-coating the truth dangerously."[6]

In contrast, the MGM Press Book quoted an unidentified scientist as saying the film provided "the average person his clearest understanding to date of the most lethal weapon ever devised by man, and the essential problems of atomic energy now confronting the world. That, to me, makes the picture of unique value to all humanity." While the film may have raised such questions, its inaccuracies such as the radiated scientist and, more importantly, the portrayal of Tibbets, may have done serious damage to the historical record.

The Beginning or the End did one more thing: It founded the myth that President Harry S. Truman actually made the decision to drop the atomic bomb. Virtually all histories and films have adopted this version of events ever since. In effect, President Franklin D. Roosevelt made the decision to drop the bomb when he determined that the United States should undertake the effort to build an atomic bomb. At best, Truman rubber stamped Roosevelt's commitment to build and to use the bomb whenever the Manhattan Project achieved its goal of creating a weapon which would end the war. Both General Groves and General Nichols always believed that the bomb they were building would be used whenever it was completed and tested, a decision which Roosevelt made when he decided to undertake the atomic bomb program.

As documentaries about the bomb have since made clear, Truman knew nothing about the Manhattan Project and its goal until thirteen days becoming the President on April 12, 1945. Only thirteen days later did General Groves and Secretary of War Henry L. Stimson brief him about the development of the bomb and its planned use. In one of the film's most egregious rewritings of history, *The Beginning or the End* portrays Roosevelt beginning a letter to his new vice president about the Manhattan Project while vacationing at Warm Springs, Georgia. A few minutes later Roosevelt suffered his fatal stroke and so failed to inform Truman about the bomb, then nearing completion. This scene has no basis in reality.

Under these circumstances with such limited information, could Truman then have decided against its use? General Nichols, for one, believed that if Truman had decided, for whatever reason, not to use the bomb, he and the Democratic Party would have been burdened with the death of every service man who died after the bomb could have been used.[7] So despite what subsequent films and books have presented, politically as well as militarily, Truman had no reason to interfere with the ultimate use of the bomb when it became available in August, 1945.

Above and Beyond (1952)

Rather than focusing on the political issues surrounding the use of the bomb, *Above and Beyond* (Melvin Frank and Norman Panama, 1952) would five years later portray how Paul Tibbets (Robert Taylor) trained his men to drop the first atomic bomb. As such, the film depicted the bombing of Hiroshima as a necessary and positive military action. Since Tibbets had sold the rights to his story in a contract which gave him final say over his portrayal, viewers came to the film with the assumption that it accurately depicted the story of the Hiroshima bombing. *Above and Beyond* did show how Tibbets had flight tested the new B-29 Super Fortress after having flown B-17s over Europe early in the war. And the film did explore the deterioration of the relationship between Tibbets and his wife Lucey (Eleanor Parker) while he trained his men for the bomb mission. This portrayal of a military wife in a Hollywood film was virtually unique as she continually demanded to know her husband's mission and complained over his many absences. Was this an accurate rendering of their domestic life? Not really. Tibbets acknowledged that the relationship was worse than portrayed in the film. In fact, the flier's place in history would outlast his marriage, although he said the divorce did not result from the wartime experience.

Where did the film go wrong? First, it did not provide an accurate account of how Tibbets received his assignment because MGM wanted to protect the flier from Lauris Norstad, the general who remained a thorn in his side more than seven years after the end of the war. At one point, Norstad had complained that bombers based in North Africa should conduct their bombing missions at 6,000 feet instead of a much higher altitude. In the course of the meeting, Tibbets told Norstad he would fly at any height the general requested if he would fly as his copilot. That ended the discussion, but Norstad never forgot the barb. Perhaps this was a noble omission by the studio, but the actual story provides an important insight into Tibbet's life and personality. (Another officer in the meeting also remembered the confrontation and later recommended Tibbets to command the atomic bomb mission).[8]

Again, the cinematic *Enola Gay* had turrets and the name on the wrong side of the plane. Although Tibbets fixes the takeoff time as 2:15 A.M. and the film recreates his wave to men on the tarmac from the cockpit in the dark, the plane takes off in bright daylight. The film also ignored the tensions between Tibbets and his co-pilot, Bob Lewis (Dick Simmons). Lewis assumed he was going to pilot the mission since he had been flying the plane during training missions over Japan. As a result, the film did not show the tension erupting during take off on August 6, when Lewis tried to grab the wheel thinking Tibbets was failing to get the plane airborne.

Like *The Beginning or the End*, *Above and Beyond* portrays Tibbets as a reluctant bomber pilot, concerned with the terrible nature of his mission. He writes to his mother, "Mom, I'm scared. Maybe I'm scared of the idea of dropping one bomb that can kill thousands of people. It's a hard thing to live with, but it's part of my job and I've got to do it." These fictional, cinematic comments bear no resemblance to Tibbet's actual feelings about dropping the bomb. Never once did Tibbets in interviews, lectures, or his own books ever express doubts or remorse about his mission. Nor did Charles Sweeney, the pilot of *Bock's Car* which carried out the Nagasaki mission, or the other fliers in the bomb unit ever question their involvement in dropping the two atomic weapons on Japan.

As he had done after reading the screenplay for *The Beginning or the End*, Admiral Parsons voiced his objections to *Above and Beyond*'s portrayal of Tibbets. Parsons wrote to screenwriters/directors Norman Panama and Melvin Frank about the script's inaccurate portrayals of Tibbets and the men involved with the A-bomb mission. In response, the filmmakers said they would make some changes based on Parsons' input. However, they explained that "we dare not portray, in an American film today, an American airman killing eighty thousand Asiatics in a flash, and expressing no feelings of conscience about this, without seriously playing into the propaganda hands of the Kremlin."[9]

The Beginning and the End and *Above and Beyond* may well have done something significant to our future view of the decision to drop the bomb: The portrayals of Tibbets expressing grave concerns may, however inaccurate they were, have made people conclude that if the man delivering the bomb had doubts, then perhaps dropping the bomb was wrong. This certainly was the conclusion in most documentaries about the use of the bomb, particularly those appearing in 1995, the 50th anniversary of Hiroshima and Nagasaki. These portrayals ultimately merged into one message: the bomb was a terrible device which should never have been used.

Documentaries: A Negative Perspective on the Bomb

The documentary *Hiroshima: The Decision to Drop the Bomb* (1995) opens with shots of the destruction of Hiroshima and dead Japanese. One former Marine then expresses his view that the bomb was a good thing because it saved American lives, perhaps his. A Hiroshima survivor counters this view when she tells of a new-born baby trying to feed from her dead mother's breast, an image followed by images of dead bodies and collapsed buildings. The film acknowledges that Japan attacked Pearl Harbor, but then contrasts the 100,000 or more dead in Hiroshima with the 2,000 or so Americans killed in Hawaii. The filmmakers then juxtapose the rise of fascism with the development of the Manhattan Project and with Truman becoming President. The film explains Japanese imperialism and militarism and observes that the U.S. and England were facing an enemy with a reputation for "ruthlessness and brutality."

However, in tracing the period from Truman's ascendancy to the presidency, the film makes it clear that the United States should not have dropped the atomic bomb. It argues that the Emperor wanted to end the war in the summer of 1945, if not before, and Japanese diplomats had been trying to have the Soviet Union act as an intermediary. At the same time, the film blames Truman and his close advisor and now Secretary of State, Jimmy Burns, for continuing to demand unconditional surrender and refusing to indicate that the Japanese could retain the Emperor. In the end, the film states that Truman was determined to use the bomb when it became available.

The film includes a commentary from Hans Bethe, a Nobel Prize–winning physicist who observes that while the bomb served as a tremendous weapon to end the Second World War, it became a menace for the future. Also, the film tries to make the case that Truman and Byrnes saw the bomb as a means to face Stalin and the Soviet Union from a position of strength. In fact, this scholarly argument ignores a simple reality. Stalin knew about the bomb almost from the beginning of the Manhattan Project. A Russian scientist had sent him a letter explaining that all scientific articles about atomic energy had ceased to appear by 1942, with the obvious conclusion that such work was being kept secret. If Stalin needed further confirmation that the United States was trying to build an atomic bomb, his spies were regularly providing information about the work done at Los Alamos.

Groves and Nichols were certain spies worked within the Manhattan Project, in part because the Soviet Union submitted requests to obtain Uranium under Lend Lease. Groves denied the requests, but could never track down the Soviet spies during the war.[10] Stalin may have known about the Trinity Test from his spies before word reached Truman at Potsdam because the Soviet dictator showed no surprise when Truman informed him of the bomb and the test. And once the Trinity Test demonstrated that an atomic bomb worked, Stalin did not need the bombs to be dropped on Japan to know that he would now have to build a bomb of his own.

In the end, *Hiroshima: The Decision to Drop the Bomb* reveals its bias when it concludes the United States had no reason to drop the bomb in August since the invasion of Japan was not to take place until November by which time, the film argues, Japan would have surrendered. Consequently, the film concludes, "the bomb was not necessary to defeat Japan." However, this and other documentaries as well as scholarly works seem to forget or ignore reality. Most obviously, even if briefly mentioning December 7, the film does not adequately remind viewers that Japan started the war with an attack on Pearl Harbor on a quiet Sunday morning when the two countries were at peace.

The film does acknowledge that the Japanese were ruthless and brutal enemies, but does not mention the Bataan Death March or the atrocities the Japanese committed against the prisoners during the war. American soldiers had continued to die, if not in the great numbers that had resulted during the invasions of Iwo Jima and Okinawa, but continually in fighting in the Philippines, Burma, China, and even in the air over Japan. American POWs, as portrayed in *The Great Raid* (John Dahl, 2005), barely survived were and facing certain execution as allied forces approached the prison camps. If Japan had truly wanted to surrender, the Emperor or a senior official simply had to broadcast its intention by radio or through Swiss diplomats in Tokyo. Finally, even after Hiroshima and Nagasaki, and after Japan announced its surrender, young officers attempted to stage a coup to prevent any surrender.

An objective scholar must therefore ask whether *Hiroshima: The Decision to Drop the Bomb* should legitimately be considered a documentary given its clear bias and at a minimum include a pro-bomb advocate to provide a contrary view. The same question must be asked of other purported documentaries including *Hiroshima Nagasaki August, 1945* (1970) and Stephen Segaller's *Rain of Ruin: The Bombing of Nagasaki* (1995). Both of these documentaries make the case that the United States was wrong and inhumane to drop the atomic bombs by showing the countless victims and defaced survivors without a mention of Pearl Harbor or the brutal nature of the Japanese warfare.

To give it some semblance of being politically neutral, the documentary *Rain of Ruin: The Bombing of Nagasaki* includes comments by revisionist historians such as Barton Bernstein who advances his argument that Truman's claim about using the bomb saved 500,000 lives is fallacious. Using Churchill's figure of 800,000 lives saved, he points out that the planned invasion was to be carried out by only 500,000 troops. The Stanford professor has ignored the Japanese casualties and his claim that the United States would have lost only 27,000 men in the invasion, even if accurate, ignores the matter of who started the war. Also, perhaps of less significance except to show that the filmmakers had no interest in getting the basic facts right, *Hiroshima: The Decision to Drop the Bomb* used a turreted B–29 to represent the *Enola Gay* and took off in daylight instead of 2:45 in the morning.

Documentaries: A Neutral or Positive View on the Bomb

The Showtime docudrama *Hiroshima* (Koreyoshi Kurahara and Roger Spottiswoode, 1995) comes about as close to an accurate and non-judgmental portrayal of the dropping of the bomb as a film can. In doing so, it uses brief footage of the actual persons, including Truman, Groves, and Tibbets as lead-ins to actors recreating the events. The film shows Truman's becoming president and shortly having to deal with the ramifications of using the atomic bomb. While it does suggest that Truman ultimately decided to use the new weapon, *Hiroshima* makes clear that the United States simply used the bomb to end the war and save lives, both American and Japanese.

Ultimately, documentary filmmakers got the story right in the Oscar nominated documentary *The Day After Trinity* (Jon Else, 1981) and in the documentary *Victory in the Pacific* (2005). *The Day After Trinity* focuses on the building of the bomb at Los Alamos with primary attention paid to J. Robert Oppenheimer, the director of the bomb laboratory. It conveys the reality that the scientists at Los Alamos were perfectly happy to work on the bomb since possibly for the first time in their lives, they had all the resources needed to conduct their research. Only after the bomb was a reality did they question what they had achieved. The most interesting element in the film is the sequence where two scientists carry the plutonium core of the Trinity bomb to the New Mexico test site. The narrator observes that, at that time, this was all the plutonium in the world which exploded on July 16. Later, on August 9, *Bock's Car* dropped yet another plutonium bomb on Nagasaki. Thus, indirectly, the narration provides an answer to the question of whether a third bomb existed since it says that Los Alamos was able to produce a plutonium bomb every three weeks, and that a third bomb would have been ready to drop at the end of August had Japan not surrendered.

While acknowledging that such a deduction had validity, General Nichols continued to believe that the possible existence of the third bomb remained classified until 1983. Then, physicist Robert Bacher related to this author how he was completing the packing of the third core for shipment on August 14, when a friend came into the room with news that the Japanese had surrendered.[11] Only then did Nichols produce a memo from General Groves to General George Marshall dated August 10, 1945.[12] In it, Groves stated that the third bomb would be ready to send to the Pacific within a week. In a handwritten reply Marshall advised Groves that the bomb should not be used without the permission of the President. (Nichols's copy of the memo was contemporaneous with the original and he apparently did not know it had been declassified more than 10 years earlier).

In any event, the film's title comes from a remark Oppenheimer later made in answer to the question of when it was too late to stop the nuclear arms race. His answer: "The day after Trinity." Albert Einstein later expressed guilt over his role in starting the Manhattan Project when he signed a letter on August 2, 1939. This letter was written by Alexander Sachs, an informal adviser to President Roosevelt, and by Leo Szilard, and it explained that it might be possible to build an atomic bomb. On the other hand, neither General Groves, General Nichols, Paul Tibbets, nor the fliers who participated in the bombings of Japan ever expressed regret or remorse over the bombing. In fact, Groves and Nichols came to the conclusion that the bomb gave the Japanese a face-saving way to surrender, believing they could not fight against a weapon of the magnitude of the atomic bomb.

Victory in the Pacific (2005) presented more or less the same story. It showed the American forces suffering heavy casualties in capturing Iwo Jima and Okinawa and suggested that Henry L. Stimson's estimated figure of 500,000 American casualties from an invasion of Japan might have been low. Countering the revisionists' rejection of the numbers, the film pointed out that the Japanese had figured out where the Americans would be landing and had been sending additional forces to the southern island of Kyushu. The narration continues that when General Marshall received that intelligence, he considered changing the landing to another Japanese island. Appearing in *Victory in the Pacific*, Dr. Bernstein essentially agreed with the film's contention that the atomic bombing of Japan was necessary to end the war. Ideally, then, *Victory in the Pacific* sent the revisionist historians into retreat and became the final cinematic word on the necessity of using the atomic bombs on Hiroshima and Nagasaki.

Perhaps a future movie will even show the *Enola Gay* as a turretless B–29 taking off in darkness on its rendezvous with destiny.

Sources

In addition to using the Manhattan Project documents in the National Archives and the Franklin Roosevelt Library, General K.D. Nichols gave me full access to his personal records and documents he had retained when he left the Manhattan project. I also interviewed, among others, the following people: Robert Bacher, physicist at Los Alamos; Jacob Besser, crew man on both atomic bomb missions over Japan; Melvin Frank, writer, director, *Above and Beyond;* Peter Goodchild, BBC Producer of the *Oppenheimer* series; Bierne Lay, writer, *Above and Beyond;* General K.D. Nichols, Manhattan District Engineer and author of *The Road to Trinity;* Stan Norris, author of *Racing for the Bomb: General Leslie R. Groves, The Manhattan Project's Indispensable Man;* Norman Panama, writer, director, *Above and Beyond;* Dore Schary, MGM executive and producer; Henry Smyth, author of *Atomic Energy for Military Purposes*, the official history of the Manhattan Project; and Paul Tibbets, pilot of the *Enola Gay* and commander of the atomic bomb squadron.

Films

Above and Beyond (Melvin Frank and Norman Panama, 1952)
Beginning or the End, The (Norman Taurog, 1947)
Day After, The (television movie, Nicholas Meyer, 1983)
Day After Trinity, The (documentary, Jon Else, 1981)
Fat Man and Little Boy (Roland Joffé, 1989)
Hiroshima (Koreyoshi Kurahara and Roger Spottiswoode, Showtime docudrama, 1995)
Hiroshima Nagasaki August, 1945 (Geof Bartz, Paul Ronder, short documentary, 1970)
Hiroshima: The Decision to Drop the Bomb (Jeremy Bennett, documentary, 1995)
Jericho (television series, CBS, 2006–2008)
Rain of Ruin: The Bombing of Nagasaki (Stephen Segaller, documentary, 1995)
Testament (Lynne Littman, 1983)
Victory in the Pacific (An American Experience, documentary, 2005)

Notes

1. MGM press kit for *The Beginning or the End*.
2. General Lesley Groves letter to Carter Barron, April 16, 1946, document in the Suid Collection in Special Collections, Georgetown University.
3. Ibid.
4. Ibid.
5. Ibid.
6. William Parsons in letter to Air Pictorial Division on December 14, 1951. The original document is in the National Archives, photocopy held in the Suid Collection, "Above and Beyond" file, Special Collections, Georgetown University.
7. Information is from an interview with Paul Tibbets conducted by the author on July 7, 1976.
8. Information is from an interview with Dore Schary conducted by the author on March 3, 1975.
9. Letter from Norman Panama and Melvin Frank to William Parsons on January 15, 1952, Suid Collection, "Above and Beyond" file, Special Collections, Georgetown University.
10. Information is from conversations the author had between 1982 and 1984 with General K.D. Nichols during Nichols' work on his autobiography *The Road to Trinity* (New York: William Morrow and Company, 1987).
11. Information is from an interview with Robert Bacher conducted by the author on September 21, 1982.
12. Copy of memo from General Groves to General George Marshall dated August 10, 1945, Suid Collection, "Manhattan Project Collection," Special Collections, Georgetown University. Original document is in the Department of Defence's records, "Manhattan Project Files," National Archives. The memo is in Major General K.D. Nichols Papers, Army Corps of Engineers History Office, Fort Belvoir, Virginia, held in the National Archives.

Part Three

Playing at War

11

The Authentic Illusion
Twentieth Century War Reenactors and the Ownership of History
JENNY THOMPSON

For those who have never "seen the elephant," war is a foreign experience.[1] Soldiers and civilians returning from battlefronts may provide vivid accounts, but the personal, life-altering experience of war can never be conveyed fully through second-hand accounts. As writer and Vietnam veteran Tim O'Brien muses, "Can the foot soldier teach anything merely for having been there? I think not. He can tell war stories."[2]

The war experience may remain personally unknown to most people. But over the course of the twentieth and twenty-first centuries, war has increasingly become a vicarious experience. War stories are available for popular consumption through myriad forms, from games and books to photographs and films.

To be sure, measuring the impact of the vicarious war experience is a difficult task. But I sought to understand something of that impact, by investigating one group of people who make war their hobby: war reenactors. In the United States, Europe, Canada, and Asia, a subculture of war reenactors has grown up over the last four decades. With their stated goal of honoring history's real soldiers and creating an "authentic" war experience for themselves, reenactors form units, dress in period uniforms, and "re-fight" the battles of the past.

From 1993 until 2000, I conducted ethnographic research on one branch of this subculture: reenactors in the U.S. who reenact twentieth-century wars, including World War I, World War II, the Korean War, and the Vietnam War.[3] Although not as large as some other reenacting enclaves (most notably American Civil War reenacting, which boasts tens of thousands of participants),[4] these reenactors take on a subject matter from history that makes them both fascinating and controversial. Because they choose to reenact more recent wars, they have available a wide variety of evidence from which they base their representation of war, including films, photographs, and oral history from living veterans (many of whom attend reenactments and even serve as unit historians). The more controversial aspects of their representation, including their portrayal of wars that are still debated and still remembered by survivors and veterans, their use of automatic weapons, and their portrayal of Nazi soldiers,[5] means that for many outsiders to "the hobby"[6] — and the many critics of reenacting — these reenactors are especially difficult, if not impossible, to understand.

But I wanted to understand, and so I embarked on a journey into "the hobby." My research primarily consisted of conducting interviews, implementing an extensive questionnaire of nearly three hundred reenactors, and, over the course of seven years, attending forty-three reenactments, or, as reenactors call them, "events." The events I attended included public events, where reenactors present displays, perform battles, and interpret the war story for the public, and private events, where reenactors spend a weekend away from spectators to live and fight like soldiers for themselves. As a participant-observer, I dressed for the part, donning what reenactors refer to as a period "impression." For World War I events, I dressed in a Red Cross motor corps uniform, for Western Front World War II reenactments, I wore a U.S. correspondent's uniform, and for Eastern Front World War II events, I went as a Soviet combat soldier.

Through the course of my research, I came to understand the reenactors' motives and points of view. The vast majority of reenactors grew up in post–World War II and Vietnam War era America; they are mostly baby boomers and Gen-X'ers, with an average age of thirty-eight. All of them recall having grown up on a steady diet of war-related representations, including books, TV shows, games, and movies. As one reenactor put, "Our heads were filled with war stories."[7] And most had relationships with veteran relatives (over eighty percent of reenactors have relatives who fought in the wars they reenact.) And thus, they explain, they grew up — and remain — fascinated by war. In particular, they are fascinated with the figure they refer to as the "common" soldier.

This notion of a common person at war is at the base of the reenactors' portrayal. Few reenactors portray real historic figures; instead, they focus on portraying what they term the "average" man or woman who experienced war. "Most people think of history as something that happened to famous people years ago," one reenactor explains. "It his become clear to me that 'war' in whatever year is made up of regular people."[8] This focus on the experience of regular people reveals the reenactors desire to portray the war experience from the ground up. To them, war is not glamorous, heroic, or a grand narrative, and those who experienced it were real; they suffered, endured hardship and confronted the "unimaginable."

In trying to understand something about an experience that has long been a mystery to them, reenactors say they wish to represent the common war experience "authentically" and go beyond what they identify as the limits of the media's war representations. And to be sure, nearly all reenactors argue that institutions that are culturally sanctioned to represent war, such as Hollywood, the book industry, and the academy, usually distort, politicize, or romanticize the war experience. Having experienced the biases and limitations of the media or the high school history book, they turn to reenacting in order to "fill in the gaps"—as one reenactor put it—left by available accounts of war. "What I believe to be one of the better about reenacting," one reenactor explains, "is that it shows the common man's view of history. While TV and books will tell you about the generals who led and the battles which were fought, reenactors will tell you how the common soldier fared, what he wore and carried, what he fought with, and sometimes, sadly, how he died."

Outsiders tend to view the reenactors' aim as "recreating" history, but reenactors willingly admit that they cannot — nor do they want to — experience real war.[9] While their understanding of war is largely based on the media's portrayal of the soldier's experience, at the same time, as they try to fill in those gaps, they also exercise their own kind of grassroots power over the representation of war. The results of this curious interplay between war's more "official" portrayal and their own reveal the complex effects of the consumption of war. And indeed, their relationship to war is far more complicated than I had thought initially.

But first, in order to illustrate my findings, I must tell a war story.

"A Magic Moment"

The thick Maryland woods are spread over steep hills, providing a challenging setting for what today serves as the Eastern Front of World War II. About fifty reenactors are here at this weekend-long, invitation-only event at a state-owned camp in Maryland, rented by reenactors for the weekend, promising complete privacy.

As we head out to begin the first combat scenario, I am accompanied by two reenactors I have known for a while, Dave Watkins and Luke Gardner, and another I have just met, John Ostroski.[10] All three are portraying Soviet privates. We're moving out into the woods to take positions and hide from the Germans, who have deployed somewhere secretly earlier in the morning. Our commander leads our group of Soviets, about twenty in all, with little comment as we make our way down a path lying at the base of a narrow valley. Our group stretches up a steep hill, climbing steadily, silent, rifles in bare hands. Several lag behind. By the time I reach the top, I find myself alone. Where are Dave and Luke? I continue walking on to a flat plateau where the woods begin to thicken. I see John up ahead, crouched behind a fallen tree, peering intently into the woods. Now what?

John turns around and indicates that I should take cover. I kneel down where I can keep an eye on him. For what seems like an eternity, I wait, crouching in silence. I see nothing but leaves. I hear nothing but an occasional rustle as John shifts his weight. He seems determined to defend this position. From what? I ask myself. But there's John, holding his silent vigil, staring in front of him, his rifle at his side. I resolve myself to eternal waiting and sit down, trying at least to get a little more comfortable, when I hear: Crunch. Crunch. Crunch. The sound of a slow step from the woods.

I sit up quickly and peer ahead. My heart leaps as the leaves give way to a single German soldier headed in our direction. He walks in slow motion, holding his rifle at the ready, turning his head cautiously from side to side, scanning the woods. John glances back to me, nods his head to acknowledge that he sees him, and then gingerly shifts his weight, moving noiselessly into firing position.

I am now paralyzed by a sense of fear; my heart is thumping in my chest and the blood racing through my veins. What next? My thoughts race as I realize that I'm entirely overwhelmed by a sense of vulnerability. After all, I hardly know these guys. What am I doing in the woods with them? Before I can answer that question, John brings his rifle to aim, pulls the trigger and — crack!—fires in the German's direction. John pulls the bolt, expends the shell, and fires again, crack! I barely see the German "take his hit" and fall before John is on his feet, signaling me to run.

A few minutes later, we stop near several towering trees. John whispers, "There are some Germans to my right." My eyes adjust to the leaves, and I shiver when I realize that there are several other Germans about thirty feet to the left. Surrounded by the dense woods, they're sitting on the ground eating lunch. They talk quietly; a big German shepherd sits near its master. (I had not seen these particular reenactors before.) "There are Germans over here too," I tell John. "Okay," he whispers, "I'm going to kill these guys," he indicates the Germans to his right. "Then let's surrender to them." He points to the lunching soldiers. "It's fun," he says, "to be captured."

As John fires to the right, I watch the members of the lunch party. Upon hearing gunfire, they spring to their feet and grab their rifles. John turns to me with a look of glee, and we move out from behind the tree. I now face three Germans walking toward us, dog in tow, their rifles high against their cheeks, muzzles pointing directly at us. They yell at us fiercely in German with a note of panic in their voices. Hands in the air, we walk toward them. As we close ranks, one indicates for us to kneel. They surround us. The officer stands at the helm, his dog panting at his side, while the two privates begin to search us. One soldier rifles through my pockets and bread bag. I'm worried that he'll get mad when he finds the "non-period" (modern) items in my bag — rolls of film, a bottle of apple juice. But he ignores them and instead concentrates on my camera. He points to it and says knowingly that I'm a spy: "*Spion*!" He glares at me, squinting his eyes. When he notices my pistol his face lights up. He takes it from me, examines it, and tucks it in his belt, smiling.

Meanwhile, John is performing much more authentically than me, shouting in Russian what I take to be unfavorable evaluations of the German army. When one of the soldiers takes John's rifle from him, John tries to explain something that seems not to be part of the game. In a combination of hand gestures and Russian, he tries to tell the German to release the bolt for safety purposes. The German holds the rifle, looking at him quizzically. He doesn't understand. Finally, John gives up and asks in English, "Would you release the bolt?"

The German nods. He fumbles around but apparently doesn't know how. He gives up and hands the rifle back to John who quickly releases it, sets the safety on, and then hands it back to his captor. After watching this exchange, the officer reprimands his private and says, also in English, "Never give a weapon back to a prisoner!" All of us try to muffle our laughter at this comical breach in authenticity.

"*Tod?*" (dead?) one soldier asks the officer after the search and interrogation are complete. "*Ja*," he responds, barely looking up. The soldier walks slowly around us and stands behind our kneeling figures. I see him from the corner of my eye as he raises his gun and rapidly fires several rounds over our heads; for a split second, I'm not sure if he has killed me, but deciding he probably has, I drop to the ground at the same time as John. I keep my eyes closed, wanting to appear dead.

When I open my eyes I see that my pistol has been returned and is lying on the ground in front of me. John stirs and asks if I'm okay. "Yes," I say weakly. "That was fun," John says, picking up his own weapon lying in front of him. He runs his hand through his hair and rests an arm on his knee.

"Yeah," I respond, feeling incapable of any deep conversation. Suddenly, the German soldier, our executioner, reappears. He is smiling. With an extended hand, he congratulates us for doing such a good job. "Thanks a lot!" he says amicably. "That was really great!" We all shake hands, and John says, "Hey, you know, you guys could have roughed us up more than you did." The German laughs. His face is ruddy with cold. His eyes are shining. "Maybe next time," he says. With a quick nod, he disappears once more into the woods.

"We're Here, We're There, This is It": The Authentic Illusion

My experience during that little scenario in the woods went a long way in explaining something about reenacting that is not usually apparent to the outsider. Acting within their generic, open-ended scenarios, reenactors neither try to relive history nor transport themselves in time. Instead, they produce and simultaneously consume their own illusions — "watching it" as reenactor Luke Gardner put it — while "acting in it." No longer are they passive viewers in a movie theater or comfortable readers lounging on a sofa. Rather, they have assumed the powerful, dual roles of creator of and participant in a war representation.

While reenactors will often explain their hobby by stating that they are trying to recreate war and thereby understand what war was like, the above experience undermined that explanation. In fact, given my initial assumption that the reenactors' ultimate aim was to recreate war authentically, I was surprised at the way the participants in the above scenario conducted themselves. Clearly, we were not trying to recreate a specific historic battle. Instead, all of us behaved as if following an unwritten generic script with a vague historical storyline: What would happen if some German soldiers captured some Soviet soldiers in the woods during World War II? The result, from the Soviets' perspective, was not very good of course, but from the reenactors' perspective, it was a success. Although our execution was enacted in a rather off-handed way, as though unbridled cruelty (never mind a war crime) was perfectly acceptable as well as authentic, it was performed within a larger context of teamwork and even friendship. One minute killed and the next congratulated by our executioner, we were clearly acting. But we were also our own audience, able to break character and evaluate the quality of our play. And there was something very playful, however macabre, about the scenario. But nowhere was there any evidence that we were truly convinced we were reliving World War II. Something else seemed to keep our behavior in check.

Certain ideas about history as much as the rules and boundaries of reenacting itself seemed to exercise more control over our actions than any effort to lose ourselves in a time-travel fantasy did. In fact, both the bolt incident and the eventual return of our weapons suggested that real-world considerations (safety and property rights) were not to be ignored even in the most authentic of scenarios.

"We had become actors in a historical play," Luke Gardner said, describing a reenacting experience that he judged a success, "that we were all benefiting from. We were all enjoying the play, we were acting in it, but we were also watching it. So it was very intriguing. That's really what the hobby can be at its best."[11]

Luke's description of what it is like to experience a scenario when things seem real describes my feeling as I watched those Germans approach us in the woods. As they walked toward us with their rifles raised, I remember thinking, "Gee, this looks really real." As I watched the incredible spectacle unfolding before me, it was hard to remember that I was also part of it. It was both thrilling and scary.

I was later able to understand my experience in terms of the larger context of reenacting. My experience was, to use a reenactor term, "a magic moment." All reenactors have their own stories of achieving a magic moment, a time when suddenly everything comes together and they achieve their goal: they have created an authentic war experience so pure that, always only for a moment, they feel as though they are "there." "We all talk about that magic moment," reenactor Scott Friewald says, "when you feel like you're back in the period you're recreating. I mean, it's easy at that point to almost forget you're in [the present]."[12]

Although a magic moment is "usually a very occasional thing to experience," as one reenactor says, it is often described as the apex of the hobby. A magic moment is "fantastic," one reenactor says simply. Another insists that it "border[s] on something spiritual." And another calls it "Nirvana." Reenactor Alain Benson struggled to give words to the sensation: "It's sort of ... is the word euphoric? You feel sort of ... it sort of makes you feel like really great because you ... it's the closest you can come to being there without really having to live through all that stuff."[13]

I knew not having to live through "all that stuff" while still achieving authenticity was the central, if contradictory, goal of a private event. And the more I noticed how action easily went in and out of certain boundaries, from period behavior (fighting, executions) to nonperiod commentary (socializing, congratulating), the more I came to believe that the terms re-creation or reenactment do not, as some reenactors themselves argue, accurately describe what goes on in a private event. (In fact, many reenactors think the term "reenactment" is a misnomer, even though they usually use it themselves.)

Not only is a private event structured by rules (helmets off to indicate that one is dead) but there are also certain limits to authenticity, times when it is acceptable to be oneself and times when it's not. Why else would a reenactor conclude an execution scenario by shaking his victim's hand? Even if some speak of achieving authenticity in terms of "feeling that you're back in the period you're recreating," I suspected this only came close to describing something hard to explain. Only after I listened to reenactors describing their magic moments and experienced my own, did I understand precisely what they were trying to achieve.

"There have been quite a few times when I've felt like I was actually there," reenactor Scott Mies answered when I asked if he had ever experienced a magic moment. He recalled an Eastern Front World War II event when he went on patrol with several other Soviet reenactors in the rain. "I was thinking to myself about actually seeing this as a real experience before my eyes," Scott remembers. As they moved cautiously through a field, single file, he was suddenly reminded of "film footage of Soviet troops, moving among this swamp area in some of the Russian back woods, and you know, a couple guys were ahead of me and even though ... I mean," Scott stumbled, "moments like that make you seem like you're actually looking at something that could be incorporated as an actual, you know, historical scene."[14]

Such a description, however confused, reveals that reenactors do not judge the authenticity of their experiences by their success at transporting them in time or recreating actual war. Instead, they judge a moment's authenticity by its success at resembling authentic *representations* of war — in Scott's case, film footage. What they strive to achieve, therefore, is not a pure re-creation of history. Rather, they try to create authentic-looking moments that are judged authentic because they resemble other representations that document history, or, more precisely, what history looks like. The creation of an authentic war experience, therefore, does not rely on replicating history, but on duplicating elements from its authentic representations. In this way, reenactors create their own war representation — an "illusion for ourselves," as reenactor John Loggia describes it[15] — that appears authentic-looking.

Once I understood this essential aspect, I understood why the vast majority of reenactors don't assume identities of actual historical individuals — a fact which surprised me at first. For, in order fully to experience the phenomenon of an illusion, they must remain themselves. Like actors, they must have an ever-present consciousness that what they are experiencing is not historically real, but only looks as if it were. Their own descriptions of magic moments universally acknowledge this near-reality. "I was really wrapped up in the intensity of it," Luke says, recalling an incredible reenacting experience. "Only because it was so real, realistic seeming."[16] John Loggia describes another realistic-seeming experience at a World War I event when he led a night attack across no-man's-land: "[We were] moving up to the Allied lines, there was smoke everywhere and there were people who were feigning death and they looked like they were really dead. There was a guy very stiff with his arm up and that was like being there ... My heart was beating because I kept thinking when are the Germans going to get us? When are they going to open up on us?"[17] Keenly aware that others were only feigning death, but looked like they were dead, John underscores how the experience of an illusion doesn't involve believing oneself to be in the past. Instead, it relies on knowing one is not.

Reenactors argue that it is only through experiencing a magic moment that they gain a deep and personal perspective on history and an insight into the experience of war. For John, such a perspective came during that scary nighttime raid; Luke says he gained perspective during a particularly memorable patrol he participated in at a Vietnam War reenactment. Just moments before an ambush, Luke says, all seemed to become intensely real as he and his unit moved cautiously through a field of high grass. Luke crouched slightly, his breath slowed, and he could hear his heart thumping in his chest. He slowly turned his head, and saw his men walking steadily, strung out through the field, their rifles at the ready, sweat pouring down their faces, their eyes scanning the woods for the enemy. Just seconds later, the ambush began. To this day, Luke describes this moment as the single best reenacting experience he has ever had. "It's amazing," he recalls. "It still sticks in my mind."[18]

Alain Benson also recalls a moment that he will not soon forget. Before a combat scenario, he and the other members of his German World War II unit were standing in the frozen January woods dressed in uniform. "It trips you out," Alain says. "You really think you're there because everything that they're wearing is real. It's exactly what they wore — it's all real. It's real equipment and uniforms and the other part is it's all used and dirty. It's exactly how the guy would have looked who had worn it probably the day when it was taken away from him." Rather than thinking that he had literally been transported back to 1942, Alain says he found himself able to imagine history by looking at the scene from the perspective of a 1942 movie camera. "It's always just a few seconds where you just sort of ... you can imagine the films that you see, the documentaries of the German soldier smoking a cigarette with a bunch of other guys at the side of a road, with the tanks driving by. It's black and white. For a few seconds you can just sort of imagine that from his perspective, taking a drag from the cigarette, that's what it looked like from his perspective, in color."[19]

By creating their own images of the past, they actually do see war from an unusual point of view — their own. Describing the awe he and his friends felt at that moment, Alain remembers: "We even like stopped. We just stopped and said, 'Check it out. Check out the mist and the snow and doesn't it remind you of the photographs and the films we've always seen so much of? We're here, we're there, this is it.'"[20]

Such a point of view, confusing in its own right (being here, being there) is one that seems unconcerned with history's big picture. Instead, revelations are far more personal. One reenactor felt closer to history by walking through a trench at dawn, the fog clinging to its rough sides. But he was not, by his own account, imagining he was a soldier. Instead, he was enraptured by the illusion. What he saw and had a part in creating, he said, looked as if it were a replication of the trench-life descriptions he had read in Paul Fussell's book *The Great War and Modern Memory*.[21] Others forge a connection by getting killed in the back of a truck and then discussing how their experience resembled an event they had read about. Others marvel at their illusion's capacity to let them "imagine," as reenactor Fred Legum said, "what that must have been like when it actually happened." [22]

Guided by their knowledge of what could have happened and what history looked like, reenactors are thus unencumbered by having to relive particular historical experiences. Instead, they step into the boots of common soldiers and walk around in them for themselves. "We're not reliving the experience," as reenactor Hank Lyle explains. "We're living it for ourselves."[23]

As my next war story shows, it is this power — this tantalizing opportunity to exercise control over history's portrayal — that captivates reenactors.

One Version of Events

By two-thirty in the afternoon the fighting at this World War II private event is in full swing. I lounge on the front seat of a World War II truck next to Brian Shore, who's happily devouring a chocolate bar. Suddenly, I notice Craig Jones, a reenactor I've known for a few years, and another fellow I don't know, standing next to the truck, dressed in GI uniforms, carrying rifles.

"Hi, Craig!"

"Hi," Craig responds nervously, a strange reaction from someone who's usually extremely gregarious. "Uh," he begins, his eyes surveying the truck.

"What's going on?"

"I'm afraid I'm going to have to ask you to get out of the truck. We're taking this truck."

"Oh," I say as I realize what's happening. Craig and his companion are Germans in disguise.

Guided by Craig's rifle, I climb into the back of the truck. Craig climbs in after me. "We're hijacking this truck and heading for the German lines," he says. Now he seems more relaxed. "We had to make our way over here and find a way back. We're on a mission from Axis HQ."

The other German is back. "Okay," he tells Craig. "I tied him up. When we're ready we'll have him drive us across to HQ."

"No way," Craig says emphatically. "You gotta drive. Just leave him tied up. We don't want any problems."

The small German pulls out a cigarette and lights it before responding. "It's like a double clutch. I don't know how to drive one of those."

"Shit," Craig sighs. "Okay, make him drive, but do it now."

But soon, the small German returns. "C'mon," he says with a frown. "We're going to have to find another vehicle. That guy claims he can't drive the truck either."

"Oh, Jesus," Craig grimaces.

"Yeah," the German responds. "He keeps stalling it."

"Okay." Craig jumps out of the truck, stomps out his cigarette, and grins. "See you later, Jenny."

As quickly as they arrived, they're gone. I get out of the truck to find Brian still in the driver's seat. When he sees me he starts laughing.

"Oh, man!" he says.

"What happened?"

"That was so funny. That guy's telling me, 'Drive! Go!' and I pretended to be all confused and nervous and like, 'I don't know how to drive this thing!' So I was grinding the gears, letting it stall, and acting like I didn't know how. The guy's really getting frustrated and he's like, 'If you don't get going, I'm going to have to kill you.' So I'm like, 'Well, if you kill me, then this truck is still staying where it is, 'cause no one else can drive it!'" Brian is exuberant, clearly proud he outwitted our would-be captors.

"Wow," I say.

After a minute Brian says, "When our guys come back, let's tell them we killed those guys." He looks at me and raises his eyebrows.

"That we killed them?" I am incredulous.

"Well, yeah," Brian says turning the ignition and expertly putting the double clutch in gear. "Let's just tell them that." He pauses. "I mean, those guys put us into their scenario. So why shouldn't we finish it the way we want to?"

"Okay," I agree, not wanting to change the course of history in this event. "We'll tell them that."

Brian smiles as he steers the truck across the ground. Several American troops are marching back from action. One flashes a victory sign at me, and I nod my head and sigh. Why not? Does it really matter that the truth of what actually happened will differ from the way Brian has decided to represent it?

Later that night, I ran into Craig. He squeezed my arm and grinned. "Now how about that!" he said laughing. "Wasn't it fun to be hijacked?"

"Yeah, at least it would have been. But it didn't happen."

Craig, still grinning, looks pleased. "Well, we figured out what happened. That guy, the driver, he just didn't want to play. You know, he just wasn't into it."

"Were you disappointed?"

"Well," he shrugs his shoulders. "That's the kind of over the edge stuff I wish more reenactors would get into. But most guys can't be forced to do things like that. They get all bent out of shape. They're just fair-weather reenactors. But it was a funny story."

Later, I realized the scenario had produced more than one story. Each of us could make up our own version of events — captured, escaped, doublecrossed — it didn't matter what had actually happened that day, or for that matter, what happened in World War II. What seemed even more important than history was what we would decide to tell everyone later, how we would choose to tell our own war stories.

Part of Our History

"People want to have their own stories and their own history," reenactor Scott Mies explains, "and sometimes they want to make their own history by going out and starting a war."[24] Speaking about actual war, Scott makes a point that applies to reenacting as well. Not only do reenactors create authentic illusions and experience magic moments, but they also take away evidence of their war experiences. And, as Brian, Craig, and I would do, they tell war stories.

"He leapt forward," a reenactor wrote of a unit member's stunning exploits, "screaming as he drew near the Soviet lines. Muzzles flashed as he entered the hellish hailstorm."[25] Some stories have become folktales among certain reenactors, such as the account of Luke's orchestration of the intense Vietnam combat patrol when all of the members of his unit reported one of the best reenacting experiences they had ever had.

Telling war stories is the verbal equivalent to an equally time-consuming activity at events: taking photographs. According to my questionnaire, nearly seventy percent of reenactors report that they take pictures with modern cameras during events, often in the midst of combat. Some even devote themselves entirely to the camera, donning the popular impression of war correspondent. In fact, so central is the taking photographs to reenacting that one Vietnam War reenactment unit in France organizes events it calls "photo-reenactments," which are designed solely for the purpose of crafting realistic-looking war images, and often even involve the staging of scenes to replicate actual period photographs.[26] While some reenactors argue that using "non-period" cameras is inauthentic, most admit that they love to have their pictures taken in uniform. The visual richness of an event, particularly to a novice, is undeniable; one reenactor, a professional photographer, said that to anyone with a camera, an event appears as a series of endless images waiting to be captured.

Even so, the ubiquity of cameras at events surprised me. At my first reenactment, as if my encounter with the mass of World War I reenactors was not enough of a shock, when several reenactors drew cameras from their kits to take pictures of me in uniform, it left me dumbfounded. It seemed incongruous that they should engage in such a self-conscious act, ill suited to what I believed then to be their wish to time travel. But I soon realized that just like a well-told war story, a reenacting photograph that "captures," as Luke says, an event's "historical quality [and] could have been shot on the scene," testifies to their success at staging war.[27] And often, they explicitly reveal their efforts to make the creation of such images possible: "We do not want to see visible, out of place, non-period/incorrect items," the rules of one event announcement read. "Anyone taking pictures of these areas should walk away with a photograph as it would have appeared in 1944."[28]

Whether admiring their own images in their reproduction *soldbuchs* (pay books) or posting reenacting photographs on a website, reenactors reveal their desire to possess an authentic (looking) representation of war that features themselves squarely in its center. Reenactor Richard Paoletti told me he spent two days before our scheduled interview trying to think up an analogy to explain this fascination: "No other collection that I can think of — like stamps or coins — you can't just shrink yourself into a stamp and put yourself in the book and go, you know, 'Oh, look! I'm a stamp!' Right? I mean this is something that you can actually collect and actually show off. Be a part of it."[29] Having invented a way to put themselves "in the book" of history, reenactors carve out a place for themselves in the long history of war: in the representations of war.

And there is no doubt that reenactors are captivated by images of war. Since 1855, during the Crimean War, when the camera was used for the first time on a battlefield, photographs have become central components to war. Since then, still and moving images, both documentary and fictional, seem to capture war's many facets of horror, devastation, fear, and even triumph. From Timothy O'Sullivan's gruesome pictures of American Civil War corpses to Steven Spielberg's jittery images of Americans landing on Omaha Beach in *Saving Private Ryan* (1998), images of war have been conveyed steadily to a public that remained far beyond the borders of a battlefield. As ardent consumers of these war images, reenactors are fascinated by their realism, citing the use of photographs as the number one most used and trusted historical source upon which they base their own representations.[30]

To be sure, reenactors place themselves in history quite literally. One reenactor uses his skills as a graphic designer to replicate period *Life* and other wartime magazine covers. On a computer, he copies the covers' original layout, removes the images of history's actual players, and replaces them with images of reenactors; others produce pseudo-documentary films shot entirely at reenactments. Reenactor William Gregory described a video his unit made called *Men Against Blanks*: "We used the opening credits of an original German newsreel and the soundtrack which described the battle, then we edited in the Battle of the Bulge from one of the Ft. Indiantown Gap battles. We then added subtitles.... It was shot in black and white and really looks like one of the original films."[31]

Alain Benson uses a 1942 Leica camera to take photographs that are, he says, "indistinguishable" from period war photographs. He showed me one of his prize examples, a black-and-white photograph of several reenactors standing at the side of a road, silhouetted by gray fog. He explained how he wanted "to create this image because, remember, two hours before this photograph ... these guys were all wearing blue jeans and T-shirts and we were driving our Volkswagens and Nissans. So I sort of—I created this moment."[32]

With great pride Alain claims that he has even fooled some top publishers into thinking his images are authentic. Many reenactors even told me that authentic-looking photographs of reenactors have been reproduced in books with captions that tout them as actual war photographs. Further, contemporary war documentaries often blend footage of reenactors with historical footage, making it extremely confusing for viewers, who don't know when they are watching film shot during a war and when they are watching footage that a documentary crew shot a few months ago. Similarly, reenactor Morris Call's own carefully produced replicas of period World War II German documents—made for reenactors—have been sold on eBay at prices that only original pieces can command. Although Morris is vehemently opposed to passing off as authentic the documents he makes, he says that other less scrupulous militaria dealers sell them under the guise of being period for as much as one hundred dollars. Another reenactor once had an extremely authentic-looking formal portrait of himself taken when his unit awarded him the Knight's Cross. Years later, he came across the photograph at a militaria show where it was being sold as authentic. "That's me!" he told the dealer.

Reenactors often use the evidence of their war experiences in the real world. During the holidays, Fred Legum and others send greeting cards straight from the trenches; others use email addresses that signify their personas (to give a hypothetical example: Britsoldier@anyoldISP.net) or business cards designed to resemble period imagery; others display formal portraits of themselves in uniform in their homes; and Tilden Scott shows videos of reenactments in which he has participated to his high school students when teaching them history.

Whatever form their war stories take, reenactors reveal their desire to involve themselves in history's representation and thereby "own" or possess history for themselves. And it is only through the hobby that a reenactor can "feel as though you are part of our history of the wars." "I have had a lifelong love of history," one reenactor explains. "But something was always missing. At my first reenactment, it all came together…. Reenacting lifts history off the page and makes it real." What was missing, of course, was themselves. Having viewed common soldiers for so long from afar, reenactors can now enjoy a connection to history that they have long imagined or desired. Further, by appropriating history for themselves, they can also assert their authority over the representation of history. Such power gives one reenactor "a sense of personal fulfillment and deep, internal joy that I never thought possible." And indeed, they delight in their ingenuity, often brimming with self-satisfaction and even arrogance as they describe their own roles in history.

The amount of time, effort, and often money, reenactors expend on their hobby means that their game is a serious one. But its seriousness also lies in the fundamental meanings associated with their endeavors. Through reenacting, they do more than play a game. They also seek to exercise their own power over the official realm of history. They are able to serve as both producers and consumers of the war story, able to judge historical evidence, create scenarios, capture images, tell war stories, and thereby "own" history for themselves.

The question of why reenactors go to such lengths to represent war by and for themselves can perhaps best be answered by understanding just how powerful and seductive the story of war is. Clearly, reenactors are not seeking true war experiences, and they repeatedly express their belief that war is horrible. But they also acknowledge that their lifelong fascination with war has been fed by countless representations of war, leading them directly to their hobby.

The reenactors' fascination with war, and their desire to study, represent, and exercise control over its representation, reveals the tremendous impact not only of war's representation on people, but also of war itself. To be sure, war's impact is not only felt by those who fight or survive it. It also extends to those who never experience it personally. In a sense, reenactors respond to a legacy of war by making their own use of that history. And their choices in representing war reveal the contemporary nature of a hobby that is ostensibly looking to the past, but is in fact, largely about the present. In short, reenactors make use of war in ways that are meaningful to their present-day concerns and desires.[33]

In the end, as reenacting shows, one does not have to "see the elephant" to feel war's repercussions. Everyone is, to some degree, shaped by war. All of us, it seems, can tell our own war stories.

Notes

1. This essay has been adapted from my book length study of reenactors, *War Games: Inside the World of 20th-Century War Reenactors* (Washington, D.C.: Smithsonian Books, 2004).

2. Tim O'Brien, *If I Die in a Combat Zone* (New York: Bantam Doubleday Dell Publishing Group, 1972), 32.

3. The reenactors who were a part of my study were primarily from states in the Northeastern and Mid-Atlantic regions of the U.S.

4. Twentieth century war reenacting largely grew out of American Civil War reenacting, which grew exponentially following the American Civil War centennial celebrations and reenactments that took place in the U.S. in the 1960s. While there are no official figures, my estimate is that there are roughly six thousand twentieth century war reenactors in the U.S.

5. Twentieth century war reenactors not only portray American soldiers, but also German, Australian, Soviet, Scottish, Japanese, Canadian, French, British, and Vietnamese troops.

6. Reenactors refer to all war reenacting as "the hobby."

7. Tilden Scott, letter to the author, February 27, 1997.

8. The quotes used here that are attributed to unnamed reenactors are drawn from reenactors' open-ended, written responses to questions on my questionnaire.

9. According to the results of my questionnaire, about one third of reenactors have served some time in the military; only a handful, however, are veterans of a war.

10. All reenactor names used here are pseudonyms.

11. Luke Gardner, interview with the author, September 1995.

12. Scott Friewald, interview with the author, March 1997.

13. Alain Benson, interview with the author, March 1996.

14. Scott Mies, interview with the author, June 1997.
15. John Loggia, interview with the author, November 1995.
16. Luke Gardner, interview with the author, September 1995.
17. John Loggia, interview with the author, November 1995.
18. Luke Gardner, interview with the author, September 1995.
19. Alain Benson, interview with the author, March 1996.
20. Ibid.
21. Paul Fussell, *The Great War and Modern Memory* (New York: Oxford University Press, 1975).
22. Fred Legum, interview with the author, May 1997.
23. Hank Lyle, interview with the author, April 1997.
24. Scott Mies, interview with the author, June 1997.
25. William Azari, "After Action Report: North Vernon 17–2–96," *Third SS Zeitung: The Official Newsletter of the Re-enactment Group "Totenkopf"* (April 1996): 18.
26. Grunts: French Vietnam War Reenactment Society, unit webpage, http://grunts.free.fr.
27. Luke Gardner, interview with the author, September 1995.
28. Event announcement, "'Anzio' Breakout from the Beachhead," World War II private reenactment, Massachusetts, U.S., sponsored by the Third Panzer Grenadier Division, August 1998.
29. Richard Paoletti, interview with the author, February 1997.
30. In putting together their impressions and in an attempt to create authentic looking events, reenactors turn to historical sources. While period photographs and other primary sources are seen as fairly trustworthy, many other sources are viewed with skepticism. The process of research and the great lengths to which reenactors go to achieve authenticity are discussed in *War Games*.
31. William Gregory, "Men Against Blanks," email posted on the World War II newsgroup, July 31, 1996.
32. Alain Benson, interview with the author, March 1996.
33. The ways in which contemporary issues and themes are played out within the hobby are discussed at length in *War Games*.

12

Digital War Games and Post 9/11 Geographies of Militarism

MARCUS POWER

Introduction: The Simulation of Digitized Superiority

> It felt like I was in a big video game. It didn't even faze me shooting back. It was just natural instinct. *Boom! Boom! Boom! Boom!* ... The insurgents were firing from the other side of the bridge.... We called in a helicopter for an airstrike.... I couldn't believe I was seeing this. It was like [the game] *Halo*. It didn't even seem real, but it was real.[1]

In the course of the Gulf War numerous news stories emerged in which U.S. troops refer to their experience of combat as "like a video game." In the quotation above, from a story written in February 2006 by a *Washington Post* journalist, Sgt. Swales likens his experience of combat in Mosul to the popular game *Halo* (Bungie Studios, 2001), and notes that the impulse to return fire seemed "natural" after years of video gaming. In his newspaper report, the *Washington Post* journalist Jose Vargas notes that many soldiers from the same battalion as Swales played games like *Halo, Full Spectrum Warrior* (FSW) and *SOCOM II: U.S. Navy SEALS*[2] during their downtime, noting that their Playstation and Xbox gaming consoles crowded the trailers that served as their barracks. The war-as-game motif is not unique to this battalion or even to this particular war but what is different is that video war games are filtering down through the ranks to the lowest levels of infantry soldiers whilst the broader vision contemplated for video games at the highest levels of the Pentagon is unprecedented. Additionally, the video games themselves are increasingly seeking to offer virtual experiences of distant (but contemporary) combat theatres relaying particular kinds of stories about America, its technologies and its "others."

12. Digital War Games and Post 9/11 Militarism (Power)

Today, digital games[3] retailers offer a range of "grittily realistic" games that seek to represent and celebrate the arts of war. Since September 11, 2001 (hereafter referred to as 9/11) the kinds of video games released by the gaming industry have increasingly sought to mirror real world conflict scenarios, particularly the recent U.S. military interventions in Afghanistan and Iraq. A particular trend is toward the popularity of games of "covert-ops" where a secretive military operation (with no international sanction) must be played out. Terrorist threats must here be neutralized only by secret and illegal actions. This theme existed prior to 9/11 but there has been a surge in the popularity of these games, not only in their production but also in terms of their consumption.[4] Almost as soon as a new rogue nation has been identified in Washington, a combat video game appears "to exploit the thrilling potential of slaughtering its people."[5] There are also games like *Conflict: Global Storm* (Pivotal Games, 2005) that involve fictional squirmishes (set in imaginary countries like Zekistan) against terrorists and guerrillas worldwide. Simulating guns, explosions, enemies and death, virtual recruits can do battle with various enemies in ways that often involve a valorization of past American military conflicts or seek to parallel contemporary American geopolitics. As they exist in video games, these racialised enemies are portrayed as specific groups of people who exist in the "real" world.[6] The Iraqi army is often present in the construction of video game narratives, firmly resurrecting the idea of the Iraqi army in the popular imagination of American gamers. Such games provide opportunities for American civilians to enlist and fight in a virtual Iraq where "to play is to be a virtual recruit in a war consumed."[7]

Given the vast amounts of money sloshing around the industry[8] and the growing popularity of digital games, it is surprising that they have not received more critical attention. It has been estimated that 75 percent of American households play digital games with 228 million digital games sold in the U.S. in 2005 alone, effectively two games for every household.[9] Popular console releases often rival Hollywood films in terms of earnings. The industry was estimated to be worth $23.2 billion in 2003 and is predicted to reach $33.4 billion in 2008.[10] Aside from being commercially very lucrative, digital war games represent a powerful medium to explore the ways in which images elicit consent for the U.S. military. Some post 9/11 video games allow players not only to do battle with familiar adversaries but also to become soldiers from the safety of their own homes, providing exposure along the way to the technological marvels of the U.S. military. Amidst the fantasy and fetish around military hardware players gain a sense that the technology on display here represents money well spent for U.S. taxpayers as well as a sense of participation in this military expenditure since the playspace of the game offers a chance to experiment with these newly acquired military toys.

Some post 9/11 games like *America's Army* (U.S. Army, 2002) exist as virtual advertisements for the present and future glory of the U.S. Armed Forces in ways that Frank Capra, director of the *Why We Fight* series of seven World War II propaganda films funded by the War Department, would have been proud of. Current video games focused on militarism and warfare are similar to the *Why We Fight* films "except they've morphed into 'how we fight' video games which takes away from a lot of the other 'why' questions, and all the moral questions that are connected to that."[11] Such games, besides primarily serving as an increasingly effective military recruitment tool and as the "next generation of wartime propaganda"[12] are a kind of "shock and awe"[13] display of what the American military is capable of without the consequences of context.

This chapter seeks to examine the increasingly close relationship between the U.S. military and the video game industry and the consequences of this for the militarization of U.S. popular culture. In particular the chapter explores the geographies of militarism[14] that digital war games produce and seeks to explore the ways in which digital war games invite Americans to "participate in a militarism of consumption and pleasure."[15] How do the military representations constructed in digital war games legitimize and justify U.S. military interventions and how are they implicated in the production of geopolitical discourses of war and security? This chapter argues digital war games present a clean, sanitized and enjoyable version of war for popular consumption, obscuring the realities, contexts and consequences of war. Additionally, digital games provide players with coping strategies in a world full of geopolitical anxiety and uncertainty.

In Search of the Last Starfighter

> There has never been, in history, a crop of young soldiers who were so pre-stuffed on so much realistic-but-not-real war-like-but-not-war material.[16]

When we talk about military power in the context of the visual, it is necessary to situate this historically. Here, then, it is important to trace the rise of video war games within what James Der Derian calls the military-industrial-media-entertainment network, the post-industrial cousin of the military-industrial complex.[17] Der Derian explores the parameters of "virtuous war" by which is meant the virtual (the disembodied simulation) and virtuous (war as clean, good, as surgical, abstract and bloodless). The history of video games is, however, complex and multifaceted, whilst pinpointing the "first" computer game is a contested issue centered upon questions of definition and chronology.[18] Many accounts focus on the Hingham Institute sponsored by the Study Group on Space Warfare, which produced the game *Spacewar* (Steve Russell, 1962) whilst the first commercial home video console was the Magnavox Odyssey launched in 1972 and developed at Sanders Associates (a military contracting firm).[19] The emergence of programmable machines or consoles in the 1970s created a flexible division of labor between hardware and software such that games software could be bought, collected, and compared in the same way as records.[20]

The games and the entertainment industry they initiated would provide a forum for the naturalization and incorporation of military technology in everyday life. As Hall has argued, integrating computer technology into entertainment "helped fuel consumers' economic and social support for the arms industry."[21] In 1972 the games company Atari was established in Silicon Valley near a Lockheed Martin missile installation and the U.S. Army later collaborated with Atari to retool the 1980 arcade game *Battlezone* (Atari, 1980) for training use. In the early 1980s, Ronald Reagan famously predicted that action video games were training a new generation of cyber/cold warriors ready to fight real foes on the real battlefield (itself computer enhanced). During the Cold War, some of the earliest games like *Missile Command* (Atari, 1980) presented a "protorealist anxiety narrative about living under the threat of nuclear annihilation."[22]

The digital games industry has thus been "heavily entangled" with military industries for many years now and from the earliest days of the space program.[23] In the 1940s the U.S. Military began pumping money into computational devices in an effort to improve code breaking and the artillery-table-calculating skills needed during the Second World War.[24] According to Manuel de Landa[25] after 1945 Command, Control and Communications (C^3) was transferred from the Military to the RAND corporation, which employed John Van Neumann and his game theory to model nuclear dissuasion during the Cold War. Thus, the U.S. nuclear strategy was partly defined using war games. The U.S. Department of Defense (DoD) has been the primary exponent of war game design since the 1950s, yet commercial game designers have also produced many of the ideas shaping the design of military simulations.[26] The U.S. Department of Defense defines a war game as "a simulation, by whatever means, of a military operation involving two or more opposing forces, using rules, data, and procedures designed to depict an actual or assumed real life situation."[27]

War games have taken many forms ranging from large-scale battlefield exercises to abstract strategy games played with maps, counters, and miniatures.[28] Military officials have utilized strategic simulations at least since *Chess* and *Go* and the development of *Kriegspiel*, a nineteenth century Prussian strategy game which featured toy soldiers, cannons and other emplacements on a table-top map which established some of the earliest conventions of war gaming.[29] By the early 1960s much more sophisticated war game designs had been developed in the commercial sector (beginning with the founding of the Avalon Game Company in 1958), games which changed the focus of game design from abstract strategy and chance to an emphasis on historical realism and simulation defined by rules and data.

The Defense Advanced Research Projects Agency (DARPA), founded in 1958 in the wake of the USSR's Sputnik launch, has been a central actor in providing the Pentagon with high-tech games. The biggest boost to military war gaming came from the construction of the DARPA-funded SIMNET (from 1982), the military's distributed simulator networking project, which sought to explore more cost effective forms of simulation. SIMNET was made operational in January 1990 and was trialed by General Schwarzkopf who prepared his staff at the U.S. Central Military Command in Florida for a potential conflict in the region by playing scenarios of the war game *Operation Internal Look*. As Schwarzkopf recalls in his memoirs: "As the exercise [*Operation Desert-Shield*] got under way, the movement of Iraq's real-world ground and air forces eerily paralleled the imagined scenario of the game."[30]

The Gulf War also led to further DARPA supported research and development efforts and the founding of the Army's Simulation Training and Instrumentation Command (STRICOM) to help manage and direct the simulation effort. STRICOM's logo is "All but war is simulation." By 1998 the total budget for modeling and simulation programs had reached in excess of $2.5 billion, funds that played a critical role in accelerating the development and dissemination of modeling and simulation technologies and in promoting the mutually beneficial synergy between the military and entertainments industries.[31] There has also been a significant amount of movement and exchanges of staff (in both directions) between military organizations and commercial gaming companies like Atari and Sega. Today, though, the offspring has outpaced the parent.[32] The establishment in 1999 of the $45 million Institute for Creative Technologies (ICT) at the University of Southern California meant that the crossovers between military simulations and the entertainment industries became much less opportunistic and spontaneous. The ICT was set up to advance military simulations yet further and enlisted Hollywood and video game designers in this process.

12. Digital War Games and Post 9/11 Militarism (Power) 203

The game *America's Army* (*AA*), released on July 4, 2002, has been deployed by the Army as a recruiting tool and has had more success than any U.S. military recruitment campaign since the Uncle Sam *I Want You* ads in the Second World War[33] with nearly eight million people registered to play worldwide as of December 2006.[34] *AA* was first developed at the Naval Postgraduate School in California through an initiative called *Operation Star Fighter* named after the 1984 movie *The Last Starfighter*, directed by Nick Castle, a film about a teenager who is recruited by aliens to fight in an intergalactic war after getting a perfect score on his local arcade machine). The U.S. military has invested millions of tax dollars in developing the game with a view to offering players the chance to virtually explore and "experience" the Army from basic training all the way up to deployment and live situations that might be found in the global War on Terror, creating "surrogate soldiers" along the way.[35] The original PC version of the game featured two parts, one a training simulator called "Soldiers" (which includes boot camp) and another more traditional FPS[36] called "Operations" in which players working in teams carry out specific missions. In late 2003 a new version of the *America's Army* format entitled *Special Forces*, was released whilst in 2005 a console version

The multiplayer first-person-shooter war computer game *America's Army* (2002) was the first of several computer games produced by the American military for purposes of public relations, recruitment, and training of soldiers.

of the game (subtitled *Rise of a Soldier*) was released for the Playstation 2. The PC game can be legally downloaded by gamers as young as thirteen and is often bundled together with gaming magazines and given away at stock-car racing events and state fairs. The game allows gamers to play at soldiers online, banding together with other internet warriors to battle national enemies in detailed and "realistic"[37] ten-minute scenarios. On a typical day more than 30,000 people log on to the Army's official servers[38] (which cost just under $1 million a year to maintain) whilst the Army's civilian developers now release updates every few months.[39] In late March 2004 a huge AA gaming tournament was held, offering hundreds of thousands of dollars in prize money and computer equipment.[40] Game tournaments are also held at Army recruiting offices and high schools.[41]

While the equipment and uniforms in the game are designed with maximum realism in mind, death and injury are treated differently. As Schiesel notes: "limbs are never blown off. Instead, wounds are marked by a puff of red smoke. Injured foes never writhe and scream in agony."[42] The deliberate censorship of explicit violence in this game further mimics the U.S. government and media censorship of images of dead American soldiers and coffins — in the game bodies vanish after being killed and so body counts do not pile up visually.[43] The games are seductive to potential recruits and may arguably suppress an aversion to killing. According to Anthony Swofford's best selling memoir, *Jarhead: A Marine's Chronicle of the Gulf War and Other Battles* (2003), soldiers in the Gulf War used scenes from antiwar movie *Apocalypse Now* (Francis Ford Coppola, 1979) to hype themselves up for combat. Perhaps in the Iraq War, video games offered an alternative means of pre-stuffing the troops and getting them "pumped" for combat? Gulf War veteran Mary Spio (now the editor of the U.S. popular culture magazine *One2one*) has argued that "[w]hat we saw in the Abu Ghraib prison scandal was the tip of the iceberg — it was a glimpse of a generation of war gamers coming of age. Video games that allow players to kill real human beings are desensitizing generations of American society."[44] While the military has concluded that there is no direct correlation between video games and an increased urge to kill, games are increasingly being used as effective training tools to preach a particular model of "hands off killing."[45]

This raises important issues about the impacts of exposure to video games on soldiers who have trained extensively on approved military simulations, soldiers who may "become 'charged' in the same way stimulated by the games and with lethal results, thanks to the 'hyper adrenalised disconnect' between 3-D flesh and blood and 2-D pixel people."[46] In 2005 the Institute for Creative Technologies initiated a project together with the Office of Naval

Research (ONR) that creates an immersive virtual reality system for the treatment of Iraq war veterans diagnosed with combat-related post-traumatic stress disorder. The treatment approach involves recycling and adding to the virtual assets that were initially built into the combat tactical simulation incorporated in the commercially available Xbox game, *Full Spectrum Warrior*.[47] The version created is designed to resemble a middle-Eastern city and outlying village and desert spaces and offers the clinician the chance to monitor the patients behavior and customize the therapy experience by placing them in virtual scenario locations that resemble the setting in which the traumatic events initially occurred. *FSW* is set in the fictional country of Zekistan but for all the dusty alleyways, mosques and Arab villages the setting could easily be Iraq or Afghanistan. Most combat video games, however, do not portray the streets of U.S. towns and cities but rather places that look like the most recent war zones visited by U.S. troops.[48] With the initiation of the ICT virtual therapy project, we seem to have come full circle then. Not only are video games used to recruit for the U.S. armed forces and to train and prepare troops after they have enlisted but they are also played by U.S. troops during a tour of duty and are even now being used to treat the consequences of combat engagement in the form of "virtual therapy" for post-traumatic stress disorder.

"Cozying up on the Couch with Operation Fallujah": Text/Medium/Player

> [T]hese games go beyond entertainment — raising some new issues not the least of which is whether gamers should be bothered about cozying up on the couch with "Operation Fallujah."[49]

More directly than *America's Army*, *Kuma\War* (Kuma Reality Games, 2004), a tactical first and third-person episodic shooter game (that comes as a set of online PC "missions") seeks to create scenarios straight off the real battlefields of Iraq and Afghanistan (alongside historical scenarios set in Iran, South Korea, Sierra Leone, and Vietnam). Contemporary missions include "Osama 2001: Tora Bora," "Abu Ghraib MP," "Fallujah: Operation al Fajr" or "Uday and Qusay's Last Stand." There are currently 74 missions available, authored by a company called Kuma Reality Games that, according to the game promo, offer "news" and all "the critical Intel you need to understand a world in crisis."[50] The company was set up in 2004 in New York by a group of retired military officers as a kind of "CNN with an itchier trigger finger."[51]

Kuma uses information culled from Fox news reports, military experts, Department of Defense records, and original research. Online episodes consist of a playable mission, extensive background text, satellite photos, and a multimedia library, often including interviews with participants in the events themselves. Thus, there is a sense in which games are intended as reporting as well as recruiting tools. The game designers aim to make the game "true to the boots on the ground" and have received a lot of interest from active soldiers and veterans. The Kumawar.com website also allows for messages of support to be left for the troops in Iraq whilst two new missions are available each month. According to Kuma Reality Games, Iraqis (who adopt the parts of Iraqi police and the National Guard) also play the missions.[52] In 2004 Kuma ran a Story From the Front-contest, in which it invited serving U.S. troops to submit accounts of gunfights, ambushes and rescues to the site. Kuma players then voted online for a winner, whose tale was made into a game.[53] In July 2006, *Kuma\War 2* was released with an expanded online multiplayer environment and improved graphics with a first mission that recreates the assassination of Abu Musab Al-Zarqawi.

The existence of games like *Kuma\War* underscores the need to think critically about the text/medium/player interface. Games are not merely watched but played and so it is no longer sufficient to talk about the visual or textual representation of meaning. As Galloway has argued, the game theorist must also talk about actions and the game worlds in which they transpire.[54] In the field of game studies (in which there has been a lively debate about this interface) Aarseth has argued for a "bottom up and emergent"[55] conception of simulation in which the reality of the simulation is essentially created through the player's own initiative, where a new emotional reality is created through gameplay. Players may play the game, however, but in an important sense *the game also plays them* in that many games have pre-scripted stories that one must complete correctly and in the right order. Also, the "gritty" realism that game developers are so keen to produce (and gamers to consume) centers on the authenticity of weapons, sounds, combat scenarios, etc. Realism is often conceived then as simply a matter of pixel density and color accuracy. So the hyper-intensive focus on the technology available during particular conflicts is an important part of how games are marketed and consumed. Why, then, are the same principles of "realism" not extended to the enemy as "other"?

Baudrillard notes that "we prefer the exile of the virtual" and his work challenges scholars of video games to explore the ways in which "virtual wars" feed our willingness to "unleash the real world."[56] So it is important to attend to the ways in which games seek to represent an emotional reality that gen-

12. Digital War Games and Post 9/11 Militarism (Power)   207

erates the desired fantasies in the minds of players and to consider the roles that digital games have as affective assemblages through which geopolitical sensibilities emerge and are amplified. In other words, what kinds of affective resonances do digital games create amongst gamers? The soundscapes constructed in digital war games in particular are often geared to inviting certain kinds of emotive affects and performances. The group Machine Head provided the music for the *Black Hawk Down* (Ritual Entertainment, 2004) and *FSW* games and the first song on their thrash metal album, "Davidian," refers to freedom ringing with a shotgun's blast. Accompanied by thrash metal, digital war games offer "an alternative posture for U.S. Americans — that of being wronged and righteous."[57]

Johan Huizinga has usefully developed the concept of a playspace[58] — referring to the interface between medium and medium-user — but how consciously do players activate playspaces? Immersive media increasingly collapse distinctions between different kinds of space, collapsing the real into the hyperreal. The problem, however, is not this leakage of the playspace into the worlds of everyday life *per se* but "an electronically induced amnesia…. Video games do not teach the wrong ethics, they teach that ethics are superfluous: only the game counts and the game can be started over and over again."[59] A big part of the appeal of digital war games is that most seek to "proudly transport the gamer into immersive, gut wrenching virtual battlefields. They persuade the gamer that, in an echo of a Second World War era journalism, "you are there"— on the beaches of Normandy, in the jungles of Vietnam, in modern military hotspots [like the deserts of Iraq]."[60] Games like *AA* and the *Kuma\War* series, in a fashion similar to wartime newsreels from the Second World War, provide a real world hook by offering privileged glimpses from the front lines and some of the backgrounds in the game are taken directly from video footage of landscapes in which the U.S. military has recently been engaged.[61]

In many ways new video war games are not realistic but *cinematic* in that they don't reproduce the real world experience of war but they do reproduce the *theatrical experience of war*.[62] So playing a game becomes like starring in a war movie since games use all of the same techniques as movies for framing shots, editing, pacing, and narration.[63] Thus digital games are not one medium, but many different media and could be understood as "interactive movies about war with all the boring parts taken out."[64] It does not matter, then, that games are not fully realistic since gamers enjoy them for what they are: immersive/interactive movies about the experience of war where they get to see themselves onscreen as the noble hero in Pentagon's latest version of the noble war fantasy. Here the *player* of the game *is* the story. This is "cinematic cotton candy"[65] which makes real and contemporary war seem heroic, necessary, fun, and exciting. Rapidly escalating defense costs also seem a little more reasonable and common-sensical to gamers as a result.

Beyond the real world hooks and privileged glimpses, games like *Conflict Desert Storm* (Ritual Games, 2002) allow players to feel as if they are "defending the country" and enables them to vent frustrations in ways which make clear the lines of division between "us" and "them," self and other, freedom fighter and terrorist. Released in October 2001 to coincide with President Bush's own upgraded call for a new war on Iraq, prospects for peace are played off in this game as unrealistic and naïve.[66] An updated version of the game was released in 2004 (also set in the Gulf War in 1991) called *Conflict: Desert Storm II: Back to Baghdad* (Ritual Games, 2003). The appearance of such games (which valorize past wars) at a time concurrent with the rising rhetoric of war in U.S. politics before the invasion of Iraq in March 2003 is not coincidental. The power in this game is not solely in the ability of its players to occupy and conquer foreign lands, nor in the mass carnage gamers can effect through carpet bombing but in the ability to transpose fear into historically-based combat scenarios[67] with clear battle lines in a war that is safe and winnable. Here the legitimacy of war is never questioned and it is almost always inferred that the product of war is national safety and security.

Whilst American foreign policy is portrayed as benign here, Arab cultures are portrayed as savage/terrorist and uncivilized, constructing racialized meaning which in turn provides an ideological sanction for the War on Terrorism and aggression in the Middle East. It is also important to remember here that communities of game players are formed through common representations of a collective enemy.[68] Only opposing soldiers can be killed by game players whilst racial stereotypes of orientalized others help fix Iraqi difference in a position of orientalized abjection and impossibility against which the supposed technological superiority of U.S. forces can be counterposed.

Conclusions: Towards a Culture of Perpetual War

>...the entertainment industry has assumed a posture of cooperation toward a culture of perpetual war.[69]

At the outset of the present War on Terrorism, President Bush reminded Americans they were all soldiers — a pronouncement that video gamers were ideally equipped to identify with.[70] Given the U.S. Presidential declaration of a war/crusade between the "forces of good and the forces of evil" it is perhaps to be expected that American cultural products such as video games might "echo this lamentable idiocy."[71] In 2003 U.S. antiwar activist Mikel Raparez held an online fundraising campaign to buy President Bush a Playstation 2, raising enough to buy the President a console and a copy of *SOCOM II: U.S. Navy SEALS* and *Conflict Desert Storm*. The letter from Raparez's campaign that accompanied the Playstation 2 noted "[w]e ask that you accept these gifts and use them, rather than the lives of Iraqi civilians and our U.S. servicemen, to fulfill any militaristic fantasies."

In the new world order military intervention has become something of a cyclical economic machine "greased by an array of media products that share an uncritical tendency to endorse any war that can be made to appear necessary."[72] Video war games put a friendly, hospitable face on the military, manufacturing consent and complicity amongst consumers for military programs, missions, and weapons, thus obfuscating the relationships between consumers, institutions, and economies of violence.[73] The representation of war and combat in U.S. popular cultural products like video games thus "sutures consumerism to citizenship within a militarised ideology," helping to "perform, practice and consume a militarised, technologically based form of citizenship training."[74] Games can also help make U.S. militarism appear benign and in a sense create a degree of intimacy between state and citizen by inviting consumers to embody the values, the authority, the force, and the power of the militarized state.[75]

It is important, however, to remember that games are often used in ways not intended or anticipated by their developers and military sponsors. Game data, rules, and codes can be modified to produce different narratives, characters, and outcomes. At the start of May 2006, the Department of Defense warned Congress that the makers of combat video games have unwittingly become part of a global propaganda campaign by Islamic militants to exhort Muslim youths to take up arms against the U.S.[76] The DoD warned that "tech-savvy" militants from al Qaeda and other groups had modified video war games so that U.S. troops play the role of bad guys in running gunfights against heavily armed Islamic radical heroes. One of the most popular games, Devlin said, was *Battlefield 2* (Digital Illusions, 2005) which had been the subject of considerable software modification, a game that ordinarily shows U.S. troops engaging forces in China or a united Middle East coalition but modified versions depict a man in Arab headdress carrying an automatic weapon into combat with U.S. invaders.

The first Arab 3D war video game, *Under Ash* (Dar Al-Fikr, 2002), later renamed *Under Siege*, was released by a Syrian publisher as a direct response to games which encourage players to bomb Arab cities. There is also *Special Force* (Hezbollah Central Internet Bureau, 2003), a first-person-shooter game based on the armed Islamic movement in South Lebanon where the central character is a holy warrior fighting against Israeli occupation. The ideological opposite of *America's Army*, these two FPS games both take the perspective of a young Palestinian participating in the Islamic Jihad and although they contain similar militaristic representations to American-made shooters and have a similar look and feel, the narratives are very different. The existence of game modifications[77] reminds us then that we should be attentive to the nascent counter-movement in the game sector and that we should look beyond the blood-and-guts marketing of combat video games, avoiding the assumption that just because a product bears a military title that its narratives cannot be read in different ways.[78]

Digital war games offer a "therapeutic way to work out 21st century angst by battling the bad guys."[79] They offer the possibility of getting back control, of overcoming fear and are fantastical and temporary: "for 45 minutes you can pretend you have some sense of agency, some control, or at the very least some part in trying to make the world a better place."[80] Games can also produce a moral and ethical distance between players and history (particularly where that history may be painful and still a little raw) allowing players to experience violence cleanly (gone in a quick puff of red smoke) and encouraging them to accept the role of perpetrators who bear no moral or ethical culpability for their actions carried out in a just/virtuous crusade against evil.[81] In experiencing death within controlled and renewable parameters an ideology of hegemony and a false sense of power and invincibility are created amongst American consumer-citizens that in turn "contributes to U.S. imperial arrogance."[82]

Death and bodily dismemberment are frequently banished from games (in much the same way images of death were excluded from images and accounts of the Second World War). American bodies are always shown intact and the gory details are removed so that war becomes more palatable, pasteurizing the "mud of battle" and creating the desired fantasy of a "virtuous war." Games thus reinforce the image of a clean war with clean battle lines, no moral questions posed, and no consideration given to the reality of taking a life. They also offer a cinematic romanticization of war that is both seductive and powerful and they can provide an (heroic) experience of winning a war single-handedly. Game producers arguably "call forth a cult of ultra-patriotic xenophobes whose greatest joy is to destroy, regardless of how racist, imperialistic and flimsy the rationale."[83] Here, the simplification of cultures and history is itself a form of violence.

For some gamers, virtual war offers the chance to correct misperceptions of history through gameplay and their appeal partly comes from their perceived ability to *teach history* and not just represent it.[84] A range of video war games offer precisely this possibility of reworking historical battles for modern-day virtuous play, from Second World War battles to Vietnam and Somalia, offering players the chance to seek "virtual revenge for American losses."[85] Others seek to restage past military engagements in ways that have a direct bearing on present-day confrontations. Games also enable the military to rewrite history such that the complexity and geopolitical "messiness" of the conflict is edited out and will not register with gamers: "[t]hey will remember military conflicts as pure contests of strategy and force, with none of the external political, moral, historical, ideological, and humanitarian factors involved."[86] Players may not learn the essence of war from fun and escapist games but these simulations embody the institutionalized conformity of the armed forces even if they don't always address the meaning of war.[87] Video games, then, can contribute to a historical myopia in ways that legitimate the "colonial present." However, real world military-issue body bags don't come equipped with a "restart" option and a "game over" screen.

Notes

1. Sgt. Sinque Swales quoted in Jose Antonio Vargas, "Virtual Reality Prepares Soldiers for Real War," *The Washington Post*, February 14, 2006, accessed from http://www.washingtonpost.com/wpdyn/content/article/2006/02/13/AR2006021302437.html/ on November 11, 2006.

2. *Full Spectrum Warrior* (Pandemic Studios, 2004) and *SOCOM II: U.S. Navy SEALS* (Zipper Interactive, 2003).

3. Aphra Kerr suggests that the term "digital games" is preferable to "video games" since it refers to the entire field and embraces arcade, computer, console, and mobile games in all their diversity. Aphra Kerr, "The Business of Making Digital Games" in *The Business and Culture of Digital Games: Gamework/Gameplay*, ed. Aphra Kerr, 36–57 (London: Sage, 2006).

4. Michelle Barron and Nina Huntemann, "Militarism and Video Games: An Interview with Nina Huntemann," Boston: Media Education Foundation, accessed from Http://wwwmediaed.org/news/articles/militarism/ on September 15, 2005.

5. Andy Deck, "Demilitarizing the Playground," *No Quarter*, p. 12, accessed from Http://artcontext.net/crit/essays/noQuarter/ on July 2, 2006.

6. Robertson Allen, "Representations of the Enemy in Conflict: Desert Storm and America's Army," p. 2. Paper presented at the University of Bergen, Aesthetics of Play Conference, October 14, 2005, accessed from Http://students.washington.edu/roballen/documents.shtml/ on November 12, 2006.

7. Roger Stahl, *War Games: Citizenship and Play in Post-Industrial Militarism*, unpublished Ph.D. thesis, Department of Communication Arts and Sciences, University of Pennsylvania State University, 2004, 151.

8. Steven Poole, *Trigger Happy: Video games and the Entertainment Revolution* (London: Arcade Publishing, 2000).

9. Adam Elkus, "Subliminal Militarization," accessed from http://82.165.179.211/warandpeace/35759/ on November 19, 2006.

10. "DFC Intelligence," 2004, Worldwide Market Forecasts for the video game and interactive software entertainment industry, San Diego, California.

11. Barron and Huntemann, "Militarism and Video Games," 3.

12. Ed Halter, "War Games: New Media Finds Its Place in the New World Order," *Village Voice*, accessed from Http://www.villagevoice.com/news/0246,halter,39834,1.html/ on May 11, 2006.

13. As if to underscore this point, console manufacturers Sony controversially tried and failed to register a trademark for "Shock and Awe" as the Iraq war was still ongoing.

14. See Rachel Woodward, "From Military Geography to Militarism's Geographies: Disciplinary Engagements With the Geographies of Militarism and Military Activities," *Progress in Human Geography* 29, 6 (2005): 1–23.

15. Stahl, "War Games," 21.

16. Cheryl Seal, "Was the Excessive violence of U.S. Troops in Iraq Fuelled by Military-Funded Computer Games?" accessed from Http://baltimore.indymedia.org/newswire/display/3836/index.php/ on May 12, 2006.

17. James Der Derian, *Virtuous War: Mapping the Military-Industrial-Media-Entertainment Network* (Boulder, CO: Westview Press, 2001).

18. John Kirriemuir, "A History of Digital Games" in *Understanding Digital Games*, eds. J. Rutter and J. Bryce, 21–35 (London: Sage, 2006).

19. Kirriemuir, "A History of Digital Games."

20. Leslie Haddon, "The Development of Interactive Games" in *The Media Reader: Continuity and Transformation*, eds. H. Mackay, and T. O'Sullivan (London: Sage, 1999), 123–147. Jennifer Johns, "Video Games Production Networks: Value Capture, Power Relations and Embeddedness," *Journal of Economic Geography* 6 (2006): 151–180.

21. Karen Hall, "Shooters to the Left of Us, Shooters to the Right: First Person Arcade Shooter Video Games, the Violence Debate," *Reconstructions* 6.1 (2006): 10.

22. Alexander Galloway, *Gaming: Essays in Algorithmic Culture* (Minneapolis: University of Minnesota Press, 2006), 73.

23. Hall, "Shooters to the Left," 9.

24. Heather Chaplin and Aaron Ruby, *Smartbomb: The Quest for Art, Entertainment, and Big Bucks in the Videogame Revolution* (New York: Algonquin Books, 2005).

25. Manuel De Landa, *War in the Age of Intelligent Machines* (Cambridge, MA: MIT Press, 1991).

26. Timothy Lenoir and Henry Lowood, "Theatres of War: The Military-Entertainment Complex" in *Kunstkammer, Laboratorium, Bühne—Schauplätze des Wissens im 17. Jahrhundert*, eds. J. Lazardzig, H. Schramm and L. Schwarte (Berlin: Walter de Gruyter Publishers, 2003), 432–64.

27. Joint Chiefs of Staff, *Publication 1, Department of Defense Dictionary of Military and Associated Terms* (Washington, DC: GPO, 1997), 393.

28. Lenoir and Lowood, "Theatres of War."

29. Thomas Allen, "The Evolution of Wargaming: From Chessboard to Marine Doom," in *War and Games*, ed. G. Ausenda, 231–250 (Rochester, NY: Boydell Press, 2002).

30. Norman Schwarzkopf, *It Doesn't Take a Hero* (New York: Bantam Press, 1992).

31. Lenoir and Lowood, "Theatres of War."

32. Chaplin and Ruby, "Smartbomb."

33. Brian Cowlishaw, "Playing War: The Emerging Trend of Real Virtual Combat in Video Games," *American Popular Culture*, Online Magazine, January 2005, accessed from

Http://www.americanpopularculture.com/archive/emerging/real_virtual_combat.htm/ on October 22, 2006.

34. *America's Army*, 2006, "Registration Figures," accessed from Http://www.americasarmy.com/ on November 16, 2006.

35. Seth Schiesel, "On manoeuvres with the Army game squad," *New York Times*, February 25, 2005, accessed from Http://www.theglobeandmail.com/servlet/story/ on May 25, 2006.

36. First-person-shooter (FPS) games purport to recreate full-scale real-world battles. The phrase "first person" refers to the players point of view — players use controls (keyboard, mouse, or game controller) to look up, down and around onscreen and often the image that appears onscreen is a pair of forearms and hands aiming a weapon "into" the screen.

37. At the electronic game world's trade show E3 in Los Angeles in May 2006, the latest version of *AA* was unveiled, a game based on actual soldiers' experiences. Players can now take control of one of nine "real" U.S. soldiers (including brief in-game biographies) whose likenesses appear in the game (with these hypermasculine soldiers also immortalized as accompanying action figures).

38. *SOCOM: U.S. Navy SEALS* (released for Playstation in two versions) also has an official website which prominently displays a link to the official Navy SEALS website. which equally prominently displays a link for those wishing to enlist in the SEALS. The game was produced with the assistance of the U.S. Naval Special Warfare Command.

39. Schiesel, "On manoeuvres."

40. Cowlishaw, "Playing War."

41. The use of video games as recruitment tools implies that video gamers' virtual prowess and enjoyment translate directly into real-world Army suitability and success.

42. Schiesel, "On manoeuvres," 3.

43. Karen Hall, "Practising Militarism: The Cultural Function of First Person Shooter Arcade Video Games," Popular Culture Association in the South, Nashville, TN, October 5–7, 2000, accessed from Http://web.syr.edu/kjhall/texts/nashville.htm/ on November 10, 2006.

44. Spio quoted in Elkus, "Subliminal Militarization."

45. Chaplin and Ruby, "Smartbomb," 210.

46. Seal, "Excessive Violence."

47. Albert Rizzo and Jarrell Pair, "A Virtual Reality Exposure Therapy Application for Iraq War Veterans with Post Traumatic Stress Disorder: From Training to Toy to Treatment," accessed from Http://doi.ieeecomputersociety.org/10.1109/VR.2006.23/ on May 10, 2006.

48. Deck, "Demilitarizing the Playground."

49. Tom Loftus, "War Games in a Time of War: Real-World Events Inspire Developers, But Results Vary," Http://www.msnbc.com/id/5318462/print/1/displaymode/1098/ on November 12, 2006.

50. *Kuma\War*, Kuma war promotional video, accessed from Http://www.KumaWar.com/ on October 22, 2006.

51. J. Sims, "When Reality Is Just an Illusion," *The Independent*, March 29, 2004.

52. Colin Freeman, "Battles Re-enacted in Video Arcades, NY Gamemaker Lets Players Portray Iraqi or U.S. Troops," *San Francisco Chronicle*, January 16, page A-4, accessed from Http://www.sfgate.com/cgibin/article.cgi?f=/c/a/2005/01/16/MNG5LAR6KU1.DTL&hw=kuma&sn=001&sc=1000 on November 11, 2006.

53. Freeman, "Battles Re-Enacted."

54. Galloway, "Gaming," 72.

55. Espen Aarseth, "Genre Trouble: Narrativism and the Art of Simulation" in *First Person: New Media as Story, Performance and Game*, eds. N. Wardrip-Fruin and P. Harrigan (Cambridge, MA: MIT Press, 2004).

56. Jean Baudrillard, *The Gulf War Did Not Take Place* (Bloomington: Indiana University Press, 1991), 27–29.

57. William Warner, "Spectacular Action: Rambo and the Popular Pleasures of Pain" in *Cultural Studies*, eds. L. Grossberg, C. Nelson, and P. Treichler (London: Routledge, 1992), 677.

58. Johan Huizinga, *Homo Ludens*, trans. George Steiner, (London: Maurice Temple Smith, 1970).

59. Randy Schroeder, "Playspace Invaders: Huizinga, Baudrillard and Video Game Violence," *Journal of Popular Culture* 30, no. 3 (1996): 153.

60. Cowlishaw, "Playing War," 1.

61. Halter, "War Games."

62. Cowlishaw, "Playing War," 6.

63. Poole, "Trigger Happy."

64. Cowlishaw, "Playing War," 6.

65. Cowlishaw, "Playing War," 7.

66. Stahl, "War Games."

67. Julian Stallabras, "Just Gaming: Allegory and Economy in Computer Games," *New Left Review* no. 198 (1993): 83–106.

68. Allen, "Representations of the Enemy."

69. Deck, "Demilitarizing the Playground," 1.

70. Hall, "Shooters to the Left."

71. Deck, "Demilitarizing the Playground," 3.

72. Deck, "Demilitarizing the Playground," 1.

73. Hall, "Shooters to the Left."

74. Hall, "Practising militarism," 1–3.

75. Hall, "Shooters to the Left."

76. David Morgan, "Islamists Using U.S. Video Games in Youth Appeal," accessed from Http://news.yahoo.com/s/nm/20060504/us_nm/ on May 26, 2006.

77. *America's Army* has spawned a very large 'mod' community of its own, visible for instance on the PlanetUnreal.com website. A group calling itself the Velvet Strike Team has similarly tried to modify the game *Counter Strike* but 'mods' do not change the overall logic of the game. A shooter is still a shooter.

78. Pat Kane, "Toy Soldiers," *The Guardian IT supplement*, Thursday, December 1, 2005.

79. Loftus, "War games," 4.

80. Barron and Huntemann, "Militarism and Video Games," 5.

81. Hall, "Shooters to the Left."

82. Ibid., 15.

83. Deck, "Demilitarizing the Playground," 5.

84. Cowlishaw, "Playing War."

85. Halter, "War Games," 2.

86. Elkus, "Subliminal Militarization."

87. Deck, "Demilitarizing the Playground."

13

The Political Battlefield of Pro-Arab Video Games on Palestinian Screens

HELGA TAWIL-SOURI

Like everyone else in the Internet café, I rely on the place to offer me a cup of strong coffee as I wait for my e-mails to download on antiquated modems. It has become part of my routine while in Ramallah in 2003. I am alone, however, in bringing ear plugs. It's not because of the bombs and shootings, although it helps (we're in the midst of the Second Intifada); but because almost every one in the center is screaming, throwing threats that bounce off the barren walls: "I'm going to get you;" "Bastard! Just wait till I get you back." No, the young men (most clients are between twelve and twenty-five, very few of them female) are not shouting at each other, but at characters in videogames. While on a visit to a family in Jenin, a girl of twelve urges me to play a videogame. "You have to play.... This is the best game ever. It's by Hezbollah ... it's the first game where you can shoot Israelis," she explains.[1] *Special Force* had just been released by Hezbollah and she had downloaded it from their website.[2] The girl gives me a videogame history lesson:

> in all the other games you can shoot Saddam [Hussein], you can shoot Iran and Libya ... Syria is also a target. My friends and I would try to turn the planes around to shoot at Israel but the game wouldn't allow it.... You can't shoot at America and Europe either.... I learned from [a friend] that Hezbollah changed the rules ... so of course all of us here now only play this ... well we also play [the] Haram ash–Sharif game [*Under Siege*] where we get to shoot the soldiers who started the Intifada[3] ... it's our revenge on Israel. We get to shoot the Israelis. We get to blow up *Markava* [Israeli military] tanks!

I had not known that war games often made their targets Arabs or Muslims and that it wasn't until these "pro–Arab" games that kids could shoot the other way. Although privileged in having Internet access in her home, this twelve-year-old was not unique in her love of pro–Arab videogames. As I discovered in for-profit Internet centers, non-profit computer labs, and living rooms across the West Bank and the Gaza Strip, these videogames were what most youth were busy doing while behind a computer. Based on field-work in 2003 and 2004 of observing computer users, interviews with players, parents, and computer center owners in the Palestinian Territories, and a survey of mainstream Western press coverage, this chapter focuses on three pro–Arab videogames. First, I describe the games; second, I provide the population's response to them; third, I look at controversies emanating from the West that surround them — from charges of propaganda to the effects of media violence; and finally, I situate the games and their controversies within the context of Palestinian society.

Rather than disdain videogames as irrelevant child's play, the concerns herein assume that videogames are no less important than other media. I address how they employ racial and national meaning and how they reinforce dominant ideas or, conversely, challenge hegemony. Moreover, given the reliance on field work and interviews with players, most of whom are teenagers, this chapter challenges theorists who eschew media use, especially with regards to children who presumably have nothing to say about their experiences. Like the work of Buckingham and others,[4] this work relies on letting children speak for themselves about their media use, and refutes simplistic panics and accusations about the negative influence of media. Finally, in the tradition of anti–Orientalists,[5] this chapter challenges essentialist explanations of the role of Islam in Arab societies, especially with respect to "fundamentalism."

What's in a Game?

The video gaming market, dominated by Western and U.S. companies (such as Electronic Arts, Activision, Nintendo and Sony), generates more than ten billion U.S. dollars annually. One analyst suggested that "as videogames acquire greater capabilities to simulate 'real' life, they are likely to outstrip Hollywood even further as America's choice source of popular entertainment,"[6] and will soon be the U.S.'s largest media export. Of the variety of genres, this chapter focuses on First Person Shooter — or FPS — games, which Neiborg defines as "a three-dimensional navigation in virtual environments, through a first person perspective, in which the player interacts in single- or multiplayer combat sequences by means of using a range of weaponry in order to complete a mission or objective."[7]

Many controversial issues surround videogames and especially FPS games. Since the turn of the millennium, there is a trend for social, political and alternative groups to use games to sell their products and ideas — what Wiltenburg has dubbed "advergaming."[8] Gay rights groups (with games such as Italian-made *Queer Power*[9]), the Christian Right (boasting games such as *Left Behind: Eternal Forces*[10] and *God Speed 3D*,[11] developed by U.S. companies) and White Supremacists (such as American-made *Ethnic Cleansing*,[12] *White Law*[13] and *Shoot the Blacks*[14]) are among such trend-setters in the West. In other parts of the world the trend has caught on too, albeit with less sophisticated technologies. *Special Force, Under Ash* and *Under Siege*, the three games discussed here, are precisely the kinds of games emerging from the Middle East that can loosely be classified as "pro–Arab."

Under Ash and *Under Siege*

Under Siege and *Under Ash* were created by the Syrian gaming company Dar al–Fikr[15] in 2001 and 2003. Both games revolve around the events of the Palestinian uprising, based on historical events with which players can interact. Although both games are based on actual history, their lure for Arab gamers has been the ability to turn the tables on Israeli power and have the upper hand in the resistance without any real-life repercussions. Both games were met with immediate success in the region and in the Palestinian Territories. By July 2004, a year and a half after its initial release, *Under Ash* had sold fifty thousand units at eight U.S. dollars apiece (*Empyre Discussion Board*).[16] However, these numbers are not true indicators of the game's popularity. It is difficult to gauge actual number of games sold, since the majority of videogames — no matter their origin — are either purchased as pirated copies or played in public venues where one copy suffices for hundreds of gamers. As one of the creators of the game, Radwan Kasmiya, explains, the number sold is considered "a hit [by the company] since ninety per cent of games are illegal copies [and considering that gamers] can jump to the nearest shop and grab a bundle of ten CD's full of games for [two dollars]."[17] *Under Ash* is also available for download from the company website. And similarly, while the number of downloads can be seen as low at two-hundred and fifty thousand, (compared to *America's Army*'s more than seven million registered users) the creators see it as a success and "a strong emotional message ... because [of] how hard it is to download fifty megabytes of [a] poorly crafted game from the internet via a 14.4 Kbit modem."[18]

The object of *Under Siege* is to relive the Intifada, sometimes in eerily similar circumstances to real life. The game opens with a fly-through over worshippers at a Hebron mosque before it is attacked by Jewish settler Baruch

Goldstein in 1994. As Goldstein opens fire on the crowd, the player must dodge bullets and shoot as quickly and accurately as possible. In another scene, the goal is to toss a canister of tear gas back at an Israeli tank. Most of the objectives feature young men who fight tanks with slingshots and stones, hurling back tear gas canisters at the soldiers. Only the experienced fighters have machine guns, a status to be achieved as each level is passed. These are accurate representations of Palestinian resistance — where the majority rely on slingshots and stones, and the older more experienced fighters have dilapidated Kalashnikovs.

Under Ash, an FPS game based on the Second Intifada, is the sequel to *Under Siege*. It revolves around a character, Ahmed, from whose perspective the game is played. The game begins with Ahmed trying to reach the Al-Aqsa mosque while dodging Isreali bullets. Once he reaches the Dome of the Rock he has to evacuate injured Palestinians, grab a rifle from an Israeli soldier and throw the soldiers out — a re-creation of the incident that marked the beginning of the Second Intifada. In subsequent levels, Ahmed has to infiltrate an Israeli settlement, raise a Palestinian flag in a forbidden area, and sneak into an Israeli army weapons depot. In the final task Ahmed takes part in a guerilla attack against an Israeli radar position in Southern Lebanon during which the soldiers are killed and the facility destroyed. Ahmed can only attack Israeli soldiers and settlers. Points can be lost or the game can end if Palestinian or Israeli civilians are killed. The creators of these games posit them as a quasi-documentaries. It is best explained on their website (in non-native English):

> when you live in the Middle East you can't avoid being part of the image. As a development company we believe that we had to do our share ... in telling the story behind this conflict and targeting youngsters who depend on videogames and movies (which always tell the counter side) to build their acknowledgement about the world.... [The game] contains graphical violence and shooting at military personal models, it does not include shooting at civilians or abusing them, it does not include suicide bombing or any terrorist simulation.... Contents are inspired by real stories of Palestinian people, they were documented by United Nations records (1978–2004).... West Bank and Gaza Strip are occupied land according to UN law, and military actions performed by local fighters against occupying forces is considered eligible. *Under Siege* is about the modern history of Palestine and it focuses on the lives of Palestinian family between 1999–2002 during the second Intifada. All levels are based on true stories [*sic*].

Special Force

In February 2003, the Hezbollah Central Internet Bureau released *Special Force*. Based on the same militaristic representation as American-made shooters, *Special Force* is inspired by Hezbollah missions during the early 1980s

Israeli invasion of Southern Lebanon. The object of the game is best described on the cover of the CD-ROM: "The designers of *Special Force* are very proud to provide you with this special product, which embodies objectively the defeat of the Israeli enemy and the heroic actions taking by heroes of the Islamic Resistance in Lebanon ... be a partner in the victory. Fight, resist and destroy your enemy in the name of force and victory."

Players have to navigate through the same real-life conditions that the fighters did — location of mines, number of Israeli soldiers, weather conditions and difficult terrain. One of the most well-known facts about this game occurs during the "training session" where players can practice their shooting skills by aiming at Israeli Prime Minister Sharon. The majority of the game is based on combat scenarios not different than most other FPS games. The pro–Arab narrative is delivered through text-based briefings of historical accounts presented at the beginning of each level, setting up the context of the ensuing mission. For example, a typical screen shot reads: "You must oppose, confront and destroy the machines of the Zionist enemy and the heroic actions taken by the heroes of the Islamic Resistance in Lebanon." Except for instances of Israeli or Hezbollah iconography such as flags and "martyr posters" pasted on walls, the game looks and feels like most other combat scenarios with mine fields, enemy tanks, and the like. As Galloway explains, "while the action in *Special Force* is quite militaristic, it feels like a simple role reversal, a transplant of its American counterparts, with Israelis as the enemies rather than dark-skinned Arabs."[19]

Special Force can certainly be seen as part of Hezbollah's larger media enterprise, what has been called a "shrewd media presence."[20] The creators of *Special Force*, just as the creators of *Under Ash* and *Under Siege*, see these games not just as propaganda but "modern history games ... based on lives of real people trying to survive ethnic cleansing [*sic*]."[21] As another creator explained, "we want the new generation, which doesn't listen to the news, to learn about the Palestinian cause."[22] Part of the point of the games is to keep the idea of resistance alive, for the "idea to live among the Arab people ... [and the] Islamic people ... we do not want the resistance concept to vanish."[23]

Rising Popularity, Rising Concerns

Computer and Internet growth in the Palestinian Territories began after the 1993 peace accords once Palestinians were allowed to develop their own media and telecommunications infrastructure — although heavily dependent on and restricted by Israeli infrastructure. Most of this growth has occurred through the establishment of school-based computer labs and computer or Internet centers, from urban refugee camps to rural villages; funded by both private and government-run foreign NGOs, with minimal assistance or funding from the Palestinian Authority. Despite the violence, increasing poverty and political standstill of the Second Intifada, computer and Internet use became one of the most feasible means of communication, education and entertainment for a population under curfews and closures, bounded by checkpoints, gun-fire and tanks. More and more Palestinians, particularly those under eighteen, were passing their time behind computer screens. By 2005 more than half of Palestinians below eighteen were regular Internet users.[24] Arguably, the driving force behind children going in droves to computer centers was not to escape violence on the streets but to participate in violence on digital screens.

Children had various ways of interpreting their interactions with pro–Arab games, from escaping reality to exacting revenge, from recognizing the political irony of being able to reverse the winners to merely a passing of time. Those who sought revenge or retribution were most often those who had directly suffered from violence in reality. For example, one eleven-year-old boy in the Gaza Strip explained, "I've watched our homes being demolished. I've watched my parents being humiliated at the checkpoint. For me, in this game, I can finally have some strength that I don't have in real life. I can fight for the dignity and honor of my parents [sic]."

Despite claiming being able to fight Israelis, or defend themselves and their families, gamers were well aware that they were interacting in a virtual world. As a fourteen-year-old boy in a West Bank village suggested, "I know this is not real. But it feels good to pretend. It feels good to ... imagine that we are not victims, but we are conquerors." Although conscious that their games were in the virtual realm, there was a recognition of the games' impact on real lives—whether on political or less serious grounds. One nine-year-old boy explained how the videogames changed the structure and hierarchy of role-playing in both virtual and real games. In their equivalent of "cowboys and Indians" Palestinian kids play "Israelis and Palestinians." In the real version, "all the boys fight to be [Israeli] soldiers, because it's always the Palestinians that lose," explained the young boy; but in the virtual games, he continued, "we finally have fights about who wants to be Palestinian. And we decide according to who loses [in the real-life games]. The loser has to take the role of Israelis and let me tell you, nobody wants to be the Israeli [in the computer games].... It's good for our national pride that now we're all wanting to be ourselves, I mean we all want to be Palestinian fighters." Overall, children had positive things to say about the games: allowing them to be proud of their heritage, entertaining them, letting them achieve something they wished they could do in real life, and so on. For some, the games were also educational, as suggested by this nineteen-year-old: "It's not just entertainment or fun, it's also a way to learn history, to know what's going on better."

The adults familiar with the game-playing had more ambivalent reactions. Negative remarks centered around concerns that gamers were not gaining "valuable" computer skills but were "wasting time playing games," as one parent put it. A computer center worker in Deir el–Balah refugee camp lamented, "I wish for them to do more educational or religious things with some of the [software] we have. Maybe learn some skills so they can get a job, or improve their English. But they prefer to play these war games." In fact, some computer centers, in the effort to encourage kids towards other virtual experiences, deleted the games all-together. And as an owner in Bethlehem quickly learned, without games his center would run out of business: "The kids won't come unless I let them play games." He continued to explain the phenomenon, "[the kids] are a radical generation. They look for shooting. It is something inside them that they need to express and release." As with adults the world over, concerns revolved around whether spending time playing videogames is as beneficial — for social, educational and technological skills — as other computer activities.

Other adults had more positive explanations. In Qalandia refugee camp, the owner of an Internet café suggested, "it's very good the kids come and play here. It's better than going to the checkpoint to throw stones." While hardly any of the adults focused on the fact that games are also part of a computer-skills repertoire, all of them suggested that the kids are better off in the centers than on "the streets." Even if they were partaking in throwing stones at Israeli soldiers in virtual and real realms, one of them was inherently safer.

Seldom did an adult take issue with the contents of these games. When violence did come up, responses were pragmatic, relating that real violence is of deeper and more serious concern. As one parent suggested, "my kid sees bullets all day. His brothers have been shot.... He slept under his bed for three months after [the incursions of 2002] were over.... He wetted his bed at least twice a night.... It's not because of the games that he's done these things or that he's scared to go downstairs [to play]. It's because of the occupation. Game or no game, it's not going to make a difference." Like this mother's concern, other parents were more worried about the real tanks on the streets, the real bullets caught in the flesh, and the real political losses. While both gamers and their adult counterparts held a matter-of-fact approach to the effects of gaming, and downplayed the propagandistic and violent effects of the games (for those were more serious in the real sphere anyway), the rest of the world was virulently protesting the fact that these games existed, assuming their popularity was a major factor in creating anti–Western terrorists.

Global Controversies

In the post 9/11 context, many Western politicians, journalists and groups have condemned pro–Arab games. An Australian parliament member called them de-humanizing since they "encourag[e] young people to become suicide bombers and to participate in attacks on people from the West."[25] Noted *New York Times* columnist Thomas Friedman fretted that "videogames do matter" in the War Against Terror, and the war over Muslim minds since they are responsible for turning Islam into a death cult, suggesting that certain games, such as *Ummah Defense I* (whose objective is to unite the world under the banner of Islam) is nothing short of hate speech.[26] Western pundits attempt to connect the games to Islamic terrorism and al–Qaeda. For example, based on reports by British police officials combing through an Islamic bookstore for clues about the 7/7 London bombings,[27] Friedman alleges that one of the bombers' frequenting of the bookstore (that sells these videogames), is enough evidence to connect the games to terrorism.[28]

The rhetorical debate in the mainstream Western press around the games parallel those around the Palestinian-Israeli conflict and the belief in a "clash of civilizations" between the West and Islam. Thus many of the protests against the games fall within the same reductionist discourse as those propagated by Samuel Huntington,[29] only this time by journalists and politicians who have probably never played the games. The fears and accusations assume the games lead to anti–Americanism (often equated with anti–Western, anti–Israeli, or anti–Semitic sentiments) which lead to violence. Especially in the case of *Special Force*, games are posited as agitprop, described as "a sign of Hezbollah's elaborate propaganda efforts. [The game's] popularity is also an indication of Hezbollah's success in permeating popular consciousness in Lebanon and in gaining political legitimacy."[30] For some, indoctrination through videogames is inseparable from the party's proselytism: "[Hezbollah] has fanned the flames of the Intifada itself by delivering weapons and know-how to Palestinian terrorist groups. And it has openly propagandized for the destruction of Israel by means of its media and Web outlets and through such wildly popular Hezbollah-sponsored videogames such as *Special Force*."[31] Hezbollah for its part has not denied the connection between videogames and its larger mission. One Hezbollah officer claims, "*Special Force* is only the first step. The movement will only become greater in time."[32] But it also recognizes the variety of ways the game is used by its players: entertainment, education, history, anger-release, political frustration, and peer pressure.

Certainly these videogames are part of the global trend whereby media have become a means of expression, advertising, and propaganda for various groups, ranging from the U.S. Army to pro–Islamists. But the Western response to pro–Arab games is based on a number of assumptions that need to analyzed. An immediate connection is made between these games and the "violent effects" they have on gamers, especially that their "realism" is more convincing than other media. Many of these claims are based on ethnocentric Western notions of war and bloodshed, positions which are reductionist, simplistic and Orientalist.[33]

Back to Violence, Race, and Media Effects

"Anyone who reads the news knows that computer games cause brain damage. They are also addictive. And, of course, they promote violence in youngsters."[34] This statement about the violent effects of videogames by a technology journalist echoes not only popular misconceptions of videogames held in society, but the fears about pro–Arab games specifically. For years, leading voices on the left and the right, inside and outside academia, have agreed that videogame use among children has deleterious consequences, ranging from aggressiveness and violence to laziness and obesity.

While the premise of "direct effects" has subsided to one of "limited effects" in discussions of media in the West, it still rages when it comes to games outside the status-quo. Much of the fear about pro–Arab videogames is firmly embedded in over-reactionary beliefs, and the controversy surrounding them is not different from the fear of a hypodermic needle injected into children immediately turning them into terrorists, without any regard to the context in which these games are created, played and popularized. As one journalist fretted,

> what if a video game rewarded you for killing Arabs? Or Israelis? Or Somalis? ... Or even just Americans? Those games are out there, and they're growing as number of organizations realize the immense marketing potential of videogames in pushing a political agenda. Some are designed to recruit young people, promote an ideology or justify policies. Others are about promoting hate.[35]

There *are* games out in the world that are purely about promoting hate. One of the most disturbing ones is *Ethnic Cleansing*, made in the U.S. where a gamer can be a Ku Klux Klansman or neo–Nazi skinhead, randomly gunning down "dark-skinned people." The game's marketing blurb alludes to its racist nature: "Your skin is your uniform in this battle for the survival of your kind. The White Race depends on you to secure its existence. Your peoples' enemies surround you in a sea of decay and filth that they have brought to your once clean and White nation."[36] There are also games that are purposeful recruitment efforts, such as *America's Army*,[37] arguably the most successful FPS game in history, launched for free on the U.S. army website in 2002 with an average of over thirty-five thousand new users every day. A U.S. Army Colonel explained that the game allows youngsters to "try the army on for size and get more information about the many job opportunities," and urging that it was crucially important to attract gamers when still young because "if don't get in there and engage them early in life about what they're going to do with their lives, when it comes time for them to choose, you're in a fallback position."[38]

There have been complaints by parental groups, journalists and academics about the glorification of violence in *America's Army* and its impact on individuals and society. But according to an Army spokesperson, "*America's Army* is about military values. And patriotism. And those are good things...."[39] The same rhetoric cannot be used however when the proponent of the game is an "enemy" of the West. Nor for that matter can the rhetoric of limited effects be used, as if direct effects apply only to Arab children simply because of their nationality.

If anything is clear from these examples, and if any trends should be alarming, it should be the troubling post–9/11 collaboration between popular culture and militarization, symbolized in the expanding cooperation between the military and videogame industries. Media theorists such as Baudrillard, Virilio, Der Derian and Žižek have interrogated the ideological, cultural and material links between war and popular culture, and the shrinking distinction between the real and the imagined in the virtual realm of war and terror.[40] There is also concern about the implications on American society and its indirect participation with war and violence, and whether its media culture is preparing young Americans for armed conflict. Leonard puts it best in the following statement:

> War videogames are no longer purely about training soldiers already enlisted; rather, they are about recruitment and developing future soldiers, while simultaneously generating support among civilian populations for increasing use of American military power. Americans of all ages are thus able to participate collectively in the War on Terror and in Operation Iraqi Freedom, just as if they were members of the military.... With a little money and the switch of a button, the divide between real and virtual — between civilian and military, between

domestic and foreign — is erased as we wage war through gaming. Yet most Americans remain on their couches, in their classrooms, and in their offices, providing consent and support through videogames — through play.[41]

But there is further fear that FPS games in particular "reinforce the idea that international conflict is not solved through diplomacy, it is solved through insurgency."[42] *America's Army* and *Special Force* are often classified together, their effects equated in statements such as:

> terrorists and soldiers, spies and businessmen, students and parents — we live in age of video game enthusiasts, and what is best and worst about our world will sooner or later be packaged into a game. As the games grow more realistic, and the players grow older, the distinctions between life and game grow grayer and more vague. We increasingly grow desensitized to the difference between simulation and reality — living in make-believe worlds in which actions have no consequences and deadly mistakes can be fixed by pressing reset.[43]

For other journalists, the differences between games like *Special Force* and *Ethnic Cleansing* are minimal, classifying both as "public relations tools" for terrorists and racists.[44]

However, there is a fundamental difference between these pro–Arab games and *Ethnic Cleansing*, in that the first do not promote random racist killing and are based on real conflicts. Moreover, in terms of their inhumanity, terror, racism, and bloodthirstiness, *Under Siege* and *Special Force* pale in comparison to games such as *Israeli Air Force*,[45] an American-made game based on the Israeli invasion of Lebanon in which players can "carpet bomb all of Beirut." Collateral damage, in military euphemism, is possible in American games, whose goals are to destroy Afghanistan, Iraq, Arab, or Muslim nations. The killing is indiscriminate. The pro–Arab games may not be any less propagandistic, but they do not mercilessly sacrifice civilians. *Special Force* doesn't include civilians, and in *Under Ash* killing civilians incurs in lost points or a "game over." Unlike their Western counterparts, while combat is central in the pro–Arab games, the slaying of civilians is not.

Comparing pro-Arab videogames to *Ethnic Cleansing* or *America's Army* denies them their political context and uniqueness — especially when played in the Palestinian Territories, where gamers are victims, not perpetrators, of war. There is a deep difference between killing for the sake of doing so (*Ethnic Cleansing*, or more popular FPS games such as *Doom*[46] or *Quake*[47]), for waging a war (*America's Army*) or in order redress your people's losses (*Under Siege*). Or as the pundits in Hezbollah have expressed in not-quite the same terms: "It seems that the [Western] media is silent when they, the Zionists, use their tanks to slaughter our children. But when our children play a shoot-em up game where they shoot Zionist tanks in return for correct answers we are accused of training terrorists and instilling hatred towards Jews!"[48]

There is an entrenched contradiction at the heart of the effects tradition: if videogames do influence children, why is there no concern about the Arab child who will see his kin as villain, evil-doer, terrorist, to be killed indiscriminately, as has been the case in games until the pro–Arab ones came along? This addresses the problems of the ethnocentrism embedded in videogames and the on-going stereotypes of Arabs, Muslims and terrorists (never mind the conflation of the three). American-made games such *Desert Storm*[49] and *America's Army* "portray Arab-Americans [and Arabs] as savages, uncivilized warriors, and terrorists. In a very real way, war games construct racialized meaning.... White people are presented as praiseworthy fighters and heroes."[50] Are these games not providing ideological sanction for America's War on Terror and its aggression in the Middle East?

As the twelve-year-old girl from Jenin made clear, none of the games that she had played before these three had allowed her *not* to shoot at Arabs; in her words "I always had to shoot at my own people." Before *Under Ash*, *Under Siege*, and *Special Force*, the Arab (and/or Muslim) was by default the enemy. For example, *Command and Conquer: Generals*' goals are to defeat an Arab guerilla force who uses sneaky and underhand tactics, as opposed to the U.S. forces' high-tech weapons, skills, and strategic abilities.[51] In its narrative it incorporates an Orientalist discourse where the Arab is the uncivilized, unmodernized and violent "Other."

There are also larger problems with focusing only on violent effects. One is the denial of the context in which games are played, and the historical conditions that have led to anti–Western sentiment. Given the history of Arab-Western relations, why would a child think anything positive of the West, when all she has known is colonization, cultural imperialism, economic exploitation of her nation's reserves, maintenance of corrupt dictatorships, waging of wars and crusades, false promises of democracy, printing of profane cartoons, and so on.

Anti-Western or anti–American sentiment cannot be blamed on games alone. Games are not influencing kids towards a particular political perspective, since it is the conditions around them that have already situated them as "pro–Arab" (and sometimes "anti–Western" and/or "anti–Israeli") subjects of larger political conditions. So while these games illustrate the conditions of contemporary culture in the Middle East, they also serve to debunk claims of violent effects and brain-washing through media. It is the larger political, economic, and social landscape around these gamers that is the stronger force in children's lives, not the fact that they can escape into a virtual world, which either recreates their life in war-torn Palestine or allows them to rewrite history so that they can be heroes. As one of the directors of *Dar al–Fikr* said:

"Children that play these videogames live in a huge irony. On one hand they sense the anger of adults about being victims of politics, victims of mental and physical violence. And on the other side, he can sit alone on his PC and transform himself into someone with strength and able to resist U.S. forces."[52]

Additionally, there is a myopic view of whose "patriotism" is justified. Why is it that Americans can excuse their pro-military propaganda and defend their political views as the correct ones and everyone else's as "terrorist"? Given the similarities between *America's Army* and *Special Force*, this seems to be the case made. For example, one scholar complains of Hezbollah's website that it "provide[s] links to downloadable children's videogames that train children to play the role of terrorists, to be suicide bombers, and to shoot actual political leaders, but fails to mention, that following that logic, American children are doing the same: accessing the U.S. Army website, downloading war games, training to be state-sponsored terrorists (depending on one's perspective) and shoot Arab leaders.[53] This mimics the rhetoric surrounding global relations, where the United States and Europe are entitled to protect, rationalize and propagate their perspectives at the expense of others. Debates about whose war is more just (America's or Iraqi insurgents), whose democracy more acceptable (Israel's denial of its Arab population of equal rights because they are not Jewish, or Hamas legitimately coming to power through elections), or whose freedom of speech more justified (European newspapers printing cartoons of Prophet Muhammad or Muslims burning flags in protest) continue to be one-sided.

While the "effects" tradition is certainly limited in its scope of analysis, there is a still deeper fear that videogames in particular are more potent: "Films and television programs can only dramatize their politics, but we now have a medium where you can interact with them, as an engaged participant."[54] This has to do with gamers being consumed in a virtual world at more intense levels than in other media, and even more so in FPS games. This leads us into the subsequent concerns about the "action" aspect of videogames and its twin "realism."

Realism on the Screens

Compared to *America's Army* and Western games these pro–Arab games are expressions of political realities that are lived on every day basis by their players, especially in the Palestinian Territories. These games bring up new issues of realism — a central theoretical issue in media studies of the connections between the virtual and real worlds.

First, there must be a distinction made between games modeled around real events and those that claim to be an extension of real life struggle. In this view, exceptional about *America's Army* is its "mimetic" realism: as a model of the experience of the American army, the game claims a real material referent that other games cannot. Games like *Special Force* are similar in representation to *America's Army*, although their narratives are different; training fighters in a virtual setting as real as possible. In the words of a Hezbollah official, "*Special Force* offers a mental and personal training for those who play it, allowing them to feel that they are in the shoes of the resistance fighters."[55]

These games challenge accepted notions of media realism and require deeper consideration than just their visual or textual representations. Because these games are not just watched, listened to, or read, but interacted with, they supplement the debate about realism and representation with the phenomenon of action. Galloway proposes that game studies define realist games "as those games that reflect critically on the minutia of everyday life, replete as it is with struggle, personal drama and injustice."[56] As such, *Under Ash* and *Under Siege* embody a new phenomenon which addresses players' real-life concerns. If we are to agree with Galloway's definition of realism as the documentary-like attention to everyday struggles, then these games are truly realist. As he explains, *Under Ash* takes a "more sober, almost educational tone ... [since] players ... have a personal investment in the struggle depicted in the game, just as they have a personal investment in the struggle happening each day around them. This is something rarely seen in the consumer gaming market [even if the game is] a cookie-cuter repurposing of an American-style shooter for the ideological needs of the Palestinian situation."[57]

One thirteen-year-old in East Jerusalem explained, "I love that I am able to shoot Israelis. Of course it's because I'm not able to shoot them in real life.... But it feels almost like the real thing, especially levels one and two, where the sceneries are from around here." Or as a seventeen-year-old in Gaza expressed about *Under Ash*, "there are times when I play this game and I imagine that I really am able to shoot the [Israeli soldiers].... I just have to think of all those times when I was angry but unable to do anything about our occupation. When I sit at the [computer] screen, I think of the real anger I feel and I play much better."

Under Ash and *Under Siege* are important for two reasons: first, their realism is not only in the narrative or the visual, but in their action; second, because of their documentary-like quality of life on the Palestinian ground — demolished houses, checkpoints, separated families, etc. — and partly because the games are "distinctly difficult to play, a sardonic instance of socio-political realism,"[58] they are not fantasy escapism alone. They are as close to a realist representation as any videogame has ever come.

Both pro–Arab and Western-made war games point to the burgeoning relationship between virtual reality and the bloodshed of the real. To return to one of the effects tradition's concerns: is there a larger militarization and violence of everyday life occurring in videogames? Here, a number of scholars have already made important contributions. Baudrillard, Virilio, Der Derian have critically engaged the ideological, cultural and material links between popular culture and war and the blur between the real and fantastically imagined.[59] They analyze the hyper-presence of war on television and videogames as war without bloodshed. Without carnage or destruction, a strategy of deception has fooled us into believing that a real war never happened. As Leonard argues, "against a background where war takes place within the hyper-real (virtual) and where war-making itself is increasingly virtual and hyper-real, [these theorists] demonstrate the importance of challenging and deconstructing videogames as part of a pedagogy of peace."[60]

But these concerns are ethnocentric. For the victims of war, such as Palestinians (Lebanese, Israeli or Iraqi for that matter), there is nothing hyper-real about being bombed, forbidden to go to school because a tank is outside your house, living with curfews and closures, or losing your parents. Nor is there anything hyper-real about resisting with stones, slingshots and homemade bombs. As such these theorists forget that in hyper-real wars there are "traditional" elements of war experienced — by the underdogs of course. The connection between the virtual field of war available to Palestinian children and the real war outside their living rooms and schoolyards is more than just "technical illusion"[61] or "hyperrealist logic."[62] And many of the Palestinian kids who play are very much aware of the (dis)connection between the two worlds. The same boy who plays better when he thinks of his real anger, explained the discrepancy between his real and virtual anger-release:

> there are times when [*Under Siege*] gets me even more frustrated, because in the game I am this strong fighter, I am able to resist, to avoid bullets, to have weapons, to do all these things I am unable to do in real life.... It is worse with [*Special Force*] because there I have this feeling that I am really beating the Israelis and winning the cause. But I know it cannot happen here. I know it is not so easy to blow up their tanks or shoot down their airplanes.

Another sixteen-year-old girl in Gaza got to the heart of the matter by situating her playing within a larger political context: "The American games give me a strange feeling. I wonder if these scenes from inside their tanks and airplanes are what the soldiers see when they're dropping bombs on Iraq.... Or that Israeli game where they are shooting Arabs. Is that a true representation of how they see things? ... It's probably close, since *Under Siege* is close to our reality." Such examples speak to the media and political savviness of these gamers, who negotiate the conflicts on their screens as much more than virtual killing fields.

Leonard further suggests that "what ... [is] frightening is that in our playtime, in our leisure time, we're engaging in fictional conflicts that are based on a terrorist threat and never asking questions."[63] Again, these concerns do not adequately apply in the Palestinian context. First, there is no leisure time. There are hardly any parks, playgrounds or soccer fields in Gaza. Kids are often locked up under curfews and closures or by their parents due to fear. Second, the militarization of everyday life is occurring in the real realm — under oppressive and deadly conditions. Third, there are many questions asked by Palestinian kids; but they're not heard. As a thirteen-year-old posed, "how come no one cares that we are being killed? [The U.S.] complains about our stone-throwing, they call us terrorists, they are angry that we play these games, but they never recognize that their weapons are the ones that kill our people.... Where is the peace that Clinton promised? Where is the state that Bush promised? Why do they keep selling us lies and then expect us to believe them and love them?"

I raise these concerns to suggest that although post-modern theorists offer critical insight into the hyper-real violence of today, they suffer from an ethnocentrism that assumes that what the West experiences on its screens is the only (hyper)reality out there. Deep-seated in their arguments is the omission that real beings are on the other side of those digital images of war; those pixelated images emanating out of tanks and little red dots from heat-sensitive satellites are real places and people. While these theorists contribute to our understanding of media representations they are guilty of denying the "Other" (in this case the proverbial Arab) his own very real experience and violent reality — which is affected by a push of a button thousands of miles away.

Responses to Western Hegemony

One of the strengths of the virtual world is that it offers a space to challenge convention and tilt the dominant world view. In great part this is what these pro–Arab games are succeeding at (while recognizing that in the political sphere many Arabs already hold "anti–Western" views). For some Western analysts, these videogames are posited as part of a larger media campaign occurring in the Middle East, claiming that *Special Force* "hopes to become the computer entertainment equivalent of what Al-Jazeera and Al-Arabiya are in the news broadcasting sector — a public Arab opposition voice against pro–Western dominance."[64] That is partially true. And some Arabs will agree, as this Lebanese journalist's remark on the games' importance: "It is easy to sneer at computer games as the silly embodiment of someone's teenage fantasies. Which they are. But at least in *Under Ash* the silly fantasy is not the product of someone else's teenage morality; this one's all our own."[65]

The fact that these games are Arab-made is a major reason for their popularity. Of course allowing kids to shoot real-life enemies, redress losses, and do so in their own language helps too. But there is more than just redressing the "balance to a genre dominated by victorious U.S. soldiers defeating Arab enemies."[66] Their popularity stems from more than just portraying Arabs as triumphant heroes, and it is something none of the Western pundits focus on. It is dignity.

Radwan Kasmiya, one of the creators of *Under Siege*, explains: "All I want is ... equality in the minds of Arabic children so they would feel digital dignity [sic]."[67] And the kids echo this. Here is how one sixteen-year-old in a Ramallah Internet café describes it,

> it's great that there is a creation now that shows our horrible conditions: the occupation, people imprisoned in jails, demolished houses, a husband and wife separated by a checkpoint ... but [these games] also give us a sense of dignity, that we are not portrayed simply as victims, but as resisters. We're not just doing nothing with our hands tied behind our backs, but we're fighting back.... You know how all other games have us there like shooting targets. This time the targets aren't us. It sounds silly, but it's a wonderful feeling.

While this young man makes clear that being on the winning side is a wonderful feeling, his comments also suggest that games serve an educational purpose in their depiction of real circumstances. As the *Special Force* design team admit, the game is intended to disseminate the group's values, concepts and ideas, but also give players a chance to feel as if they were taking part in the attacks. Mahmoud Rayya, an official from Hezbollah, explains succinctly, "this game is resisting the Israeli occupation through the media."[68] *Under Siege* and *Under Ash* are arguably more educational than *Special Force*: their opening scenes made up of mini-documentaries of Palestinian history. Their visuals may well be a historical archive. The games are filled with documentary-style oral narratives, interviews and confessions from various Palestinians. These games, it becomes clear, are not just about entertainment, but about education. One only has to reconsider one of the central objectives according to the creators, that of building gamers' historical and world knowledge.

These games are part of the larger, contemporary practice of Arabs' (and, what is often seen in the mainstream Western press, as their fundamentalist Islamic threads') response to Western influence and hegemony. In a sense the creation of videogames symbolizes the cooption of Western technologies for "anti-modern" means. Some see the fact of "anti–Western Muslim extremists using the West's own technologies against it ... [as an] irony."[69] They hold simplistic views, explaining it as a "paradox ... that many extremists wish to purge their territories of Western influence, media, and related technology"[70] and yet play videogames — or worse yet, use jets to fly into buildings. But reality is much more complicated. Palestinian gamers have learned that they can be both "modern" and "fundamental" simultaneously. They can play on the Internet in virtual wars like their Western counterparts *and* support "fundamentalist" groups. Thus, an individual's fundamentalist orientation does not prevent her from adopting modernistic approaches. Through these videogames, Arab kids and groups such as Hezbollah exploit the very tools of modern society to strengthen and re-institutionalize the fundamental core of their Islamic faith and political objectives. Religion can no longer be seen simply as impervious to change and irrelevant to modernization. The task therefore becomes one of reconciling anachronistic values with time-honored assumptions about the content, nature, and direction of modernizing change and the role of technology therein. As such, these games and the trends behind them fly in the face of modernization theorists. Since Daniel Lerner,[71] the West has assumed that its model of modernization exhibits elements and consequences whose relevance is universal, much of which happens through the great multiplier of the media. All one needs is to supply Arabs with digital technologies, and they will be on the road to modernity. From there it is just a short step to the excessive importance that post-modernists and proponents of globalization assign to mass consumerism and popular culture in the framing of everyday life and redefining basic values. The works of Francis Fukuyama, Samuel Huntington, Benjamin Barber and recent work by Bernard Lewis[72] remain in that tradition. They continue to distinguish conflict in the region as a by-product of monolithic and overarching thoughts — "the triumph of liberalism" or "the clash of civilizations." Rather than thinking of a possibility of reconciliation between the two forces, these Orientalists see the homogenized McWorld of Barber rapidly eroding local identities. And it is to their surprise when they do not see this happening with increasing Internet usage or videogames.

There is little of such sharp dichotomies in the Palestinian Territories. Global expectations are being reshaped to accommodate local needs and preferences, just as the local is not averse to experimenting with more global encounters and cultural by-products. These games are symbolic of the variety possible as technologies are spread "Eastward," and of the impossibility of a lasting homogenization of Western media. This observation is not just text-centric (the messages inside these games), but an industry-wide one: those voices so long oppressed, stereotyped, vilified, or negated, are learning that their master's tools can be put to very different uses than the master intended. This is not to suggest that power in the digital realm will immediately result in power in the real political one. If anything, the reality of Palestinians shows otherwise.

Conclusion

Pro-Arab games are entering a landscape already gripped by political unrest, displacement and collective violence. The spaces of war have manifestly asserted their logic on every part of public and private space — and now virtual space. Instead of the Western concern about how virtual violence may seep into the realms of social and political life, for Palestinian kids the issue is reversed. Of concern should be the fact that with the rise of these videogames, the few spaces of non-violence available to Palestinian youth are all but disappearing. The Second Intifada, following years of occupation and corruption, destroyed common and porous spaces such as parks and playgrounds. Combined with Israeli policies of physical fragmention, it also encouraged the formation of separate, isolated and exclusive spaces, transforming the use of space in a more compelling sense: real playgrounds into battlegrounds, and now battlegrounds into virtual playgrounds.

Throughout the Intifada, and arguably since 1948, the majority of Palestinians have been trapped negotiating, constructing, and reconfirming an unsettled pattern of identity. They are homeless in their own homes. Like other displaced groups, they become disoriented and distressed because there is no longer a neighborhood for them to live in, play in, and rely on. They become homeless in at least three existential senses, as Khalaf[73] describes of the Lebanese: they suffer the angst of being dislodged from their most enduring attachments and familiar places; they suffer banishment; and are impelled by an urge to reassemble a damaged identity and broken history. Imagining old places and recreating history to preserve the places and politics as they would prefer them serve as a reprieve from the uncertainties and anxieties of today. The components of these videogames that serve as "digital memorials" do precisely that: re-construct Palestinian spaces and history, preserving them for younger generations to keep remembering. The fears emanating from the

West posit Arab children without a social, religious, political and spatial identities. This myopia is an extension of the effects tradition, combined with the added component of racist stereotypes, and a negation of the reality of war in these children's everyday lives. The perspective is also reductionist in the assumption that Arab children are more gullible to propaganda than Western children. These approaches fail to acknowledge the realities behind these games, that identities are more complex than simply a reaction or negotiation with what is happening on computer screens, but must take into account the array of factors in social life, and in this context specifically, the impact of constant violence, oppression and war. They also fail to recognize that identities are dynamic and subject to change, narratives that evolve and form over time and in time.

Special Force, *Under Siege*, and *Under Ash* are no longer alone as pro–Arab videogames. New games have arrived on the scene which will undoubtedly continue to raise the issues discussed above. *Ummah Defense*'s[74] objective is to unite the world under Islam, *Islam Fun*[75] introduces young children to Islam, *Maze of Destiny*[76] has players rescue chapters of the Quran from thieves. A new version of *Special Force* has been released based on the Summer 2006 Hezbollah-Israel war; and it won't be long before a game showcases the latest row "between East and West," perhaps with Danes drawing enflaming cartoons and Pakistanis burning down embassies. Pundits will myopically focus on the games' ideological underpinnings, forgetting the intricacies inside and beyond the screens. As a tagline at the end of level four of *Under Ash* suggests, the same applies here as a conclusion: "A real life story or a political propaganda? You have the right to decide."

Notes

1. For anonymity, interviewees are not mentioned by name.
2. www.specialforce.net.
3. Haram ash–Sharif refers to the Dome of the Rock (or Temple Mount) in Jerusalem, the site from which the Second Intifada "began" in September 2000.
4. David Buckingham, *After the Death of Childhood: Growing Up in the Age of Electronic Media* (Maldem: Polity Press, 2000); Ien Ang, *Desperately Seeking the Audience* (New York: Routledge, 1998); David Morley, *Television Audiences and Cultural Studies* (New York: Routledge, 1992); Ellen Seiter, *Television and New Media Audiences* (Oxford: Oxford University Press, 1999); and Lynn Schofield-Clark, *From Angels to Aliens: Teenagers, the Media and the Supernatural* (New York: Oxford University Press, 2003).
5. Edward Said, *Orientalism* (New York: Vintage Books, 1994); Mahmoud Mamdani, *Good Muslim, Bad Muslim: America, the Cold War, and the Roots of Terrorism* (New York: Pantheon Books, 2004).
6. "Life Is Just a Game," *New Atlantis* 4, Winter (2004): 105–108, accessed from www.thenewatlantis.com/archive/4/soa/videogames.htm.

7. David B. Neiborg, "America's Army: More Than a Game," in *Transforming Knowledge Into Action through Gaming and Simulation*, ed. Thomas Eberle Willy Christian. International Simulation and Gaming Association, (Munich: SAGSA, 2004). CD-Rom.
8. Mary Wiltenburg, "More Than Playing Games," *Christian Science Monitor*, April 3 (2003): 14.
9. *Queer Power*, Molleindustria, 2004, online game, www.molleindustria.it.
10. *Left Behind: Eternal Forces*, Left Behind Games, 2006, online game, www.leftbehindgames.com/pages/the_games.htm.
11. *GodSpeed 3D*, Inspired Idea, 2002, CD-Rom.
12. *Ethnic Cleansing*, Resistance Records, 2002, online game, www.resistance.com/ethniccleansing/index.htm.
13. *White Law*, Resistance Records, 2003, online game, www.resistance.com.
14. *Shoot the Blacks*, World Church of the Creator (Year Unknown), www.wcotc.com.
15. The name Dar al–Fikr loosely translates to "house of thought." Both games are available at www.underash.net.
16. Empyre Discussion Board, "Politics, Reality, Violence and a Video Game," accessed from http://mail.cofa.unsw.edu.au/pipermail/empyre/2004–July/ on February 1, 2006. Empyre Discussion Board is a web-based discussion board established in Australia where gamers and game creators often share opinions together. The discussion board also includes an in-depth email interview with one of the creative directors of *Under Ash*.
17. Empyre Discussion Board.
18. Empyre Discussion Board.
19. Alexander Galloway, "Social Realism in Gaming," *Game Studies* vol. 4, issue 1 (2004), accessed from www.gamestudies.org/0401/galloway/ on November 25, 2005.
20. Daniel J. Wakin, "Video Game Mounts Simulated Attacks Against Israeli Targets," *New York Times*, 24, May 18, 2003.
21. Special Force website, www.specialforce.net.
22. Quoted in Nick Lewis, "Dangerous Games: How the Seductive Power of Videogames Is Being Harnessed to Push Deadly Agendas." *Calgary Herald*, C11, July 9, 2005.
23. Quoted in Wakin, "Simulated Attacks," 24.
24. Internet growth rate increased at around eight percent a year during the Intifada years, from 2000 to 2004, so that by the end of 2005, fifteen percent of the total population were regular Internet users. For those under the age of eighteen, who have computer and Internet access in schools as well as local centers, usage rates at the end of 2005, were at 52 percent. Internet World Stats, "Internet Usage in the Middle East"(September 30, 2005), accessed from www.internetworldstats.com on October 5, 2005; PCBS, *Palestinians at the End of Year 2005* (Ramallah: Palestinian Central Bureau of Statistics, 2006).
25. Quoted in Alfred Hackensberger, "Shooting Baruch Goldstein, Carpet Bombing Beirut." *Qantara*, accessed from www.qantara.de/webcom/show_article.php/_c-478/_nr-310/i.html on November 25, 2005.
26. Thomas L. Friedman, "Giving Hatemongers No Place to Hide," *The New York Times*, A19, July 25, 2005.
27. Ed Johnson, "Investigators Pursue Clues to Bombings in Leeds, Pakistan," *Associated Press*, July 18, 2005.
28. Friedman, "Hatemongers."
29. Samuel Huntington, "The Clash of Civilizations," *Foreign Affairs*, Vol. 72, No.3 (Summer 1993).
30. Wakin, "Simulated Attacks," 24.
31. Gal Luft, "Hizballahland," *Commentary Magazine*, July–August, 2003, n.p.
32. Quoted in Hackensberger, "Shooting Baruch," n.p.
33. Said, *Orientalism*.

34. Paul Hyman, "War! What Is It Good for?" *Computer User*, September 1, 2003, accessed from www.computeruser.com/clickit/printout/articles/daily/4992,80/ on February 1, 2006.

35. Lewis, "Dangerous Games."

36. Social Impact Games, "Political and Social Games," accessed from www.socialimpactgames.com on February 1, 2006.

37. *America's Army: Special Forces 2.0*, U.S. Army, 2003, online game, www.americasarmy.com.

38. Quoted in David Leonard, "Unsettling the Military Entertainment Complex: Videogames as a Pedagogy of Peace," *Studies in Media and Information Literacy Education*, vol. 4, issue 4, November (2004), www.utpjournals.com/.

39. Quoted in Hyman, "War!"

40. Jean Baudrillard, *The Gulf War Did Not Take Place* (Bloomington: Indiana University Press, 1991); Paul Virilio, *Strategy of Deception* (New York: Verso, 2000); Paul Virilio, *Ground Zero* (New York: Verso, 2002), James Der Derian, *Virtuous War: Mapping the Military Industrial-Media-Entertainment Network* (Boulder, CO: Westview Press, 2001); and Slavoj Žižek, *Welcome to the Desert of the Real: Five Essays on September 11 and Related Dates* (New York: Verso, 2002).

41. Leonard, "Pedagogy of Peace," n.p.

42. Ibid., n.p.

43. "Life is Just a Game," n.p.

44. Hyman, "War!"; Lewis, "Dangerous Games."

45. *Israeli Air Force*, Electronic Arts, 1998, CD-Rom.

46. *Doom*, IdSoftware and Activision, 1993, CD-Rom, www.idsoftware.com/games/doom/doom3/.

47. *Quake*, IdSoftware, 1996, CD-Rom, www.idsoftware.com/games/quake/quake.

48. Special Force website, www.specialforce.net.

49. *Desert Storm*, Sci Entertainment Group, 2002, CD-Rom.

50. Leonard, "Pedagogy of Peace," n.p.

51. *Command and Conquer: Generals*, Electronic Arts, 2003, CD-Rom.

52. Empyre Discussion Board.

53. Bruce Klopfenstein, "Terrorism and the Exploitation of New Media" in *Media, Terrorism, and Theory*, ed. Anandam Kavoori and Todd Fraley, 112 (Boulder, CO: Rowman & Littlefield, 2006).

54. Lewis, "Dangerous Games," n.p.

55. Special Force website.

56. Galloway, "Social Realism," n.p.

57. Ibid., n.p.

58. Ibid., n.p.

59. Baudrillard, *The Gulf War Did Not Take Place*; Virilio, *Strategy of Deception*; Der Derian, *Virtuous War*.

60. Leonard, "Pedagogy of Peace," n.p.

61. Virilio, *Strategy of Deception*.

62. Baudrillard, *The Gulf War Did Not Take Place*.

63. Leonard, "Pedagogy of Peace," n.p.

64. Hackensberger, "Shooting Baruch," n.p.

65. Habib Battah, "Syrian-developed PC Game Portrays Palestinian Anguish," *The Daily Star*, October 21 ,2004, accessed from www.dailystar.cin.lb.

66. Rebecca Armstrong, "Jihad: Play the Game," *The Independent*, August 17, 2005, accessed from web.lexis-nexis.com.

67. Empyre Discussion Board.

68. Quoted in Armstrong, "Jihad," n.p.

69. Klopfenstein, "Terrorism and the Exploitation," 113.
70. Ibid., 113.
71. Daniel Lerner, *The Passing of Traditional Society: Modernizing the Middle East* (New York: The Free Press, 1958).
72. Francis Fukuyama, *The End of History and the Last Man* (New York: Avon Books, 1992); Samuel Huntington 1993; Benjamin Barber, *Jihad vs. McWorld: How Globalism and Tribalism Are Reshaping the World* (New York: Ballantine Books, 1996); and Bernard Lewis, *What Went Wrong? The Clash Between Islam and Modernity in the Middle East* (New York: Oxford University Press, 2002).
73. Samir Khalaf, *Cultural Resistance: Global and Local Encounters in the Middle East* (London: Saqi Books, 2001).
74. *Ummah Defense*, IslamGames, 2001, CD-Rom.
75. *Islam Fun*, Innovative Minds, 2002, CD-Rom, www.inminds.co.uk.
76. *Maze of Destiny*, IslamGames, 2002, CD-Rom.

14

Manufacturing Militainment
Video Game Producers and Military Brand Games

MATTHEW THOMAS PAYNE

The U.S. Military and the U.S. Department of Defense have enjoyed close working relationships with the computer simulation and modeling industries for decades.[1] Yet over the last fifteen years, this collaboration has increasingly focused on producing military-themed video games for military and non-military audiences; contributing to a production dynamic that some have called the Military-Entertainment Complex.[2] And because today's armed forces are all but reliant on private, networked interactive entertainment firms to produce their in-house training software *and* their consumer-brand of electronic games, video game producers emerge from this new media production matrix as highly influential decision-makers. Drawing from hours of original, in-depth interviews conducted with the producers of *America's Army* (2002), *America's Army: Rise of a Soldier* (2005), and *Full Spectrum Warrior* (2004), this article argues that these production professionals function as techno-cultural brokers who fuse state-sponsored militarism and private-sector entertainment to produce video games that blur the lines between fantasy and fact, recreation and training, and entertainment and war.

Introduction

In the premiere issue of *Wired*, cyberpunk fiction author Bruce Sterling penned the magazine's first feature piece, "War Is Virtual Hell," about his recent trip to the annual Interservice/Industry Training Systems and Education Conference in November 1992.[3] The conference and trade show, which has been going strong since its inception in 1966, is aimed at promoting — in the organization's own words—"cooperation among the Armed Services, Industry, Academia and various Government agencies in pursuit of improved training and education programs, identification of common training issues and development of multiservice programs."[4] Among the trade show's aisles of military innovations was a digital mapping tool called Project 2851. If realized, the technology would allow numerous military machines to access and share databases of digital maps and navigational coordinates. But in Sterling's view, the project is about something far more profound—it is nothing less than "the virtual reproduction and archiving of the entire planet."[5] "It means," Sterling portends, "that soon there will be no such thing as 'unknown territory' for the United States military.... It will know other countries better than those countries know themselves."[6] Technologies like Project 2851 find a compelling analog in Benedict Anderson's *Imagined Communities*.[7] Anderson positions nation-building technologies, such as the modern map, the census, and the museum, as knowledge-producing and identity-forming techniques that allow a nation-state to delimit spaces, populations, and cultural histories for the purposes of controlling discourses and human resources which perpetuate the fiction of their own nationhood.[8] The real-time charting capabilities of Project 2851 are simply the realization of Anderson's maps in a digital age, whereby surveillance and tracking systems support the military's ability to digitally reify the controlling state's fictive ontology through quick and accurate geopolitical information production. Ever the futurist, Sterling speculates that the military's digital production will move beyond virtual topographies and maps, and that they will, with the help of private firms, soon realize their mantra to "Simulate before you build."[9] This means that emergent weapons and war technologies will be generated, tested, and replaced "before a nail is ever hammered."[10]

Yet in spite of the innumerable advances in military technologies, the most difficult war-fighting tool to reliably construct is still the human one. Historian of technology Lewis Mumford describes how a standing army poses a number of production and maintenance difficulties for the modern state. "An army is a body of pure consumers. As the army grew in size it threw a heavier burden upon the productive enterprise: for the army must be fed and housed and equipped, and it does not, like the other trades, supply any service in return except that of 'protection' in times of war. In war, moreover, the army is not merely a pure consumer but a negative producer: that is to say, it produces illth ... instead of wealth—misery, mutilation, physical destruction, terror, starvation and death characterize the process of war and form a principal part of the product."[11]

How, then, can the military hope to "simulate before building" when it comes to manufacturing human war fighters? That is, how can the Department of Defense manufacture experienced soldiers short of actually sending them to war? The Defense Department's working hypothesis since the 1950s has been through computer-based simulation and modeling war game technologies.[12] Within the last decade, the world's militaries have forged increasingly closer ties to networked interactive entertainment firms to supplement their in-house capabilities of generating virtual theaters of war. These training programs are administered to educate soldiers on proper combat protocols and to virtually expose them to the decision-making opportunities that they might encounter on real-world battlefields. And while the vast majority of these war simulations have been application-specific, stand-alone technologies, there has been a significant trend towards making these technologies networked, interoperable, and increasingly game-like over the last ten years, which brings us to this paper's primary object of study: commercially available military video games. Sterling's prescient musings about future military technologies are a convenient springboard for thinking about how the Department of Defense's institutional logic has been marching towards appropriating PC and console game technologies for years. What, then, are the guiding principles and strategic techniques used by interactive media producers to embed authorized military protocol and values into commercial video games?

Research Methodology

One productive approach for addressing this research question is through the social construction of technology (SCOT) tradition. Defined broadly, this critical stance is a direct and oppositional response to technological determinism, and maintains that humans and other social forces, such as law, economics, and organizations, shape the development, production, and usage of technologies. Moreover, SCOT proponents contend that innovations come out of historically specific social milieus and material modes of production and not some ethereal or Platonic plane.

SCOT is not without its own critics, however. In particular, philosophy of technology scholars have criticized social constructivists for ignoring the wider effects of technology by giving too much attention to the stages of technological development; granting excessive agency to human actors while marginalizing other generative forces; of being preoccupied with debunking technological determinism (which is often wielded as a fallacious "straw man" argument); and for avoiding moral language so as to elide questions regarding technologies' ethical implications.[13]

With these criticisms in mind, this paper seeks to answer its research question by way of a dual-pronged methodological approach. First, an organizational view explains how these producers generate and exercise power, and accrue substantial social capital as media brokers. Second, this paper uses two analytic tools common to the SCOT approach — the *technological frame* and the *technological script*— to examine how these creatives manufacture their authorized military titles. Both concepts, which will be explained shortly, illuminate how gaming technologies reflect their producers' views of the military, and their beliefs about the imagined game-playing audience. These two SCOT tools are applied to a series of in-depth interviews conducted with the head producers of *America's Army* (2002), *America's Army: Rise of a Soldier* (2005), and *Full Spectrum Warrior* (2004) in Spring 2006. Such a multifaceted methodological approach agrees with Wiebe Bijker and John Law's "postulate of heterogeneity," which holds that technical and cultural forces not only mutually constitute our everyday technologies, but that "Social classes, occupational groups, organizations, professions — [are also] held in place by intimately linked social and technical means."[14] Indeed, the organizational relationships and creative justifications offered by these media professionals evidence that militarized media cannot be reduced to technological or social forces alone.

Military video game producers are new media cultural brokers who communicate Defense Department needs to interactive entertainment firms, thus operating as human linchpins within their inter-firm media production configurations. During this collaboration they impart, onto the process and onto the texts, a militarized worldview. And though these creative professionals are unquestionably central to this specific media production process, it is too reductive to attribute a totalizing or even primary authorial voice to these specialists alone. A SCOT-based research agenda affirms this disinclination to locate "final causes, for there are no final causes. Rather, [the investigator's job] is to unearth [techno-social] schemes and expose their contingency."[15] Working from largely shared frames of meaning, these producers benefit from their vocational positioning between their information flows, and use their technical know-how and trans-network access to inscribe preferred readings and uses into their commercial wares. Pursuing their craft thusly legitimizes them as a practically minded, informed, and occasionally inspired interactive media elite, even as their creative and administrative skills propagate a military message. The analysis that follows is derived primarily from six hours of in-depth phone interviews that I conducted with three video game producers in the Spring of 2006 about their work on commercial military-themed video games. These individuals were selected because of the popularity of their titles, and because their games are marketed as realistic and authentic virtual military experiences based on established combat protocols.

The Military Video Game Producer as a Techno-Cultural Broker

Two concepts common to organizational communication, *social capital* and *structural hole theory*, illustrate how a producer engenders and maintains a privileged position within a production dynamic by bridging the considerable institutional divide between the military and the game firm. *Social capital*, or the advantages enjoyed by those participating in or between different groups or organizations, has been an important — if sometimes slippery — concept in sociology, political science, and communication studies since at least the 1970s (though the term's conceptual roots are traceable to the nineteenth century). Unlike human capital, which is based on the personal qualities of individuals, social capital is generated between people or groups. The concept of social capital agrees especially well with SCOT's emphasis on the necessary interplay between social forces in technological development. But this cooperative value production is not just some random externality that happens by virtue of growing one's network associations. Instead, according to Nan Lin, "The premise behind the notion of social capital is rather simple and straightforward: [there is an] *investment in social relations with expected returns.*"[16] People network and interact with one another to produce and accrue profits.[17] But not all networks are created equal, and not all social value is produced similarly. The degree of social success also varies with a range of factors (e.g., location in an organization, strength of weak and strong ties, number of associations). For information managers, the preeminent variable for social value is their number of peers, with the result being that, "Social capital is more valuable to the manager with few peers."[18] The interviewed creative directors are without organizational redundancy; they are the primary information linkages between the Defense Department and the game company. These are simple but important interrelated points: the fewer the number of working military game producers, the more social capital these specialists accrue, and the more important social capital becomes as a result of their centrality to this production dynamic.

In addition to their singularity, these media producers also benefit from their unique placement in between their network flows. Ronald S. Burt's *structural hole theory* is an especially useful concept for arguing how "social capital is a function of brokerage opportunities in a network."[19] According to

Burt: "The structural hole argument defines social capital in terms of the information and control advantages of being the broker in relations between people otherwise disconnected in a social structure. The disconnected people stand on opposite sides of a hole in a social structure. The structural hole is an opportunity to broker the flow of information between people and control the form of projects that bring together people from opposite sides of the hole."[20] The professionals interviewed for this project affirm this type of organizational linkage by connecting two university-based research institutes (one of which employs designers, the other sub-contracts a game firm) and a private entertainment company to military interests. Burt is good to acknowledge that just because people work in different information flows, it does not necessarily mean that they are unaware of others.[21] The point, rather, is that as more information flows become linked (or, as more gaps are bridged) the network's information gains increase, as does the social capital of those agents who connect previously unlinked groups. It is not surprising, then, to find that as the military video games near fruition, the producer becomes the primary liaison between the government officials and the design team. While much of this seems intuitive enough, *structural hole theory* and *social capital* together support this study's findings that game producers know how to pair the military's content and usage desires with their design team's specific production capabilities, and profit by managing this unique information gap.

Technological Frames of Meaning

Producers do not arrive at their proverbial drawing boards devoid of social biases just as technologies are not delivered to us from up on high. The guiding principles and core assumptions that technologists carry with them undergird their decisions about how a particular media technology or artifact should be coded, how it should work, and how it should be adopted by society. These often implicit normative values are known as a *frame of meaning*, and is defined by Bijker and Law as, "a combination of the explicit theory, tacit knowledge, general engineering practice, cultural values, prescribed testing procedures, devices, material networks, and systems used in a community."[22] Bijker and Law note that this conceptual frame is not limited to technologists but is applicable to any community that shares procedures and resources. The production managers examined here clearly have strong feelings about both the military and video games that guide their decision-making processes. But these normative frames are neither totalizing nor are they static or uniformly shared, though they do evidence compelling similarities. Of course, innovators need not be fully cognizant of their own values to succeed as inventors. They must, however, have some basic understanding of how their work environments and information networks operate in order to survive professionally. Indeed, inventors prosper precisely because, "they understand the values, institutional arrangements, and economic notions of that culture."[23] Frames of meaning inform the creative act, and are in turn affected by technological successes and failures; they are socially constructed, generative fictions that are always subject to change. Successful information managers and media production specialists, including this study's game producers, each have their own sets of guiding values. The most common frames of meaning for these military game productions are the ideas of *positive realism*, *negative realism*, and the conviction that these games serve a *social good*.

Fighting for Positive Realism

Military-themed video games privilege realist gameplay aesthetics that focus on combat operations and resource management challenges. To maximize the verisimilitude of their games, military game designers aspire to faithfully replicate real world topographies, physics, and ballistics in their game worlds. As far as the producers are concerned, any gameplay element that accurately simulates corporeal reality is positive realism, whereas any element that deviates from the codes and conventions of military realism is deemed to be negative. It is not surprising then that the three producers' teams began their projects by taking research trips to military posts (e.g., Ft. McClellan, Ft. Lewis, and Ft. Benning) for data collection and hands-on, immersive training drills. At these "greening-up" events, the design teams took part in tactical maneuvers, used various pieces of gear, and experimented with weapons (including a live grenade in one team's case). The groups also collected digital images of the training facilities, all of which appear in varying capacities in their respective titles. The producers stressed their faithful adherence to the military's own reference documents, and the digital images collected at the training facilities. Michael Zyda, the Development Director for *America's Army*, notes, "[my team] would always go back to the reference material [and ask], 'Okay, what do the signs on the wall really say at these places?' And, 'what does the dirt look like?' These guys were taking pictures of the dirt, taking pictures of the blistered paint, and reproducing it in the game."[24] The teams also relied on images from the internet and from broadcast and newspaper journalists to confirm that their virtual environments resembled geographical regions.

The teams' field trips generated numerous digital assets and gave designers a better appreciation for their projects' goals, but the most utilized and authoritative information source throughout the development stages were the teams' Subject Matter Experts (SMEs). These military specialists educated the designers on a variety of institutional issues, command protocols, and most salient to the purposes of building an authentic military game, combat tactics. For instance, Rachel Hardwick, the producer of *America's Army: Rise of a Soldier*, credits her team's four SMEs with supplying the majority of their military knowledge. "[We would ask them,] 'If you had these mountains to climb, [or if you're in] this kind of environment ... this country side, or here's how many people you have on your squad, and you're facing this geopolitical background, what kind of tactics would you use?' And we would talk to them about specifics. [They would tell us], 'Here's what a squad is.... Here's what the pecking order is.... Here's the range of rank that you'd have.... Here's how you'd move.' So we were involved with the SMEs on a detail-by-detail basis."[25] The Subject Matter Experts were both retired officers and active duty personnel, all of whom had different levels of involvement for the three projects; though it bears noting that the games all had at least one military SME on staff throughout their development phases. While a few of these experts only fielded technical queries, most of the SMEs actually played the games — with and against the design teams — and even one expert lent his voice to a game as a drill sergeant. The SMEs played the games as they were being built to head off potential problems and maximize the games' military authenticity within authorized limits (explained in the following section). Hardwick emphasizes her team's reliance on their Subject Matter Expert, saying: "[The SME] would play levels with our designers and a couple of our programmers so that they could see the behavior, [and demonstrate that], 'This is how we need to emulate,' and, 'This is how the [Artificial Intelligence] needs to emulate the movement.' What we actually need to convey to the [production] team is the ... authentic military experience. We want this to be as real as possible, we wanted the weapon settings to be real, we wanted the recoil to be real, we wanted the movement to be as real as possible."[26]

Each game also had its own regularly scheduled conference calls and interim progress reports about art assets, production plans, code, et cetera, in addition to the more vibrant and enjoyable game testing sessions. This strong and reliable feedback loop engendered a genuine feeling of professional camaraderie between the groups, while offering a check against errant or erroneous material. The threat of incorrect information was one of James

Korris' foremost concerns. Korris is the Creative Director for the Institute for Creative Technologies at the University of Southern California, and headed the *Full Spectrum Warrior* production effort. Like the other producers, Korris believes that he has an ethical obligation not to produce sloppy or inaccurate products that might endanger U.S. troops or civilians. Korris notes: "I must tell you [*Full Spectrum Warrior*] received an exhaustive operational security review before it was released.... There were people in the Pentagon that looked at this for weeks. Notwithstanding the fact that every single thing that's depicted in that game, you can find on the Internet. When we started developing the game, you could even download the field manuals from the training and doctrine command that explained how to do everything, okay? So it wasn't like we were giving away secrets.... [That said,] you never [want] to put something out there where the consequences would be that people would get hurt."[27] Overall, the producers characterize their working relationships with the military representatives as pleasant and collaborative, though there was never any question as to the military's ultimate authority. Hardwick claims that working with the military on *Rise of a Soldier* was "much more of a licensor-licensee kind of relationship.... We had to get everything approved by them and they did a lot of guiding."[28] The production dynamic was slightly different for Zyda's *America's Army* team, as it was composed of military buffs who had already internalized many of the Army's core values and the technical specifications of its standard issue weapons. In his view, Zyda enjoyed the ideal scenario for any military game project supervisor: "[A] lot of the guidelines were just in our heads from many of the discussions we had with all the various people in the Army.... [Everyone on the design team] was a huge fan of the Army. A lot of these guys knew every single weapon system in the Army and knew all about the operations [before we started the project]. We had a weapons expert who grew up with weapons his whole life and amazingly knew everything about the Army's weapon inventory and could create them in 3D fully with textures. So it was like, 'Wow!' Basically, what you want to hire is a bunch of 'obsessives' who each have talents that [can be directed] and that's what you end up doing."[29] As Zyda makes clear, a successful game producer assembles a team that internalizes the core values of a project so that the organizational or ideological differences that may separate the groups is effectively mitigated. The political and/or interpersonal affinity does not generate any more formal organizational linkages. Yet by fostering inter-organizational kinship concerning military culture writ large, the producer profits from a wellspring of mutually beneficial social capital.

Fighting Against Negative Realism

Within game design discourse, "realism" is a ubiquitous term that production leaders regularly utilize to communicate their aesthetic needs to their artists, programmers, and designers. These producers rarely acknowledge realism as an artistic construct during the interviews, but they are acutely wary of introducing any unsanctioned information into these games lest they be censored and forced to sacrifice precious development time. When programmed realism resembles classified military reality or is perceived to undercut the military's cause, those elements are quickly eliminated.

The interviews reveal instances when aspirations to realism either failed to satisfy the military's needs, violated a more sacred imperative, or did not present the military in a favorable light. For example, as interested as these teams were in replicating authentic military realities, there was a reluctance to locate the combat in any factual place, or model missions after historical firefights.[30] Hardwick asserts that the Army did not want to identify a specific country or conflict in the game for two reasons. First, "because it could be highly offensive to anyone who is [from there]; [and second, because] the game [is] not about a specific environment or a specific conflict."[31] Thus, the game teams were charged with constructing realistic theaters of war without being geo-politically specific. In all likelihood, the decision to omit real and identifiable locations in these titles was to avoid backlash from political or ethnic groups that might be implicated in the game. A few highly faithful weapons models also did not survive the games' beta stages. When one team's Subject Matter Expert saw that some unknowingly classified weapon systems had been given digital life, they too were nixed. And in at least one case, actual ballistic fidelity was the target of some popular scorn. Hardwick explains her game's bind, saying: "One of the things that we [were criticized for] on the [Xbox reviews for *Rise of a Soldier*] is about the behavior of the grenade launcher in the grenadier missions. The thing is, everybody in the Army — I get random emails from guys in the Army — they've all said that of all of the shooters they've played, we are absolutely the most accurate in terms of the realistic sighting."[32] In at least this one instance, the decision to remain faithful to a military reality (i.e., that is how the weapon actually operates) was criticized for violating a more sacred game convention (i.e., ease of use) by the non-military public.

In a rare moment of uniform disagreement, the designers each criticize some aspects of their peers' games. Hardwick's team opted against programming explicit language into *Rise of a Soldier* after hearing their lead Subject Matter Expert reject it as unrealistic and in bad taste. Hardwick notes: "One of the things that [the lead SME] had said was he and a bunch of people were so disgusted because of the swearing ... that they turned it off immediately, and said that it absolutely did not depict anything in terms of real tactics. And that was one of the goals of [*Full Spectrum Warrior*]. [Our team] wanted to throw some swearing in there, but that would have changed the rating from Teen to Mature and [the Army] wanted, very specifically, a Teen rated game."[33] While Hardwick's SME found the explicit language objectionable, the choice to omit such language from *Rise of a Soldier* most likely had more to do with producing a less objectionable product for a younger demographic than it did with modeling proper battlefield decorum.

Interestingly, *Full Spectrum Warrior*'s James Korris critiques *America's Army* for its limitations as a first-person-shooter (FPS) marketing tool, and for being incapable of serving as a training device (although Korris' appraisal is more critical of the FPS genre writ large than *America's Army* specifically). Korris states: "... whether [FPS games] are in outer-space or if they're in the fifteenth century, or if they're on the beaches of Omaha, they are basically ... games where you have a variety of weapons, you run around trying to find people to shoot, they shoot you and that's the game. And I've got to tell you, that's not what the military is...."[34] Zyda would dispute this characterization, arguing that *America's Army* does indeed have a value system at its core and that it has been utilized for training purposes. According to Zyda: "The Army has this value system that they claim guides their way. It's a scaffolding for a career in the Army and [they are] good values.... And I would say we put [the value system] in there. So [*America's Army* is] really the first, first-person-shooter that had this belief system underneath it.... The game is an official product of the U.S. Army and so it's going to have those value-systems because that's what the Army believes itself [to be]."[35] Zyda was also pleased to learn from a Staff Sergeant at Fort Benning that *America's Army* was being used to help new recruits pass parts of the obstacle course and rifle range. So even though the game was designed as a marketing and recruiting tool, it proved to have some educational applications.[36] The question of "proper" military education introduces the final recurrent frame of meaning throughout these interviews — games as a *Social Good*.

Fighting for the Social Good

The producers concur that their military games serve a public good[37] by introducing gamers to the military's core values, and that these games provide a much-needed corrective to the spectacular violence common to most

FPS games and *Rambo*-style combat films. The military's values are communicated foremost through these titles' exacting gameplay demands. There are few opportunities to explore the game worlds outside of the missions' primary objectives, and most actions that oppose the stated orders or violates the game's code of ethics (e.g., shooting civilians in *Full Spectrum Warrior*, or harming a fellow soldier in *Rise of a Soldier*) is immediately disciplined. Hardwick states without qualification that, "[*Rise of a Soldier*] is about ... getting to the core Army values. You're always rewarded for healing your teammates, you always want to bring everyone in your squad through [even] if it you have to choose between a mission objective and saving your squad."[38] For Korris' *Full Spectrum Warrior*, the game's values are embedded in its modeling of proper combat maneuvering. "Mainly what [*Full Spectrum Warrior*] teaches are battle drills. How are you supposed to behave in various situations? And what you are trying to learn from it is tactical maneuver and fire. Because ... what [does] a soldier do? It's shoot, move, and communicate. [*Full Spectrum Warrior* is] trying to teach you how to lead soldiers who do that."[39] Zyda too believes that *America's Army* models positive military values, but concedes that his team's project does not have the same educational potential as other serious games. He states, "The official Army line is that *America's Army* is a 'first-person mission experience.' Which is complete nonsense, right? That's what the Army wanted us all to say in the official press. [*America's Army*] gives you the experience of training and the [running] missions the way the Army would do it. But in the end, it's a first-person-shooter."[40] Zyda's comments demonstrate competing frames of meaning about how best to estimate *AA*'s legacy. During the interview, he trumpets *America's Army* as having "founded the serious game genre,"[41] thereby contributing to the social good. But Zyda immediately tempers that praise by recognizing the game's inherent limitations as a first-person-shooter marketing device, suggesting that the game possesses some gameplay elements (such as negative realism), which undermine its ultimate viability as a training tool.

These producers see their games as offering a corrective to the spectacular and manifestly unreal militarized violence common to other popular entertainment fare. For Hardwick, "anything that you can do to put a more realistic idea ... out there to counter the Hollywood idea of big explosions and overdramatized [action], and ... the over-dramatization of either war or the military ... I think it's a good thing. Being able to get a more realistic perspective out there is a good thing."[42] Korris concurs: "I feel good about the fact that we are trying to present ... a more accurate, a more sober, view of what [war] ... really is. [A war is] the nastiest place you can be on Earth and it is the meanest aspect of the human condition. I do not believe it is possible to have any more horrid thing happen than to be in warfare."[43] The producers' pronouncements against spectacular media violence is intimately linked to their perceived professional and personal responsibilities to the GIs. The producers often position their wares within the serious game genre for a reason. They believe that their games are instructive, and that they teach useful skills and promulgate a positive image of the U.S. armed forces. It is no surprise, then, given the gravity of the subject and their close working relationships with military personnel, that these producers see their games' lack of sensational viciousness (again, as compared to other FPS games) as a remarkable and respectful, creative accomplishment.

Technological Script

As similar as these games are in content, thematic concerns, and targeted demographics — males in their teens and early twenties — the games' variation in design reveals how these producers each sought out different game playing audiences. It is not unusual for technologists to inscribe their preexisting notions of user behavior into the material fabric of their inventions. In her chapter, "The De-scription of Technical Objects," Madeleine Akrich asserts that a "large part of the work of innovators is that of 'inscribing' [a] vision of (or prediction about) the world in the technical content of the new object."[44] Akrich calls this predictive engineering a work's *script*; thus when someone uses a technology in an unanticipated way, they have gone off-script. The interviews conducted for this paper do not indicate how gamers might be playing these titles "against the grain," but they absolutely demonstrate how these producers wanted their games to be played, and what gamers should ideally take away from their game playing experiences. Akrich also notes that the "technical realization of the innovator's beliefs about the relationships between an object and its surrounding actors is thus an attempt to predetermine the settings that users are asked to imagine for a particular piece of technology and the pre-scriptions ... that accompany it."[45] Thus technologies are simultaneously predictive *and* prescriptive. Fortunately for this chapter, the interviewees discuss their admittedly incomplete notions of their audiences, and state unequivocally what gamers should think after playing their games.

America's Army: Rise of a Soldier's major affective aspiration, according to its producer, is to leave a positive image of the U.S. Army in its players' minds. It was not crafted as a recruiting tool, but as a public relations toy that introduces its male target audience to the infantry's military specialties and to its core combat values. The game was neither designed to net enlistees, like *America's Army*, nor was it produced to improve tactical decision making, like *Full Spectrum Warrior*. Hardwick states that the "goal [of *Rise of a Soldier*] is to ... give the Army a positive image in the industry and with their target market. But it wasn't a direct recruiting device as much as [it was a] kind of an image enhancement or ... realistic depiction." [46] Interestingly, many of the game's most ardent fans are current enlistees. In fact "[One of the SMEs] ... said he went to Afghanistan for a year, and they sent a copy of the game and [soldiers] were ... playing 8 on 8 ... in these [recreational] areas they've got set up."[47] When GIs play a military game in a combat zone (and *Rise of a Soldier* is not the only game soldiers play) that leisure practice performs a number of services for a title: it reinforces the text's authenticity; it increases its cultural capital within gaming communities; and it reifies its producers' technological frames of meaning. After all, what group of gamers could give more credence to a military game's veracity than soldiers stationed in theaters of war?

Interestingly, James Korris largely defines his project in opposition to games like *America's Army* and *Rise of a Soldier*. Korris's team was charged with creating an educational console game that would improve the decision-making abilities of enlisted servicemen, and that is how he understands and characterizes *Full Spectrum Warrior*. When asked about his thoughts on the game's over-the-counter availability, Korris notes, "In terms of the general public playing *Full Spectrum Warrior*, I'll tell you what I like about it. And the first thing is that we have never made a recruiting product. I don't think anyone has ever joined the Army because they [played] *Full Spectrum Warrior*."[48] Korris calls his team's work social engineering because he does not view his game as either a recruiting tool, or as an entertainment-only game, though he is not dismissive of the importance of playability. Note Korris' game designer language when he says: "Our games just happen to be built around social engineering that is trying to get you to develop a capability of observation and decision-making.... And the one thing that we never overlooked was — these have got to be good games. So I just have the same question. People come in and they use this thing where they are taking the role of a platoon leader or a company leader or ... whatever. And I ask them, 'how was the game?' 'Did you want to keep playing it?' And if the answer is 'yes,' then I've got a good game."[49]

In contrast to *Full Spectrum Warrior*, *America's Army* was from its very beginnings a recruiting tool that sought as wide an audience as possible. Michael Zyda contends that it not only kick-started the serious game movement, but it also completely changed the way that the Army thought of marketing itself. This free PC game targets teenage audiences in the hopes of cultivating a contemporary fan base that will spawn future infantrymen. Zyda explains the Army's position regarding the game's rating. "Let me give you the official answer and then the real answer, okay? The official answer is it's a Teen-rated game, which means you must be at least 13 years old to play this game.... But what the Army really, really wanted was between 11 to 14. But you can't say that if you are making a T-rated game. Because you are saying, 'Well, wait a second, T-rated is 13.' But what does the Army know? The Army knows that kids who play with GI Joes between the ages 11 to 14 have twice the propensity to consider a career in the Army when they turn 18. This is opposed to kids who don't play with GI Joes. And it's that small scrap of information that got them to want to build a game."[50] *America's Army*'s raison d'être explains why it is a far less disciplining title than *Full Spectrum Warrior* or *Rise of a Soldier*. Its technological script encourages gamers to "play military" rather than to "play seriously," which is a reasonable strategy since the game's stated goal is to stimulate an interest in the Army, not to give regimented training drills to a lay gaming community.

In addition to tailoring game technologies to preferred audiences for a desired end, producers also control how easily their wares can or cannot be altered through the game's format. For instance, popular platforms like the Playstation 2 and Xbox run game discs that are not reprogrammable on the user end. They are "plug and play" technologies where the code is safeguarded from user manipulation. Players are therefore forced to remain "on script" if they are to play the game. This architecture of exclusion also poses barriers to the game's own developers, though. Once a console title has been produced, the costs of subsequent modifications are exorbitant. Korris explains this difficulty, saying: "...if I want to change some code and make a 1.1 modification on a piece of [console] software, I've got to go through minimally $75,000 process with Microsoft. That's why [console] games ... are so bug free. There are extremely rigorous quality assurances on them.... Every time you want to change the code ... you have go through a $75,000 quality control cycle and then put out a technical reprint, recall all the SKUs — it's a nightmare. [With the PC, it is] very easy, you write some code, you recompile it, you [post the update online], you're done."[51] In a rare move for a console title, Korris's team embedded two versions of *Full Spectrum Warrior* onto the commercially released game disc; the consumer version was easier and more fun game, while the "secret" military version was more demanding and also less enjoyable. The creative director explains: "We stuck [the Army training application] on the disc and put an unlock code on it. Although, there's nothing in it that's sacred, it's not classified content. We knew you could get the unlock code on the Internet. But that's why we released [*Full Spectrum Warrior*] commercially, because we couldn't get on the Xbox any other way."[52] Indeed, the code needed to access the military version of the game was available in less than twenty-four hours after the game's launch.[53]

Conclusion

Recognizing game producers as vital production nexuses adds nuance and specificity to our understanding of how commercial video games emerge from our Military-Entertainment Complex. The interviews reveal that these game producers share common practices and attitudes about bringing their military employers' visions to digital fruition. They enjoy creative latitude regarding gameplay design and have remarkable decision-making power because of their unique location in their inter-organizational media production network. Game producers utilize similar technological frames of meaning, which directly impact their research practices and creative decisions, buttress their unqualified commitment to U.S. soldiers, and are reflected in their similar ideas about their imagined game playing audiences; ideas which manifest themselves in the unique "scripts" of their game technologies. But these professionals' comments are most illuminating when they discuss the social value of their craft, believing that there is common good to promoting the military's values and tactics through the video game form. Yet these producers are not naïve or disinterested about how their wares are shaped and deployed by the Department of Defense, and are at times critical of the military titles produced by rival game firms. If Bruce Sterling is right, and modern war is evermore a virtual hell, then our understanding of war as entertainment is incomplete without recognizing how video game producers often negotiate the military's and entertainment firms' needs to produce titles that blur the boundaries between fiction and reality, between education and gaming (such as serious games), and between militarism and entertainment.

Notes

1. For more information on this history see: Manuel De Landa, *War in the Age of Intelligent Machines* (New York: Zone Books, 1991); and Timothy Lenoir, "All But War is Simulation: The Military-Entertainment Complex," *Configurations* 8, no. 3 (Fall 2000): 289–335.
2. For accessible conceptualizations of the Military-Entertainment Complex see: Timothy Lenoir and Henry Lowood, "Theaters of War: The Military-Entertainment Complex," (2002), accessed from http://www.stanford.edu/class/sts145/Library/Lenoir-Lowood_TheatersOfWar.pdf on August 15, 2006; and Stephen Stockwell and Adam Muir,

"The Military-Entertainment Complex: A New Facet of Information Warfare," *Fibreculture* 1, (2003), accessed from http://journal.fibreculture.org/issue1/issue1_stockwellmuir.html on December 1, 2006.

3. Bruce Sterling, "War Is Virtual Hell," *Wired* no. 1.01, (March/April 1993), accessed from http://wired.com/wired/archive/1.01/virthell_pr.html on December 1, 2006.

4. Interservice/Industry Training Systems and Education Conference, "About Page," accessed from http://www.iitsec.org/about.cfm on December 1, 2006.

5. Sterling, "War Is Virtual Hell," paragraph 6 under "Today Kuwait, Tomorrow the World."

6. Ibid., paragraph 7 under "Today Kuwait, Tomorrow the World."

7. Benedict Anderson, *Imagined Communities: Reflections on the Origin and Spread of Nationalism* (New York: Verso, 1991).

8. Ibid., Chapter 10.

9. Sterling, "War Is Virtual Hell," paragraph 18 under "Today Kuwait, Tomorrow the World."

10. Ibid., paragraph 19 under "Today Kuwait, Tomorrow the World."

11. Lewis Mumford, *Technics and Civilization* (New York: Harcourt Brace, 1962), 93.

12. Live-action war games are a formal training technique that date back to the nineteenth century.

13. All of these criticisms are summarized in Langdon Winner's article, "Upon Opening the Black Box and Finding it Empty: Social Constructivism and the Philosophy of Technology," *Science Technology & Human Values* 18, no. 3 (Summer 1993): 362–378.

14. Wiebe Bijker and John Law, "Postscript: Technology, Stability, and Social Theory" in *Shaping Technology / Building Society: Studies in Sociotechnical Change*, ed. Wiebe Bijker and John Law, 290 (Cambridge, MA: The MIT Press, 1992).

15. Ibid., 292.

16. Nan Lin, "Building a Network Theory of Social Capital," *Connections* 22, no. 1 (1999): 30. Italics in original.

17. Ibid., 31.

18. Ronald S. Burt, "The Contingent Value of Social Capital," *Administrative Science Quarterly* 42, no. 2 (June 1997): 339–365, 345.

19. Ibid., 340.

20. Ibid., 339.

21. Ibid., 341.

22. Bijker and Law, "Postscript: Technology, Stability, and Social Theory," 301.

23. W. Bernard Carlson, "Artifacts and Frames of Meaning: Thomas A. Edison, His Managers, and the Cultural Construction of Motion Pictures," in *Shaping Technology / Building Society: Studies in Sociotechnical Change*, ed. Wiebe Bijker and John Law, 175–198, 175 (Cambridge, MA: The MIT Press, 1992).

24. Michael Zyda. Spring 2006. Interview conducted by Matthew Thomas Payne. Audio Recording. Austin, Texas.

25. Rachel Hardwick. Spring 2006. Interview conducted by Matthew Thomas Payne. Audio Recording. Austin, Texas.

26. Ibid.

27. James Korris. Spring 2006. Interview conducted by Matthew Thomas Payne. Audio Recording. Austin, Texas.

28. Hardwick, Interview.

29. Zyda, Interview.

30. A private game business like *Kuma* does the opposite by selling virtual combat experiences modeled after recent real-world firefights (see www.kumawar.com).

31. Hardwick, Interview.

32. Ibid.

33. Ibid.
34. Korris, Interview.
35. Zyda, Interview.
36. *America's Army* also had the Army's "combat life-saving" lectures built into it (they are virtual renditions of the Army's PowerPoint lectures on the topic) to help soldiers pass the off-line tests.
37. It is definitely debatable as to what exactly constitutes a public good. For example, who are these games good for, and for what public(s) or constituencies exactly are they benefiting? What is most salient here is that these producers recognize that their wares are met with mixed reactions, and they frame their works' social impacts accordingly.
38. Hardwick, Interview.
39. Korris, Interview.
40. Zyda, Interview.
41. Though definitions differ, the *serious games* label generally refers to titles that have educational aims and are played in non-traditional learning environments.
42. Hardwick, Interview.
43. Korris, Interview.
44. Madeline Akrich, "The De-scription of Technical Objects," in *Shaping Technology / Building Society: Studies in Sociotechnical Change*, ed. Wiebe Bijker and John Law (Cambridge, MA: The MIT Press, 1992), 208.
45. Ibid., 208.
46. Hardwick, Interview.
47. Ibid.
48. Korris, Interview.
49. Ibid.
50. Zyda, Interview.
51. Korris, Interview.
52. Ibid.
53. This begs the question that if the creators anticipated that the code would be made widely available, why then bother making the military version secret?

15

War/Games
The Art of Rules and Strategies
BO KAMPMANN WALTHER

Thinkers like Paul Virilio and James Der Derian have pointed out the many and intricate similarities between games and war.[1] When taking into account the distinctiveness of war, the domains of art and games seem to be intuitive points of comparison. Given the explosion in media and information technologies in recent decades it would also be fair to think of entertainment as a common source. Historically, games and game scenarios have played a decisive role in the planning, simulation, and training of potential as well as actual combat. War games have pretty much existed as long as there have been wars. The idea of simulating battles without the personal hazards can be traced back to ancient Sumer (today Southern Iraq) more than four thousand years ago. Chess and Go, two of the oldest games in the world, arose from war games. Contemporary war games originated in Prussia at the turn of the nineteenth century. The game *Kriegspiel* (War Game) introduced the ideas of arranging markers on a sand table and using a dice to determine any random elements in the battle. After the Franco-Prussian war, the English came up with their own version and they began to be used wisely by armed services to train in tactics and predict military outcomes. In our modern society we learn all there is to know about armed conflict through the first person shooter *Doom Marine* and via highly enjoyable online role-playing games such as *America's Army*. War has been an easy pick for game design. Digital games are squad-based (terrorists on one side confronting anti-terrorists on the other) and they involve tactics (though, as we shall see, not all of them) and an impressive degree of realism, as in *Battlefield 2, Counter-Strike,* and *Ghost Recon*.

The reason for all the hype surrounding the war-games-complex is threefold. First, games and war meet in a common "third": the simulation. Not quite a game and not quite warfare, a simulation is rather something in between: a training ground, a real-life simulacrum, and an entertaining behavioral system. At a safe distance the soldier learns to drop bombs efficiently over the Iraq desert or is taught how to drive a tank through the sand in the same hostile region thousands of miles away. Second, complex ties between Hollywood and Pentagon as well as the many "infotaining" facilities across the U.S. military system further accentuate the idea of an increasing war-game intimacy. The connection between military and entertainment go beyond gaming. Nowadays, movies are supported by the military, there is cooperation with the military to develop games and television series and the sponsoring of game events. *Full Spectrum Warrior 04* was initially developed as a training tool for the U.S. army but is now available in shops. The same goes for *Close Combat*, which was originally crafted for marine training (see Matthew and Marcus, this volume). Third, rhetoric helps, as when leading officers involuntarily or not use the vocabulary of (computer) games to communicate the tensions and essences of prevailing war. Simulation, Hollywood, and words all point to the strong linkage of war and games. Yet this linkage is highly debatable which explains the clumsy grammar of the headline. You may read the slash mark as simultaneously a point of contact or as a deep abyss.

Games and war share a number of key formal traits. Both have *rules*. In fact, rules seem to be an invariant feature in each case, whether we conceive of the war-game complex in conceptual or "real-life" schemes. Without rules both would simply seize to exist. Both rely strongly on long-term *strategies* and short-term *tactics*. And, moreover, games and war exhibit a list of *interaction patterns*, when the player engages in the game worlds of today's compelling leisure and when the soldier carries out his duties in a dangerous combination of knowing the rules and mapping the right (or wrong) strategy.

Especially the historical roots of the various links between war and games have been the focus of many hitherto enquiries. Besides some short remarks on this otherwise fascinating marriage I will not elaborate further on this. Rather, what interests me is the formal or ontological rationality of war and games. Does it make any sense formally to proclaim that war is (a) game? Can the soldier be likened to a computer game player? We find that the ontological enquiry is deeply entangled in a perhaps foggy onto-teleological uncertainty. To ask about the "being-ness" of games and war in order to face up to their mutual similarities and differences not only implies how they "are" but also, and maybe even more so, what is the purpose of their being. Games and war have rules and essentially this is their ontology. Yet, they also have *goals*, i.e., teleology. Unite rules and goals in a formal analysis of war/games and what we have is a quest for the onto-teleological nature of war/games.

My point is admittedly very simple. While computer games and war plainly share vital features, and just as evidently seem to go hand in hand in sociological and historical terms, they are, even so, miles apart when it comes to human involvement and, especially, human consequences. Warfare is lethal. Computer games are not. In the former you die; in the latter you merely move the queen across the board. The million-dollar question is of course whether moral justification (or disapproval) of war and war games is rooted in the *rules* or in what those rules *represent*. But society often sees it differently because the existence of the simulation — in its entire technological splendor across the military-entertainment complex — inevitably throws the war-games encounter into an ethical battlefield. Is it not wrong, one might ask, to master life and death by moving pieces on a floorboard or by controlling a jet engine from across the globe with almost speed of light and with apparently no physical or mental contact what so ever? Are FPS (first person shooter) games "murder simulations" or "training tools"? The imperative lesson would be to blame not the games and their ontology but, rather, the way we *conceive* them, and hence to take seriously the differentiation of rules and representation in both war and games.

Let us begin with the core building blocks of games by drawing on basic economic game theory, and then move on to the different types of war, war games, and game tactics.

Rules

Economic game theory is a set of mathematical methods of decision-making in which a competitive, "risky" situation is analyzed to determine the optimal course of action for a player. John von Neumann and Oscar Morgenstern were the founders of game theory. According to von Neumann and Morgenstern a game consists of a set of rules governing a competitive situation in which two to n individuals or groups of individuals choose strategies designed to maximize their own winnings or to minimize their opponent's winnings. The rules specify the possible actions for each player, the amount of information received by each as play progresses, and the amounts won or lost in various situations. Neumann and Morgenstern restricted their attention to games in which no player can gain except at another's expense (so-called zero-sum games).[2]

Later John F. Nash revolutionized game theory by demonstrating that in noncooperative games there are sets of optimal strategies (so-called Nash equilibria) used by the players in a game such that no player can benefit by unilaterally changing his or her strategy if the strategies of the other players remain unchanged.[3]

Drawing on economic game theory we can now define games as complex, rule based interaction systems consisting of these three key mechanisms: a) absolute *rules*, b) contingent *strategies*, and c) possible *interaction patterns*. Game rules are *absolute* in the sense that while the players may question the rationality of the rules at hand, they are nevertheless obliged to obey, to "play by the rules." Rules are therefore absolute commands and unquestionable imperatives.[4] They transcend semantic issues, cultural signification, moral agendas, etc. This does not, incidentally, preclude the fact that game rules are *discussed* in a cultural or ethical milieu. In contrast to rules, strategies are *contingent*, nonabsolute entities since they count as the more or less detailed plans for the execution of turns, choices, and actions in the game. Other strategies than the ones actually carried out could have been outlined and performed. Both in the shape of short-term tactics and as long-term schemes, strategies are contingent. In economic game theory, a strategy is an overall plan for how to act in the assembly of different states that the game may be in.[5] Game theory studies the affiliations of the rules and the strategic behavior in competitive situations.[6] Finally, interaction patterns are the moves and choices that become part of the game being played thus interfering with the restrictions and options of the game. As the implementation of game strategies tend to cluster in selected regions of the possibility space of the game (in approximation of what is known as the "dominant strategy" in game theory) forming a path through the game space, we may even insinuate that the interaction patterns, taken as a whole, *are* the game itself— especially if we view it from the perspective of the player.[7] Interaction patterns are the *possible* as opposed to necessary combinations or the emergent outcome of rules and strategies.

This differentiation can be listed even more briefly: Rules are *commands*. Strategies are *plans* for game executions. Interactions patterns define the actual *path* through the game and specify the topography of human-computer (or player versus rule) dynamics.

The notion of game play involves all three levels of a game which also explains the difficulty in defining the concept properly. Game play is the actualization of a specific stratification of rules, strategies, and interactions as well as the realization of a certain amalgamation of commands, plans, and paths. For a player, a successful game play means a delicate balance between knowing the rules and mapping one's strategy in accordance with both rules and the possible actions of opponents. Games should be equally challenging and rewarding, hovering between boredom and anxiety hereby assuring a space of flow through the network of choices. For a computerized game system, a successful game play implies a balance between fixed rules and the control of player input in variable settings.

What defines a rule? A rule, being algorithmic in its core design, consists of a simple, unequivocal sentence, e.g., "you are not allowed to use hands while the ball is on the pitch." Hereby a rule constitutes the possibility space of a game by clearly stating limitations (not use hands) as well as opportunities (the ball is on the pitch). It is always possible to define a game both in negative and positive terms: rules limit actions; they determine the range of choices in the possibility space; they encircle the arenas to be played in; yet they also frame what *can* be done.

At this point I am speaking of *all* games, i.e., both traditional games, including sports, and computer games, not to mention the range of war games. *Heroes of Might and Magic* rests on rules stored in and processed by a computer. Chess or *Monopoly*, by contrast, relies on rules not accumulated in the database and algorithms of a computer but written down on paper and stored in the players' mind during the play. In a game of soccer, for example, a referee administers such rules. Implicit rules that are normally considered exterior to the "real" rules (e.g., clock in chess matches) must be engaged explicitly in digital games. These rules have to be programmed as well. Weather conditions or the general physics of a soccer game are usually taken as "out-of-game" features in the real world. When we simulate a soccer game in a computer, however, the rules of soccer *and* the general physics (including random variables such as surface granularity, crowds, time of day, etc.) must be built into the rule algorithms and the input-output control of the computer.

Rules specify the constitution of the playing "deck" or, more broadly, the playing "field." In games, behavioral patterns inside this field are limited, constrained, and highly codified.[8] Rules are guidelines that direct, restrict, and channel behavior in a formalized, closed environment so that artificial and clear conditions inside the "magic circle" of play are created.[9] The outside of this circle, reality or nonplay, is essentially irrelevant to game play. Confronted with unambiguous rules, strategies (or tactics) might entail best practice solutions variable to the given rule constraints. Hereafter, interaction patterns map the various player interventions and can hence be viewed as a texture of moves and choices overlain on top of the possibility space of the game. Furthermore, interaction patterns can refer to the social and competitive intermingling of players during the fulfillment of the game. In that respect, the patterns correspond to the outcome of absolute rules and social dynamics.

Rules have the following qualities: They limit and restrict player action. Thus, they tell what can be done and what cannot be done with the objects associated with the game. They are unambiguous, explicit, and finite (which is why they are easily incorporated in computer algorithms). All players of a game must share them. Rules are fixed, i.e., unchangeable (if they do change, we rather refer to local or "house" rules). They are binding, i.e., nonnegotiable, and, finally, they can be repeated which means that they are portable and work independent of technology platform or fictional representation.

The formal organization of games can be regarded as a parameter space. In this space, the current state of the game counts as a point and ultimately a dimension in the parameter space. A played game has therefore n possible state dimensions. In tic-tac-toe, for instance, the nine squares constitute the parameter space of the game and thus the possibility domain for the arrangement of the board pieces. The rules of the game define the possible edges in the space connecting states.

Rules define the *possible* game, whereas a *particular* game is a path through the state space. The crucial factor is that there can be no variability or multiple paths through the possibility space of a game without the compulsory parameters of the game. Hence, the parameter space constitutes the *transcendental* level of the game, whereas the particular game path expresses the contingent *realization* of the space.

This dialectic between parameter space and actual game path also sheds some light on why games are complex; basically it is because there is an uneven relation between the unchanging set of rules and the actual and changing realization of a particular game. This asymmetrical tie between rules and realization (or rules and strategies) can be termed game *emergence*. Most often it is impossible to predetermine the actual moves and outcome of a game only by knowing the set of rules. Also, most games are games of imperfect information.[10] At the outset, the rules of chess are simple and yet the wealth of distinct chess playing tactics is quite enormous. A child can memorize chess rules, but to master all grand openings in the actual game is probably a lifetime achievement.

When it comes to computer games we must be careful not to confuse two distinct yet closely associated levels of rules. One level, which is the algorithmic source code of the game, consists of an unambiguous list of specifications for what can be done and what cannot be done, i.e., what counts as edge in the parameter space. On another level, rules designate the ability of the computer to keep track of the players' interaction with the different states that the game system can be in. We can specify the former level the *rule system* of the computer and we will name the latter level its *interaction system*. While the rule system contains the data structures that enable the initial set-up of the game as well as determine the constraints and possibilities of the game, the interaction system evidently operates in a dynamic framework whose prime function is to control the executing of new outputs relative to the player's real-time inputs.

Another way of explaining the difference between the two levels is that the rule system is responsible for the *initial framing* of the game by setting up the possibility space for the game and for the player's actions and choices, whereas, in a slightly different way, the interaction system links to the *actual game play*. The latter is the realization of, or a given path through, the possibility space.

Strategies

One of the arguably most effective ways to seduce adolescents into military service is through partaking in vast, online based first person shooters. These games hinge profoundly on perception, motoric skills, and low-level tactical abilities. As noted by Virilio, gaining a clear view of the battlefield is critical.[11] This is true in traditional, rural environments such as in the Second World War of *Battlefield 1942*, and equally so in present day urban warfare like the game *Delta Force*. Virilio links the evolvement of military technology with the rapid maturity of "seeing" devices and other instrumental and operational devices aimed at optimizing the range of perception. Motoric skills lie at the very heart of computer games, and in FPS they involve the infamous formula of "FIND, FIX, FIGHT, and FINISH the enemy," known simply as "FFFF."

When it comes to tactical nuances, however, the FPS genre is rather low-key. According to Edward N. Luttwak's highly influential book *Strategy: The Logic of War and Peace* from 2001 the five common levels of strategy are: 1) technical level: weapons, 2) tactical, 3) operational, 4) "theater" (the "imposing European spectacle" etc.), and 5) grand strategy, most often diplomacy and politics.[12] Most FPS's only cover the lowest of these levels, thus focusing unerringly on perception and bodily skills. Although *Battlefield 2* has the operational level as well — a commander has a bird vision of the battleground — other, high-level regulations of war (intrusion by NGO's, interrogations of war prisoners, logistic complexities when waiting for war) are conveniently absent in FPS's. We can therefore conclude that just as there is a prominent tension in all games between the boredom of easiness and the anxiety of difficulty, as presented in the previous section, there is a structurally similar tension or negotiation in war games between the goal to entertain and the need to offer an "authentic" experience.

According to David Nieborg this tension leads to two paradoxes in FPS's and other computerized simulation devices: First, the paradox of *reductiveness*: every simulation involves some reduction of course. The FPS genre, for instance, cannot sufficiently cover the higher levels of tactics and should therefore be labeled as abstract simulation of certain aspects of "real" war. This is especially prevalent in quick, level-oriented games like *Counter-Strike*. Second, the paradox of *fairness* (or symmetry): the modeling of the opposing teams in most online FPS's makes it impossible to emphasize the asymmetrical role of technology within the military. Weapons and gears are carefully balanced since each player (or group of players) must enjoy equal options and means to success. The paradox of fairness makes it thus impracticable to simulate the alleged superiority of American soldiers.[13]

I am not so sure whether "paradox" is the right term here. Maybe "compulsory representational techniques" would be better (and less captivating). To profess the paradoxes of reductiveness and fairness may seem reductive and unfair in itself. Computer games that simulate aspects of war are much more concerned with matters of *consistency* than the 1:1 elements of realism. Topics in social life as well as in politics are massively significant in actual warfare (and peace negotiation) and perhaps the most direct and cognitively honest form of realism lies in the graphical quality of games. And yet only a portion of complex diplomacy or multifaceted social communication is in most cases enough to provide a realistic simulation — which is, incidentally, never the real deal (the matrix is only "the matrix" because we are not in it). Moreover, graphical authenticity in advanced video games is very often a cover-up for two important aspects of consistent gameplay. Rather than a complete real-life mimesis, this authenticity is provided on a graphical and spatial level in order to facilitate the plane projection of images in a 3D environment. Computer games combine perception of static images with the need for action-packed changes in vision and viewpoints. Also, the acquired authenticity works to secure a vital sense of *level connectedness*. Rather than enjoying the full assortment of colors, nuances, and "dirt" of scenery the average gamer wants to "map" the world that he or she is immersed in. A consequence of this cognitive and spatial mapping is the gamer's constant lookout for bridging possibilities, i.e., those places and/or gadgets that provide access from one level to the next. Rather than being hidden stories, computer games must be conceived as spatial frames for structural progression that also justifies their inclusion of only the lower levels of war tactics. It is simply a matter of gameplay consistency (finding the best weapon), not of simulating every corner and detail of reality (waiting in vain for the convoy).

In general, the creation of new and powerful game technologies is correlated with realistic renderings of textures in 3D spaces by using real-time based motion procedures that are represented relatively to the user's perspective. Action ranges over ornamental imagery. Lurking snipers are superior to granular perfection on the walls. There are basically two ways of doing this: In *binocular parallax* the user's vision and body is tied to an exact point in space. The optical performance can easily be experienced by focusing on a spot in front of the eye while the other eye is covered — and vice versa.

What happens is that space itself seems to move! More advanced is *motion parallax* that simulates the fact that body movements create different visual inputs. Computer games simulate this simulation technique: when playing a game it is not the physical body movements themselves that modify the game space (that would be genuine virtual reality); rather it is the *represented* body, i.e., the corporeal viewpoint, which is transferred into the space of the game. Canonical 3D shooters such as *Doom* and *Duke Nukem* suffer from visually imperfect textures, which are easier to render than bitmap images and high-polygons, and, at times, flickering depth perception. These games favour the freedom of motion feedback over image depth and photorealistic neutrality. The *Half-Life* modification *Counter-Strike* exploits to a large extent textures as a cover-up for geometrical forms, and the so-called "blurring" that is produced by photo technical distortion, sharpening of edges, use of patina, etc., is far from realistic. Similarly, the central perspective in the game (or, rather, in the copious *maps*) is basically accurate, but the manufacturing of shadow effects is rather simple, and the texture gradients are reduced to blurring.[14]

Yet, the consistency of computer game spatiality not only bases itself on the capacity of the 3D engine, which is the "motor" that quantizes ("calculates") the images on the screen as well as renders them (i.e. by "moving" them). The consistency is further tied to constituents of *genre* and hereby intimately related to the user's expectations prior to the game. Take adventures as an example: *Grim Fandango* is not realistic and action packed like the current successor of *Doom, Doom 3*. The former game primarily consists of static, cartoon-like scenes. When the avatar, Manny, enters a new location within the "Land of the Dead," the game immediately switches camera mode, lighting angle, and architectural structure. Indeed, modern adventure games are much more attracted to mood, graphical richness, and narrative complexity than to the user's physical presence, real-time rendering, and the facilitation of simple conflict schemes. Thus, the crucial aspect of space representation in adventures, as opposed to action packed and fast paced shooters and war games, becomes the constant and "natural" transformation of centre and periphery in the depicted game world. The entire aesthetic effect is based on this realistic potential of transformation, which is obvious in games like *The Longest Journey* and *Myst III: Exile*.

A typical combat game with only low-level tactics included still struggles with the fact that the user's orientation in the 3D space is established using central perspective and not through the singular textures that one encounters during the spatial journey. In *Counter-Strike,* the player needs to navigate quickly in space. Where are the snipers? Where is the bomb located? Will the competing team reach the target before us? That is why the space in *Counter-Strike* is not crammed with niceties and interesting objects, whether they are visual or spatial or belong to a social domain. If they do exist it is likely because they serve a functional role: The user can climb up the ladder and get a better view of the killings at hand or he may hide behind the wall of a run-down country house and take the terrorists by surprise. In adventure games, it is the other way round. Here, constant orientations within space are not the average requirement. Spaces in *Myst* and *Riven* are highly complex — so what one does is draw a map, learn about the structure of the landscape one is traversing, and enjoy the details.

However, this mapping of spatial information is grounded in a functional desire for control. Playing *Myst* is not just about envisioning and seeing the sights of a remarkable world. Also, and more decisively, the player's desire to uncover the "secret" structure underneath the surface is triggered, tracing the atlas behind the puzzles. As Guattari puts it: "We're strict functionalists: What we're interested in is how something works, functions — finding the machine. But the signifier is still stuck in the question 'what does it mean'?"[15]

Let us now look at three different types of war games and see how they each comprise combat realism and tactical inclusion. From a ludological angle, the quandary is that the first game simulates too little (which might be just enough), the second simulates way too much (which is exactly the point of its design), and the third simulates merely on a meta-level (which makes it great to reflect upon and dull to play).

In 1962 a young computer programmer from MIT, Steve Russell, fueled with inspiration from the writings of E. E. "Doc" Smith, led the team that created the first computer game. It took the team about 200 man-hours to write the first version of *Spacewar*. The game was written on a PDP-1, an operating system that was the first to allow multiple users to share the computer simultaneously. This was perfect for playing *Spacewar,* which was a two-player game involving warring spaceships firing photon torpedoes. Each player could maneuver a spaceship and score by firing missiles at his opponent while avoiding the gravitational pull of the sun. Later on Russell transferred to Stanford University where he introduced computer game programming and *Spacewar* to an engineering student, Nolan Bushnell. The latter went on to write the first coin-operated computer arcade game and start Atari Computer. The rest is history.

As part of the sixties' development in computer technology, including a strong belief in cybernetic control and artificial intelligence, the interface of *Spacewar* has strong ties to air surveillance and computer tools. Although the aesthetic side, or the expressive component of *Spacewar* as fiction, has been significant in the diffusion of the computer, Russell's invention clearly resides on the threshold between the computer as weapon, tool, and toy.[16] Today, it is easier to see the inherent complexity in *Spacewar*. On the one hand the game is a simple, almost naive, skeleton version of our days' *Counter-Strike*, and precursor of *Pong*, which revolutionized the fast growing consol market in the seventies. On the other hand *Spacewar* may be interpreted as the entertaining side effect of Cold War tech implementations that also gave birth to such disparate phenomena as the U.S. Semi-Automated Ground Environment (SAGE)—an automatization of counterattack possibilities against the Soviet Union—and Stanley Kubrick's political satire *Dr. Strangelove*.

My second example is a vast array of hardware and software presently run by the U.S. Department of Defense (DoD) called the Sentient World Simulation (SWS). According to a concept paper for the project, SWS will be a synthetic mirror of the real world with automated continuous calibration with respect to current real-world information. The DoD is on the brink of developing a parallel to Planet Earth, almost similar to The Matrix (the fictional computer program in the film *The Matrix*), with billions of "nodes" representing everything from individuals, financial institutions, utilities, and down to the local Pizza Hut. By applying theories of economics, demography, and—in particular—behavioral psychology the developers are certain that they can predict actions and responses of both individuals and mobs, all of which is highly relevant for military and intelligence services.

According to the Danish new media specialist Peter Bøgh Andersen a simulation must automatically possess three elements to count as proper: 1) It acts as a replacement for a real entity or real experience; 2) it always contains a model of the simulated reality; and 3) the simulated model expresses the engineer's perception of this reality.[17] In other words: a simulation is *an engineered model-reality*. There is a clear materialistic epistemology underpinning this assumption of effectively copying and thus manipulating the nature of reality. The centre image is that of a "black box." One cannot know what goes on inside it (like when positivist epistemologies do not care about any world below, inside, or behind the kind of reality that we can measure). But one can calibrate, monitor, and thus control the behaviors and values assigned to anything that enters and leaves the box. In the words of Sherry Turkle, simulations are power tools, as people who understand the distortions imposed by simulation are in a position to call for more direct economic and political feedback, new kinds of representation, and more channels of information.[18]

What makes a simulation such a powerful form of communication is that it is, like most events, non-linear. A book or film is linear. The author leads you from point to point, with no deviation allowed. Simulations, and games in general, are non-linear. That is, you can wander all over the place and still be somewhere. Flip through a book, and you pick up pieces out of context. Make different moves in a game, and you have a context, because the game allows, even encourages, deviating from the historical events.

The nature of this non-linearity does not imply that it is impossible to be in command of the design and thus the experience of the simulation. As it were, this "hidden" control is not the order of things but rather the *parametrical values* assigned to the "nodes" of the simulation. This non-linear, parametrical level of control is precisely part and parcel of *The Sims'* success. *The Sims* can ultimately be regarded as a mundane allegory of the Sentient World Simulation. Electronic Art's game invites you to prepare, not for combat and weapons fight, but for the logics of household, love affairs, and job searching. As computer game theoretician Miguel Sicart has pointed out, "winning" lies beyond the scope of *The Sims*.[19] Instead, the players need to understand the parameters and variables of the game thus realizing and in a way "concurring" the demarcations already set up by the game. You can be a dad with a lover and an angry teenage daughter or even a gay person with a promiscuous *modus vivendi*; but you cannot play the part of Kurt Cobain's "I'm only happy when I'm sad" eulogy. The parametrical standards of *The Sims* simply do not allow you to.

If the Sentient World Simulation were to be malformed into a computer game other than *The Sims*, what would it look like? The DoD's enormous AI must never be mistaken for a game, since there is no clear-cut win-code or valorized outcome attached to the system. Also, it is quite simply too big, too inclusive. When we might think of it as a game anyhow, besides the vague familiarity with the concept of "virtuality," we do so by means of *representation*. Might not the Sentient World Simulation be spectacular as a plot in a movie, or perhaps serving as the background story of a hybrid action-strategy-adventure game? Think *Enemy of the State* (the movie) meets *Deus Ex* (the game). In both cases outcome (the win-lose option) and representation (from chaotic network to complex plot) rest on an inevitable reduction technique.

The third example stems from a former school turned art gallery in contemporary Israel. Two projected images on the wall show scenes from the Palestinian Intifada. One of them is a game called *The Stone Throwers* in which the user assumes the role of a young Palestinian man placed in front of the al–Aqsa mosque in the old neighborhoods of Jerusalem. He is armed with stones and to win the game he must throw them at the Israeli soldiers coming towards him on the screen.

At the outset this may seem like an updated version of *Spacewar* but in a different setting. However, once the game ends a message appears on the screen in English: "Well maybe you have killed some of the Israeli soldiers in the computer world, but this is the real world." Afterwards we are shown a photograph of a group of people carrying the open coffin of a boy draped in what looks like the Palestinian flag. The text goes on: "Stop the killing of the innocents in Palestine before the game is really over."

The other game on the wall is also named after the Intifada, only this time it has Israeli roots. The game centers on a lone Israeli soldier facing a violent Palestinian demonstration. Lots of guns are at the player's disposal, ranging from sophisticated live ammunition to wooden clubs. However, to win the player must stay alive and disperse the crowd while injuring or killing as few Palestinians as possible.

The Israeli game is subtler since it puts the political message inside the very rules; to progress properly the player has to convey some sort of humanistic understanding and, in addition, he has to possess a bare minimum of strategic know-how. Instead of throwing stones and killing fervently at the monstrosities appearing randomly in front of the avatar, the Israeli shooter is not in want of an "extra-ludic" text that utters the inevitable morale. As ludic toy *and* as a means to communication the Israeli FPS comes out, then, as the better game.

Interactions

In computer game research, also today known as ludology, there seems to be an unbridgeable divide between those who put emphasis on the representational gambit of games as opposed to those who focus on games as formal rule systems.[20] When we look back into the history of games, including sports, or even speculate freely on their possible semantics, it is almost unfeasible *not* to think of war in its widest usages as a universal starting place. While chess may not mean anything on the level of stringent rules it is nevertheless all about attacking and defending. In fact, *Chaturanga*, considered by most historians to be the predecessor of chess, was a sort of war game played in India during the seventh century. For the Brazilians, "soccer" translates into *jogo bonito* ("the beautiful game") but essentially the pitch consists of two "fortresses," one in attack and one in defense, with a middle field — or, as it were, battle field — in between. "Hold the line," shouts General Maximus in the beginning of the film *Gladiator*. Italian soccer player and central defender, Fabio Cannavaro, uses the same words when he leads the four men in the back a few yards up the pitch to lure the opposing team into offside.

However, as Jesper Juul has suggested, games are both. They are "half-real," meaning that they consist of rules *and* fiction.[21] You do something that the rules require you to do; and you do so within an environment, a story. Once there is a story involved, the very same rules, which are essentially non-semantic strings of algorithms, suddenly open up for intentionality, meaning, performance, societal codes, and the like. Similarly we can note in the tradition of sociologists like Gregory Bateson and Niklas Luhmann that the central mark of "play" (and "gameplay") is the participants' ability to invest in something that is both "real" and, at the same time, "not real."

Bateson's own prime example is monkeys fooling around.[22] They bite, and they do not bite. In fact, monkeys are good at "not-biting," producing that particular bite which is simultaneously a bite and not a bite. Monkeys take fun very seriously: they bite the not-real bite for real. The distinctive cognition here, *pace* Bateson, is not the predicative nor transformative quality of the bite (the bite "is" or the bite "stands for") but rather the word "not"— as in "this is *not* a bite" *and* "this is *not* a non-bite," at the same time. Empirically speaking, a monkey's playful bite should not be hard, but not too soft. Not soft, but not too hard.

The monkey illustration is analogous to the whereabouts of human players. One *really* puts an effort into killing foes in *Counter-Strike*; and yet one is closely aware, since this is part of playing's tacit knowledge, that *in reality* those teams are merely pixels and virtual illusion. Once players lift the illusionisms of gameplay out into reality and violently transgress the confines of the magic circle, two things happen: Either the game turns into a "serious" game as in our previous discussion of the Middle East meta-game, a game about what it means to play a game, or it vaporizes into no game at all. When contestants fervently argue over a referee's decision in a game of soccer, then their quarrel is definitely part of the game and furthermore a proof of how the interaction system communicates with itself and thereby keeps track of the rule system. But to insist that the absolute goal of soccer is *not* to win would be a poisonous abortion of the very reality of the circle's ontology.

In play, the deep fascination therefore lies in the oscillation between play and nonplay, which is the "other" of play usually considered to be "reality." In the playing of games we are more fixated on progressing in the prior structure that is the game.[23] Gaming presupposes the tension or the initial transgression in which we constantly resist falling out of the fantasy context of play. Furthermore, gaming also presupposes focus on a second, higher transgression in which success and failure is measured against our achievement of defined objectives. Thus, in playing a computer game, we work in a second simulacrum, an "as if structure" overlain on top of the first initial transgression that makes play possible in the first place.

We can paraphrase this from a gamer's point of view, stating that as long as any communication on teleological concerns (the purpose, rights and wrongs of this and that) is enacted within the ontology of the game, it is acceptable. If the communication takes place outside of this "sacred" being it immediately becomes obscure, dangerous and, exactly, beside the point.

As one commentator on an Internet war game forum puts it: "A game where peace is the ultimate objective would not be fun at all. What would be the thrill of sitting in a room full of the world's leaders and negotiating a treaty? What would motivate people to bring more peace? People want action and adventure, not to pore over volumes of text and watch people NOT die."

Besides the obvious lesson that the success of games follows from their degree of consistency (i.e., their onto-teleological existence), contrary to the level of their realism, the comment is disturbing because it means that while one is *always* obliged to follow the rules (anything else would be cheating or otherwise disrupting the boundaries of the magic circle), one is *not* always obliged to follow the "fiction" attached to the rules. And one is *certainly* not obliged to partake in the debate surrounding the eventual positive or negative aspects of a game and its rules.

How can this be explained in formal terminology? Once a game, including war games and those who simulate human aggression, are played out in real life, the game's interaction system bifurcates into two levels. Sometimes these two levels correspond, sometimes they don't. The levels are exactly that of the game's fiction or story, plus a larger and fuzzier societal context. The obtrusive word, of course, is "real." In reality you can move from "I killed a member of the blue team" to "this is good because I belong to the red anti-terror squad" to concerned pacifists asking "why kill?" The computer makes sure that there is a nice and subtle balance between the first two usages thus linking the dual factors of "real" rules and fiction, or rules and interaction, to each other. In contrast to this, the bifurcation is very troubling (or annoying) because there is a huge difference between "ten down, one to go" and "why make eleven people suffer?"

All games contain rules, strategies, and interaction patterns. So, too, does war, which is fundamentally a highly professional and formalized input/output system set within an ostentatious social or political framework. Troubles of ethical and socio-philosophical character surface when one unrelentingly compares the interaction system of a game with the representational values of war.

Notes

1. Paul Virilio, Sylvère Lotringer and Mark Polizzotti, *Pure War*, revised edition (New York: Semiotext(e), 1997); James Der Derian, *Virtuous War: Mapping the Military-Industrial-Media-Entertainment Network* (Boulder, CO: Westview Press, 2001).
2. John von Neumann and Oskar Morgenstern, *Theory of Games and Economic Behavior* (Princeton, NJ: Princeton University Press, 1953).
3. John F. Nash, *Essays on Game Theory* (London: Edward Elgar, 1997).
4. Neumann and Morgenstern, *Theory of Games*.
5. Jesper Juul, *Half-Real: Video Games Between Real Rules and Fictional Worlds* (Cambridge, Mass.: MIT Press, 2005).
6. Jonas Heide Smith, "The Games Economists Play: Implications of Economic Game Theory for the Study of Computer Games," *Game Studies* 6.1 (2006), accessed from http://gamestudies.org/0601/articles/heide_smith on June 1, 2008.
7. John H. Holland, *Emergence: From Chaos to Order* (Oxford: Oxford University Press, 1998).
8. See Johan Huizinga, *Homo Ludens. Vom Ursprung der Kultur im Spiel* (Reinbek: Rowohlt, 1994), original 1938; Roger Caillois, *Man, Play, and Games* (Urbana: University of Illinois Press, 2001), original 1958; Bo Kampmann Walther, "Playing and Gaming: Reflections and Classifications," *Game Studies* 3.1 (2003) accessed from http://www.gamestudies.org/0301/walther/ on June 1, 2008.
9. Katie Salen and Eric Zimmermann, *Rules of Play: Game Design Fundamentals* (Cambridge, Mass.: MIT Press, 2004).
10. Nash, *Essays*.
11. Virilio, Lotringer and Polizzotti, *Pure War*.
12. Edward N. Luttwak, *Strategy: The Logic of War and Peace* (Cambridge, Mass.: Belknap Press, 2002).
13. David B. Nieborg, "First Person Paradoxes—The Logic of War in Computer Games" in *Game Set and Match II: On Computer Games, Advanced Geometries and Digital Technologies*, ed. K. Oosterhuis and L. Feireiss, 107–115 (Rotterdam: Episode Publishers, 2006).
14. Søren Kolstrup, "Ecological Optics and Virtual Space" in *Virtual Space: The Spatiality of Virtual Inhabited 3D Worlds*, ed. Lars Qvortrup (Springer Verlag: Berlin, 2002), 216.
15. Guattari quoted in Gilles Deleuze, *Negotiations 1972–1990* (Columbia University Press: New York, 1995), 21f.
16. Christian Ulrik. Andersen, "The Computer as Weapon, Tool and Toy" in *Digital*

Art & Culture, ed. Søren Pold and Lone Kofoed Hansen (Aarhus: Aarhus University Press, 2007), 43–80.

17. Peter Bøgh Andersen, "Ships and Movies," in *Cognition, Technology & Work*, no. 4, December (2003): 294–301.

18. Sherry Turkle, *Life on the Screen: Identity in the Age of the Internet* (New York: Simon & Schuster, 1995), 163.

19. Miguel Sicart, "Family Values: Ideology, Computer Games & Sims," working paper presented at DIGRA Conference, 2003.

20. Gonzalo Frasca, "Ludologists Love Stories, Too: Notes From a Debate That Never Took Place," accessed from http://www.ludology.org/articles/Frasca_LevelUp2003.pdf on June 1, 2008.

21. Juul, *Half-Real*, 58.

22. Gregory Bateson, *Mind and Nature* (London: Bantam Books, 1979).

23. Graeme Kirkpatrick, *Critical Technology: A Social Theory of Personal Computing* (Aldershot: Ashgate, 2004), 74.

Abbreviations, Acronyms and Terms

AA: *America's Army*, computer game produced by the U.S. Army for public relations and recruitment purposes, a tactical multiplayer first-person–shooter game, released on July 4, 2002.

AI: artificial intelligence.

C3: Communications, Command, and Control, expression used by the military about technologies of communications. C4 refers to Command, Control, Communications, and Computers.

DARPA: the Defense Advanced Research Projects Agency, an agency under the United States Department of Defense, founded in 1958 and responsible for the development of new technology for use by the military.

DoD: U.S. Department of Defense.

FPS game: a first-person-shooter game.

FSP: *Full Spectrum Warrior*, computer game released on June 1, 2004.

Hezbollah: Arab word meaning *party of God*, a Shi'a political party with seats in the Lebanese government and a paramilitary force based in Lebanon. Listed as a terrorist organization by six countries, among them the United States, but in most of the Arab and Muslim world considered a legitimate resistance movement.

Intifada: Arab word meaning *shaking off*, an expression used about the first armed uprising of Palestinians against the Israeli occupation of the West Bank and Gaza Strip in the late 1980s and early 1990s and today a term meaning popular resistance to oppression.

ICT: Institute for Creative Technologies, a research institute at the University of Southern California, created 1999 in collaboration between the U.S. military, the entertainment industry, and University of Southern California to develop virtual reality and simulation technology.

MIC: the military-industrial complex, composed of a nation's armed forces, its suppliers of weapons systems, supplies and services, and its civil government. The term was made famous when President Dwight D. Eisenhower used it in his Farewell Address to the Nation on January 17, 1961.

MIME-network: In his book *Virtuous War: Mapping the Military-Industrial-Media-Entertainment Network* (2001) James Der Derian coined the expression "MIME-network," alluding to the military-industrial complex, MIC (see above), and incorporating the connections to the media and entertainment industry as it has evolved in recent years.

ONR: the Office of Naval Research.

RAND Corporation, the: Research And Development, an American global policy think tank set up in 1946 by the United States Army Air Force, offering research and analysis to the United States armed forces.

SIMNET: the military's distributed simulator networking project with vehicle simulators and displays for real-time distributed combat simulation used by the United States military, developed in the 1980s, fielded in 1987, used for training during the Gulf War, and replaced in the 1990s by other simulation programs.

SME: Subject Matter Expert, a military specialist who helps computer game designers create aesthetic verisimilitude in a computer game.

STRICOM: the U.S. Army's Simulation, Training and Instrumentation Command set up in 1992 to help manage and direct simulation.

SWS: the Sentient World Simulation, a project initiated by the U.S. Joint Forces Command and located at Purdue University. SWS consists of a vast array of hardware and software that simulate a mirror model of the real world which is used to predict and evaluate future events and courses of actions. It is a further development of SEAS, the Synthetic Environment for Analysis and Simulations, also located at Purdue University.

VR: virtual reality.

WoW: *World of Warcraft*, massively multiplayer online role-playing game (MMORPG) released on November 23, 2004.

About the Contributors

Sue Collins, Ph.D., is a professor in the Department of Media, Culture, and Communication at New York University. Her dissertation research explored the U.S. domestic propaganda campaign of World War I and its recruitment of stardom as a source of political authority and mechanism of governance. She has published on the political economy of reality TV celebrity and on celebrity activism.

Erika Doss is professor and chair of the Department of American Studies, University of Notre Dame, Indiana. She is the author of numerous books and articles on modern and contemporary American public cultures including the forthcoming *Memorial Mania: Self, Nation, and the Culture of Commemoration in Contemporary America*.

Anne Gjelsvik, Ph.D., is an associate professor at the Department of Art and Media Studies at the Norwegian University of Science and Technology (NTNU) in Trondheim, Norway. Her latest book (in Norwegian) is on violence in fiction film. Among her publications are *Femme Fatalities: Representations of Strong Women in the Media* (2004) co-edited with Rikke Schubart. She was chief editor of the Norwegian media studies journal *Norsk Medietidsskrift*, 2002–2006. She is currently working on a book about fatherhood in contemporary American cinema.

Mette Mortensen, Ph.D., holds a postdoctoral fellowship at the University of Copenhagen. She is co-editor of *Passports: Identity, Culture, and Borders* (Informations Forlag, 2004) and *Geometry of the Face* (Royal Danish Library, 2003). She has written numerous articles on representations of war, the history of photography, and contemporary art.

Matthew Thomas Payne is a doctoral student in the Department of Radio, and Film at the University of Texas at Austin. His research focuses on the social impact of communication technologies and new media, video games, alternative media practices, and teaching film and video production. Matthew has previously served as the coordinating editor for FlowTV (www.flowtv.org), an online journal and forum dedicated to television and new media culture.

Marcus Power is a reader in human geography at the University of Durham, UK. His research interests include postcolonial geographies, geopolitics and imperialism, and visuality and "popular" geopolitics. He is co-editor of *Cinema and Geopolitics* (2007) with Andrew Crampton.

Rikke Schubart is an associate professor at the University of Southern Denmark. Among recent publications are *Super Bitches and Action Babes: The Female Hero in Popular Cinema, 1970–2006* (McFarland, 2007) and *Femme Fatalities: Representations of Strong Women in the Media* (2004), co-edited with Anne Gjelsvik. She has written about the horror film, the action cinema, and contemporary American film. She is currently working on a book about the American war movie after 1991. She published her first novel, *Bid*, in 2008.

Lawrence H. Suid, Ph.D., is a film and military historian. His books include *Guts & Glory* (2002), a study of the relationship between the United States armed services and the American film industry, *Sailing on the Silver Screen* (U.S. Naval Institute Press, 1996), an account of the relationship between the U.S. Navy and Hollywood, and *Stars and Stripes on Screen* (Scarecrow Press, 2005) with Dolores A. Haverstick, a guide to the portrayal of the U.S. military in motion pictures. He is currently writing a biography of Fred Zinnemann.

Yvonne Tasker is professor of film and television studies at the University of East Anglia, UK. She is the author and editor of various books and collections exploring popular cinema including *Working Girls: Gender and Sexuality in Popular Cinema* (1998) and (with Diane Negra) *Interrogating Postfeminism: Gender and the Politics of Popular Culture* (2007). Her forthcoming book *Soldier's Stories: Military Women in Cinema and Television Since World War II* will be published by Duke University Press.

Helga Tawil-Souri is an assistant professor in the Department of Media, Culture, and Communication at New York University. Her research focuses on various aspects of Palestinian and Arab media practices, including analyses of local broadcasting industries, the relationship between the Internet and national/economic development, and issues around social and political spaces. She is also a photographer and documentary filmmaker.

Tanja Thomas is a professor at the Institute of Applied Cultural Sciences, University Lüneburg, Germany. Her research focuses on critical media theory, cultural studies; gender studies; governmentality studies. She is co-editor (with Fabian Virchow) of *Banal Militarism* (2006); *Medien — Diversität — Ungleichheit: Zur medialen Konstruktion sozialer Differenz* (Media — Diversity — Inequality: Mediated Constructions of Social Differences, 2008) and editor of *Medienkultur und soziales Handeln* (Media Culture and Social Action, 2008).

Jenny Thompson has an M.A. and a Ph.D. in American studies and has taught history and American studies at the University of Maryland and at Roosevelt University in Chicago. She is the author of *War Games: Inside the World of Twentieth-Century War Reenactors* (2004) and editor of *My Hut: A Memoir of a YMCA Volunteer in France During World War One* (2006). She is the curator of education at the Evanston History Center in Evanston, Illinois.

Fabian Virchow, Ph.D., lectures at the University of Marburg and the University of Lüneburg. His fields of research are military sociology, political culture, the sociology of the history of ideas, social/political movements and political communication. He is co-editor of *Banal Militarism* (2006), and author of *Gegen den Zivilismus* (2006) which deals with the far right's approaches to foreign and defense policy. His articles have appeared in reviewed journals including *Civil Wars, Patterns of Prejudice* and *Peace & Change*. He is currently working on a book titled *Media and the Far Right in Contemporary Europe—Theoretical Considerations and Case Studies*.

Bo Kampmann Walther, Ph.D., is associate professor and head of research in media studies, University of Southern Denmark. He is a soccer columnist for the Danish newspaper *Information* and a jazz musician. He writes, lectures, and teaches extensively on new media, computer games, and modern soccer. See more at www.sdu.dk/hum/bkw.

Debra White-Stanley is completing her Ph.D. dissertation, "Foreign Bodies: Military Medicine, Modernism and Melodrama," in the Department of English at the University of Arizona. Her publications include "'God Give Me Strength': The Melodramatic Soundtracks of Allison Anders," *Velvet Light Trap,* vol. 51 (Spring 2003), and "Sound Sacrifices: Representing the Pain of War on the Cinema Soundtrack" (in *Lowering the Boom: New Essays on the History, Theory and Practice of Film Sound,* 2008, University of Illinois Press).

Index

AA *see America's Army*
Aarseth, Espen 206
Above and Beyond 170, 172
Abu Ghraib 26, 46–7; pictures 48, 50–2; prison 53; scandal 6, 151, 154, 157, 159, 204
"acts of war" 77
Adams, Eddie 49
Akrich, Madeleine 250
Al-Arabiya 231
Albrecht-Heide, Astrid 100
Alda, Alan 134, 140
Ali, Muhammad 87, 88
Al-Jazeera 63, 231
Al Qaeda 47
Altman, Robert 134
America: A Tribute to the Heroes 5, 79, 82–5, 87–91
American-British War of 1812 120
America's Army 3, 8, 200, 203, 205, 207, 210, 217, 224, 225–8, 238, 241, 244, 246, 248–49, 252, 256, 273
America's Army: Rise of a Soldier 8, 238, 241, 245–47, 249–52
America's Army: Special Forces 203
Andersen, Peter Bøgh 266
Anderson, Benedict 239
Apelt, Maja 100
Apocalypse Now 204
Aristotle 117
Artefact emotions (A-emotions) 124–25
Attacke! Frauen ans Gewehr 105
Auslander, Philip 89

Bacevich, Andrew 18
banal militarism 40, 97
banal nationalism 6, 40, 97
Barber, Benjamin 232
Barthes, Roland 62, 68
Bateson, Gregory 269
Battlefield 1942 262
Battlefield 2 209, 256, 262
Battlezone 7, 201
Baudrillard, Jean 2, 4, 7, 17, 206, 224, 229
The Beginning or the End 7, 167–9, 171–2

Beloved 152
Bennett, Tony 79–80
Bettany, Paul 119, 120
Biedermann, Jeanette 109
Bijker, Wiebe 241, 243
Billig, Michael 6, 40, 97
Bin Laden, Osama 2
Black Hawk Down 3, 64–5, 207
Bourriard, Nicolas 55
Bradshaw, Peter 123, 126
Bragg, Rick 66
Brenner, Christina Maria 110
British Royal Navy 121
Brothers in Arms: D-Day 15
Bruckheimer, Jerry 65
Buckingham, David 216
Budd, Mike 135
Bundesluftwaffe (German Air Force) 104
Bundesmarine (German Navy) 105
Bundeswehr (unified armed forces of the Federal Republic of Germany) 31–34, 37, 39, 98, 100–4, 107, 109, 110–11
Burt, Ronald S. 242
Bushnell, Nolan 266
Butler, Judith 24, 56

C3 *see* Command, Control and Communications
Caarby, Hazel 154
Call of Duty 15
Capa, Robert 49, 58
Capra, Frank 200
Carey, Mariah 107
Carrey, Jim 84
Carroll, Andrew 25
Chaturanga 269
Civil War 23, 194
Clinton, Hillary 164
Clooney, George 84, 107
Close Combat 257
Close Combat: Invasion Normandy 15
CNN: War in the Gulf 2
Cobain, Kurt 267
Cold War 18, 48, 156, 201, 266
Collins, Sue 5, 77
Command and Conquer: Generals 226

Command, Control and Communications
  (C3) 201, 273
Concert for New York 5
Condon, Richard 6, 150
Conflict Desert Storm 208–9
Conflict: Desert Storm II: Back to Baghdad
  208
Conflict: Global Storm 199
Connell, Robert 100
Coppola, Francis Ford 204
Cops 65
Counter-Strike 256, 263–66, 269
Courage Under Fire 161
Crimean War 47, 194
Crowe, Russell 116, 127
Cruise, Tom 84

Dahl, John 174
Damon, Matt 107
Dar al-Fikr 226
d'Arc, Jeanne 69
DARPA *see* Defense Advanced Research Projects Agency
The Day After 167
The Day After Trinity 175
Debord, Guy 85
Defense Advanced Research Projects Agency
  (DARPA) 202, 273
de Gaulle, Charles 35
Delacroix, Eugène 69
DeLillo, Don 32
Delta Force 262
Demme, Jonathan 6, 150, 152, 159
De Niro, Robert 64
Department of Defense: Danish 55; German
  102; United States 26, 48, 53, 159, 201, 209,
  240, 242, 253, 266–7, 273
Der Derian, James 2, 3, 7, 56, 200, 224, 229
Desert Storm 20, 226
Deus Ex 267
Dion, Celine 84, 90
Dirty Harry 88
Dr. Strangelove 266
DoD *see* Department of Defense, U.S.
Doom 225, 264
Doom Marine 256
Doom 3 264
Doonesbury 27
Doss, Erika 4, 13
Duke Nukem 264

Eastwood, Clint 53, 84, 88
Ebert, Roger 118
Edwards, James 151
Eifler, Christine 101
Elise, Kimberly 160
Elkins, James 57
Elsaesser, Thomas 155
Else, Jon 175
Elshtain, Jean Bethke 163
Enemy of the State 267

Enloe, Cynthia 145
Ethnic Cleansing 217, 223

The Far Side of the World 118, 120
Fat Man and Little Boy 168
Federal Republic of Germany 5
Feldtagebuch—Allein unter Männern 105
Fiction emotions (F-emotions) 124
Flags of Our Fathers 53
Ford, John 68
Foucault, Michel 80
Franco-Prussian War 256
Franke, Ulrike 105
Frankenheimer, John 150, 156
Franz, Dennis 87
Frasier 88
Frauen am Ruder 104
Freedman, Carl 134, 138–9
Freeland, Cynthia 123, 124
French, Philip 123
Freud, Sigmund 154
Frye, Northrop 68
Fukuyama, Francis 232
Full Spectrum Warrior (FSW) 8, 198, 205,
  238, 241, 246, 248–49, 251–52
Full Spectrum Warrior 04 257
Fuller, Samuel 151
Fussell, Paul 190

Galloway, Alexander 206, 228
Garcia, Andy 107
Gelbert, Larry 143, 148
Geneva Conventions 53
German Democratic Republic (GDR, East
  Germany) 5, 33
German Federal Armed Forces 31–33, 38
German Navy 31
Germania 69
Geyer, Horst 37
Ghost Recon 256
Gitlin, Todd 138–9
Gjelsvik, Anne 6, 115
Gladiator 269
Global War on Terror (GWOT) 163–4, 203,
  208, 222, 224, 226
God Speed 3D 217
Goette, Aelrun 105
Goldberg, Whoopi 85
Gordon, Max 53
Grammer, Kelsey 88
The Great Raid 174
Grieswelle, Detlef 34
Grim Fandango 264
Guattari, Felix 265
Guernica 27
Gulf War 2, 18, 21, 46, 62, 155, 159, 198, 202,
  204, 208
Gunter, Gabriel 105–6, 108

Haiti Dreams of Democracy 152
Half-Life 264

Index

Hall, Karen 201
Halliwell, Geri 107
Halo 198
Hanks, Tom 77, 87
Hansen, Jonathan 18
Hardwick, Rachel 245–47, 249, 251
Heroes of Might and Magic 260
Hill, Faith 90
Hiroshima 174–5
Hiroshima: The Decision to Drop the Bomb 172–4
Hiroshima Nagasaki August, 1945 174
Hoffman, Dustin 64
Höpfl, Heather J. 24
Huizinga, Johan 8, 207
Huntington, Samuel 222, 232
Hussein, Saddam 62; execution of 46, 50, 58; palace of 70

I Am a Soldier, Too: The Jessica Lynch Story 66
Inglesia, Enrique 90
Intifada 217, 222, 268, 273
Iraq War 150–2, 155; torture scandal 158
Irvine, Ian 133
ISAF (International Security Assistance Force) 44
Islam Fun 234
Israeli Air Force 225
Iwo Jima 44, 53

Jarhead 53
Jean, Wyclef 90
Jeffords, Susan 157, 164
Jenkins, Charles Robert 150
Jericho 167
Jerslev, Anne 120
Jets — Leben am Limit 104
Joffé, Roland 168
Johnson, Shoshana 69
Juul, Jesper 9, 269

Kaplan, Amy 18
Keenan, Thomas 51
Keller, Jörg 103
Kennedy, John F. 35, 88
Khalaf, Samir 233
King, Barry 86
King Arthur 123
Kingdom of Heaven 123
Klein, Uta 99, 102, 111
Kold, Claus 47
Korean War 6, 18, 20, 132, 135, 138, 140, 147, 150–2, 181
Korean War Veterans Memorial 22
Korris, James 246, 248–49, 251–52
Kriegspiel 202, 256
Kubrick, Stanley 266
Kuma\War 205–6; series 207
Kuma\War 2 206
Kümmel and Werkner 101
Kurahara, Koreyoshi 174

The Last Starfighter 203
Late Night 87
Law, John 241, 243
Lears, Jackson 18, 79
Left Behind: Eternal Forces 217
Leigh, Janet 159–60
Lennon, John 90
Leonard, David 224, 230
Lerner, Daniel 232
Letters Home 25, 26
Levinson, Barry 64
Levinson, Jerrold 116, 123
Lewis, Bernard 232
La Liberté Guidant le Peuple 69
Limp Bizkit 90
Lin, Maya 4, 18, 19, 24
Lin, Nan 242
Lincoln Memorial 15
Die Lindenstraße 103
Linville, Larry 137
Linville, Susan 161
Lippold, Friederike 108
Littman, Lynne 167
Liu, Lucy 88
LiveLeak 5, 44–45, 49, 50
Loan, Nguyen Ngoc 49
Loeken, Michael 105
The Longest Journey 265
Lopez, Jennifer 107
Lord of the Rings trilogy 123
Luhmann, Niklas 269
Luttwak, Edward N. 262
Lynch (incident) 62
Lynch, Jessica 5, 63, 64, 66–7, 70–3, 151; case 5, 61; incident 62; story 65, 69; war hero 62
Lyotard, Jean-Francois 3

The Manchurian Candidate (novel, 1959) 150
The Manchurian Candidate (1962) 150–1, 156, 159–60
The Manchurian Candidate (2004) 6, 150–3, 159–61, 164
Mann, Anthony 151
Marc, David 132, 138
Marianne 69
Marine Corps Memorial 53
Markle, Peter 3
Marley, Bob 90
Marshall, David 82, 86–7, 89
M*A*S*H: movie 134; television series 6, 132–5, 137–40, 142–5, 148
Master and Commander: The Far Side of the World 6, 115–6, 118, 120–5, 127
The Matrix 9
Maze of Destiny 234
McHale's Navy 133
McLagan, Meg 86
Medal of Honor: Allied Assault 15
Mendes, Sam 53
Mexican American War 20
Meyer, Nicholas 167

Index

MIC *see* military-industrial complex
Milestone, Lewis 151
military-entertainment complex 238, 253
military-industrial complex 200, 273
military-industrial-media-entertainment network 200; *see also* MIME-network
Miller, Patrick 69
Miller, Toby 80
Miller and Lewis 82
MIME-condition 3, 4, 9
MIME-network 2, 4, 7, 274; *see also* military-industrial-media-entertainment network
Mirzoeff, Nicholas 46, 132
Missile Command 201
Mitchell, W.J.T. 58
Morgenstern, Oscar 258
Morrison, Toni 152
Mortensen, Mette 5, 44
Mosse, George L. 5, 69
Mumford, Lewis 239
Myer and Gamson 86
MySpace 48
Myst 265
Myst III: Exile 265

Napoleonic War 118, 120–1
Nash, John F. 258–9
National D-Day Memorial 13–15, 21, 26
National World War I Memorial Museum 20
National World War II Memorial 15–16, 27
NATO 44, 48, 52
Neale, Steve 122
Neiborg, David B. 216
Nelson, Willie 89
new eyewitness 46
Nicholson, Jack 85
Nicht von Schlechten Eltern 103
Nieborg, David 263
Nielsen, Holger K. 48
9/11 1, 5, 77, 199, 222, 224
NYPD Blue 87

O'Brian, Conan 87
O'Brian, Patrick 118–9
O'Brien, Tim 181
Omaha Beach 13, 20, 118
ONR (Office of Naval Research) 273
Operation Desert Storm 152
Operation Internal Look 202
Operation Iraqi Freedom 6, 224
Orientalist 223, 226, 232

Pacino, Al 85
Palestinian uprising 217
Panama, Norman 170
paradox of fiction 123
paradox of tragedy 116, 123
Pardell, Christopher 25–6
Parker, Eleanor 171
Parker, Sarah Jessica 87
Paul, William 134

Payne, Matthew Thomas 8, 238
Pearl, Daniel 150
Pearl Harbor 1, 9, 15
Pearl Harbor (movie) 1, 16
Pearl Harbor: Attack on America 17
Pearl Harbor: Zero Hour 17
Pentagon 48
Petty, Tom 88
The Phil Silvers Show 133, 135
Picasso, Pablo 27
Piestewa, Lori 69
Pietà 69
Pink Floyd 90
Pitt, Brad 85, 107
Pleitgen, Ulrich 103
Poetics 117
Pong 266
Power, Marcus 7, 198
pro–Arab computer games 3, 8, 215, 217, 220, 222–23, 225–27, 229–30, 233–34
Profiles from the Front Line 65

Quake 225
Queer Power 217

Rain of Ruin: The Bombing of Nagasaki 174
RAND Corporation (Research and Development) 201, 274
reenactments 7, 181–82, 186–90, 192–96
relational aesthetics 55
The Rescue of Jessica Lynch 3
"Respect for America's Fallen Heroes Act" 27
Die Rettungsflieger 104
Revolutionary War 25
Richards, Cliff 110
Riven 265
Roberts, Julia 107
Rojek, Chris 82
Rose, Nicolas 81
Rosenberg, Emily 16
Rosenthal, Joe 44, 53–54
Roush, Matt 78
Rumsfeld, Donald 46, 53
Russell, Steve 265–66
Ryan, Meg 85, 161
Rzenzik, John 90

Saving Private Ryan 15, 53, 116–7, 126, 194
Schiesel, Seth 204
Schießer, Sylvia 102, 103
Schubart, Rikke 1, 5, 61
Schweiger, Til 103
Scott, Ridley 3, 64–65
The Searchers 68
Second Intifada 215, 218, 220, 233
Segaller, Stephen 174
Seifert, Ruth 101
Sentient World Simulation (SWS) 266–7, 274
Serlin, David 26
7/7 London bombings 222
Sex and the City 87

Index

Sherry, Michael 17
Shoot the Blacks 217
SIMNET 202, 274
Simon, Paul 89
The Sims 267
Simulation, Training and Instrumentation Command 202, 274; *see also* STRICOM
Sinatra, Frank 151, 160
Sirk, Douglas 151
Slotkin, Richard 5, 62, 67–8, 70
SME *see* Subject Matter Expert
Smith, E.E. "Doc" 265
Smith, Will 87
Smits, Jimmy 87
social construction of technology (SCOT) 240–42
SOCOM II: U.S. Navy SEALS 198, 209
Soldatenglück und Gottes Segen 105
Sontag, Susan 49, 51, 58, 154
Spacewar 7, 201, 265–66, 268
Spanish Civil War 27, 58
Special Force 3, 8, 210, 215, 217–19, 222, 225–31, 234
Spence, Donald P. 71
Spielberg, Steven 15, 53, 117, 194
Spigel, Lynn 83–84
Spottiswoode, Roger 174
Springsteen, Bruce 89, 90–1
Stallone, Sylvester 85
Steinman, Clay 135
Sterling, Bruce 238–40, 253
Stiller, Ben 85
Sting 89
The Stone Throwers 268
Streep, Meryl 160–2
STRICOM 202, 274; *see also* Simulation, Training and Instrumentation Command
Subject Matter Expert (SME) 245, 247–48, 274
Suid, Lawrence H. 6, 167
Swit, Loretta 137
Swofford, Anthony 204
SWS *see* Sentient World Simulation

Taliban 47, 54
Tan, Ed 124–5, 127
Tasker, Yvonne 6, 132
Taurog, Norman 7
Taves, Brian 120
Tawil-Souri, Helga 3, 8
Taylor, Robert 170
Tearing Down the Spanish Flag 1
Testament 167
Thomas, Tanja 6, 97
Thompson, David 133
Thompson, Jenny 7, 181
Tillman, Pat 36
Tora! Tora! Tora! 17
Trudeau, Gary 27

Turkle, Sherry 9
Turner, Bryan 24
Turner, Joseph M.W. 127–8

U2 89–90
Ummah Defense I 222, 234
Under Ash 8, 209, 217–19, 225–26, 228, 231, 234
Under Siege 3, 8, 209, 215, 217–19, 226, 228–31, 234
Ut, Huynh Cong (*also called* Nick Ut) 58

van Munster, Bertram 65
Van Zandt, Steven 90
Vedder, Eddie 90
Veit, Philipp 69
Victory in the Pacific 175–6
Vietnam Veterans Memorial 18–19, 21, 24
Vietnam War 6, 19–20, 46, 143, 181–82, 193, 121
Virchow, Fabian 4, 31, 97
Virilio, Paul 224, 229, 262
Voight, Jon 155
von Neumann, John 258

Wag the Dog 64
The Wall 18
Walther, Bo Kampmann 8, 9, 256
war-games complex 256
War Spin 65
Washington, Denzel 151, 153, 160, 164
Washington Monument 15
Wayne, John 68
Weir, Peter 6, 115–6, 119
West Wing 87
White Law 217
White-Stanley, Debra 6, 150
Why We Fight 200
Williams, Robin 84
Wiltenburg, Mary 217
Winkler, Hartmut 108
Winter, Edward 136
Wonder, Stevie 89–90
World of Warcraft 28, 274
World Trade Center 53
World War I 23, 26, 181–82, 189, 193
World War II 14–6, 20, 22–3, 54, 99, 118, 121, 181–83, 186, 189–90, 192, 194, 200, 201, 203, 207, 210–11, 262
WoW *see* World of Warcraft
Wright, Jeffrey 151, 153

Young, Neil 89, 90
YouTube 5, 44, 48–9, 50, 55
Yuval-Davis, Nira 99, 101

Zizek, Slavoj 1, 224
Zwick, Edward 161
Zyda, Michael 244, 246, 248–49, 251–52

www.ingramcontent.com/pod-product-compliance
Ingram Content Group UK Ltd.
Pitfield, Milton Keynes, MK11 3LW, UK
UKHW041929140426
5217IPUK00014B/377